New General Mathematics 3

J B Channon MA
formerly Assistant Master at Rugby School

A McLeish Smith BA
formerly Second Master at Lawrence Sheriff School, Rugby

H C Head MA
Assistant Master at Rugby School

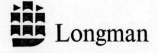

Longman

LONGMAN GROUP LIMITED
London

Associated companies, branches and representatives throughout the world

First edition © J. B. Channon and A. McLeish Smith 1958
New edition © Longman Group Ltd 1971

First published 1958
New edition 1971

ISBN (with answers) 0 582 31845 9
ISBN (without answers) 0 582 31844 0

Printed in Great Britain by Butler & Tanner Ltd, Frome and London

Preface

This set of four books is based on the authors' **General Mathematics** series, which has been completely rewritten in order to meet modern demands. Decimal currency has been used throughout, and in Books 1 and 2 the metric system of measures has supplanted the Imperial system almost completely, though a few questions and examples still remain in which Imperial units are used. Books 3 and 4 are completely metric. SI units have been used extensively but not exclusively; in particular the eminently useful centimetre and litre have been retained.

With the introduction of decimal currency it is assumed that pupils at primary level will have acquired some knowledge of decimal notation—place value, multiplication and division by a whole number and so on.

The more ponderous and less useful features of traditional textbooks will not be found here, and their omission has left room for chapters on those new topics which appear to the authors to be of permanent value, and which are in no danger of being eliminated from the syllabus once the experimental period of trial and error is over. Such topics as binary numbers, statistics, set theory, matrices, vectors, probability and linear programming must find a place in any series of books which is attempting to fit pupils for the modern world of technological development, and all of these subjects are dealt with in this series.

At the time of writing the future of geometry is still in a state of considerable uncertainty and, for this reason, more of the subject is retained than some teachers may consider necessary. These chapters can of course be disregarded by those who wish to do so, but they are there for those who believe that the study of geometry still has something to offer to the intelligent pupil.

J.B.C.
A.McL.S.
H.C.H.

Rugby 1971

Contents

Contents

Chapter 1

Indices.   Logarithms (1)

In Book 2, Chap. 1, the principles of indices were explained and the three fundamental laws set out: they are

$$\textbf{1 } a^x \times a^y = a^{x+y}$$
$$\textbf{2 } a^x \div a^y = a^{x-y}$$
$$\textbf{3 } (a^x)^y \quad = a^{xy}.$$

In Chap. 2 only positive integral (whole number) values for a, x and y were considered, but the laws are in fact true for all real values of a, x and y, whether they are positive, negative, integral or fractional.

(i) *To find a meaning for* $x^{\frac{1}{3}}$.
$$x^{\frac{1}{3}} \times x^{\frac{1}{3}} \times x^{\frac{1}{3}} = x^{\frac{1}{3}+\frac{1}{3}+\frac{1}{3}} = x^1$$
$$\therefore (x^{\frac{1}{3}})^3 = x$$
$$\therefore x^{\frac{1}{3}} = \sqrt[3]{x}.$$
Similarly $x^{\frac{2}{3}} = x^{\frac{1}{3}\times 2} = (x^{\frac{1}{3}})^2 = (\sqrt[3]{x})^2$
or $x^{\frac{2}{3}} = x^{2\times\frac{1}{3}} = (x^2)^{\frac{1}{3}} = \sqrt[3]{x^2}.$

(ii) *To find a meaning for* x^0.
$$x^0 \times x^3 = x^{0+3} = x^3.$$
Divide both sides by x^3.
Then $x^0 = x^3 \div x^3 = 1.$

(iii) *To find a meaning for* x^{-3}.
$$x^{-3} \times x^3 = x^{-3+3} = x^0 = 1$$
$$\therefore x^{-3} = 1 \div x^3 = \frac{1}{x^3}.$$
Similarly $x^{-\frac{2}{3}} = \frac{1}{x^{\frac{2}{3}}} = \frac{1}{\sqrt[3]{x^2}}$ or $\frac{1}{(\sqrt[3]{x})^2}.$

These results can be summarised as follows:

$$4 \quad a^{\frac{1}{n}} = \sqrt[n]{a}$$
$$5 \quad a^0 = 1$$
$$6 \quad a^{-n} = \frac{1}{a^n}$$
$$7 \quad a^{\frac{x}{y}} = \sqrt[y]{a^x} \quad \text{or} \quad (\sqrt[y]{a})^x.$$

Example 1 *Simplify* $9^{\frac{1}{2}}$, $8^{\frac{1}{3}}$, $8^{-\frac{2}{3}}$, $4^{\frac{1}{6}} \times 4^{\frac{1}{3}}$, $\left(\frac{16}{81}\right)^{-\frac{3}{4}}$.

$$9^{\frac{1}{2}} = \sqrt{9} = \pm 3$$
$$8^{\frac{1}{3}} = \sqrt[3]{8} = 2$$
$$8^{-\frac{2}{3}} = \frac{1}{8^{\frac{2}{3}}} = \frac{1}{(\sqrt[3]{8})^2} = \frac{1}{2^2} = \frac{1}{4}$$
$$4^{\frac{1}{6}} \times 4^{\frac{1}{3}} = 4^{\frac{1}{6}+\frac{1}{3}} = 4^{\frac{1}{2}} = \sqrt{4} = \pm 2$$
$$\left(\frac{16}{81}\right)^{-\frac{3}{4}} = \frac{1}{\left(\frac{16}{81}\right)^{\frac{3}{4}}} = \left(\frac{81}{16}\right)^{\frac{3}{4}} = \left(\frac{\pm 3}{\pm 2}\right)^3 = \pm \frac{27}{8}.$$

Exercise 1a

Simplify

1 $2a \times 3a^2$	**2** $2a \times (3a)^2$	**3** $(2a)^2 \times 3a$
4 $4^{\frac{1}{2}}$	**5** $27^{\frac{1}{3}}$	**6** $125^{\frac{1}{3}}$
7 $\sqrt[3]{2^6}$	**8** $8^{\frac{2}{3}}$	**9** 2^{-2}
10 3^{-3}	**11** $9^{\frac{1}{2}}$	**12** $9^{-\frac{1}{2}}$
13 $(25a^2)^{\frac{1}{2}}$	**14** $2a^{-1}$	**15** $(2a)^{-1}$
16 $4^{\frac{3}{2}}$	**17** $2^{-2} \times 2^3$	**18** $(2^2)^2$
19 10^{-2}	**20** $\sqrt{1\frac{9}{16}}$	**21** $3a^{-2}$
22 $(3a)^{-2}$	**23** $\sqrt{3^4}$	**24** $(a^2)^{-\frac{1}{2}}$
25 $(\frac{1}{9})^{-1}$	**26** $(\frac{1}{4})^{-\frac{1}{2}}$	**27** $3^{\frac{1}{2}} \times 3^{\frac{3}{2}}$
28 $(\frac{1}{27})^{-\frac{2}{3}}$	**29** $3^{\frac{1}{2}} \times 3^{-\frac{3}{2}}$	**30** $0.04^{\frac{1}{2}}$
31 $2a^{-1} \times 3a^2$	**32** $(2a)^{-1} \times 3a^2$	**33** $2a^{-1} \times (3a)^2$

34 $16^{-\frac{3}{2}}$ **35** $2^{\frac{1}{2}} \times 2^{\frac{3}{2}}$ **36** $(2^6)^{-\frac{2}{3}}$

37 $125^{-\frac{2}{3}}$ **38** $3^x \times 3^{-x}$ **39** $16^{-\frac{3}{4}}$

40 $0{\cdot}027^{\frac{2}{3}}$ **41** $2a \times 3a^{-2}$ **42** $2a \times (3a)^{-2}$

43 $4^{-\frac{3}{2}}$ **44** $\left(\frac{8}{27}\right)^{-\frac{2}{3}}$ **45** $\dfrac{1}{3^{-2}}$

46 2×2^{-3} **47** $\sqrt[3]{4^{1{\cdot}5}}$ **48** $3^{n-1} \times 3^{1-n}$

49 $64^{-\frac{2}{3}}$ **50** $\sqrt[3]{8a^{-6}}$ **51** $2x^{\frac{1}{2}} \times 3x^{-\frac{5}{2}}$

52 $0{\cdot}125^{-\frac{1}{3}}$ **53** $\left(\frac{16}{9}\right)^{-\frac{3}{2}}$ **54** $\sqrt[4]{16a^{-12}}$

55 $4a^3b \times 3ab^{-2}$ **56** $4a^3b \times (3ab)^{-2}$ **57** $\sqrt{(125^2)^{-\frac{1}{3}}}$

58 $\dfrac{75a^2b^{-2}}{5a^3b^{-3}}$ **59** $(2x)^{\frac{1}{2}} \times (2x^3)^{\frac{3}{2}}$ **60** $\left(\frac{18}{32}\right)^{-\frac{3}{2}}$

Rewrite the following expressions, using positive indices only $\left(\text{e.g. } x^{-2} = \dfrac{1}{x^2}\right)$:

61 a^{-2} **62** b^{-1} **63** $c^{-\frac{2}{3}}$ **64** xy^{-1}

65 $(xy)^{-1}$ **66** $a^{-2}b^3$ **67** ab^{-3} **68** $(ab)^{-3}$

69 $2x^{-\frac{1}{2}}$ **70** $3y^{-\frac{2}{3}}$

Solve for x the following equations:

71 $x^{\frac{1}{2}} = 2$ **72** $x^{\frac{1}{3}} = 3$ **73** $x^{-1} = 2$

74 $x^{-2} = 9$ **75** $2x^3 = 54$ **76** $x^{-\frac{1}{2}} = 5$

77 $x^{-\frac{2}{3}} = 9$ **78** $2x^{-3} = -16$ **79** $5x = 40x^{-\frac{1}{2}}$

80 $x = 9\sqrt{9x^{\frac{1}{2}}}$

Logarithms

'Logarithms are numbers invented for the more easie working of questions in arithmetike and geometrie . . . by them all troublesome multiplications and divisions are avoided and performed onlie by addition instead of multiplication, and by subtraction instead of division. The curious and laborious extraction of roots are also performed with great ease.'

3

This was written by Mr Briggs in 1631 in introducing the tables which are now used and which were invented by Napier as a way of reducing the enormous labour of calculation involved as the sciences of astronomy and navigation advanced and demanded ever more accurate numerical calculation.

The basic principle is simple. $10^1 = 10$ and $10^2 = 100$, so that any number between 10 and 100 must lie between 10^1 and 10^2, and is therefore 10 to the power of 'one point something'.

In fact tables of logarithms are simply lists of the powers to which 10 has to be raised in order to give any number required, and the word 'logarithm' denotes that power:

$$1\ 000 = 10^3 \quad \therefore \text{ the logarithm of } 1\ 000 \text{ is } 3$$
$$100 = 10^2 \quad \therefore \ \log 100 = 2$$
$$10 = 10^1 \quad \therefore \ \log 10 \ = 1$$
$$1 = 10^0 \quad \therefore \ \log 1 \ \ = 0.$$

Consider the number 3·7, using the log-tables. Its logarithm is 0·568 2, since these are the figures which appear in the tables immediately after 37: also, since 3·7 lies between 1 and 10, its logarithm lies between 0 and 1.

$$37 = 3.7 \times 10 = 10^{0.568\ 2} \times 10^1 = 10^{0.568\ 2+1} = 10^{1.568\ 2}$$

Hence $\quad \log 37 = 1.568\ 2.$

$$3\ 700 = 3.7 \times 1\ 000 = 10^{0.568\ 2} \times 10^3 = 10^{0.568\ 2+3} = 10^{3.568\ 2}$$

Hence $\quad \log 3\ 700 = 3.568\ 2.$

In the logarithm of any number the decimal part is called the **mantissa** and the integer before the decimal point is called the **characteristic.**

It should now be clear that the logarithms of all the numbers 3·7, 37, 370, 3 700 and so on have the same mantissa, while the characteristic is found by noticing that it is always one less than the number of figures before the decimal point. For example, there are 8 figures in 37 000 000, therefore the characteristic is 7,

$$\therefore \ \log 37\ 000\ 000 = 7.568\ 2, \text{ etc.}$$

Now consider the number 37·4.

To find its logarithm, first write down the characteristic (which is 1): then locate the row beginning with 37 and go along it until the column with 4 at the top is reached: this gives the figures 572 9.

$$\log 37 \cdot 4 = 1 \cdot 572\,9$$
$$\log 374 = 2 \cdot 572\,9, \text{ etc.}$$

Exercise 1b

Express as powers of 10:

1 2·65, 26·5, 26 500, 265

2 9·13, 9 130, 913, 9 130 000

Write down the logarithms of:

3 4·58, 458, 458 000, 45·8

4 7·06, 70 600 000, 70·6, 7 060

To look out the logarithm of 3·746, begin by finding the logarithm of 3·74 as already explained (i.e. 0·572 9), and add to it the number in the column headed 6 on the extreme right-hand side of the page in the tables, keeping on the same horizontal line all the time. This number is 7. Therefore the figures in the mantissa are 572 9 + 7, i.e. 573 6.

$$\log 3 \cdot 746 = 0 \cdot 573\,6 \quad \text{or} \quad 3 \cdot 746 = 10^{0 \cdot 573\,6}.$$

Express as powers of 10:

5 7·241   **6** 7·248   **7** 7·246   **8** 7·243

Write down the logarithms of:

9 5·136, 5 136, 51·36, 513 600

10 8·403, 840·3, 8 403 000, 84 030

11 75·12   **12** 4 137   **13** 208·5   **14** 294 100

15 82 460 000   **16** 65 160   **17** 12·05   **18** 397·3

19 40·02   **20** 100·6

21 Draw the graph of log x for values of x from 1 to 100, first completing the table

x	1	10	20	30	...	100
$\log x$	0·1	1·0	1·301	1·477	...	2·0

New General Mathematics

Read off the logarithms of 15, 47, 73, 9, 91. Find also the numbers whose logarithms are 0·5, 1·1, 1·75, 1·33, 0·86. Use log-tables to check the answers.

To find the number whose logarithm is given, the reverse of the previous process may be used (as for finding θ when $\tan\theta = 2\cdot173\ 4$), but it is often convenient to use the tables of **anti-logarithms.**

Only the mantissa has to be looked out, since the characteristic exists solely to show how many figures there are before the decimal point in the final number.

To find $10^{2\cdot754\ 7}$ (*i.e. the number whose logarithm is* $2\cdot754\ 7$).
·754 7 in the anti-log tables gives 5 684.

The characteristic 2 shows that there are 3 figures before the decimal point.

∴ the number whose logarithm is 2·754 7 is 568·4

or $10^{2\cdot754\ 7} = 568\cdot4.$

To find $10^{5\cdot391\ 4}$.
·391 4 in the anti-log tables gives 2 462.

The characteristic 5 shows that there are 6 figures before the decimal point.

∴ $10^{5\cdot391\ 4} = 246\ 200.$

Exercise 1c

Write down the values of:

1 $10^{0\cdot638\ 2}$, $10^{3\cdot638\ 2}$, $10^{2\cdot638\ 2}$, $10^{5\cdot638\ 2}$

2 $10^{0\cdot951\ 7}$, $10^{2\cdot951\ 7}$, $10^{4\cdot951\ 7}$, $10^{7\cdot951\ 7}$

Write down the numbers whose logarithms are:

3 0·714 2, 1·714 2, 6·714 2, 3·714 2

| **4** 2·181 4 | **5** 4·210 5 | **6** 1·563 8 | **7** 6·298 3 |
| **8** 3·448 5 | **9** 5·081 3 | **10** 1·109 1 | **11** 2·008 8 |

12 Draw the graph of $y = 10^x$ for values of x from 0 to 1. Read off the logarithms of 5, 8 and 9, and also the anti-logarithms of 0·15, 0·36 and 0·87.

'Troublesome multiplication and division'

Example 2 *Evaluate* 34·83 × 5·427.

$$34\cdot83 \times 5\cdot427 = 10^{1\cdot542\ 0} \times 10^{0\cdot734\ 6}$$
$$= 10^{1\cdot542\ 0+0\cdot734\ 6} \qquad \textbf{Law 1} \quad a^x \times a^y = a^{x+y}.$$
$$= 10^{2\cdot276\ 6}$$
$$= 189\cdot1.$$

Check 35 × 5 = 175.

N.B. Such checks will not generally be very close to the correct answer, but they should be close enough to reveal any serious mistake, and will certainly point out whether or not the decimal point is in the right place.

Example 3 *Evaluate* 4 562 ÷ 98·76.

$$4\ 562 \div 98\cdot76 = 10^{3\cdot659\ 2} \div 10^{1\cdot994\ 6}$$
$$= 10^{3\cdot659\ 2-1\cdot994\ 6} \qquad \textbf{Law 2} \quad a^x \div a^y = a^{x-y}.$$
$$= 10^{1\cdot664\ 6}$$
$$= 46\cdot19.$$

Check 4 600 ÷ 100 = 46.

Exercise 1d

Work out the following, giving a rough check in every case:

1 2·413 × 3·092	**2** 9·475 ÷ 6·13	**3** 3·802 × 2·09
4 8·735 ÷ 3·909	**5** 3·338 × 2·074	**6** 98·15 × 7·264
7 46·31 ÷ 8·742	**8** 45·34 × 16·21	**9** 176·3 ÷ 92·48
10 26·52 × 9·184	**11** 16·83 ÷ 8·992	**12** 912·4 ÷ 53·55
13 18·1 × 60·27	**14** 527·2 ÷ 94·35	**15** 43·14 × 8·932
16 43·14 ÷ 8·932	**17** 286·3 ÷ 17·08	**18** 34·07 × 1·007
19 705·6 × 85·04	**20** 45·80 ÷ 6·392	

New General Mathematics

Example 4 *Evaluate* $53 \cdot 75^3$.

$$53 \cdot 75^3 = (10^{1 \cdot 730\,4})^3$$
$$= 10^{1 \cdot 730\,4 \times 3} \qquad \textbf{Law 3} \quad (a^x)^y = a^{xy}.$$
$$= 10^{5 \cdot 191\,2}$$
$$= 155\,300.$$

Check $50^3 = 125\,000$

Exercise 1e

Work out, giving a rough check whenever reasonable:

1 $5 \cdot 037^2$	**2** $61 \cdot 03^2$	**3** $2 \cdot 938^3$	**4** $12 \cdot 94^3$	**5** $3 \cdot 572^5$
6 $252 \cdot 8^2$	**7** $7 \cdot 214^3$	**8** $2 \cdot 539^5$	**9** $5 \cdot 632^4$	**10** $19 \cdot 18^3$

'The curious and laborious extraction of roots'

Example 5 *Evaluate* $\sqrt[3]{350}$.

$$\sqrt[3]{350} = (10^{2 \cdot 544\,1})^{\frac{1}{3}}$$
$$= 10^{2 \cdot 544\,1 \div 3}$$
$$= 10^{0 \cdot 848\,0} \qquad \sqrt[n]{a} = a^{\frac{1}{n}}.$$
$$= 7 \cdot 047.$$

Check $7^3 = 343$.

Exercise 1f

Work out, giving a check whenever reasonable:

1 $\sqrt{26 \cdot 21}$	**2** $\sqrt[3]{26 \cdot 21}$	**3** $\sqrt[5]{31 \cdot 60}$	**4** $\sqrt{2\,621}$	**5** $\sqrt[3]{6 \cdot 392}$
6 $\sqrt[5]{3\,160}$	**7** $\sqrt[4]{35 \cdot 81}$	**8** $\sqrt[3]{927 \cdot 8}$	**9** $\sqrt[10]{2 \cdot 882}$	**10** $\sqrt[6]{35 \cdot 81}$

Having grasped the fundamental principle that logarithms depend upon indices and are all based upon powers of 10, it is possible to adopt a simpler method of setting out the work: for instance Examples 2 and 3 could be set out as follows:

Example 2

Evaluate 34·83 × 5·427.

No.	Log.
34·83	1·542 0
5·427	0·734 6
189·1	2·276 6

Check 35 × 5 = 175.
Ans. 189·1.

Example 3

Evaluate 4 562 ÷ 98·76.

No.	Log.
4 562	3·659 2
98·76	1·994 6
46·19	1·664 6

Check 4 600 ÷ 100 = 46.
Ans. 46·19.

Example 6 *Evaluate* 42·87 × 23·82 × 1·127.

No.	Log.
42·87	1·632 1
23·82	1·377 0
1·127	0·051 8
1 150	3·060 9

Check 40 × 25 × 1 = 1 000.

Ans. 1 150.

Example 7 *Evaluate* $\sqrt[3]{\dfrac{218}{3·12}}$.

No.	Log.
218	2·338 5
3·12	0·494 2
4·119	1·844 3 ÷3 = 0·614 8

Check $\sqrt[3]{\dfrac{210}{3}} = \sqrt[3]{70} = 4·\ldots$

$(4^3 = 64)$

Ans. 4·119.

Example 8 *Evaluate* 45·23² − 24·72².

45·23² − 24·72²
= (45·23 + 24·72)(45·23 − 24·72)
= 69·95 × 20·51
= 1 435. *Ans.*

No.	Log.
69·95	1·844 8
20·51	1·312 0
1 435	3·156 8

Check 45² − 25² = (45 + 25)(45 − 25) = 70 × 20 = 1 400.

9

Example 9 *Evaluate* $\dfrac{17\cdot83 \times 246\cdot9}{256\cdot2 \times 3\cdot28}$.

No.	Log.	
17·83 246·9	1·251 1 2·392 5	
Numerator	3·643 6	3·643 6
256·2 3·28	2·408 5 0·515 9	
Denominator	2·924 4	2·924 4
5·238		0·719 2

Check $\dfrac{18 \times 250}{250 \times 3} = 6.$

Ans. 5·238.

Example 10 *Evaluate* $\dfrac{(36\cdot12)^3 \times 750\cdot9}{(113\cdot2)^2 \times \sqrt[3]{92\cdot5}}$.

No.	Log.	
36·12³ 750·9	1·557 7 × 3 = 4·673 1 2·875 6	
Numerator	7·548 7	7·548 7
113·2² $\sqrt[3]{92\cdot5}$	2·053 9 × 2 = 4·107 8 1·966 1 ÷ 3 = 0·655 4	
Denominator	4·763 2	4·763 2
610·2		2·785 5

Check $\dfrac{40 \times 40 \times 40 \times 700}{120 \times 120 \times 5} = 622\cdot2.$

Ans. 610·2.

Exercise 1g

Simplify the following, checking the answer whenever it is reasonable to do so:

1 6·26 × 23·83 **2** 14·28 × 843·7 **3** 675·2 ÷ 35·81

4 1 200 ÷ 85·25 **5** 409 × 6·932 **6** 63·75 ÷ 8·946

7 5·932 × 8·164 × 18·51 **8** 8·4 × 19·7 × 51·5

9 $\dfrac{86 \cdot 23 \times 4\,058}{913 \cdot 6}$ **10** $\dfrac{29 \cdot 86 \times 105 \cdot 2}{685 \cdot 3}$

11 $3 \cdot 925^2$ **12** $5 \cdot 103^3$ **13** $2 \cdot 895^4$

14 $\sqrt[3]{210 \cdot 4}$ **15** $\sqrt[4]{83 \cdot 64}$ **16** $\sqrt[5]{31 \cdot 64}$

17 $2 \cdot 96^2 \times 8 \cdot 542$ **18** $\left(\dfrac{95 \cdot 32}{8 \cdot 971}\right)^2$

19 $\sqrt[3]{3 \cdot 172 \times 19 \cdot 86}$ **20** $\sqrt{56 \cdot 3 \times 39 \cdot 5 \times 8 \cdot 64}$

21 $2 \cdot 973^3$ **22** $\sqrt[3]{128 \cdot 7}$ **23** $85 \cdot 73 \div 39 \cdot 63$

24 $\sqrt[5]{3 \cdot 865 \times 8 \cdot 835}$ **25** $3 \cdot 86^3 \times 8 \cdot 63$

26 $(11 \cdot 62 \div 3 \cdot 95)^2$ **27** $\dfrac{36 \cdot 84 \times 2 \cdot 95}{18 \cdot 52}$

28 $8 \cdot 3 \times 22 \cdot 4 \times 19 \cdot 6$ **29** $\sqrt[3]{19 \cdot 63 \times 12 \cdot 28 \times 74}$

30 $\sqrt[5]{6 \cdot 838^3}$ **31** $\sqrt[4]{83 \cdot 67}$

32 $1 \cdot 084^{10}$ **33** $\sqrt{31 \cdot 87 \times 1 \cdot 863}$

34 $3 \cdot 95^3 \times 62 \cdot 5$ **35** $\sqrt[3]{\dfrac{1\,067}{29 \cdot 4}}$ **36** $5 \cdot 836^2 \times 1 \cdot 283^3$

37 $\sqrt{3 \cdot 892^3}$ **38** $\left(\dfrac{403 \cdot 9}{79 \cdot 62}\right)^3$

39 $\sqrt[3]{\dfrac{218 \times 37 \cdot 2}{95 \cdot 43}}$ **40** $\sqrt[3]{75 \cdot 2^2 - 24 \cdot 8^2}$

41 $\sqrt{254 \cdot 6 \times 3 \cdot 876}$ **42** $3 \cdot 857^{0 \cdot 6}$

43 $(36 \cdot 92 \div 8 \cdot 15)^3$ **44** $29 \cdot 3 \times \sqrt[5]{3 \cdot 87}$

45 $\sqrt[3]{65\,210 \div 8 \cdot 673}$ **46** $\sqrt[3]{130} - \sqrt[3]{130}$

47 $\sqrt[3]{29 \cdot 62^2 - 10 \cdot 36^2}$ **48** $2 \cdot 908^3 + \sqrt[5]{248 \cdot 4}$

49 $\sqrt{28 \cdot 4 \times 3 \cdot 82 \times 15 \cdot 64 \times 9 \cdot 47}$ **50** $\sqrt[3]{9 \cdot 58^3 - 7 \cdot 63^3}$

51 $\dfrac{28 \cdot 61 \times 74 \cdot 23}{355 \cdot 9 \times 2 \cdot 547}$ **52** $\dfrac{315 \cdot 6 \times 95 \cdot 47}{456 \cdot 2 \times 31 \cdot 88}$

11

53 $\dfrac{943}{11\cdot 64 \times 7\cdot 189}$

54 $\dfrac{35\cdot 2}{7\cdot 165 \times 3\cdot 92}$

55 $11\cdot 65 \times 91\cdot 21 - 11\cdot 65^2$

56 $\dfrac{1\,936}{28\cdot 3} - \dfrac{1\,462}{98\cdot 41}$

57 $\dfrac{(17\cdot 2)^2 \times 4\cdot 93}{\sqrt[3]{6\,750\,000}}$

58 $\sqrt[3]{\left(\dfrac{38\cdot 32 \times 2\cdot 964}{8\cdot 637 \times 6\cdot 285}\right)^2}$

59 $\dfrac{3\cdot 786^3 + 5}{3\cdot 786^3 - 5}$

60 $\dfrac{(18\cdot 43)^3 \times (15\cdot 36)^2}{(45\cdot 38)^2 \div \sqrt[3]{18\,780}}$

It must be remembered that logarithms are not absolutely accurate: the results obtained with four-figure logarithms are in fact accurate only in the first three figures, but this degree of accuracy is often sufficient.

If greater accuracy is required, as for instance in nautical or astronomical calculations, five- or seven-figure logarithms can be used, which are worked on the same principles as those of four-figure logarithms.

Use of negative index in abbreviations

In Books 1 and 2 the abbreviation used for a speed such as 8 kilometres per hour was 8 km/h. Now that a meaning has been established for a negative index, and using the fact that speed $= \dfrac{\text{distance}}{\text{time}}$, the standard abbreviation km h^{-1} will be used,

e.g. 8 kilometres per hour   8 km h^{-1}
      7 metres per second   7 m s^{-1}
      950 revolutions per minute   950 rev min^{-1}
      12 grammes per cubic centimetre   12 g cm^{-3}

Example 11 *Find, to three significant figures, the area of a flat circular washer 6·84 cm in diameter, the hole being 2·96 cm in diameter. Take log $\pi = 0\cdot 4971$.*

Area $= \pi 3 \cdot 42^2 - \pi 1 \cdot 48^2$ cm²

$\quad = \pi(3 \cdot 42^2 - 1 \cdot 48^2)$ „

$\quad = \pi(3 \cdot 42 + 1 \cdot 48)(3 \cdot 42 - 1 \cdot 48)$ „

$\quad = \pi \times 4 \cdot 9 \times 1 \cdot 94$ „

$\quad = 29 \cdot 86$ „

$\quad \simeq 29 \cdot 9 \text{ cm}^2$

No.	Log.
π	0·497 1
4·9	0·690 2
1·94	0·287 8
29·86	1·475 1

Exercise 1h

In this exercise take $\log \pi = 0 \cdot 497\ 1$, and give all answers to three significant figures.

1 Find the area of a rectangle 3·85 m long and 2·37 m wide.

2 Find the area of a square of side 2·83 cm.

3 Find the volume of a cube of side 8·24 cm.

4 Find the area of a circular disc 5·86 cm in diameter.

5 What is the mass in kg of a rectangular piece of metal 15·7 cm long and 12·9 cm wide, if the mass of 1 cm² is 38·1 g?

6 A rectangle of area 209·8 cm² is 10·4 cm long. Find its width.

7 Calculate the length of the side of a square of area 508·5 cm².

8 Find the length of the edge of a cube of volume 129·7 cm³.

9 Find the volume of a circular cylinder of diameter 5·93 cm and length 10 cm.

10 A room contains 156·1 m³ of air: the length is 7·2 m and the breadth 4·97 m. What is its height?

11 What is the depth in cm of a cubical tank of capacity 30 litres?

12 What is the area in hectares of a rectangular field 126 m long and 97 m wide?

13 If the area of a square playing field is 3·95 hectares, what is the length of a side of the field in metres?

13

14 1 km being equal to 0·54 of a sea mile, find the number of metres in a sea mile. Find also (i) 33 knots in km h⁻¹, (ii) 32 km h⁻¹ in knots (1 knot is a speed of 1 sea mile per hour).

15 Find the area of the stained-glass window shown in Fig. 1, the dimensions given being in metres.

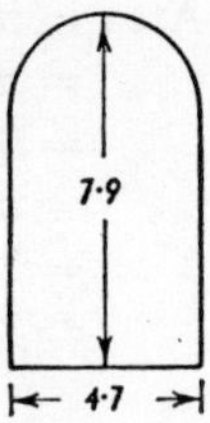

16 If £1 = $2·39, find the value of (i) £3·42 in dollars, (ii) $16 to the nearest penny.

7·9

← 4·7 →

Fig. 1

17 Find the area of metal in a circular washer of diameter 3·42 cm, having a 1-cm diameter hole in the centre.

18 What is the length of a solid cylinder of diameter 7·3 cm and volume 435 cm³?

19 Find the capacity in litres of a cylindrical tank 23·6 cm in diameter and 37·8 cm deep.

20 What is the mass in kg of a rectangular billet of metal 1 m long and 17·2 cm by 8·9 cm in section if the density of the metal is 7·21 g cm⁻³?

21 At what rate in km h⁻¹ is a boat moving if it covers a distance of 6·8 km in 19 min 17 s?

22 The mass of a cubic metre of iron is 7·85 tonnes. If an iron pillar of diameter 15·6 cm has a mass of 334 kg, what is its length in metres?

Chapter 2

Areas of parallelograms, triangles and trapeziums

Distance between parallel lines

$\overline{LM}$, $\overline{PQ}$ are two parallel lines. If from a point A on $\overline{LM}$ a perpendicular to $\overline{PQ}$ is drawn, meeting $\overline{PQ}$ in B, then $\overline{AB}$ is also perpendicular to $\overline{LM}$, for $L\hat{A}B = ABQ$ (alt.).

i.e. $L\hat{A}B$ is a right-angle.

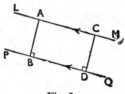

Fig. 2

Also, if from another point C on $\overline{LM}$ a perpendicular $\overline{CD}$ is drawn to meet $\overline{PQ}$ in D, then AB = CD, for ACDB is a rectangle, and its opposite sides are equal.

The length of any such perpendicular to $\overline{PQ}$ from a point on $\overline{LM}$ is said to be the distance between the two parallel lines.

Parallelograms and triangles lying between the same parallels

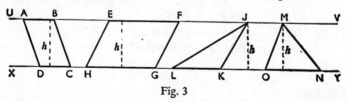

Fig. 3

In Fig. 3, $\overline{UV}$ and $\overline{XY}$ are parallel lines, and ‖gms ABCD, EFGH are drawn with their bases $\overline{DC}$, $\overline{HG}$ lying on $\overline{XY}$, and the opposite sides $\overline{AB}$, $\overline{EF}$ on $\overline{UV}$. Also △s JKL, MNO are drawn with their bases $\overline{LK}$, $\overline{ON}$ lying on $\overline{XY}$, and the vertices J, M on $\overline{UV}$. The four figures are said to lie **between the same parallels** $\overline{UV}$ and $\overline{XY}$.

Notice that the altitudes of the four figures are all equal, since each altitude is the distance between the two parallel lines $\overline{UV}$ and $\overline{XY}$.

Theorem 9

Parallelograms on the same base and between the same parallels are equal in area.

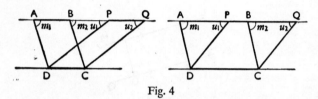

Fig. 4

Given ‖gms ABCD, PQCD on the same base $\overline{DC}$, and between the same ‖s $\overline{AQ}$, $\overline{DC}$.

To prove that ‖gm ABCD = ‖gm PQCD.

Proof In △s APD, BQC

$$m_1 = m_2 \qquad\qquad corr.,\ \overline{AD}\ \|\ \overline{BC}$$
$$u_1 = u_2 \qquad\qquad corr.,\ \overline{PD}\ \|\ \overline{QC}$$
$$AD = BC \qquad opp.\ sides\ of\ \|gm\ ABCD$$
$$\therefore \triangle APD \equiv \triangle BQC \qquad\qquad AAS$$
$$\therefore \text{fig. } AQCD - \triangle APD = \text{fig. } AQCD - \triangle BQC$$
$$\therefore \|gm\ PQCD = \|gm\ ABCD.$$

Corollary

A parallelogram is equal in area to a rectangle on the same base and between the same parallels.

16

Areas of parallelograms, triangles and trapeziums

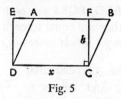

Fig. 5

Area of ‖gm ABCD = area of rect EFCD
$$= DC \times CF$$
$$= xh.$$

i.e. **the area of a parallelogram is the product of the base and the perpendicular height.**

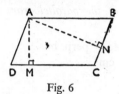

Fig. 6

Notice that either $\overline{DC}$ or $\overline{CB}$ can be taken as the base, and that each has its corresponding altitude.

Hence, in Fig. 6, the area of ‖gm ABCD is $DC \times AM$ or $CB \times AN$.

Corollary

Parallelograms on equal bases and between the same parallels are equal in area.

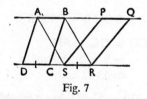

Fig. 7

In Fig. 7, ‖gms ABCD, PQRS have equal bases $\overline{DC}$, $\overline{SR}$ and lie between the same ‖s $\overline{AQ}$, $\overline{DR}$.

Join $\overline{AS}$, $\overline{BR}$ and prove that ABRS is a ‖gm.

17

New General Mathematics

Then since ‖gms ABCD, PQRS are each equal to ‖gm ABRS (*same base, same ‖s*), they are equal to each other.

As an exercise, the pupil should write out this proof in full.

Alternatively, if the perpendicular distance between $\overline{AQ}$ and $\overline{DR}$ is h,
area of ‖gm ABCD = DC × h
„ „ ‖gm PQRS = SR × h
But DC = SR   *given*
∴ ‖gm ABCD = ‖gm PQRS.

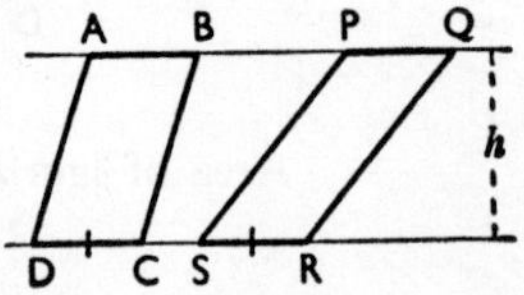

Fig. 8

Example 1 *The area of the parallelogram in Fig. 9 is 44 cm². Find x.*

Area = base × perp. ht.
     = 8x cm²
∴ 8x = 44
∴ x = $\frac{44}{8}$
    = 5½.

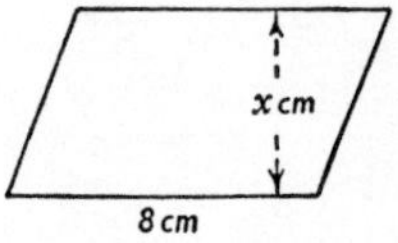

Fig. 9

Example 2 *Find the area of a parallelogram* ABCD *in which* DA = 7 *cm*, DC = 9 *cm*, $\hat{D}$ = 58°.

Draw the altitude $\overline{AM}$, and let its length be h cm.

Then $\dfrac{h}{7}$ = sin 58°

Fig. 10

∴ h = 7 sin 58° = 7 × 0·848 0 = 5·936 0

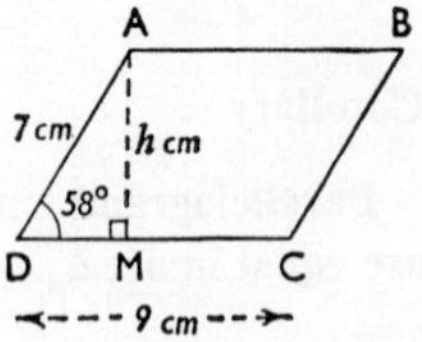

∴ area of ‖gm ABCD = DC × AM
                   = 9 × 5·936 cm²
                   ≃ 53·42 cm².

Notice that 9 × 5·936 = 53·424, but it would not be sensible to have an answer with 5 significant figures when the working involves a reading from 4-figure tables. It would, in fact, be quite reasonable to give the answer as 53·4 cm².

18

Exercise 2a

Find the areas of the parallelograms in Fig. 11, the dimensions being in centimetres.

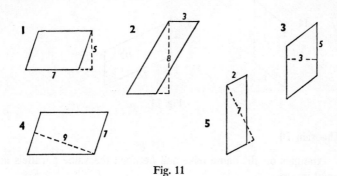

Fig. 11

In each of the parallelograms in Fig. 12 find the value of x.

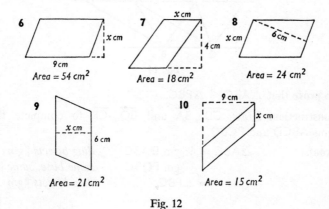

Fig. 12

Find the areas of the parallelograms in Fig. 13, the dimensions being in centimetres (3 sig. fig.).

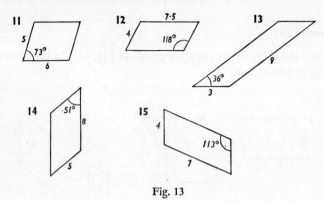

Fig. 13

Theorem 10

Triangles on the same base and between the same parallels are equal in area.

Given △s ABC, PBC on the same base $\overline{BC}$, and between the same ∥s $\overline{AP}$, $\overline{CB}$.

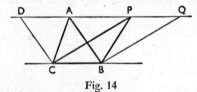

Fig. 14

To prove that △ABC = △PBC.

Construction. Draw $\overline{CD} \parallel \overline{BA}$ and $\overline{BQ} \parallel \overline{CP}$ to complete the ∥gms ABCD and PCBQ.

Proof.

$$\triangle ABC = \tfrac{1}{2} \parallel\text{gm DABC} \qquad \textit{diag bisects } \parallel gm$$
$$= \tfrac{1}{2} \parallel\text{gm PQBC} \qquad \textit{same base, same } \parallel s$$
$$= \triangle PBC. \qquad \textit{diag bisects } \parallel gm$$

Corollary

Triangles on equal bases and between the same parallels are equal in area.

Areas of parallelograms, triangles and trapeziums

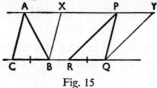

Fig. 15

In Fig. 15, ABC and PQR are the given $\triangle$s.

Complete the ∥gms ACBX, PRQY of which the given $\triangle$s are respectively the halves.

Then since the ∥gms are equal in area, their halves are equal to each other.

Corollary

If a triangle and a parallelogram are on the same base and between the same parallels, the area of the triangle is half the area of the parallelogram.

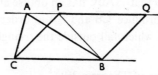

Fig. 16

In Fig. 16, ABC is the given $\triangle$ and PQBC is the given ∥gm.

Join $\overline{PB}$, which bisects the ∥gm.

Then
$$\triangle ABC = \triangle PBC$$
$$= \tfrac{1}{2}\text{∥gm PQBC}.$$

Corollary

The area of a triangle is half the product of the base and the perpendicular height (altitude).

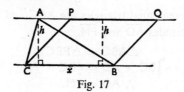

Fig. 17

21

In Fig. 17, $\triangle ABC = \frac{1}{2}\|gm\ PQBC$
$$= \frac{1}{2}xh.$$

Notice that any of the three sides of a triangle can be taken as the base, each having its corresponding altitude.

Hence in Fig. 18,

area of $\triangle ABC = \frac{1}{2}BC \times AD$ or $\frac{1}{2}CA \times BE$ or $\frac{1}{2}AB \times CF$.

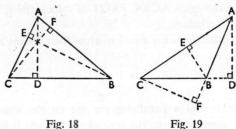

Fig. 18   Fig. 19

Notice in Fig. 19 that $\triangle ABC$ has an obtuse angle at B, and that it is necessary to produce $\overline{CB}$ and $\overline{AB}$ in order to draw the altitudes $\overline{AD}$ and $\overline{CF}$, which fall outside the triangle.

Corollary (Converse of Theorem 10)

Equal triangles on the same base and on the same side of it are between the same parallels.

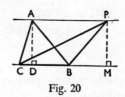

Fig. 20

In Fig. 20 the given equal triangles are ABC and PBC.

Draw their altitudes $\overline{AD}$ and $\overline{PM}$.

Then since
$$\triangle ABC = \triangle PBC$$
$$\frac{1}{2}BC \times AD = \frac{1}{2}BC \times PM$$
$$\therefore AD = PM.$$

But $\overline{AD}$, $\overline{PM}$ are both $\perp$ $\overline{BC}$.

$$\therefore \text{ APMD is a rect}$$
$$\therefore \overline{AP} \parallel \overline{DM}$$
$$\text{i.e. } \overline{AP} \parallel \overline{CB}.$$

Example 3 *Find the area of* $\triangle ABC$ *if* $BA = 6$ *cm*, $BC = 7$ *cm*, $\hat{B} = 34°$.

Let the altitude AD be x cm.

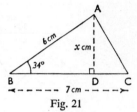

Fig. 21

Then
$$\frac{x}{6} = \sin 34°$$

$$\therefore x = 6 \sin 34°$$
$$= 6 \times 0.559\,2$$
$$= 3.355(2).$$

$\therefore$ area of $\triangle ABC = \frac{1}{2}BC \times AD$

$$= \frac{1}{2} \times 7 \times 3.355 \text{ cm}^2$$
$$= \frac{1}{2} \times 23.48(5) \text{ cm}^2$$
$$= 11.74 \text{ cm}^2$$
$$\simeq 11.7 \text{ cm}^2.$$

Example 4 *Find the area of* $\triangle PQR$ *if* $PR = 5$ *cm*, $QR = 6$ *cm*, $P\hat{R}Q = 118°$.

Let the altitude PD be x cm.

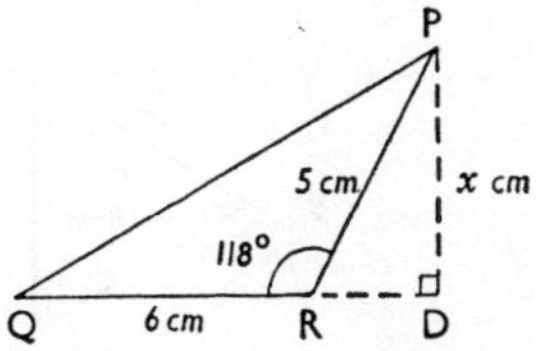

Then
$$P\hat{R}D = 180° - 118° = 62°$$

$$\therefore \frac{x}{5} = \sin 62°$$

$$\therefore x = 5 \sin 62° = 5 \times 0.882\,9$$
$$= 4.414(5).$$

Fig. 22

$$\therefore \text{ area of } \triangle PQR = \frac{1}{2}QR \times PD$$
$$= \frac{1}{2} \times 6 \times 4.414(5) \text{ cm}^2$$
$$= 13.24 \text{ cm}^2$$
$$\simeq 13.2 \text{ cm}^2.$$

23

Exercise 2b

Find the areas of the triangles in Fig. 23, the dimensions being in centimetres.

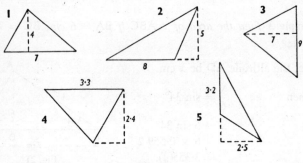

Fig. 23

In each of the triangles in Fig. 24 find the value of *x*.

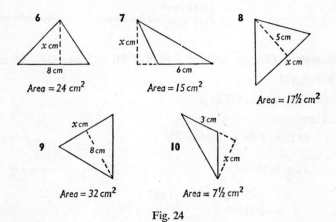

Fig. 24

Find the areas of the triangles in Fig. 25, the dimensions being in centimetres (3 sig. fig.).

Areas of parallelograms, triangles and trapeziums

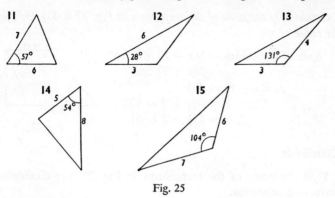

Fig. 25

Trapezium

Area of a trapezium. In Fig. 26, ABCD is a trapezium with $\overline{AB} \parallel \overline{DC}$.

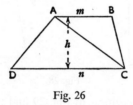

Fig. 26

Let the lengths of $\overline{AB}$ and $\overline{DC}$ be m and n respectively, and let their perpendicular distance apart be h.

Join $\overline{AC}$.

Area of trap ABCD

$$= \text{area of } \triangle ABC + \text{area of } \triangle ACD$$
$$= \tfrac{1}{2}mh + \tfrac{1}{2}nh$$
$$= \tfrac{1}{2}h(m + n) \quad \text{or} \quad \tfrac{1}{2}(m + n)h$$

Hence the area of a trapezium is half the product of the sum of the parallel sides and the perpendicular distance between them.

25

Example 5 *If the area of the trapezium in Fig. 27 is* $40\frac{1}{2}$ *cm², find the value of* x.

Area of trapezium $= \frac{1}{2}(x + 8) \times 6$ cm²
$$= 3(x + 8) \text{ cm}^2$$
$$\therefore 3(x + 8) = 40\tfrac{1}{2}$$
$$\therefore x + 8 = 40\tfrac{1}{2} \div 3 = 13\tfrac{1}{2}$$
$$\therefore x = 13\tfrac{1}{2} - 8 = 5\tfrac{1}{2}.$$

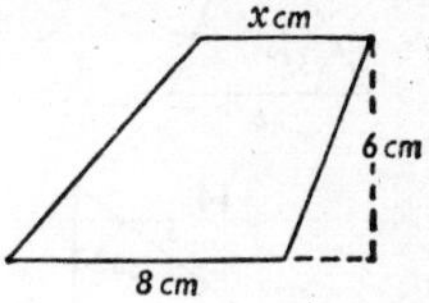

Fig. 27

Exercise 2c

Find the areas of the trapeziums in Fig. 28, the dimensions being in centimetres.

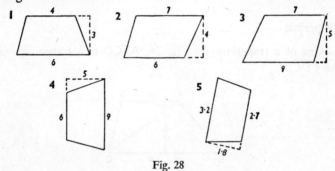

Fig. 28

In each of the trapeziums in Fig. 29 find the value of x.

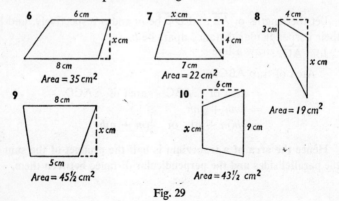

Fig. 29

Find the areas of the trapeziums in Fig. 30, the dimensions being in centimetres (3 sig. fig.).

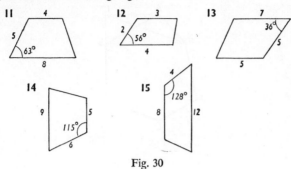

Fig. 30

Construction 7

To construct a triangle equal in area to a given quadrilateral.

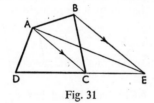

Fig. 31

Given a quad ABCD.

To construct a △ of equal area.

Construction Join $\overline{AC}$.

Through B draw a line ∥ $\overline{AC}$ to meet $\overline{DC}$ produced in E.
Join $\overline{AE}$.
Then △AED is the required △.

Proof   △ABC = △AEC *same base* $\overline{AC}$, *same* ∥s $\overline{AC}$, $\overline{BE}$
∴ △ABC + △ACD = △AEC + △ACD
∴ quad ABCD = △AED.

This construction may be applied to any polygon, the result being a polygon of equal area but with one side fewer than the original polygon.

B

27

For example (Fig. 32), starting with the hexagon ABCDEF,

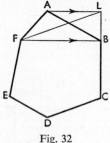

Fig. 32

the △ABF is cut off and replaced by the equal △LBF. Then the pentagon LCDEF is equal to the given hexagon.

The process may be repeated (cutting off △LCF) and the pentagon reduced to a quadrilateral of equal area.

This quadrilateral may in turn be reduced to an equal triangle.

A median bisects a triangle

In Fig. 33 the median $\overline{AM}$ of △ABC bisects $\overline{BC}$.

Hence △s ABM, ACM have equal bases and the same altitude, and are therefore equal in area.

Fig. 33

This may be regarded as a special case of triangles on equal bases and lying between the same parallels.

If triangles have the same altitude, their areas are in the ratio of their bases.

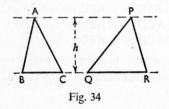

Fig. 34

In Fig. 34 the △s ABC, PQR have the same altitude *h*.

Then
$$\frac{\triangle ABC}{\triangle PQR} = \frac{\frac{1}{2} \times BC \times h}{\frac{1}{2} \times QR \times h}$$
$$= \frac{BC}{QR}.$$

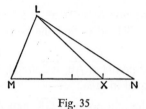

Fig. 35

Hence (Fig. 35), if for example MX = 3XN, then
$$\triangle LMX = 3 \times \triangle LXN.$$

Exercise 2d

1 Draw a rectangle measuring 10 cm by 8 cm. Construct a rhombus, equal in area to the rectangle, with sides of 10 cm. Measure the shorter diagonal of the rhombus.

2 A rectangle 9 cm long is equal in area to a square which measures 6 cm each way. Find the width of the rectangle.

3 A line parallel to the side $\overline{QR}$ of △PQR meets $\overline{PQ}$, $\overline{PR}$ in X, Y respectively. Prove that △s PXR, PYQ are equal in area.

4 A is any point in the side $\overline{PQ}$ of parallelogram PQRS. Prove that △APS + △AQR = $\frac{1}{2}$ ‖gm PQRS.

5 Find the length of a side of the square which is equal in area to a rectangle measuring 45 cm by 5 cm.

6 PQRS is a trapezium in which $\overline{PQ}$, $\overline{SR}$ are the parallel sides, and X is the mid-point of $\overline{SR}$. Prove that the trapeziums PQRX, PQXS are equal in area.

7 Draw a rectangle of altitude 5 cm with a base of length 7 cm. On the same base construct a parallelogram of equal area,

29

with an angle of 70°. Measure the lengths of the diagonals of the parallelogram.

8 ABCD is a parallelogram in which AB = 7 cm and AD = 5 cm. $\overline{AX}$ and $\overline{AY}$ are the perpendiculars from A to $\overline{BC}$, $\overline{CD}$ respectively. If AY = 4 cm, calculate the area of the parallelogram, and hence find AX.

9 The area of a trapezium is 14·7 cm². If 5·3 cm, 3·1 cm are the lengths of the parallel sides, find the perpendicular distance between them.

10 In △ABC the mid-points of $\overline{AB}$, $\overline{AC}$ are H, K. Prove that △s BHK, CHK are equal in area.

11 In △PQR, M is the mid-point of $\overline{QR}$, and A is any point on $\overline{PM}$. Prove that △s APQ, APR are equal in area.

12 PQRS is a quadrilateral in which $\overline{PQ}$, $\overline{SR}$ are parallel. If the diagonals meet at O, prove that △s POS, QOR are equal in area.

13 PQR is any triangle, and X is any point on $\overline{QR}$ produced. Give, with proof, a construction for finding a point Y in $\overline{PQ}$ such that △s QXY, PQR are equal in area.

14 Draw a parallelogram with sides of 6 cm and 8 cm, and an angle of 81°. Construct a rhombus with sides of 8 cm, equal in area to the parallelogram. Measure the shorter diagonal of the rhombus.

15 A triangle is equal in area to a rectangle which measures 10 cm by 9 cm. If the base of the triangle is 12 cm long, find its altitude.

16 Three buoys A, B, C are placed so that B is due E of A, and C is on a bearing S 38° W from A. If AB = 250 m and AC = 350 m, find the area of △ABC in m² correct to 3 sig. fig.

17 ABCD is a ∥gm. S, Q are points on $\overline{AD}$, $\overline{BC}$ such that $\overline{SQ} \parallel \overline{AB}$. P, R are any points on $\overline{AB}$, $\overline{CD}$ respectively. Prove that quad PQRS = $\frac{1}{2}$ ∥gm ABCD.

18 PQRS is a trapezium in which $\overline{PQ}$, $\overline{SR}$ are the parallel sides. X, Y are points in $\overline{SR}$ such that SX = YR. Prove that the trapeziums PQXS, PQRY are equal in area.

19 Draw a regular pentagon with sides each 5 cm long, and then construct a triangle of equal area.

20 ABCD is a quadrilateral, and E is a point in $\overline{CD}$ such that $\overline{AE}$, $\overline{BC}$ are parallel. Prove that quad ABED and $\triangle$ACD have equal areas.

21 Give, with proof, a construction for drawing a parallelogram whose area is twice the area of a given quadrilateral.

22 In Fig. 36 the lengths given are in centimetres. Find the areas

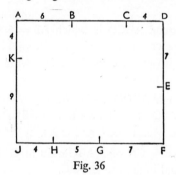

Fig. 36

of $\triangle$ABK, $\triangle$DKE, $\triangle$ABG, $\triangle$HEG, trap CDFJ, ‖gm CDHJ, trap ADGH, $\triangle$AGE, quad BEHK, $\triangle$CGK.

23 D is a point on the side $\overline{BC}$ of $\triangle$ABC such that BD = 2DC. E is a point on $\overline{AD}$ such that DE = 2EA. Prove that $2\triangle$ABC $= 9\triangle$ABE.

24 $\overline{BM}$, $\overline{CN}$ are altitudes of $\triangle$ABC. If AB = 3·5 cm, AC = 3·2 cm, BM = 2·1 cm, calculate the area of $\triangle$ABC and hence find CN.

25 ABCD is a parallelogram and $\overline{AM}$, $\overline{AN}$ are the perpendiculars from A to $\overline{BC}$, $\overline{CD}$ respectively. If AB = 6·3 cm, AD = 4·9 cm, AN = 4·2 cm, calculate the area of the parallelogram, and hence find AM.

31

26 AXY, BXY are △s on the same base $\overline{XY}$ and between the same ‖s $\overline{AB}$, $\overline{XY}$. If $\overline{BX}$ bisects $\overline{AY}$ at E, prove that E is also the mid-point of $\overline{BX}$.

27 A is any point in the side $\overline{PQ}$ of a square PQRS, and B is the mid-point of $\overline{AR}$. Prove that the area of △ABS is a quarter of the area of the given square.

28 Given a triangle ABC with X any point in $\overline{BC}$, show how to construct a trapezium ABXY equal in area to △ABC (two possibilities). Prove that your construction is correct.

29 In the rectangle ABCD, P is any point on $\overline{AB}$. If AB = 11 cm and AD = 8 cm, find the sum of the areas of △APD and △BPC.

30 Construct a quad ABCD in which AB = 6·8 cm, AC = 8·3 cm, AD = 6·2 cm, BC = 4·7 cm, DC = 6·2 cm. Construct △AED equal in area to quad ABCD, with E lying on $\overline{DC}$ produced. Measure AE.

31 Draw a rectangle ABCD having AB = 5·7 cm, AD = 7·2 cm. Construct △AED equal in area to rect ABCD, with E lying on $\overline{DC}$ produced. Measure DE and check by calculation.

32 The medians $\overline{BM}$, $\overline{CN}$ of △ABC meet at O. Prove that quad AMON is equal in area to △BOC.

33 $\overline{AM}$ is a median of △ABC, and D is the mid-point of $\overline{AM}$. Prove that △ABD = △CDM.

34 Draw a rectangle ABCD in which AB = 12 cm and AD = 8 cm. On $\overline{AB}$ mark a point E such that AE = 10 cm, and join $\overline{DE}$. Draw $\overline{CF}$, the perpendicular from C to $\overline{DE}$. Measure DE and CF, and find their product. What do you notice? Why?

35 A, B, C are three hill-top points of observation. B is 2·4 km from A on a bearing of 142°. C is 3·2 km from A on a bearing of 209°. Find the area of △ABC in square kilometres, correct to 3 sig. fig.

36 RSTU is a quad such that $\overline{SU}$ bisects $\overline{RT}$. Prove that △s RSU, TSU are equal in area.

37 Calculate the area of a rhombus with diagonals of 10 cm and 7 cm.

38 $\overline{AM}$, $\overline{BN}$ are altitudes of $\triangle ABC$ in which $AC = \frac{1}{2}BC$. Prove that $BN = 2AM$.

39 Show how to construct the parallelogram ABCD, given that its area $= 48$ cm², $AB = 8$ cm, $BD = 13$ cm.

40 ABCD is a parallelogram, and a line through D meets $\overline{AB}$ at E, and $\overline{CB}$ produced at F. Prove that $\triangle ADF = \triangle CDE$.

41 E is any point on the side $\overline{AB}$ of a parallelogram ABCD. $\overline{AC}$ cuts $\overline{DE}$ at F. Prove that $\triangle CDF = \triangle AEF + \triangle BCE$.

42 Give, with proof, a construction for drawing an isosceles triangle equal in area to a given square, the base of the triangle being a diagonal of the square.

43 H, K are any points on the sides $\overline{AB}$, $\overline{AD}$ respectively of ‖gm ABCD. Prove that $\triangle s$ CBK, CDH are equal in area.

44 A line parallel to the diagonal $\overline{AC}$ of ‖gm ABCD meets $\overline{AD}$, $\overline{CD}$ in X, Y respectively. Prove that $\triangle ABX = \triangle BCY$.

45 Draw a ‖gm PQRS in which $\hat{S} = 60°$, $PS = 8$ cm, $RS = 10$ cm. Construct a ‖gm ABRS equal in area to PQRS and having $SB = SR$. Measure BR.

46 In $\triangle$ PQR, M is the mid-point of $\overline{QR}$, and X is any point in $\overline{QM}$. A line through M parallel to $\overline{XP}$ meets $\overline{PR}$ in Y. Prove that $\triangle XYR = \frac{1}{2}\triangle PQR$.

47 $\overline{AB}$, $\overline{CD}$, $\overline{EF}$ are three parallel straight lines, $\overline{CD}$ lying between the other two. X and Y are points on $\overline{CD}$, and the straight lines $\overline{PYQ}$, $\overline{MYN}$ meet $\overline{AB}$ in P, M, and $\overline{EF}$ in Q, N. Prove that $\triangle PXQ = \triangle MXN$.

48. In $\triangle XYZ$, M is the mid-point of $\overline{YZ}$, and the perpendiculars from M to $\overline{XY}$, $\overline{XZ}$ are $\overline{MD}$, $\overline{ME}$. If $XY = 9$ cm, $XZ = 6$ cm, and the area of $\triangle XYZ$ is 36 cm², calculate MD and ME.

49 O is any point inside a rectangle ABCD. Prove that $\triangle OAB + \triangle OCD = \triangle OAD + \triangle OBC$.

New General Mathematics

50 PQRS is a trapezium in which the parallel sides are $\overline{PQ}$, $\overline{SR}$, and PQTS is a parallelogram. If $\overline{PR}$, $\overline{QT}$ (produced if necessary) meet at U, prove that $\triangle QRU = \triangle STU$.

51 The area of the parallelogram ABCD is 43 cm², AB = 7 cm, BC = 9 cm. Calculate $A\hat{B}C$, given that it is acute.

52 ABCD is a trapezium in which the parallel sides are $\overline{AB}$ and $\overline{DC}$. The mid-point of $\overline{BC}$ is M. Prove that the area of $\triangle AMD$ is equal to half the area of the trapezium ABCD.

53 $\overline{PM}$, $\overline{XYZ}$, $\overline{NQ}$ are three parallel straight lines, $\overline{XYZ}$ lying between the other two. $\overline{PYQ}$, $\overline{MYN}$ are straight lines and $\overline{MX}$ is parallel to $\overline{ZN}$. Prove that $\overline{PX}$ and $\overline{ZQ}$ are parallel.

54 In a $\triangle ABC$, D divides $\overline{AB}$ in the ratio 2 : 3, and E divides $\overline{AC}$ in the ratio 3 : 4. Find the ratio of $\triangle BCD$ to $\triangle ABC$ and the ratio of $\triangle ABE$ to $\triangle ABC$. Hence find the ratio of $\triangle ABE$ to $\triangle BCD$.

55 In a $\triangle ABC$, D divides $\overline{BC}$ in the ratio 4 : 5, and E divides $\overline{AD}$ in the ratio 1 : 2. Find the ratio of $\triangle ABE$ to $\triangle ABC$.

Chapter 3

Pythagoras' Theorem
Square root tables

In a right-angled triangle the longest side, opposite the right angle, is called the hypotenuse. If squares are drawn on the three sides, the square on the hypotenuse is equal in area to the sum of the squares on the other two sides. The discovery of this fact is attributed to Pythagoras, a Greek philosopher who lived in the sixth century B.C.

A proof of the theorem will be given later in this chapter, but two demonstrations of the truth of the statement are given here.

1. Fig. 37 may be enlarged and cut out in cardboard to make a working model.

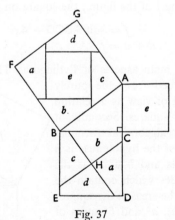

Fig. 37

$\overline{AB}$ is the hypotenuse of $\triangle ABC$ and $\overline{BC}$ is the larger of the other two sides.

The centre of the square BCDE is H (the point of intersection of the diagonals). Through H lines are drawn respectively parallel and perpendicular to $\overline{AB}$, dividing the square into four identical

35

quadrilaterals marked *a*, *b*, *c*, and *d*. It will be found that these quadrilaterals, together with the square *e*, may be fitted exactly on to the square ABFG.

2. In Fig. 38, $\overline{PQ}$ is the hypotenuse of $\triangle PQR$, and the squares

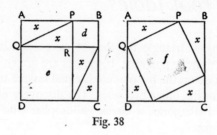

Fig. 38

on $\overline{PR}$ and $\overline{QR}$ are *d* and *e*. From the figure it should be clear that

$$d + e = \text{squ ABCD} - 4x.$$

In the second part of the figure, the square on $\overline{PQ}$ is *f*, and

$$f = \text{squ ABCD} - 4x$$
$$\therefore d + e = f.$$

There are two main aspects of Pythagoras' Theorem. Firstly, it may be regarded from the purely geometrical point of view as a relation between areas of squares. Secondly, it gives rise to an algebraical formula, for if the length of the hypotenuse is *h* units, with *a* units and *b* units as the lengths of the sides which contain the right angle, then the areas of the squares are respectively h^2, a^2 and b^2 units of area.

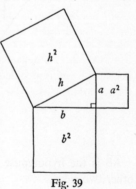

Fig. 39

Hence $h^2 = a^2 + b^2.$

This formula may also be expressed in the forms

$$a^2 = h^2 - b^2 \quad \text{and} \quad b^2 = h^2 - a^2.$$

If the lengths of two of the sides are given, the length of the remaining side may be found by substitution in the formula. For example, if the sides containing the right angle have lengths of 5 m and 12 m,

$$\begin{aligned} \text{then} \quad h^2 &= 5^2 + 12^2 \\ &= 25 + 144 \\ &= 169 \\ \therefore h &= \sqrt{169} = 13. \end{aligned}$$

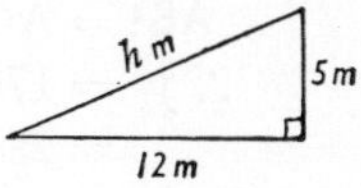

Fig. 40

∴ the length of the hypotenuse is 13 m.

If the length of the hypotenuse is 5 m and another side is of length 3 m,

$$\begin{aligned} \text{then} \quad b^2 &= 5^2 - 3^2 \\ &= 25 - 9 \\ &= 16 \\ \therefore b &= \sqrt{16} = 4. \end{aligned}$$

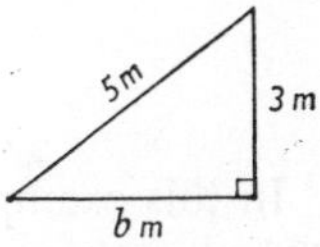

Fig. 41

∴ the length of the remaining side is 4 m.

This last example of a right-angled triangle with sides of 3, 4 and 5 units is extensively used for practical purposes, and is commonly referred to as a '3, 4, 5 triangle'. Multiples of these lengths may of course be used, such as 6, 8, 10; 9, 12, 15; 30, 40, 50 and so on.

A builder pegging out the foundations of a house would almost certainly not possess a surveyor's theodolite, an instrument which is unnecessarily complicated and expensive for this purpose. Having decided on the position A of one corner of the house, and the direction $\overline{AD}$ of one wall, he would mark off along $\overline{AD}$ a length AB of 12 m. Then with stout cords of lengths 9 m and 15 m respectively, attached to pegs at A and B, he would easily find the position of C such that $B\hat{A}C$ is a right angle.

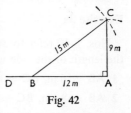

Fig. 42

In the same way a groundsman would establish his right angles when marking out games pitches.

Example 1 *In Fig. 43 if* AC = 17 *cm*, BC = 8 *cm*, CD = 12 *cm*, *find* AD.

Let AD = x cm and AB = y cm.
In rt.-∠d △ABC,

$$AB^2 = AC^2 - BC^2$$
$$\therefore y^2 = 17^2 - 8^2$$
$$= 289 - 64 = 225.$$

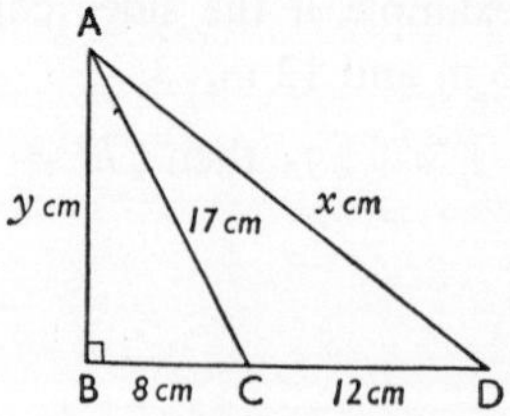

In rt.-∠d △ABD,

$$AD^2 = AB^2 + BD^2$$
$$\therefore x^2 = y^2 + 20^2$$
$$= 225 + 400 = 625$$
$$\therefore x = \sqrt{625} = 25$$
$$\therefore AD = 25 \text{ cm.}$$

Fig. 43

In this example, notice that when y^2 has been found equal to 225, there is no need to find y, since it is y^2 that is needed in the subsequent working.

Notice also the following method of calculation which will often save much numerical working:

$$d^2 = 65^2 - 33^2$$
$$= (65 + 33)(65 - 33)$$
$$= 98 \times 32$$
$$= 49 \times 2 \times 32$$
$$= 49 \times 64$$
$$\therefore d = 7 \times 8$$
$$= 56.$$

Exercise 3a

Nos. 1–10 refer to △ABC in which $\hat{B} = 90°$. In each case find the length of the side which is not given.

1 AB = 6 m, BC = 8 m

2 AB = 8 cm, BC = 15 cm

3 AC = 26 m, AB = 10 m

4 AC = 25 cm, BC = 24 cm

5 AC = 41 cm, BC = 9 cm

6 AB = 20 m, BC = 21 m

7 AC = 37 m, AB = 12 m

8 AC = 61 cm, BC = 60 cm

9 AB = 28 cm, BC = 45 cm

10 AC = 65 m, AB = 56 m

In nos. 11–15 find the value of x.

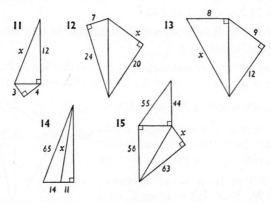

Fig. 44

16 A goat is tethered by a rope 13 m long to a post which is 12 m from a hedge. What length of hedge is within reach of the goat?

17 The heights of two vertical masts are 55 m and 66 m, and they stand 60 m apart on the horizontal ground. Find the length of a taut wire (assumed to be straight) joining the tops of the masts.

18 George and Tom stand together at a corner flag of a football pitch. George walks 9 metres along the goal line to a point A, and Tom walks 12 metres along the touch line to a point B. How far apart are they? George stands still at A, and Tom walks a further 20 metres in a direction at right angles to $\overline{AB}$. What is then the distance between them?

19 Calculate the length of a diagonal of a square with sides each 7 cm long. (3 sig. fig.)

20 In quad ABCD, $\hat{A}$ is a right-angle, AB = 7 cm, BC = 15 cm, CD = 20 cm, DA = 24 cm. Prove that $\hat{C}$ is also a right angle.

21 In ∥gm ABCD the bisectors of $\hat{C}$ and $\hat{D}$ meet at E. Prove that CÊD is a right angle. Hence calculate CD if EC = 2·8 cm and ED = 4·5 cm.

22 In △ABC, AB = 26 cm, BC = 28 cm and the altitude AD = 24 cm. Calculate AC.

23 Calculate the altitude of an equilateral triangle with sides each 8 cm long. (3 sig. fig.)

24 A vessel leaves port and steams 11 km north, then 21 km east, and then 9 km north. How far is it then from the port?

25 In Fig. 45, calculate AC, AD, BD.

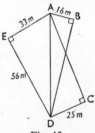

26 Find the length of the longest needle that can be put inside a rectangular box measuring 6 cm by 3 cm by 2 cm.

27 A is 280 m from C on a bearing N 32° W. B is 450 m from C on a bearing N 58° E. Find the distance from A to B.

Fig. 45

28 In the parallelogram PQRS the diagonal $\overline{PR}$ is at right angles to $\overline{PQ}$. If PR = 6 cm and QS = 10 cm, calculate the area of the parallelogram.

29 A rectangle is 2·8 cm wide, and the length of each diagonal is 5·3 cm. Calculate the length of the rectangle and its area.

30 If △ABC is right-angled at B, and AB = 2 m, BC = 2·1 m, calculate the length of the altitude $\overline{BD}$. (3 sig. fig.)

31 Starting from the ground, a helicopter rises 168 m vertically, then travels 576 m horizontally towards the south, and then 110 m horizontally towards the west. How far is it then from its starting point?

32 △ABC is right-angled at B. If AB = 7 cm and AC = 25 cm, calculate the median AM. (3 sig. fig.)

33 ABC is an isosceles triangle in which AB = 5 cm = AC, BC = 6 cm. Calculate the altitudes AM and BN.

34 ABC is an isosceles triangle in which the equal sides are $\overline{AB}$, $\overline{AC}$. If BC = 16 cm and altitude AD = 15 cm, calculate AB. Find also the altitude BE correct to 3 significant figures.

35 The altitude of a pyramid is 12 cm, and its base is a square measuring 10 cm each way. Find the area of each sloping face, and the length of each sloping edge.

Square root tables

The examples that have just been done in Ex. 3a were mostly arranged so that when the square root of a number was needed it could be found by inspection or by a short calculation. However, in a few cases the square root did not work out exactly, and it will be appreciated that in such cases some laborious effort will be saved if the square root can be found from tables.

It should be noticed that the tables, although sufficiently accurate for present purposes, give only four significant figures. For example, if the square root of 3 728 624 is needed, the nearest that the tables will give is the square root of 3 729 000. Similarly for $\sqrt{27\cdot342\,6}$ look for $\sqrt{27\cdot34}$. The results obtained are correct to four significant figures, so that the final digit cannot be assumed to be exact.

The following is an extract from square root tables:

	0	1	2	3	4	5	6	7	8	9	1	2	3	4	5	6	7	8	9
56					2396											1			
57					7576											4			
58																			

It will be noticed that the tables show no decimal points. These must be supplied by inspection.

As an example, when finding $\sqrt{5\cdot746}$, the first step is to decide roughly what the result is to be, before looking at the tables. Since 5·746 lies between 4 and 9, $\sqrt{5·746}$ must lie between 2 and 3, i.e. $\sqrt{5·746}$ is '2-point-something'.

In the tables, look for the first two digits, 57, in the extreme left-hand column. The next digit is 4, so look across the row until in the column headed 4, where a choice of 2 396 and 7 576 is given. Since the required result is to begin with the digit 2, ignore 7 576 and concentrate on 2 396. The fourth digit is 6, so look in the 'difference columns' on the right, where under 6 will be found the numbers 1 and 4. The 1 is level with 2 396 and must be added to it, giving 2 397. Hence the required result is 2·397.

The other result is clearly needed when looking up the square root of 57·46. Since this number lies between 49 and 64 its square root lies between 7 and 8. The tables give 7 576 with a difference of 4 to be added, making 7 580. Hence $\sqrt{57·46} = 7·580$.

Notice also that $\sqrt{574·6} = 23·97$ ($\sqrt{400} = 20$ and $\sqrt{900} = 30$), and $\sqrt{5\,746} = 75·80$ ($\sqrt{4\,900} = 70$ and $\sqrt{6\,400} = 80$).

For more complicated requirements such as $\sqrt{574\,600\,000}$ and $\sqrt{0·000\,057\,46}$ it is usually necessary to go through the initial stages of finding a square root by the 'long method', as shown below:

$$
\begin{array}{r}
2\ \ *\ \ *\ \ *\ \ * \\
2\ \overline{\smash{\big)}\ 5\,{}_{\backslash}74\,{}_{\backslash}60\,{}_{\backslash}00\,{}_{\backslash}00} \\
4 \phantom{\,{}_{\backslash}74\,{}_{\backslash}60\,{}_{\backslash}00\,{}_{\backslash}00}
\end{array}
$$

The digits are marked off in groups of two in the way that should already be familiar, and each group gives one digit in the answer. The result in this case is a number containing five digits, of which the first is 2.

Hence $\qquad \sqrt{574\,600\,000} = 23\,970$.

Similarly for $\sqrt{0·000\,057\,46}$

$$
\begin{array}{r}
0·\ 0\ \ \ 0\ \ \ 7 \\
7\ \overline{\smash{\big)}\ 0·00\,{}_{\backslash}00\,{}_{\backslash}57\,{}_{\backslash}46} \\
49 \phantom{{}_{\backslash}46}
\end{array}
$$

$\therefore\ \sqrt{0·000\,057\,46} = 0·007\,580$.

Finally it must be repeated that results obtained from the tables must not be assumed to be exact.

$\sqrt{5\cdot746}$ was found to be 2·397, but if 2·397 × 2·397 is worked out it will be found to be 5·745 609.

Exercise 3b

Use the tables to find the square roots of the following numbers:

1 29·53	**2** 2·953	**3** 295·3	**4** 2 953
5 3·902	**6** 0·039 02	**7** 0·390 2	**8** 4 139
9 0·928 3	**10** 38	**11** 382	**12** 0·000 87
13 127	**14** 53	**15** 931·2	**16** 105·6
17 78·3	**18** 8	**19** 29	**20** 463
21 80	**22** 0·7	**23** 61·3	**24** 613
25 0·09	**26** 0·9	**27** 0·005 2	**28** 430
29 2 500	**30** 250	**31** 500	**32** 72 300
33 5 940 000		**34** 0·000 000 594	
35 0·000 003		**36** 902 500	
37 0·000 81		**38** 0·000 063 94	
39 240 000 000		**40** 3 740 000 000	

Example 2 *An aircraft is heading NW at 330 km h⁻¹, but a wind blowing at 70 km h⁻¹ from the NE takes it off course. Find how far it travels in an hour relative to the ground, and in what direction.*

In an hour in still air the aircraft would fly 330 km NW from A to B. In the same time the wind carries it 70 km towards the SW, so that it arrives at C.

$A\hat{B}C = 90°$

$\therefore AC^2 = 330^2 + 70^2$

$\qquad = 108\ 900 + 4\ 900 = 113\ 800$

$\therefore AC = \sqrt{113\ 800} = 337$ approx.

$\cot \theta = \dfrac{330}{70} = 4\cdot714\ 3$

$\therefore \theta = 12°$ nearly.

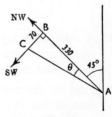

Fig. 46

43

∴ $\overline{AC}$ makes an angle of (45° + 12°) with north.

∴ in an hour the aircraft travels 337 km in a direction N 57° W.

Exercise 3c

Give answers correct to 3 significant figures where necessary, unless directed otherwise.

Nos. 1–6 refer to △PQR in which $\hat{Q} = 90°$. In each case find the length of the side which is not given.

1 PQ = 3 cm, QR = 5 cm

2 PQ = 4 m, PR = 9 m

3 PR = 7 cm, QR = 6 cm

4 PQ = 6·5 cm, QR = 5·2 cm

5 PR = 9·6 cm, QR = 3·6 cm

6 PQ = 21 m, PR = 28 m

In nos. 7–12 find the value of *x*.

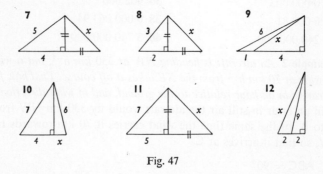

Fig. 47

13 A mast 62 m high is supported by wires attached to its top and to points on the level ground 21 m from the foot of the mast. Find the length of each wire.

14 Find to the nearest centimetre the length of the longest straight line that can be drawn on a rectangular blackboard measuring 2·16 m by 1·68 m.

15 A square has sides of length 7 cm. Find the distance from the mid-point of one side to either end of the opposite side.

16 A ladder 7 m long leans against a wall, with its foot 2 m from the wall. Find how far up the wall the ladder reaches. Find also its inclination to the ground.

17 A vessel goes 11 km due east, and then 4 km due north. What is then its distance and bearing from its starting point?

18 $\triangle$PQR is right-angled at R, and S is a point in $\overline{QR}$. If SP = 6 cm, SQ = 8 cm, SR = 3 cm, calculate PQ.

19 In Fig. 48 a batsman at A hits a cricket ball over the pavilion to land at C. If AB = 82 m, BC = 23 m, $\widehat{B} = 90°$, find the length of the hit.

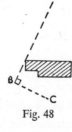

Fig. 48

20 An aircraft is heading due north at 280 km h^{-1}, but a wind blowing at 60 km h^{-1} from the west carries it off course. Find how far the aircraft travels in an hour relative to the ground, and on what bearing.

21 PQR is a triangle in which PQ = PR = 11 cm, QR = 10 cm. Calculate the lengths of the altitudes $\overline{PX}$, $\overline{QY}$.

22 Q is 1·4 km from P on a bearing N 23° E. R is 4·2 km from P on a bearing S 67° E. Find QR.

23 ABC is an isosceles triangle in which AB = BC = 17 cm, and the altitude AD = 15 cm. Calculate AC.

24 ABCD is a rectangle in which AB = 5 cm, AD = 4 cm. E is a point in $\overline{AB}$ such that CDE is an isosceles triangle whose equal sides are $\overline{DC}$, $\overline{DE}$. Calculate EC.

25 An aircraft is heading NE at 430 km h^{-1}, but is carried off course by a wind of 70 km h^{-1} blowing from the NW. Find

45

how far the aircraft travels in an hour relative to the ground, and in what direction.

26 In $\triangle ABC$, $AB = 9$ cm, $BC = 6$ cm, altitude $AD = 5$ cm, and $\hat{B}$ is acute. Calculate AC.

27 Fig. 49 shows a rectangular block measuring 6 cm by 4 cm

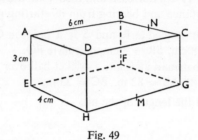

Fig. 49

by 3 cm. M, N are the mid-points of $\overline{HG}$, $\overline{BC}$. Calculate AH, EM, AM, CM, BD, DF, MN, NG, ND, NH.

28 If $\triangle ABC$ is right-angled at B, and $AB = 7\cdot2$ cm, $BC = 10\cdot8$ cm, calculate the length of the altitude $\overline{BD}$.

29 ABCD is a rectangle in which $AB = 6$ cm and $AD = 4$ cm. E is a point on $\overline{AB}$ such that $AE = 5$ cm, and $\overline{CF}$ is the perpendicular from C to $\overline{DE}$. Calculate DE and CF.

30 A circular cylinder 10 cm long has a diameter of 7 cm, and a piece of string is wound round it in an even spiral (Fig. 50). Find the length of the string if it goes round the cylinder three times.

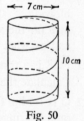

Fig. 50

Proof of Pythagoras' Theorem

Theorem 11

In a right-angled triangle the square on the hypotenuse is equal to the sum of the squares on the other two sides.

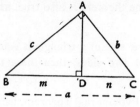

Fig. 51

Given $\triangle ABC$ with a rt. $\angle$ at A, and sides $\overline{BC}$, $\overline{CA}$, $\overline{AB}$ of lengths a, b, c units respectively.

To prove that $a^2 = b^2 + c^2$.

Construction Draw the alt. $\overline{AD}$, and let the lengths of $\overline{BD}$, $\overline{DC}$ be m, n units resp.

Proof In $\triangle ABC$, $\cos B = \dfrac{c}{a}$

In $\triangle ABD$, $\cos B = \dfrac{m}{c}$

$$\therefore \frac{c}{a} = \frac{m}{c}$$

$$\therefore c^2 = am$$

Sim. $\qquad b^2 = an$

$$\therefore b^2 + c^2 = an + am$$
$$= a(n + m)$$
$$= a \times a$$
$$= a^2.$$

Alternatively, $\qquad \cos B = \dfrac{m}{c}$ and $\cos C = \dfrac{n}{b}$

$$\therefore m = c \cos B \quad \text{and} \quad n = b \cos C$$
$$\therefore a = m + n$$
$$= c \cos B + b \cos C$$
$$= c \times \frac{c}{a} + b \times \frac{b}{a}$$
$$\therefore a^2 = c^2 + b^2.$$

47

The converse of the theorem is also true, and may be stated as follows:

If the square on one side of a triangle is equal to the sum of the squares on the other two sides, then those two sides contain a right angle.

Another proof of Pythagoras' Theorem, using similar triangles, will be found in Book 4.

Example 3 $\overline{AB}$, $\overline{AC}$ *are the equal sides of an isosceles triangle* ABC, *and* $\overline{AD}$ *is an altitude. Prove that*

$$AB^2 + AC^2 = 2AD^2 + \tfrac{1}{2}BC^2.$$

Given $\triangle ABC$ in which AB = AC. $\overline{AD}$ is an altitude.

To prove $AB^2 + AC^2 = 2AD^2 + \tfrac{1}{2}BC^2$.

Proof Since $\triangle ABC$ is isosceles, the altitude bisects the base.

$$\therefore BD = DC = \tfrac{1}{2}BC.$$

Since $\triangle s$ ABD, ACD are right-angled at D,

$$
\begin{aligned}
AB^2 + AC^2 &= (AD^2 + BD^2) + (AD^2 + DC^2) \\
&= AD^2 + (\tfrac{1}{2}BC)^2 + AD^2 + (\tfrac{1}{2}BC)^2 \\
&= AD^2 + \tfrac{1}{4}BC^2 + AD^2 + \tfrac{1}{4}BC^2 \\
&= 2AD^2 + \tfrac{1}{2}BC^2.
\end{aligned}
$$

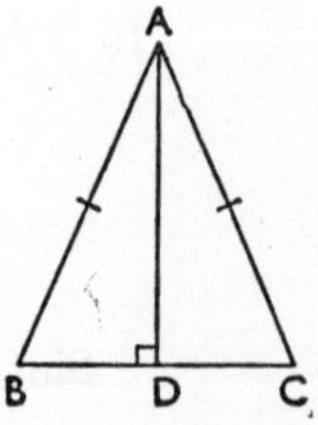

Fig. 52

Example 4 ABC *is an isosceles triangle, and* P *is any point in the base* $\overline{BC}$. *Prove that* $AB^2 - AP^2 = BP \times PC$.

Given $\triangle ABC$ in which AB = AC. P is any point in $\overline{BC}$.

To prove $AB^2 - AP^2 = BP \times PC$.

Construction Draw the altitude $\overline{AM}$.

Proof Since $\triangle ABC$ is isosceles, the altitude bisects the base.

$$\therefore BM = MC.$$

Since $\triangle s$ ABM, APM are right-angled at M,

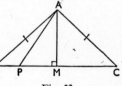
Fig. 53

48

Pythagoras' Theorem. Square root tables

$$AB^2 - AP^2 = (AM^2 + BM^2) - (AM^2 + PM^2)$$
$$= BM^2 - PM^2$$
$$= (BM - PM)(BM + PM)$$
$$= BP(MC + PM) \qquad BM = MC, \text{ proved}$$
$$= BP \times PC.$$

Exercise 3d

1 $\triangle ABC$ is right-angled at A, and $AB = 2AC$. Prove that $BC^2 = 5AC^2$.

2 Prove that, in any rectangle, the sum of the squares on the diagonals is equal to the sum of the squares on the four sides.

3 LMN is an equilateral triangle, and X is the mid-point of $\overline{LN}$. Prove that $MX^2 = \frac{3}{4}MN^2$.

4 ABCD is a quadrilateral in which the angles at A and C are right angles. Prove that $AB^2 - CD^2 = BC^2 - AD^2$.

5 The quadrilateral ABCD is such that its diagonals intersect at right angles. Prove that $AB^2 + CD^2 = AD^2 + BC^2$.

6 Find the area of a square with diagonals each 12 cm long.

7 Find the length of a diagonal of the square whose area is 128 cm².

8 Prove that, in any rhombus, the sum of the squares on the diagonals is equal to four times the square on a side.

9 ABC is an isosceles triangle in which the equal sides are $\overline{AB}$, $\overline{AC}$. If $\overline{AD}$ is an altitude and $BC = \frac{1}{2}AB$, prove that $AD^2 = 15BD^2$.

10 The quadrilateral ABCD is such that $D\hat{A}C = 90° = D\hat{B}C$. Prove that $AC^2 - BC^2 = BD^2 - AD^2$.

11 Show how to construct a line of length $\sqrt{2}$ cm. Hence construct lines of length $\sqrt{3}$ cm, $\sqrt{4}$ cm, $\sqrt{5}$ cm, $\sqrt{6}$ cm and so on. By measurement write down the values of $\sqrt{3}$ and $\sqrt{5}$ in decimals as accurately as you can. Check from the tables.

12 Give, with proof, a construction for drawing a square whose area is twice that of a given square.

49

13 PQRS is a rectangle and O is any point (i) inside it, (ii) outside it. Prove that, in both cases, $OP^2 + OR^2 = OQ^2 + OS^2$.

14 $\triangle ABC$ is right-angled at C, and the perpendicular bisector of $\overline{AB}$ meets $\overline{BC}$ (or $\overline{BC}$ produced) at L. Prove that
$$LB^2 - LC^2 = AC^2.$$

15 A triangle has sides of lengths $(a^2 + b^2)$ cm, $(a^2 - b^2)$ cm and $2ab$ cm. Prove that the triangle is right-angled. Which side is the hypotenuse?

16 If $\overline{PX}$ is an altitude of $\triangle PQR$, prove that
$$PQ^2 + RX^2 = PR^2 + Q X^2$$

17 $\triangle ABC$ is right-angled at B, and $BC = 2AB$. If $\overline{AM}$ is a median, prove that $AM^2 = \frac{2}{5}AC^2$.

18 $\triangle ABC$ is right-angled at B, and X is any point in $\overline{BC}$. Prove that $BC^2 - BX^2 = AC^2 - AX^2$.

19 The side $\overline{DC}$ of a square ABCD is produced to any point E. Prove that $AC^2 = 2(BE^2 - CE^2)$.

20 $\triangle ABC$ is right-angled at B, and $BC = 3AB$. If Q is the point of trisection of $\overline{BC}$ nearer to C, prove that $AC^2 = 2AQ^2$.

21 $\overline{AL}$, $\overline{BM}$ are medians of $\triangle ABC$ which is right-angled at C. Prove that $AL^2 + BM^2 = 1\frac{1}{4}AB^2$.

22 $\overline{AD}$ is an altitude of an equilateral triangle ABC, and M is the mid-point of $\overline{BD}$. Prove that $16AM^2 = 13BC^2$.

23 ABC is an isosceles triangle, and the base $\overline{BC}$ is produced to any point P. Prove that $AP^2 - AB^2 = PB \times PC$.

24 Quadrilateral ABCD is right-angled at B and D. $\overline{AB}$ and $\overline{DC}$ are produced to meet at E. If $CE = DC$, prove that $AB^2 - BE^2 = AD^2$.

25 $\triangle ABC$ is right-angled at A, and $\overline{AX}$ is an altitude. Y is a point in $\overline{BC}$ such that $BX = CY$. Prove that the difference of the squares on AB and AC is equal to the product of BC and XY.

26 The side $\overline{QR}$ of an equilateral triangle PQR is produced to S so that $QR = RS$. Prove that $PS^2 = 3QR^2$.

27 $\overline{AD}$ is an altitude of $\triangle ABC$. If $BD = \frac{3}{4}AD$ and $CD = \frac{4}{3}AD$, prove that $B\hat{A}C$ is a right angle.

28 ABC is a triangle in which $AB > AC$, and $\overline{AD}$ is an altitude. Prove that $AB^2 - AC^2 = BC(BD - DC)$. Prove further that $AB^2 - AC^2 = 2BC \times MD$, where M is the mid-point of $\overline{BC}$.

29 PQRS is a square, and X is any point on $\overline{SR}$ produced. Prove that $2SR \times RX = SX^2 - QX^2$.

30 $\triangle ABC$ is right-angled at A, and $AB < AC$. X, Y are the points of trisection of $\overline{BC}$, and $\overline{AX}$ is an altitude. Prove that $AB^2 = \frac{1}{3}BC^2$ and $AC^2 = \frac{2}{3}BC^2$.

51

Chapter 4

Quadratic equations (2)

If $d^2 = 25$, then $d = \pm 5$, since $(+5)^2 = 25$ and $(-5)^2 = 25$.

$$\therefore \text{ if } (x - 2)^2 = 25$$
$$\text{then } x - 2 = \pm 5$$
$$\therefore \ x = 2 \pm 5$$
$$= 7 \text{ or } -3 \qquad (2 + 5 = 7, 2 - 5 = -3)$$

Example 1 *Solve the equation* $(x + 3)^2 = 7$.

$$(x + 3)^2 = 7$$
$$\therefore \ x + 3 = \pm \sqrt{7}$$
$$\therefore \ x = -3 \pm \sqrt{7}.$$

A result such as this may be expressed approximately in decimals by putting $\pm \sqrt{7}$ as $\pm 2 \cdot 65$, but for Exercise 4a it will be sufficient if the answers are given as shown above.

Exercise 4a

Solve the equations

1 $(x - 2)^2 = 9$ **2** $(x - 7)^2 = 4$ **3** $(x + 3)^2 = 4$

4 $(x + 2)^2 = 25$ **5** $(x - 1)^2 = 2$ **6** $(x + 4)^2 = 3$

7 $(x - 3)^2 = 5$ **8** $(x + 2)^2 = 2$ **9** $(x - 2)^2 = \frac{1}{4}$

10 $(x - 6)^2 = 36$ **11** $(x - 4)^2 = 10$ **12** $(x + 5)^2 = \frac{1}{9}$

13 $(x + 3)^2 = 49$ **14** $(x - 1)^2 = 7$ **15** $(x - 8)^2 = 3$

16 $(x - 1)^2 = \frac{9}{25}$ **17** $(x + 1)^2 = 2\frac{1}{4}$ **18** $(x + 7)^2 = 6$

19 $(x + \frac{1}{3})^2 = \frac{4}{9}$ **20** $(x + 9)^2 = 3$ **21** $(x - 6)^2 = 5$

22 $(x - 2\frac{1}{2})^2 = 6\frac{1}{4}$ **23** $(x + 10)^2 = 8$ **24** $(x - 6)^2 = 2\frac{7}{9}$

25 $(x + 1\frac{1}{4})^2 = 1\frac{9}{16}$

Completing the square

Example 2 *What must be added to $x^2 + 6x$ to make the expression a perfect square?*

Suppose $x^2 + 6x + k$ is a perfect square, and that it is equal to $(x + a)^2$.

It is known that $(x + a)^2 = x^2 + 2ax + a^2$

$\therefore$ $x^2 + 2ax + a^2$ and $x^2 + 6x + k$ are identically equal.

$\therefore$ comparing coefficients of x,

$$2a = 6$$
$$\therefore a = 3$$
$$\therefore x^2 + 6x + k = (x + 3)^2$$
$$= x^2 + 6x + 9.$$

$\therefore$ 9 must be added (and $k = 9$).

Then $\qquad\qquad x^2 + 6x + 9 = (x + 3)^2.$

In practice the quantity to be added is **the square of half the coefficient of x** (or whatever letter is involved). In Example 2 the coefficient of x is 6, half of 6 is 3, and the square of 3 is 9. Hence 9 must be added.

Example 3 *What must be added to $d^2 - 5d$ to make it into a perfect square, and of what expression is the result the square?*

The coefficient of d is -5, half of this is $-\frac{5}{2}$, and the square of $-\frac{5}{2}$ is $+\frac{25}{4}$.

$\therefore$ $\frac{25}{4}$ must be added, and then

$$d^2 - 5d + \tfrac{25}{4} = (d - \tfrac{5}{2})^2$$
$$\text{i.e.} \quad d^2 - 5d + 6\tfrac{1}{4} = (d - 2\tfrac{1}{2})^2.$$

Check by squaring out the bracket.

Example 4 *Add a term to make $n^2 + 1\frac{1}{2}cn$ into a perfect square, and express the result as the square of a bracketed expression.*

The coefficient of n is $1\frac{1}{2}c$, i.e. $\frac{3}{2}c$,

half of this is $\frac{3}{4}c$,

and the square of $\frac{3}{4}c$ is $\frac{9}{16}c^2$

$\therefore$ $\frac{9}{16}c^2$ must be added, and then

$$n^2 + 1\tfrac{1}{2}cn + \tfrac{9}{16}c^2 = (n + \tfrac{3}{4}c)^2.$$

Check by squaring out the bracket.

Exercise 4b

In each of the following examples add the term that will make the given expression into a perfect square, and then write the result as the square of a bracketed expression. No explanation need be given.

1 $a^2 + 8a$	**2** $b^2 + 10b$	**3** $c^2 - 4c$
4 $d^2 - 6d$	**5** $x^2 + 5x$	**6** $y^2 - 3y$
7 $z^2 - 7z$	**8** $m^2 + 2m$	**9** $n^2 - n$
10 $u^2 - \frac{1}{2}u$	**11** $v^2 + \frac{1}{4}v$	**12** $h^2 + \frac{2}{3}h$
13 $k^2 - 1\frac{1}{3}k$	**14** $g^2 - 4\frac{2}{3}g$	**15** $a^2 + \frac{3}{5}a$
16 $b^2 - \frac{4}{5}b$	**17** $c^2 - 1\frac{1}{2}c$	**18** $m^2 - 8m$
19 $m^2 - 8mn$	**20** $a^2 - 6ad$	**21** $x^2 + 10xy$
22 $m^2 + 3mn$	**23** $u^2 - 1\frac{3}{5}u$	**24** $v^2 - \frac{3}{4}v$

Example 5 *Solve the equation* $x^2 - 8x + 3 = 0$.

The L.H.S. does not factorise, and so the equation is first rearranged to make the L.H.S. a perfect square.

$$x^2 - 8x + 3 = 0.$$

Subtract 3 from both sides.

$$x^2 - 8x = -3.$$

Add 16 to both sides.

$$x^2 - 8x + 16 = -3 + 16$$
$$\therefore (x - 4)^2 = 13$$
$$\therefore x - 4 = \pm\sqrt{13}$$
$$\therefore x = 4 \pm \sqrt{13}.$$

Example 6 *Solve the equation* $a^2 + 3a - 2 = 0$.

The L.H.S. does not factorise.

$$a^2 + 3a - 2 = 0$$
$$\therefore a^2 + 3a = 2.$$

Add to both sides the square of $\frac{3}{2}$.

$$a^2 + 3a + (\tfrac{3}{2})^2 = 2 + \tfrac{9}{4}$$
$$= \frac{8+9}{4}$$
$$\therefore (a + \tfrac{3}{2})^2 = \tfrac{17}{4}$$
$$\therefore a + \tfrac{3}{2} = \pm\sqrt{\tfrac{17}{4}}$$
$$= \pm\frac{\sqrt{17}}{2}$$
$$\therefore a = -\tfrac{3}{2} \pm \frac{\sqrt{17}}{2}$$
$$= \frac{-3 \pm \sqrt{17}}{2}.$$

If the L.H.S. will factorise it is better to use the method of factorising, instead of completing the square, e.g.

$$x^2 - 7x + 10 = 0 \; \textit{rather than} \; x^2 - 7x + 10 = 0$$
$$\therefore (x-5)(x-2) = 0 \qquad\qquad \therefore x^2 - 7x = -10$$
$$\therefore x = 5 \text{ or } 2. \quad \therefore x^2 - 7x + (\tfrac{7}{2})^2 = -10 + \tfrac{49}{4}$$
$$= \frac{-40+49}{4}$$
$$\therefore (x - \tfrac{7}{2})^2 = \tfrac{9}{4}$$
$$\therefore x - \tfrac{7}{2} = \pm\tfrac{3}{2}$$
$$\therefore x = \tfrac{7}{2} \pm \tfrac{3}{2}$$
$$= \tfrac{10}{2} \text{ or } \tfrac{4}{2}$$
$$= 5 \text{ or } 2.$$

Exercise 4c

Solve the following equations. Factorise where possible, but otherwise solve by completing the square. Do *not* put the answer in decimal form.

1 $a^2 + 4a - 21 = 0$ **2** $b^2 - b - 12 = 0$

3 $c^2 - 4c - 2 = 0$ **4** $d^2 + 2d - 2 = 0$

5 $n^2 + 4n + 4 = 0$ 6 $p^2 - 10p + 15 = 0$

7 $q^2 + 10q + 22 = 0$ 8 $t^2 - 6t + 9 = 0$

9 $m^2 + 6m + 7 = 0$ 10 $y^2 - 3y + 1 = 0$

11 $z^2 - 5z + 6 = 0$ 12 $h^2 + 5h + 4 = 0$

13 $k^2 - 5k + 2 = 0$ 14 $g^2 + 5g + 2 = 0$

15 $x^2 - 8x - 1 = 0$ 16 $a^2 - a - 1 = 0$

17 $b^2 + b - 3 = 0$ 18 $y^2 + 7y - 30 = 0$

19 $m^2 - 7m + 11 = 0$ 20 $x^2 + 3x - 2 = 0$

21 $x^2 - 10x + 25 = 0$ 22 $v^2 + 9v + 19 = 0$

23 $n^2 - 12n + 1 = 0$ 24 $u^2 - 14u - 3 = 0$

In the solution of some quadratic equations it will be necessary to simplify expressions such as $2·83 - 6·39$, and some preliminary practice will be found useful.

The rule has already been established that for an expression such as $3 - 10$, the sign of the answer is the sign of the larger number, and the size of the answer is found by taking the smaller from the larger. Thus $3 - 10 = -7$, ($10 - 3 = 7$, and the sign is minus because the larger number 10 has a minus sign). Also $-3 - 10 = -13$ (13 is the *sum* of 3 and 10).

Hence
$$2·83 - 6·39 = -(6·39 - 2·83) = -3·56$$
$$-2·83 - 6·39 = -(2·83 + 6·39) = -9·22$$
$$-4·23 \pm 5·74 = -4·23 + 5·74 \text{ or } -4·23 - 5·74$$
$$= 5·74 - 4·23 \text{ or } -(4·23 + 5·74)$$
$$= 1·51 \text{ or } -9·97$$

Exercise 4d

Simplify

1 $7·28 + 2·43$ 2 $7·28 - 2·43$

3 $2·43 - 7·28$ 4 $-2·43 - 7·28$

5 $-5·31 + 4·76$ 6 $-1·16 - 5·34$

7 $2·06 - 0·48$ 8 $3·263 - 6·587$

9 $-2 \cdot 839 - 1 \cdot 916$ **10** $6 \cdot 723 - 7 \cdot 089$

11 $5 - 3 \cdot 74$ **12** $7 - 9 \cdot 38$

13 $-6 + 5 \cdot 83$ **14** $-1 + 0 \cdot 93$

15 $-3 + 6 \cdot 74$ **16** $-6 \cdot 15 \pm 3 \cdot 42$

17 $1 \cdot 92 \pm 4 \cdot 97$ **18** $-3 \cdot 123 \pm 5 \cdot 425$

19 $2 \cdot 916 \pm 8 \cdot 499$ **20** $6 \cdot 43 \pm 5 \cdot 96$

Example 7 *Solve the equation* $h^2 + 6h - 5 = 0$*, giving the answer correct to two decimal places.*

$$h^2 + 6h - 5 = 0$$
$$\therefore h^2 + 6h = 5.$$

Add 9 to both sides to make the L.H.S. a perfect square.

$$h^2 + 6h + 9 = 5 + 9$$
$$\therefore (h + 3)^2 = 14$$
$$\therefore h + 3 = \pm\sqrt{14}$$
$$= \pm 3 \cdot 742 \text{ approx.}$$
$$\therefore h = -3 \pm 3 \cdot 742$$
$$= -3 + 3 \cdot 742 \text{ or} -3 - 3 \cdot 742$$
$$= 0 \cdot 74 \text{ or } -6 \cdot 74 \text{ to 2 dec. pl.}$$

Check Sum of roots $= 0 \cdot 74 - 6 \cdot 74 = -6$.
Coeff. of h in the given equation is $+6$.
Product of roots $= 0 \cdot 74 \times (-6 \cdot 74) = -4 \cdot 99$ approx.
Absolute term in the given equation is -5.

Example 8 *Solve the equation* $2x^2 - 14x + 9 = 0$ (2 *decimal places*).

First make the coefficient of x^2 **unity,** by dividing both sides by 2. Then the equation becomes

$$x^2 - 7x + 4\tfrac{1}{2} = 0$$
$$\therefore x^2 - 7x = -4\tfrac{1}{2}$$

Make the L.H.S. a perfect square by adding to both sides the square of half the coefficient of x.

57

Then $\quad x^2 - 7x + (\tfrac{7}{2})^2 = -4\tfrac{1}{2} + \tfrac{49}{4}$

$$\therefore (x - \tfrac{7}{2})^2 = \frac{-18 + 49}{4}$$

$$= \tfrac{31}{4}$$

$$\therefore x - \tfrac{7}{2} = \pm\sqrt{\tfrac{31}{4}}$$

$$= \pm\frac{\sqrt{31}}{2}$$

$$\therefore x = \tfrac{7}{2} \pm \frac{\sqrt{31}}{2}$$

$$= \frac{7 \pm 5\cdot568}{2} \text{ approx.}$$

$$= \frac{12\cdot568 \text{ or } 1\cdot432}{2}$$

$$= 6\cdot28 \text{ or } 0\cdot72 \text{ to 2 dec. pl.}$$

It is often easier to introduce decimals earlier in the working,

e.g. $\quad (x - \tfrac{7}{2})^2 = \tfrac{31}{4}$

$$\therefore (x - 3\cdot5)^2 = 7\cdot75$$

$$\therefore x - 3\cdot5 = \pm\sqrt{7\cdot75}$$

$$\therefore x = 3\cdot5 \pm 2\cdot78 \text{ to 2 dec. pl.}$$

$$= 6\cdot28 \text{ or } 0\cdot72 \text{ to 2 dec. pl.}$$

Check From the coefficients in the given equation,

sum of roots should be $+\tfrac{14}{2}$, i.e. 7

product ,, ,, ,, ,, $+\tfrac{9}{2}$, i.e. $4\tfrac{1}{2}$

$6\cdot28 + 0\cdot72 = 7 \quad$ and $\quad 6\cdot28 \times 0\cdot72 = 4\cdot52 \ldots$

Example 9 *Solve the equation $5a^2 + 7a + 1 = 0$.*

$$5a^2 + 7a + 1 = 0$$

Divide through by 5 to make the coefficient of a^2 unity.

$$\therefore a^2 + \tfrac{7}{5}a = -\tfrac{1}{5}$$

$$\therefore a^2 + \tfrac{7}{5}a + (\tfrac{7}{10})^2 = -\tfrac{1}{5} + \tfrac{49}{100}$$

$$\therefore (a + \tfrac{7}{10})^2 = \frac{-20 + 49}{100}$$

$$= \tfrac{29}{100}$$

$$\therefore\ a + 0\!\cdot\!7 = \pm\sqrt{0\!\cdot\!29}$$
$$\therefore\ a = -0\!\cdot\!7 \pm 0\!\cdot\!54 \text{ approx.}$$
$$= -0\!\cdot\!16 \text{ or } -1\!\cdot\!24 \text{ to 2 dec. pl.}$$

Check From the coefficients in the given equation,

sum of roots should be $-\frac{7}{5} = -1\!\cdot\!4$

and product ,, ,,　　　,, ,, $\frac{1}{5} = 0\!\cdot\!2$

$-0\!\cdot\!16 - 1\!\cdot\!24 = -1\!\cdot\!4$　and　$-0\!\cdot\!16 \times -1\!\cdot\!24 = 0\!\cdot\!198 \ldots$

Exercise 4e

Solve the following equations by factorising if possible, but otherwise by completing the square. If the roots involve decimals, give them correct to two places. Square root tables may be used.

1 $m^2 - 2m - 2 = 0$ **2** $n^2 - 2n - 1 = 0$

3 $x^2 - 2x - 4 = 0$ **4** $y^2 + 2y - 1 = 0$

5 $z^2 + 2z - 3 = 0$ **6** $a^2 - 4a = 5$

7 $b^2 - 4b + 1 = 0$ **8** $c^2 - 8c + 13 = 0$

9 $d^2 + 6d + 7 = 0$ **10** $e^2 - 6e + 4 = 0$

11 $h^2 + 4h = 11$ **12** $k^2 + 4k + 2 = 0$

13 $x^2 - 3x + 2 = 0$ **14** $y^2 - 3y - 11 = 0$

15 $m^2 + 5m = 1$ **16** $n^2 = n + 5$

17 $2d^2 - 4d + 1 = 0$ **18** $2e^2 - e - 1 = 0$

19 $3m^2 = 6m + 2$ **20** $p^2 - 10p + 5 = 0$

21 $y^2 + y = 8$ **22** $x^2 = x + 6$

23 $a^2 - 6a - 3 = 0$ **24** $2b^2 = 8b + 11$

25 $2c^2 - 3c - 9 = 0$ **26** $x^2 - 10x + 23 = 0$

27 $h^2 = 3h + 40$ **28** $4c^2 - 8c + 1 = 0$

29 $d^2 = 12d - 35$ **30** $e^2 = 3e + 11$

31 $x^2 + 5x = 15$ **32** $3m^2 - 5m + 2 = 0$

33 $4h^2 = 8h + 3$ **34** $3k^2 = 9k - 2$

35 $b^2 = 11b + 26$ **36** $5f^2 = 20f + 28$

c

37 $5e^2 + 15e + 1 = 0$ **38** $y^2 - 9y + 15 = 0$

39 $3a^2 - 12a - 2 = 0$ **40** $2d^2 + 10d + 5 = 0$

Example 10 *Solve the equation* $\frac{1}{3}d^2 - 2d = 4$.

Multiply both sides by 3 to make the coefficient of d^2 unity.

$$\frac{1}{3}d^2 - 2d = 4$$
$$\therefore\ d^2 - 6d = 12$$
$$\therefore\ d^2 - 6d + 9 = 12 + 9$$
$$\therefore\ (d - 3)^2 = 21$$
$$\therefore\ d - 3 = \pm\sqrt{21}$$
$$= \pm 4\cdot58 \text{ approx.}$$
$$\therefore\ d = 3 \pm 4\cdot58$$
$$= 7\cdot58 \text{ or } -1\cdot58 \text{ to 2 dec. pl.}$$

Example 11 *Solve the equation* $\dfrac{3}{x} = \dfrac{2x - 7}{5}$.

$$\frac{3}{x} = \frac{2x - 7}{5}$$

Multiply both sides by $5x$ to clear the fractions.

$$\therefore\ \frac{3}{x} \times 5x = \frac{2x - 7}{5} \times 5x$$
$$\therefore\ 15 = x(2x - 7)$$
$$\therefore\ 15 = 2x^2 - 7x$$
$$\therefore\ 2x^2 - 7x - 15 = 0$$
$$\therefore\ (x - 5)(2x + 3) = 0$$
$$\therefore\ x - 5 = 0 \text{ or } 2x + 3 = 0$$
$$\therefore\ x = 5 \text{ or } 2x = -3$$
$$\therefore\ x = 5 \text{ or } -1\tfrac{1}{2}.$$

Example 12 *Solve the equation* $(5m - 2)(2m + 1) = m(6m - 7)$.

$$(5m - 2)(2m + 1) = m(6m - 7)$$
$$\therefore\ 10m^2 + m - 2 = 6m^2 - 7m$$
$$\therefore\ 10m^2 + m - 2 - 6m^2 + 7m = 0$$
$$\therefore\ 4m^2 + 8m - 2 = 0$$
$$\therefore\ m^2 + 2m = \tfrac{1}{2}$$

$$\therefore\ m^2 + 2m + 1 = \tfrac{1}{2} + 1$$
$$\therefore\ (m + 1)^2 = 1{\cdot}5$$
$$\therefore\ m + 1 = \pm 1{\cdot}22 \text{ approx.}$$
$$\therefore\ m = -1 \pm 1{\cdot}22$$
$$= 0{\cdot}22 \text{ or } -2{\cdot}22 \text{ to 2 dec. pl.}$$

Imaginary roots

Example 13 *Solve the equation* $x^2 - 4x + 13 = 0$.

$$x^2 - 4x + 13 = 0$$
$$\therefore\ x^2 - 4x = -13$$
$$\therefore\ x^2 - 4x + 4 = -13 + 4$$
$$\therefore\ (x - 2)^2 = -9$$
$$\therefore\ x - 2 = \pm\sqrt{-9}$$

The square of 3 is 9, and the square of -3 is also 9. In fact there is no ordinary number which when multiplied by itself makes -9. Because of this, $\sqrt{-9}$ is said to be **imaginary.**

Hence the roots are imaginary.

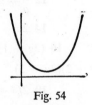

Fig. 54

In Book 2, Chap. 24, it was seen that when an attempt is made to solve graphically a quadratic equation whose roots are imaginary, the curve does not cut the axis in real points. The graph is of the kind illustrated in Fig. 54.

Example 14 *Solve the equation* $3x^2 - 4x + 5 = 0$.

$$3x^2 - 4x + 5 = 0$$
$$\therefore\ x^2 - \tfrac{4}{3}x = -\tfrac{5}{3}$$
$$\therefore\ x^2 - \tfrac{4}{3}x + (\tfrac{2}{3})^2 = -\tfrac{5}{3} + \tfrac{4}{9}$$

61

$$\therefore (x - \tfrac{2}{3})^2 = \frac{-15 + 4}{9}$$

$$= -\tfrac{11}{9}$$

$$\therefore x - \tfrac{2}{3} = \pm\sqrt{-\tfrac{11}{9}}, \text{ which is imaginary.}$$

∴ the roots are imaginary.

Exercise 4f

Solve the following equations by factorising if possible, but otherwise by completing the square. If the roots involve decimals, give them correct to two places. Square root tables may be used.

1 $3a^2 - 7a + 4 = 0$ **2** $3d^2 - 8d + 4 = 0$

3 $3u^2 - 7u + 5 = 0$ **4** $3v^2 - 8v + 5 = 0$

5 $2m^2 + 5m - 20 = 0$ **6** $2n^2 - 3n - 3 = 0$

7 $x^2 + 11x - 14 = 0$ **8** $y^2 + 2y + 3 = 0$

9 $\tfrac{1}{2}m^2 + m - 5 = 0$ **10** $\tfrac{1}{3}a^2 - 2a + 2 = 0$

11 $\dfrac{x}{6} + \dfrac{3}{2x} = 1$ **12** $\dfrac{4}{a} = \dfrac{3a + 10}{2}$

13 $2u^2 + 2u - 1 = 0$ **14** $2v^2 - 3v - 2 = 0$

15 $t^2 - 4t + 5 = 0$ **16** $(3g + 1)(2g - 3) = g(2g - 11)$

17 $(3a - 1)(a + 2) = (a + 2)(2a - 3)$

18 $3b^2 = 2b + 27$ **19** $2f^2 + 7f + 2 = 0$

20 $2c^2 = c + 3\tfrac{1}{2}$ **21** $2d + \dfrac{1}{d} = 5 - \dfrac{1}{d}$

22 $\dfrac{x - 2}{4} = \dfrac{x + 2}{x}$ **23** $4n^2 = 3n + 7$

24 $4m^2 = 4m - 1$ **25** $3y^2 = 5y + 10$

26 $\dfrac{6}{x} = \dfrac{5x - 1}{3}$ **27** $\tfrac{2}{3}a^2 - a + 2\tfrac{1}{3} = 0$

28 $(2d - 3)(3d + 1) = d(2d - 11)$

29 $6b^2 + 1 = 5b$ **30** $\tfrac{2}{3}a^2 = 1\tfrac{2}{3}a + 1$

31 $(2x + 3)(x - 2) = x(x + 1)$

32 $(3a + 2)(4a - 3) = 10a(a + 1)$

33 $\frac{1}{4}y^2 - 2y - 3 = 0$ **34** $x^2 + 15 = 7x$

35 $2x^2 - 15 = 7x$ **36** $5z^2 + 12z + 3 = 0$

37 $2a^2 + 4a + 9 = 0$ **38** $3c^2 + 8c + 2 = 0$

39 $3e^2 + 2e + 4 = 0$ **40** $\dfrac{2m + 3}{m} = \dfrac{1 - m}{6}$

41 $\dfrac{n - 5}{2n} = \dfrac{n - 4}{3}$ **42** $\frac{3}{4}p^2 - 3p + 1 = 0$

43 $9q^2 + 12q + 4 = 0$ **44** $4w^2 = w + 2$

45 $2h^2 = 3h + 11$ **46** $3k^2 + 10k = 21$

47 $4e(3e - 1) - 2 = (2e - 1)(5e + 1)$

48 $2a^2 + 3a - 16 = 0$

49 $(2t + 1)(5t - 4) = (3t - 2)^2$

50 $(4w - 3)(3w + 2) - (5w + 2)(2w - 1) = 0$

Graphical solution

Example 15 *Draw the graph of $2x^2 - 3x - 7$ and from it read off the roots of the equations*

  (i) $2x^2 - 3x - 7 = 0$,   (ii) $2x^2 - 3x - 7 = 2$,

(iii) $2x^2 - 3x = 0$,   (iv) $2x^2 - 3x - 13 = 0$,

 (v) $2x^2 - 3x + 5 = 0$,   (vi) $2x^2 - 3x = 4$.

A table of values is constructed, and the graph drawn in the usual way (Fig. 55).

x	-1	-2	0	1	2	3	4
$2x^2$ $-3x$ -7	2 3 -7	8 6 -7	0 0 -7	2 -3 -7	8 -6 -7	18 -9 -7	32 -12 -7
$2x^2 - 3x - 7$	-2	7	-7	-8	-5	2	13

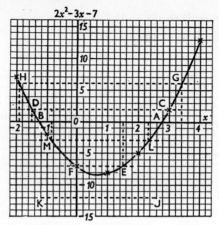

Fig. 55

(i) $2x^2 - 3x - 7 = 0$.

$2x^2 - 3x - 7$ is equal to 0 along the x axis. Hence the points on the curve at which $2x^2 - 3x - 7 = 0$ are where it cuts the x axis, i.e. at A and B.

Hence, reading from the graph,

$$2x^2 - 3x - 7 = 0 \quad \text{where} \quad x = 2.8 \text{ or } -1.3.$$

(ii) $2x^2 - 3x - 7 = 2$.

$2x^2 - 3x - 7$ is equal to 2 along the line which cuts the curve at C and D.

At these points $\qquad x = 3 \quad \text{or} \quad -1.5$.

(iii) $2x^2 - 3x = 0$.

Subtract 7 from both sides.

Then $2x^2 - 3x - 7 = -7$, and this is true at the points E and F.

Hence $\qquad x = 1.5 \quad \text{or} \quad 0$.

(iv) $2x^2 - 3x - 13 = 0$.

$$\therefore 2x^2 - 3x = 13$$
$$\therefore 2x^2 - 3x - 7 = 13 - 7$$
$$\therefore 2x^2 - 3x - 7 = 6,$$

and this is true at the points G and H.

Hence $\qquad x = 3.4 \quad \text{or} \quad -1.9$.

(v) $2x^2 - 3x + 5 = 0$.

$$\therefore \quad 2x^2 - 3x = -5$$
$$\therefore \quad 2x^2 - 3x - 7 = -5 - 7$$
$$\therefore \quad 2x^2 - 3x - 7 = -12.$$

The curve does not cut the line $\overline{JK}$ in real points.
Hence the roots are imaginary.

(vi) $2x^2 - 3x = 4$.

$$\therefore \quad 2x^2 - 3x - 7 = 4 - 7$$
$$\therefore \quad 2x^2 - 3x - 7 = -3.$$

and this is true at the points L and M.

Hence $\qquad\qquad x = 2\cdot3(5) \quad \text{or} \quad -0\cdot8(5).$

Exercise 4g

1 Draw the graph given in Example 15 to as large a scale as possible. Try to read off the roots of the equations correct to two decimal places.

2 Solve graphically the equation $x^2 - 3x - 4 = 0$, taking values of x from 5 to -2 in constructing the table of values. Use the same graph to read off the roots of the equations:

$x^2 - 3x + 1 = 0 \qquad x^2 - 3x + 5 = 0 \qquad x^2 - 3x = 0$
$x^2 - 3x = 6 \qquad x^2 - 3x - 2 = 0$

3 Solve graphically the equation $x^2 - 4x - 3 = 0$ (take values of x from 6 to -2). Use the same graph to solve the equations:

$x^2 - 4x - 9 = 0 \qquad x^2 - 4x + 4 = 0 \quad x^2 - 4x + 6 = 0$
$x^2 = 4x \qquad x^2 - 4x = 6$

4 Draw the graph of $x^2 + 3x - 2$ (taking values of x from 2 to -5), and from it read off the roots of the equations:

$x^2 + 3x - 2 = 0 \qquad x^2 + 3x - 8 = 0 \qquad x^2 + 3x = 4$
$x^2 + 3x + 2 = 0 \qquad x^2 + 3x + 5 = 0 \qquad x^2 + 3x + 7 = 0$

5 Solve graphically the equation $x^2 + 5x = 0$ (taking values of x from 3 to -8), and using the same graph solve the equations:

$x^2 + 5x = 20 \qquad x^2 + 5x + 10 = 0 \qquad x^2 + 5x - 10 = 0$
$x^2 + 5x + 5 = 0 \qquad\qquad x^2 + 5x - 6 = 0$

6 Draw the graph of $x^2 - 2x - 8$, and read off the roots of the equations:

$$x^2 - 2x - 8 = 0 \quad x^2 - 2x - 5 = 0 \quad x^2 - 2x + 1 = 0$$
$$x^2 - 2x = 0 \quad\quad x^2 - 2x = 15 \quad x^2 - 2x + 5 = 0$$

7 Solve graphically the equation $2x^2 + 4x - 7 = 0$ (taking values of x from 3 to -5), and from the same graph read off the roots of the equations:

$$2x^2 + 4x - 21 = 0 \quad 2x^2 + 4x + 2 = 0 \quad 2x^2 + 4x = 11$$
$$2x^2 + 4x + 5 = 0 \quad\quad 2x^2 + 4x = 0$$

8 Draw the graph of $4x^2 - 12x - 3$, and read off the roots of the equations:

$$4x^2 - 12x - 3 = 0 \quad\quad 4x^2 - 12x + 11 = 0$$
$$4x^2 - 12x + 9 = 0 \quad\quad 4x^2 - 12x - 13 = 0$$
$$4x^2 - 12x + 3 = 0 \quad\quad 4x^2 - 12x - 16 = 0$$

9 Draw the graph of $3x^2 - x - 7$ (take values of x from 3 to -3), and read off the roots of the equations:

$$3x^2 - x - 7 = 0 \quad\quad\quad 3x^2 - x = 2$$
$$3x^2 - x - 18 = 0 \quad\quad\quad 3x^2 = x + 24$$
$$3x^2 - x + 3 = 0 \quad\quad\quad 3x^2 - x - 14 = 0$$

10 Solve graphically the equation $2x^2 + 3x - 8 = 0$. From the same graph read off the roots of the equations:

$$2x^2 + 3x - 14 = 0 \quad\quad\quad 2x^2 + 3x - 2 = 0$$
$$2x^2 + 3x + 2 = 0 \quad\quad\quad 2x^2 + 3x - 20 = 0$$
$$2x^2 + 3x + 1 = 0$$

Problems leading to quadratic equations

Example 16 *A lawn measures 12 m by 8 m and is surrounded by a flower-bed whose area is 52 m². Find the width of the bed, correct to 3 significant figures.*

Let the width of the bed be x m.

Then in Fig. 56 the outer rectangle measures $(2x + 12)$ m by $(2x + 8)$ m.

Hence area of outer rectangle

$$= (2x + 12)(2x + 8) \text{ m}^2$$

and area of inner rectangle

$$= 12 \times 8 \text{ m}^2.$$

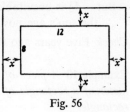

Fig. 56

The difference between the areas of these two rectangles is the area of the bed.

$$\therefore (2x + 12)(2x + 8) - 12 \times 8 = 52$$
$$\therefore 4x^2 + 40x + 96 - 96 = 52$$
$$\therefore 4x^2 + 40x - 52 = 0$$
$$\therefore x^2 + 10x - 13 = 0.$$

The L.H.S. does not factorise, so complete the square.

$$x^2 + 10x - 13 = 0$$
$$\therefore x^2 + 10x + 25 = 13 + 25$$
$$\therefore (x + 5)^2 = 38$$
$$\therefore x + 5 = \pm 6\cdot164 \text{ approx.}$$
$$\therefore x = -5 \pm 6\cdot164$$
$$= 1\cdot164 \text{ or } -11\cdot164$$

But $-11\cdot164$ is unsuitable,

$\therefore$ width of bed is $1\cdot16$ m, correct to 3 sig. fig.

Check Area of outer rectangle $= 14\cdot32 \times 10\cdot32 \text{ m}^2 \simeq 147\cdot8 \text{ m}^2$

$\therefore$ area of bed $= (147\cdot8 - 96) \text{ m}^2 = 51\cdot8 \text{ m}^2 \simeq 52 \text{ m}^2.$

Example 17 *A man is four times as old as his son, and five years ago the product of their ages was* 234. *Find their present ages.*

Let the son's age now be x years.

Then the father's age now is $4x$ years.

Five years ago their respective ages were $(x - 5)$ years and $(4x - 5)$ years.

$$\therefore (x - 5)(4x - 5) = 234$$
$$\therefore 4x^2 - 25x + 25 - 234 = 0$$
$$\therefore 4x^2 - 25x - 209 = 0$$
$$\therefore (x - 11)(4x + 19) = 0$$
$$\therefore x = 11 \text{ or } -4\tfrac{3}{4}$$

67

But $-4\frac{3}{4}$ is unsuitable,

$\therefore$ the son's age now is 11 years, and the father's 44 years.

Check Five years ago their ages were 6 and 39, and $6 \times 39 = 234$.

Example 18 *A piece of wire 56 cm long is bent to form the perimeter of a rectangle of area 171 cm². Find the dimensions of the rectangle.*

The sum of the length and width of the rectangle is half the perimeter, i.e. 28 cm.

$\therefore$ if the length is x cm, the width is $(28 - x)$ cm,

$\therefore$ the area of the rectangle is $x(28 - x)$ cm²

$$\therefore x(28 - x) = 171$$
$$\therefore 28x - x^2 = 171$$
$$\therefore x^2 - 28x + 171 = 0$$
$$\therefore (x - 19)(x - 9) = 0$$
$$\therefore x = 19 \text{ or } 9$$

If $x = 19$, the length is 19 cm and the width is $(28 - 19)$ cm, i.e. 9 cm.

Alternatively, if $x = 9$, the length is 9 cm and the width 19 cm. In either case the rectangle measures 19 cm by 9 cm.

Check Area $= 19 \times 9$ cm² $= 171$ cm²

Perimeter $=$ twice $(19 + 9)$ cm $= 2 \times 28$ cm $= 56$ cm.

Exercise 4h

1 Find the whole number such that three times its square added to twice the number makes 16.

2 A rectangle measures 12 cm by 8 cm. When the length and breadth are both increased by the same amount the area becomes 221 cm². Find the increase in length and breadth.

3 Find the whole number such that twice its square subtracted from seven times the number makes 3.

4 Find the number such that twice its square is equal to six times the number.

5 The width of a room is equal to the height, the length is 4 m, and the area of the walls is 42 m². Find the width.

6 A man is now four times as old as his son, and 8 years ago the product of their ages was 108. Find their present ages.

7 Find the ages of a lady and her daughter if the lady was 23 years old when her daughter was born, and the product of their ages now is 174.

8 Find the whole number such that twice its square is 11 more than 21 times the original number.

9 Three times the square of a certain integer is 16 less than 26 times the integer. Find the integer.

10 The length of a page of a book is 4 cm more than the width, and the area is 132 cm². Find the length in centimetres, correct to 2 decimal places.

11 A caterer buys a certain quantity of cake for £4·40, and the number of kilos that he buys is 2 more than the number of pence that each kilo costs him. Find the price per kilo.

12 A square carpet is laid in one corner of a room, leaving strips of uncovered floor 2 m wide along one side, and 1 m along the other. If the area of the room is 56 m², find the dimensions of the carpet.

13 A garage is 5 m long, the area of the walls is 34 m², and the height is $1\frac{1}{2}$ m less than the width. Find the height.

14 Find two consecutive numbers such that the sum of their squares is equal to 145.

15 Find two consecutive even numbers such that the sum of their squares is equal to 244.

16 A stone is thrown down a mine-shaft, and the formula $d = 6t + 5t^2$ gives the distance d m that it has fallen after t seconds. How long does it take to reach a depth of 155 m.

17 The area of a rectangular picture is 160 cm², and the width is 4 cm less than the length. Find the width in cm, correct to 3 sig. fig.

69

18 The base of a triangle is 2 cm more than the altitude, and the area of the triangle is 40 cm². Calculate the altitude.

19 The perimeter of a right-angled triangle is 56 cm, and the length of the hypotenuse is 25 cm. Calculate the lengths of the other two sides.

20 A piece of wire 90 cm long is bent to form the perimeter of a rectangle of area 500 cm². Find the lengths of the sides.

21 A picture, 10 cm long and 8 cm wide, is surrounded by a frame of area 63 cm². Find the width of the frame.

22 The area of a triangle is 14 cm², and the altitude is $4\frac{1}{2}$ cm more than the base. Calculate the length of the base.

23 The altitude of a triangle is 3 cm less than the base, and the area of the triangle is 12 cm². Calculate the length of the base, correct to 3 sig. fig.

24 A picture-mount measures 16 cm by 13 cm. A picture is placed on it so that the area of mount showing is 100 cm², and consists of strips of equal width on all four sides of the picture. Find the width of these strips.

25 The hypotenuse of a right-angled triangle is 4 cm long, and the perimeter is 9 cm. Find the lengths of the other two sides, correct to 3 sig. fig.

26 When a stone is thrown upwards, its height h m after t seconds is given by the formula $h = 30t - 5t^2$. How long after being thrown is it at a height of 25 m? Why are there two answers, and what do they mean?

27 A rectangular lawn measures 20 m by 15 m, and is surrounded by a path of uniform width. If the area of the path is 156 m², find its width.

28 Find two consecutive odd numbers such that the square of the smaller one added to twice the square of the greater is equal to 211.

29 Find two consecutive even numbers such that three times the square of the smaller one added to the square of the greater is equal to 84.

30 The formula $S = \frac{1}{2}n(n + 1)$ gives the sum S of the numbers 1, 2, 3 etc. up to n. Find n if $S = 136$.

31 If a straight-sided figure has n sides it has $\frac{1}{2}n(n - 3)$ diagonals. If a figure has 27 diagonals, how many sides has it?

32 An area is paved with square tiles of a certain size, and 192 are needed. If the tiles had measured 2 cm less each way, 300 would have been needed. Find the size of the larger tiles.

33 When 6 is divided by a certain number, the result is the same as when 5 is added to the number and that sum divided by 6. Find the number.

34 Find the number such that when it is added to 3 and the sum halved, the result is the same as when 5 is divided by the number.

35 A farmer uses 60 m of fencing to make three sides of a rectangular sheep pen, the fourth side being a wall. Find the length of the shorter sides of the pen if the area enclosed is 448 m².

36 A path 2 m wide surrounds a circular pond, and the area of the path is $\frac{1}{2}$ that of the pond. Find the radius of the pond in metres, correct to 3 sig. fig.

Chapter 5

Ratio. Rate. Scales.
Proportional parts

Exercise 5a   Revision

Express the following ratios in their simplest forms:

1 14 : 21	**2** 25 to 15	**3** 12 kg to 30 kg
4 75 cm : 1 m	**5** £1·25 : 75p	**6** $\frac{3}{4} : \frac{1}{2}$
7 $1\frac{1}{2}$ to $3\frac{1}{2}$	**8** 50 s to $1\frac{1}{2}$ min	**9** 1 litre : 350 cm³

10 75 mm² to 4·5 cm²

Complete the following ratios:

11 9 : 24 = 3 :	**12** 4 : 9 = : 63
13 25 : = 5 : 6	**14** : 13 = 15 : 39
15 12 : = 3 : 7	**16** 24 : 8 = : 7
17 15 : 20 = 18 :	**18** $\frac{30}{6} = \overline{9}$
19 $\frac{}{8} = \frac{21}{24}$	**20** $\frac{4}{7} = \frac{20}{}$

Find the result of

21 increasing	16p	in the ratio			7 : 4
22	„	21 m	„	„ „	10 : 7
23	„	45 s	„	„ „	5 : 3
24 decreasing	£1·25	„	„	„	3 : 5
25	„	84 km	„	„	6 : 7
26	„	$4\frac{1}{2}$ weeks	„	„	5 : 9
27 increasing	75 cm	„	„	„	9 : 5
28	„	91p	„	„	9 : 7
29 decreasing	1 h 3 min	„	„	„	7 : 9
30	„	1·35 m²	„	„	5 : 9

Rate

It will have been noticed in the preceding exercise that a ratio compares two quantities which are of the **same kind,** e.g. 4 kg : 7 kg or $3\frac{1}{2}$ m : 10 m. The **units** may be different, e.g. 9 min 30 s : 2 h, but the quantities are of the same kind, and hours or minutes or seconds may each be expressed in terms of the other two.

Quantities of **different** kinds may be connected in the form of a **rate,** e.g.

   (i) a workman is paid £4·80 for an 8 hour day, which is at the rate of 60p an hour;
  (ii) a cyclist travels 18 km in $1\frac{1}{2}$ hours, which is at the rate of 12 km an hour;
 (iii) a 4-m girder of uniform cross-section with mass 90 kg is said to have a mass of $22\frac{1}{2}$ kg per metre ($22\frac{1}{2}$ kg m^{-1});
 (iv) a piece of metal of volume 70 cm³ and mass 700 g has a mass of 10 g cm^{-3}. (This is called its **density.**)

However, a rate may also connect quantities of the same kind, e.g. the price of an article may be reduced from £4 to £3·52 which is a reduction at the rate of 12p in the £.

Exercise 5b

1 Find the rate at which tennis balls are sold per dozen, if 16 of them cost £3·20.

2 A house is rented at £163·80 per annum. Express this as a weekly rental.

3 Find in kilometres per hour the rate at which a car travels if it goes $38\frac{1}{2}$ km in 35 minutes.

4 A steel girder 5·2 m long has a mass of 137·8 kg. Find its mass in kg m^{-1}.

5 A shop has a sale, and reduces all prices by 15p in the £. Find the sale price of an article marked at £7·40.

6 A bankrupt pays his creditors at the rate of 36p in the £. How much was owing to a creditor who receives £150·21?

7 Find the mass of a uniform wooden beam in kg m⁻¹ if it is 6·5 m long and has a mass of 46·8 kg.

8 If a cricketer takes 59 wickets for 703 runs, find his bowling average in runs per wicket. (2 dec. pl.)

9 If 42·5 cm³ of sea-water has a mass of 43·69 g, find its density in g cm⁻³.

10 A man is paid £7·54 after working for 14½ hours. Find his rate of pay per hour.

11 A salesman receives commission on his sales at the rate of 8p in the £. Find his commission on sales which total £53·75.

12 How much income tax does a man pay on £212·25 at the rate of 36p in the £?

13 A town levies rates at 86p in the £. Find the sum which has to be paid on property with a rateable value of £123.

14 A bridge is 220 m long and has a mass of 11 220 tonnes. Find its mass in t m⁻¹.

15 A car engine has a mass of 152 kg and a maximum output of 57 kW. Express this in kW kg⁻¹.

16 In 1968 a motor-car firm produced 9 324 cars. Allowing a fortnight for holidays and a further 50 Saturdays and 50 Sundays, find the rate of production in cars per day.

17 A co-operative society pays a dividend of £1·18 on purchases to the value of £14·75. What rate in the £ is this?

18 A car consumes petrol at the rate of a litre for every 11 km. If the price of petrol is 8p per litre, find the cost of the petrol used for a journey of 891 km.

19 A shop has a sale, and an article originally marked at £8·75 is sold for £6·65. Find the rate of reduction as pence in the pound.

20 A salesman earns £5·13 commission at the rate of 6p in the £. Find the total value of his sales.

21 In a town with a population of 53 280 there are 562 deaths in one year. Find the death-rate per 1 000 inhabitants, correct to 2 decimal places.

22 In no. 21, if the same town had 613 live births registered, find the birth-rate per 1 000. (2 dec. pl.)

23 A car has a mass of 1 140 kg and its engine can produce a maximum power of 92 kW. Express this in kW t^{-1} (3 sig. fig.).

24 Find the rate in the £ at which a salesman earns commission if he receives £9·36 on sales of £62·40.

25 A bankrupt pays £47·61 to a creditor to whom he owes £132·25. How much does he pay in the £?

Comparison of ratios

A ratio may be expressed in the form $n : 1$, where n is a whole number, a fraction, or a decimal calculated to any required degree of accuracy. This is particularly useful when comparing ratios.

Example 1 *Express the ratio of* £4·10 : £1·90 *in the form* $n : 1$.

$$\frac{£4·10}{£1·90} = \frac{4·1}{1·9}$$

$$= \frac{41 \div 19}{1} \text{ dividing num. and denom. by 19}$$

$$= \frac{2·16}{1} \text{ correct to 2 decimal places.}$$

$\therefore$ the ratio is 2·16 : 1 approximately.

Example 2 *Find which ratio is the greater,* 7 : 13 *or* 8 : 15.

$\frac{7}{13} = 0·538 \ldots$ i.e. 7 : 13 = 0·538 . . . : 1.

$\frac{8}{15} = 0·533 \ldots$ i.e. 8 : 15 = 0·533 . . . : 1.

$\therefore$ the first ratio is the greater.

Sometimes the following method for comparing ratios is easier.

Example 3 *Find which ratio is the greater,* 9 : 16 *or* 7 : 12.

$\frac{9}{16} = \frac{27}{48}$ and $\frac{7}{12} = \frac{28}{48}$ (48 is the L.C.M. of 16 and 12)

or $\qquad$ 9 : 16 = 27 : 48 and 7 : 12 = 28 : 48.

$\therefore$ the second ratio is the greater.

75

For maps and plans the ratio is usually in the form $1:n$. For example, if the scale is 5 cm to the kilometre, 5 cm on the map represents 1 kilometre on the ground.

$$5 \text{ cm} : 1 \text{ km} = 5 \text{ cm} : 100\,000 \text{ cm}$$
$$= 1 : 20\,000$$
$$\therefore \text{ the } \textbf{scale} \text{ of the map is } 1 : 20\,000$$

The fraction $\frac{1}{20\,000}$ is called the **representative fraction** (R.F.). Notice that a scale of $1:16$ is **greater** than a scale of $1:17$, since $\frac{1}{16}$ is greater than $\frac{1}{17}$.

Example 4 *Express the ratio* $8:13$ *in the form* $1:n$.

$$\frac{8}{13} = \frac{1}{13 \div 8} \text{ dividing num. and denom. by 8.}$$

$$= \frac{1}{1 \cdot 625}$$

$$\therefore \text{ the ratio is } 1 : 1 \cdot 625.$$

Example 5 *A plan is made of a school playing field, and it is found that the length of the pavilion, 15·6 m, is represented on the plan by a line 7·8 cm long. Find the scale and the R.F.*

$$\frac{7 \cdot 8 \text{ cm}}{15 \cdot 6 \text{ m}} = \frac{7 \cdot 8 \text{ cm}}{1\,560 \text{ cm}} = \frac{78}{15\,600} = \frac{1}{200}$$

$$\therefore \text{ the scale is } 1 : 200 \text{ and the R.F. is } \tfrac{1}{200}.$$

(This result means that 1 cm represents 200 cm, i.e. 2 m, so that the scale may be quoted as 1 cm to 2 m, or $\frac{1}{2}$ cm to 1 m.)

Exercise 5c

In nos. 1–30 give results correct to 3 significant figures where necessary.

Express the following ratios in the form $n:1$:

1 $3:8$ **2** $7:5$ **3** 14 to 3

4 4 to 7   **5** £29 to £4   **6** 6 m to 8 m

7 2·4 m : 1·5 m   **8** 25 cm : 11 cm

9 80p to £2   **10** £4·25 : £2·50

Express the following ratios in the form 1 : *n*:

11 4 to 11   **12** 9 : 13   **13** 7 : 2   **14** 8 to 3

15 2·5 m : 4 m   **16** 1·5 g to 48 g   **17** 0·5 cm : 6·6 m

18 2·5 kg to 0·7 kg   **19** 8 cm to 633·6 m   **20** 5 cm : 1 km

Complete the following:

21 15 : 4 =   : 1   **22** 8 : 5 = 1 :   **23** 1 : 4·5 = 3 :

24 6·2 : 1 =   : 5   **25** 4 : 1 = 9 :   **26**   : 3·6 = 4 : 1

27   : 1·6 = 1 : 4·8   **28** 2 cm :   = 1 : 396

29   : 36 kg = 1 : 1 800   **30**   : 1 km = 1 : 4 000

Find which of the following pairs of ratios is the greater:

31 18 : 5, 11 : 3   **32** 11 : 6, 13 : 7   **33** 5 : 8, 4 : 7

34 15 : 7, 13 : 6   **35** 1 : 7, 1 : 8   **36** 7 : 15, 8 : 17

37 17 : 6, 20 : 7   **38** 11 m : 13 m, 7 g : 8 g

39 1·5 m : 40 cm, $6\frac{1}{2}$ s : $1\frac{3}{4}$ s   **40** £1·70 : 90p, £3 : £1·60

Find the R.F. of a map on which

41   1 cm represents 10 m

42 10 cm   „   1 km

43   4 cm   „   600 m

44   5 cm   „   1·5 km

45 20 cm   „   5 km

46 One road has a slope of 3 in 19, and another rises 5 in 32. Which has the steeper slope?

47 Oranges on one stall are priced at 7 for 17p, and on another at 29p a dozen. Which is cheaper?

48 A house covers a rectangle of ground measuring 15·7 m by 12·3 m. On the architect's plan the length of the rectangle is 78·5 cm. What scale does the architect use, and what is the width of the house on his plan?

49 Find the R.F. of a map drawn on a scale of 5 km to the centimetre. Also find, in centimetres, the distance on the map between Rugby and Cambridge (94 km).

50 One boy cycles 16 km in an hour, and another goes 4·4 m in a second. Which goes faster?

51 A distance of 23 km is represented on a map by 9·2 cm. Find the scale in km to the cm. Find also the R.F. of the map.

52 The mass of 47 cm³ of mercury is 638·73 g. The mass of 1 cm³ of water is 1 g. Find the ratio of the masses of equal volumes of mercury and water, in the form $n:1$. (This ratio is called **specific gravity.**)

53 For the athletic sports of a school there is a trophy for the house scoring most points per boy. The results on one occasion were: A, 95 boys, 752 points; B, 108 boys, 853 points; C, 102 boys, 829 points; D, 97 boys, 785 points. Which of the four houses won the trophy?

54 The R.F. of the plan of a garden is $\frac{1}{250}$. Find in square metres the area of a lawn represented on the plan by a rectangle measuring 9·3 cm by 6·4 cm.

55 From 250 cm³ of acid 90 cm³ is taken and diluted with 325 cm³ of water. The remainder is mixed with 575 cm³ of water. Which solution is more concentrated?

Graphical treatment of ratios

Direct variation If a man walks steadily at $5\frac{1}{2}$ km h⁻¹ a graph can be drawn as in Fig. 57, showing the distance gone in a given time, or the time taken to walk a given distance.

The distance **varies directly** as the time, since in 4 hours he goes four times as far as in 1 hour, and so on.

Also the ratio of two times is equal to the ratio of the corresponding distances. For example $\dfrac{6 \text{ hours}}{3 \text{ hours}} = \dfrac{2}{1}$, and the ratio of the corresponding distances is $\dfrac{33 \text{ km}}{16\frac{1}{2} \text{ km}} = \dfrac{2}{1}$.

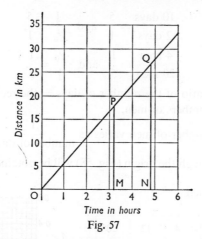

Fig. 57

The graph is a straight line through the origin, since if P and Q are any two points on the graph, then

$$\frac{PM}{OM} = \frac{QN}{ON} \quad \text{or} \quad \frac{PM}{QN} = \frac{OM}{ON}.$$

OPM and OQN are similar triangles, and $\overline{OPQ}$ is a straight line.

Inverse variation If a certain piece of work can be done in 10 days by 4 men, then it can be done in 5 days (half as long) by 8 men (twice as many), in 2 days (one-fifth of the time) by 20 men (five times as many), and so on.

The time taken **varies inversely** as the number of men. Alternatively it may be said that the time taken **varies as the reciprocal** of the number of men, so that

$$\text{time varies as } \frac{1}{\text{number of men}}$$

and number of men varies as $\frac{1}{\text{time}}$.

For example,

10 days is the time for   4 men,
2   „   „   „   „   „   „ 20   „

79 ·

$$\frac{10 \text{ days}}{2 \text{ days}} = \frac{5}{1} \quad \text{and} \quad \frac{\frac{1}{4}}{\frac{1}{20}} = \frac{5}{1},$$

or

$$\frac{4 \text{ men}}{20 \text{ men}} = \frac{1}{5} \quad \text{and} \quad \frac{\frac{1}{10}}{\frac{1}{2}} = \frac{1}{5}.$$

Hence the ratio of the number of days = the reciprocal of the ratio of the numbers of men.

Since the number of men varies as $\dfrac{1}{\text{number of days}}$, a straight-line graph through the origin (Fig. 58) will be obtained by plotting $\dfrac{1}{\text{time}}$ against men.

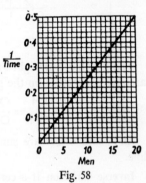

Fig. 58

Men	4	12	20
Time in days	10	$3\frac{1}{3}$	2
$\dfrac{1}{\text{Time}}$	0·1	0·3	0·5

From the graph, 16 men gives a reading of 0·4 for $\dfrac{1}{\text{time}}$. Hence 16 men would take $\dfrac{1}{0·4}$ days = $2\frac{1}{2}$ days.

Exercise 5d

1 Given that £1 is equivalent to 11·80 French francs, draw a graph and from it read off the value of
  (i) 21p, 46p in francs
  (ii) 9·91F, 7·20F in pence.

2 Three men travel at speeds of 5 km h^{-1}, 15 km h^{-1} and 18 km h^{-1} respectively, starting together. On one set of axes draw graphs to show the distances covered at any time up to 5 hours. (Take time in hours on the horizontal axis and distance in kilometres on the vertical axis.)

3 Three men travel a distance of 60 kilometres at speeds of 12 km h⁻¹, 15 km h⁻¹ and 20 km h⁻¹ respectively, starting together. On one set of axes draw graphs to show their positions at any time.

4 A man travels a distance of 60 kilometres. Find how long he would take at 6 km h⁻¹, 12 km h⁻¹ and 30 km h⁻¹, and complete a table of values like the one given below. Use decimals for $\dfrac{1}{\text{time}}$.

Speed in km h⁻¹			
Time in hours			
$\dfrac{1}{\text{Time}}$			

Taking speed along the horizontal axis and $\dfrac{1}{\text{time}}$ on the vertical axis, draw a graph connecting speed and reciprocal of time.

Read off the value of $\dfrac{1}{\text{time}}$ corresponding to a speed of 15 km h⁻¹, and hence find the time taken at this speed. Find also the speed corresponding to a time of 7½ hours.

5 Given that 50 litres of petrol cost £3·50, draw a graph and from it read off

   (i) the cost of 11, 32, 45 litres

   (ii) the number of litres that can be bought for £1·33, £1·89, £2·87.

6 Given that the mass of 16 litres of petrol is 12·4 kg, draw a graph and from it read off

   (i) the mass of 6, 10, 14 litres

   (ii) the amount of petrol that has a mass of 4, 7, 11 kg.

7 A man has £6 with which to buy a number of things which are all of the same price. Draw a straight-line graph to connect the reciprocal of the number of things with the price of one, the latter being anything from 5p to 50p.

How many things can be bought at 24p each? If 15 things are bought, what is the price of one?

8 Given that the mass of 100 cm³ of a certain metal is 254 g, draw a graph connecting mass with volume up to 100 cm³. Read off

    (i) the mass of 37 cm³, 64 cm³ of the metal

    (ii) the volume which has a mass of 100 g, 208 g.

9 A small workshop produces components for a car manufacturer. The overhead cost of maintaining the workshop is £32 per week, even when no components are made. The total cost of making 100 components is £212. Draw a graph and from it read off

    (i) the cost of making 27, 79 components

    (ii) the number of components that can be made for £95, £140.

10 A quantity of gas was kept under constant pressure and steadily heated. The temperatures (degrees C) and corresponding volumes in cm³ were observed as follows:

Temp.	17·5	21·0	33·5	42·8	56·2	66·8	75·3	86·0
Vol.	7·30	7·36	7·66	7·90	8·22	8·50	8·70	8·98

Show graphically that changes in volume are proportional to changes in temperature.

Read off from the graph

    (i) the volume at 60° C

    (ii) the temperature giving a volume of 7·8 cm³.

Two quantities may be connected in other ways than by direct or inverse ratio. For example:

    (i) The area of a square is proportional to the square of the

82

length of a side, i.e. the area **varies directly as the square** of the side.

(ii) The resistance of the air to a car's motion is approximately proportional to the square of the speed, i.e. the resistance **varies directly as the square** of the speed. The resistance at 60 km h^{-1} is four times as great as the resistance at 30 km h^{-1}.

(iii) When a piece of steel is placed at a distance from a magnet, the pull of the magnet **varies inversely as the square** of the distance, i.e. pull varies as $\dfrac{1}{(\text{distance})^2}$. If the pull at 4 cm is a force of 12 newtons, the pull at 8 cm is 3 newtons. (If the distance is multiplied by 2, the pull is divided by 4.)

(iv) The volume of a cube is proportional to the cube of the length of an edge, i.e. the volume **varies directly as the cube** of an edge.

Variations of these kinds give graphs which are curves, and not straight lines. Nos. (i) and (iv) are dealt with (not graphically) in Chap. 6. Types of variation like (ii) and (iii) will be found in Book 4.

Proportional parts

To divide a quantity into two parts which are in the ratio 2 : 5, first split it into 7 equal divisions (since $2 + 5 = 7$). The required parts will then be respectively 2 and 5 of these equal divisions, i.e. they will be $\frac{2}{7}$ and $\frac{5}{7}$ of the original quantity.

Example 6 *Divide* 1·17 *kg of sweets between Mary and John so that their shares are in the ratio* 8 : 5.

$$8 + 5 = 13$$
$$\tfrac{1}{13} \text{ of } 1\cdot17 \text{ kg} = 0\cdot09 \text{ kg}$$
$$\therefore \text{ Mary receives } 0\cdot09 \text{ kg} \times 8 = 0\cdot72 \text{ kg}$$
$$\text{and John } \quad ,, \quad 0\cdot09 \text{ kg} \times 5 = \underline{0\cdot45 \text{ kg}}$$
$$\textit{Check} \qquad \text{Sum} = \overline{1\cdot17 \text{ kg}}$$

New General Mathematics

Example 7 *Divide* 299 *into* 3 *parts in the ratio* $\frac{1}{3} : \frac{5}{6} : \frac{3}{4}$.

$\frac{1}{3} : \frac{5}{6} : \frac{3}{4} = 4 : 10 : 9$ (multiplying each by 12)

$4 + 10 + 9 = 23$

$\frac{1}{23}$ of $299 = 13$

$\therefore \frac{4}{23}$,, ,, $= 13 \times 4 = 52$

$\frac{10}{23}$,, ,, $= 13 \times 10 = 130$

$\frac{9}{23}$,, ,, $= 13 \times 9 = 117$

Check   Sum $= 299$.

Example 8 *Share* £2·53 *between* X, Y *and* Z *so that* Y *has half as much again as* X, *and* Z *has twice as much as* Y.

If X has 1 share, Y has $1\frac{1}{2}$ shares and Z has 3 shares.

$\therefore$ they receive sums in the ratio $1 : 1\frac{1}{2} : 3$

$= 2 : 3 : 6$.

$2 + 3 + 6 = 11$

$\frac{1}{11}$ of £2·53 = £0·23

$\therefore$ X receives £0·23 $\times$ 2 = £0·46

Y   ,,   £0·23 $\times$ 3 = £0·69

and Z   ,,   £0·23 $\times$ 6 = £1·38

Check   Sum = £2·53

Notice in the following example that a unit, 'cow-days', has been made up as a convenient means of expressing the shares of the partners. A similar unit, 'man-hours', is very familiar in everyday life. For example, if a stretch of road can be surfaced by a gang of 6 men working for 18 hours, the job is said to involve 108 man-hours.

Example 9 *Two farmers, Giles and Brown, share the grazing of a field. Giles puts in* 12 *cows for* 18 *days, and Brown puts in* 15 *cows for* 16 *days. How should they share the payment of* £8·55 *rent?*

Giles   has 12 $\times$ 18 cow-days = 216 cow-days

Brown   ,, 15 $\times$ 16   ,,   ,, = 240   ,, ,,

$\therefore$ their shares are in the ratio of 216 : 240

$= 9 : 10$ (dividing each by 24)

$9 + 10 = 19$

$\frac{1}{19}$ of £8·55 = £0·45

$$\therefore \text{ Giles } \text{ pays } £0·45 \times 9 = £4·05$$
$$\text{and Brown } \text{ ,, } £0·45 \times 10 = £4·50$$

Check Sum = £8·55

A similar problem might involve partners, A and B, who invest money in their business. If they invest respectively £525 for 4 months, and £900 for 3 months, a unit such as '£-months' could be used.

A supplies 2 100 £-months and B supplies 2 700 £-months.

∴ they should share profits in the ratio 2 100 : 2 700, and so on.

Exercise 5e

Divide

1 98p	into 2 parts in the ratio					5 : 9
2 £5·76	,, 3	,,	,,	,,	,,	1 : 3 : 5
3 96 m	,, 3	,,	,,	,,	,,	3 : 4 : 5
4 56 kg	,, 2	,,	,,	,,	,,	$4\frac{1}{3} : 2\frac{3}{5}$
5 153	,, 4	,,	,,	,,	,,	5 : 2 : 6 : 4
6 £33·76	,, 3	,,	,,	,,	,,	2 : 5 : 9
7 10·80 kg	,, 2	,,	,,	,,	,,	11 : 7
8 22·95 m	,, 2	,,	,,	,,	,,	5 : 12
9 £5·39	,, 3	,,	,,	,,	,,	$1\frac{1}{3} : \frac{1}{2} : 2\frac{1}{4}$
10 28·6 kg	,, 4	,,	,,	,,	,,	4 : 5 : 6 : 7

11 Two gardeners share 11 tonnes of rockery stone so that one has half as much again as the other. The total cost, including delivery charges, is £22·75. How much does each pay?

12 Two farmers share a field. A puts in 24 cows for 15 days, and B puts in 18 cows for 12 days. How should they share payment of rent of £5·60?

13 Three relatives share £599·20 so that the first has twice as much as the second, and the second has twice as much as the third. How much does the first receive?

14 Three partners Evans, Jones and Davies start a business together. Evans advances £750 for 8 months, Jones £600 for 5 months, and Davies £450 for 10 months. Find their shares in profits of £1 575.

15 Three beakers have capacities of 250, 650 and 200 cm³ respectively, and 682 cm³ of water is poured into them so that the same fraction of each is filled. Find the three volumes into which the water is divided.

16 Two farmers rent a field jointly. The first puts in 52 sheep for 15 days, and the second 42 sheep for 26 days. If the first farmer pays £5·45 towards the rent, what does the second pay?

17 A, B and C share £7·56 so that A has $2\frac{1}{2}$ times as much as C, and B has $3\frac{1}{2}$ times as much as C. Find their shares.

18 Bronze is an alloy made up of 95 parts of copper, 4 of tin and 1 of zinc. Find the amount of tin in 87·75 kg of bronze.

19 What mass of bronze would contain 5·7 kg of copper?

20 Three boys A, B and C together spend 35p on some sweets which they eat at different rates. By the time A has eaten 2, B has had 3; and for every 4 that B has, C has 5. How should they share the cost?

21 A, B and C are three cigar-makers. A can make 9 while B makes 8, and B can make 6 while C makes 7. How many has each made when their total is 1 659 cigars?

22 A, B and C share £8·55 in such a way that A has $2\frac{1}{2}$ times as much as B, and B has 4 times as much as C. Find their shares.

23 A man begins to trade with £371. Later on a partner joins him, bringing £636 into the business. At the end of the first year's trading the two men share the profits equally. When did the second partner join the first?

24 A, B and C undertake to dig a plot of land between them. A and B start together at 08.00, and C joins them at 09.15. A goes at 10.45, B goes at 11.30, and C carries on to finish the job at 13.00. Find their shares in a payment of £4·80.

25 Phosphor-bronze is an alloy of copper, tin and phosphorus in the ratio 185 : 14 : 1. Find the amount of copper in a phosphor-bronze casting of mass 27·2 kg.

26 A demolition job is shared by three contractors. A has 30 men working for 9 days, B 18 men for 10 days, and C 24 men for 15 days. Find their shares in a payment of £855.

27 Divide £29·75 among A, B, C and D so that, for every £1 that A receives, B receives 25p, C £1·75 and D £1·25.

28 A man takes a litre can of white paint, a 2-litre can of yellow paint and a 4-litre can of blue paint, and mixes the contents together in a bucket. If he now fills the original three cans with the mixture, how much white paint will there be in the largest can?

29 A dock is built by three firms working together, employing 1 209, 1 568, 1 723 men respectively. If the contract is worth £2 250 000, how much should each firm receive?

30 A man invests £1 000 in a business and his partner invests £1 600. They arrange that in any year 35% of the profits shall be divided equally between them, and the remainder in the ratio of their capital investments. Find their shares of a year's profit of £1 080.

Chapter 6

Areas and volumes of similar figures

Consider two rectangles which are of different sizes but similar in shape. Suppose the smaller measures 7 cm by 3 cm. Then if the larger is 28 cm long (i.e. 4 times as long) its width must be 12 cm (i.e. 4 times as wide). Their areas are 21 cm^2 and 336 cm^2 respectively.

Ratio of corresponding lengths $= \frac{28}{7} = \frac{4}{1}$
or $\frac{12}{3} = \frac{4}{1}$

Ratio of areas $= \frac{336}{21} = \frac{16}{1} = (\frac{4}{1})^2$.

Hence the ratio of the areas is the square of the ratio of corresponding lengths.

If the larger rectangle is 4 times as long as the smaller it must also be 4 times as wide. Hence its area is 16 (i.e. 4^2) times as great.

Again, consider two circles whose radii are 3 cm and 5 cm. Their areas are $\pi \times 3^2$ cm^2 and $\pi \times 5^2$ cm^2 respectively.

Ratio of radii $= \frac{3}{5}$

Ratio of areas $= \frac{\pi \times 3^2}{\pi \times 5^2} = \frac{3^2}{5^2} = \left(\frac{3}{5}\right)^2$ or $\frac{9}{25}$.

In general, **the ratio of the areas of similar figures is the square of the ratio of corresponding lengths.**

The ratio of similar volumes may be found in the same kind of way.

Consider a rectangular block measuring 5 cm by 2 cm by 1 cm and a similar block measuring 15 cm by 6 cm by 3 cm, i.e. 3 times as great in each direction. Their volumes are 10 cm^3 and 270 cm^3 respectively.

Ratio of corresponding lengths $= \frac{5}{15} = \frac{1}{3}$

Ratio of volumes $= \frac{10}{270} = \frac{1}{27} = (\frac{1}{3})^3$.

Hence the ratio of similar volumes is the cube of the ratio of corresponding lengths.

Example 1 *Two jugs, similar in shape, are respectively 21 cm and 14 cm high. If the smaller jug holds 1·2 litres, find the capacity of the larger one.*

$$\text{Ratio of corresponding lengths} = \frac{21 \text{ cm}}{14 \text{ cm}} = \frac{3}{2}$$

$$\therefore \quad \text{,, \quad ,, \quad ,,} \quad \text{volumes} = \left(\frac{3}{2}\right)^3 = \frac{27}{8}$$

The smaller jug holds 1·2 litres

$\therefore$,, larger ,, ,, $1 \cdot 2 \times \frac{27}{8}$ litres

$\qquad\qquad\qquad = 4 \cdot 05$ litres

Example 2 *The masses of two dolls are 960 g and 405 g respectively, and they are identical in design. If the larger doll wears an apron of area 120 cm², find the area of the apron worn by the smaller doll.*

$$\text{Ratio of volumes} = \text{ratio of masses}$$

$$= \frac{960 \text{ g}}{405 \text{ g}}$$

$$= \frac{64}{27}$$

$$= \frac{4^3}{3^3} = \left(\frac{4}{3}\right)^3$$

$\therefore$ ratio of corresponding lengths $= \frac{4}{3}$

$\therefore$,, ,, ,, areas $= \left(\frac{4}{3}\right)^2$

$\qquad\qquad\qquad\qquad\qquad = \frac{16}{9}$

Area of larger apron $= 120$ cm²

$\therefore$,, ,, smaller ,, $= 120 \times \frac{9}{16}$ cm²

$\qquad\qquad\qquad = 67\frac{1}{2}$ cm²

Exercise 6

In this set of examples it is assumed that the objects being compared are geometrically similar.

1 A tea-tray measuring 40 cm by 30 cm costs £1·28. What should be the price of a tray of similar proportions but 50 cm long?

New General Mathematics

2 A statue is of mass 640 kg and an exact model of it is made which is one-eighth of its height. Find the mass of the model.

3 A sports trophy is in the form of a cup 30 cm high, and winners of the event for which it is awarded are given replicas of it $7\frac{1}{2}$ cm high. If a replica holds one-tenth of a litre, find the capacity of the cup.

4 A cat has whiskers 10 cm long and its mass is 5 kg. Find the mass of a similar cat with whiskers 6 cm long.

5 Two pieces of plywood are in the form of isosceles right-angled triangles. One costs 48p and its hypotenuse is 40 cm long. Find the cost of the other piece if its hypotenuse is 45 cm long. (Nearest penny.)

6 Out of a set of similarly shaped jugs two are selected with heights of 16 cm and 10 cm. If the smaller holds three quarters of a litre, find the capacity of the larger.

7 Two conical vessels, made of the same material, are similar in shape, their heights being 75 cm and 125 cm. If the material for making the first cost 54p, find the cost for the second.

8 If in no. 7 the second vessel holds $187\frac{1}{2}$ litres, find the capacity of the first.

9 A soap-bubble 4 cm in diameter is blown out until its diameter becomes 8 cm. What multiple of the original surface is the new one, and how is the thickness of the soap-film affected?

10 A piece of dough on a pastry-board is square in shape and has a uniform thickness of 3 cm. It is rolled evenly so that it remains square but becomes half as long again as before. Find its new thickness.

11 A cylindrical oil-drum 70 cm long and 30 cm in diameter is made of sheet metal which costs $62\frac{1}{2}$p. Find the cost of the metal for a similar drum 84 cm long.

12 Two marble pillars are similar in shape and their masses are respectively 2 058 kg and 1 296 kg. If the first is 2·94 m high, find the height of the second.

13 A statue stands on a base of area 1·08 m², and a model of it

has a base of area 300 cm². Find the mass of the statue (in tonnes) if the model is of mass 12·5 kg.

14 A locomotive is of mass 72 tonnes and is 11 m long. An exact model is made of it and is 44 cm long. Find the mass of the model.

15 If the tanks of the model in no. 14 hold 0·8 litres of water, find the capacity of the tanks of the locomotive.

16 A garden has an area of 3 025 m², and it is represented on a plan by an area of 144 cm². Find the actual length of a wall which is represented on the plan by a line 8·4 cm long.

17 In a plan of a house and garden a window 120 cm wide is represented by a line 15 mm long. Find the area of the garden if the corresponding area on the plan is 2 025 cm².

18 A wooden model 40 cm high is made of a marble statue which is 3·2 m high. The model is of mass 12 kg. If the densities of wood and marble are in the ratio of 16 : 85, find the mass of the statue in tonnes.

19 A toy motor car is an exact replica of a real one. The windscreen of the toy measures 35 cm by 10 cm, and the other has a windscreen of area 0·315 m². If the mass of the toy is 25 kg, find the mass of the real car.

20 A doll's house is a scale model of a real house. The volumes of air in the drawing-rooms are respectively 27 500 cm³ and 220 m³. The front door of the real house has an area of 7 m². Find the area of the front door of the doll's house.

Chapter 7

Logarithms (2)

Standard form

$$1\ 000 = 10^3$$
$$100 = 10^2$$
$$10 = 10^1$$
$$1 = 10^0$$
$$0{\cdot}1 = \frac{1}{10} = 10^{-1},$$

dividing both sides of the previous line by 10.

$$0{\cdot}01 = \frac{1}{100} = \frac{1}{10^2} = 10^{-2}$$

$$0{\cdot}001 = \frac{1}{1\ 000} = \frac{1}{10^3} = 10^{-3}, \text{ etc.}$$

$$234 = 2{\cdot}34 \times 100$$
$$= 2{\cdot}34 \times 10^2$$
$$4\ 231 = 4{\cdot}231 \times 1\ 000$$
$$= 4{\cdot}231 \times 10^3$$
$$0{\cdot}23 = 2{\cdot}3 \times 0{\cdot}1$$
$$= 2{\cdot}3 \times 10^{-1}$$
$$0{\cdot}031 = 3{\cdot}1 \times 0{\cdot}01$$
$$= 3{\cdot}1 \times 10^{-2}$$

A number expressed in the form $a \times 10^b$, where a is a number between 1 and 10 and b is a positive or negative integer, is said to be in **standard form.**

If a number is expressed in standard form, it is very easy to see what the characteristic of its logarithm is,

e.g. $\log 234 = \log (2{\cdot}34 \times 10^2)$ has the characteristic 2,
$\log 4\ 231 = \log (4{\cdot}231 \times 10^3)$ has the characteristic 3.

Logarithms (2)

Logarithms of numbers less than 1

A number lying between 0·01 and 0·1 lies between 10^{-2} and 10^{-1}, and its logarithm is '-2 plus a decimal'.

For instance

$$0·037 = 3·7 \div 10^2 = 10^{0·568\ 2} \times 10^{-2} = 10^{0·568\ 2-2}$$
$$= 10^{-2+0·568\ 2}.$$

This logarithm is written as $\bar{2}·568\ 2$ (called 'bar two point five . . .').

The difference between $\bar{2}·568\ 2$ and $-2·568\ 2$ must be clearly understood, the former meaning $-2 + 0·568\ 2$ (which equals $-1·431\ 8$) and the latter $-2 - 0·568\ 2$.

In practice the rule is that the characteristic is numerically one greater than the number of noughts immediately following the decimal point,

e.g. $\log 0·041\ 32 = \log(4·132 \times 10^{-2})$ has the characteristic $\bar{2}$,
  $\log 0·000\ 87 = \log(8·7 \times 10^{-4})$ has the characteristic $\bar{4}$.

Exercise 7a

Express in standard form:

1 32·4 **2** 0·471 **3** 3 472 000 **4** 0·000 613 1

5 4 576 **6** 51 720 **7** 0·043 81 **8** 0·000 000 231

9 623 000 000 **10** 0·003 471 21

Express as powers of 10:

11 2·517, 0·025 17, 0·000 025 17, 0·251 7

12 7·306, 0·007 306, 0·730 6, 0·000 730 6

Write down the logarithms of

13 5·192, 0·051 92, 0·519 2, 0·000 519 2

14 0·038 62 **15** 0·000 197 **16** 0·650 4 **17** 0·000 000 32

18 0·000 025 14 **19** 0·8 **20** 0·800 4

Write down the numbers whose logarithms are

21 0·364 5, $\bar{3}$·364 5, $\bar{1}$·364 5, $\bar{6}$·364 5

22 $\bar{2}$·499 7 **23** $\bar{4}$·893 9 **24** $\bar{1}$·789 2 **25** $\bar{3}$·573 9

The following examples show how 'bar' logs should be manipulated: notice, in subtraction, the application of the algebraic rule 'change the sign of the bottom line and add'.

(i) $\bar{3}\cdot2 + \bar{5}\cdot4 = \bar{8}\cdot6$

(ii) $\bar{3}\cdot7 + \bar{5}\cdot8 = \bar{8} + 1\cdot5 = \bar{7}\cdot5$

(iii) $\bar{2}\cdot9 + 5\cdot6 = \bar{2} + 6\cdot5 = 4\cdot5$

(iv) $3\cdot5 - 6\cdot1 = -3 + 0\cdot4 = \bar{3}\cdot4$

(v) $3\cdot4 - 6\cdot9 = 2\cdot5 - 6 = \bar{4}\cdot5$

(vi) $\bar{5}\cdot7 - \bar{2}\cdot3$ $\quad -5 + 0\cdot7$
$$\underline{\qquad\quad -2 + 0\cdot3}$$
$$-3 + 0\cdot4 = \bar{3}\cdot4$$

(vii) $\bar{2}\cdot7 - \bar{5}\cdot3$ $\quad -2 + 0\cdot7$
$$\underline{\qquad\quad -5 + 0\cdot3}$$
$$3 + 0\cdot4 = 3\cdot4$$

(viii) $\bar{5}\cdot3 - \bar{2}\cdot7$ $\quad -5 + 0\cdot3 = -6 + 1\cdot3$
$$\underline{\qquad\qquad\qquad\qquad -2 + 0\cdot7}$$
$$-4 + 0\cdot6 = \bar{4}\cdot6$$

(ix) $\quad -3\cdot2 = -4 + 4 - 3\cdot2 = -4 + 0\cdot8 = \bar{4}\cdot8$

(x) $\bar{2}\cdot6 \times 4 = (-2 + 0\cdot6) \times 4 = -8 + 2\cdot4 = \bar{6}\cdot4$

(xi) $\bar{6}\cdot9 \div 3 = (-6 + 0\cdot9) \div 3 = -2 + 0\cdot3 = \bar{2}\cdot3$

(xii) $\bar{4}\cdot7 \div 3 = (-4 + 0\cdot7) \div 3 = (-6 + 2\cdot7) \div 3$
$$= -2 + 0\cdot9 = \bar{2}\cdot9$$

Notice particularly no. (xii). In this example -4 cannot be divided exactly by 3: it is therefore transformed into $-6 + 2$, so that the negative part of the characteristic is exactly divisible by 3.

Exercise 7b

Simplify the following, expressing the answers in 'bar' notation and without bars $\quad (e.g.\ \bar{2}\cdot5 + \bar{3}\cdot8 = \bar{5} + 1\cdot3 = \bar{4}\cdot3 = -3\cdot7)$.

1 $\bar{2}\cdot6 + \bar{3}\cdot1$ **2** $\bar{1}\cdot5 + \bar{2}\cdot5$ **3** $\bar{2}\cdot8 + \bar{1}\cdot3$ **4** $\bar{5}\cdot4 - 1\cdot1$

5 $\bar{5}\cdot4 - \bar{1}\cdot2$ **6** $\bar{5}\cdot7 + 2\cdot5$ **7** $\bar{3}\cdot8 - 5\cdot2$ **8** $\bar{3}\cdot4 - \bar{4}\cdot2$

9 $\bar{3}{\cdot}5 - \bar{1}{\cdot}7$ **10** $\bar{4}{\cdot}3 \times 2$ **11** $\bar{2}{\cdot}5 - \bar{4}{\cdot}8$ **12** $\bar{3}{\cdot}8 \times 3$

13 $\bar{3}{\cdot}6 \div 3$ **14** $\bar{2}{\cdot}5 \div 5$ **15** $\bar{4}{\cdot}3 + \bar{1}{\cdot}8$ **16** $\bar{2}{\cdot}6 \times 4$

17 $\bar{2}{\cdot}3 \div 5$ **18** $\bar{3}{\cdot}2 \div 4$ **19** $\bar{2}{\cdot}6 - \bar{1}{\cdot}8$ **20** $\bar{3}{\cdot}2 - \bar{3}{\cdot}8$

21 $\bar{3}{\cdot}8 \div 4$ **22** $\bar{2}{\cdot}5 - \bar{4}{\cdot}7$ **23** $\bar{6}{\cdot}5 \div 5$ **24** $\bar{7}{\cdot}2 \div 4$

25 $\bar{3}{\cdot}2 + \bar{2}{\cdot}6 - \bar{4}{\cdot}4$ **26** $\bar{2}{\cdot}6 - 1{\cdot}2 + \bar{3}{\cdot}8$

27 $\bar{3}{\cdot}7 \div 4$ **28** $\bar{3}{\cdot}3 - \bar{4}{\cdot}4$ **29** $\bar{2}{\cdot}9 \times \frac{4}{5}$ **30** $\bar{1}{\cdot}7 \times \frac{2}{3}$

Example 1 *Evaluate* $0{\cdot}768\ 5 \times 0{\cdot}034\ 15$.

No.	Log.
0·768 5	$\bar{1}$·885 7
0·034 15	$\bar{2}$·533 4
0·026 25	$\bar{2}$·419 1

Check $0{\cdot}8 \times 0{\cdot}03 = 0{\cdot}024$.

Ans. 0·026 25.

Example 2 *Evaluate* $0{\cdot}768\ 5 \div 0{\cdot}034\ 15$.

$$\frac{0{\cdot}768\ 5}{0{\cdot}034\ 15} = \frac{76{\cdot}85}{3{\cdot}415},$$ multiplying numerator and denominator by 100.

No bars are left: proceed as in Chap. 1.

Example 3 *Evaluate* $0{\cdot}045\ 62 \div 0{\cdot}987\ 6$.

$$\frac{0{\cdot}045\ 62}{0{\cdot}987\ 6} = \frac{45{\cdot}62}{987{\cdot}6}$$

No.	Log.
45·62	1·659 2
987·6	2·994 6
0·046 19	$\bar{2}$·664 6

Check $\frac{45}{1000} = 0{\cdot}045$.

Ans. 0·046 19.

Example 4 *Evaluate* $(0{\cdot}032\ 7)^2 \div (0{\cdot}736)^3$.

No.	Log.
0·032 7²	$\bar{2}$·514 5 × 2 = $\bar{3}$·029 0
0·736³	$\bar{1}$·866 9 × 3 = $\bar{1}$·600 7
0·002 681	$\bar{3}$·428 3

Check $\dfrac{0{\cdot}03^2}{0{\cdot}7^3} = \dfrac{0{\cdot}000\ 9}{0{\cdot}343}$

$\simeq \dfrac{0{\cdot}009}{3}$

$= 0{\cdot}003$

Ans. 0·002 681.

Exercise 7c

Simplify the following, checking every result.

1 $3.925 \times 0.031\ 75$ 2 $0.764\ 2 \times 0.350\ 7$

3 $0.673\ 5 \times 0.928$ 4 $0.093\ 5 \times 8.672$

5 $0.342\ 6 \times 0.193\ 8$ 6 $0.067\ 2 \times 0.098\ 53$

7 $0.569\ 2 \div 0.094\ 3$ 8 $29.57 \div 119.8$

9 $9.43 \div 56.92$ 10 $5.673 \div 98.42$

11 $0.52 \div 0.092\ 35$ 12 $0.766\ 2 \div 9.325$

13 $8.686 \times 0.507\ 2$ 14 $0.838\ 4 \div 0.900\ 6$

15 $3.925 \div 0.031\ 75$ 16 $0.296 \times 0.008\ 2 \times 5.437$

17 $\dfrac{9.23 \times 87.6}{991.7}$ 18 $\dfrac{0.096\ 1 \times 4.873}{0.834\ 5}$

19 $\dfrac{0.254\ 3}{0.085\ 72}$ 20 $0.964\ 2 \times 0.424\ 3$

21 $\dfrac{2.647 \times 0.009\ 21}{0.057\ 38}$ 22 $0.264 \times 0.008\ 35 \times 10.4$

23 $0.348 \times 0.088\ 6 \times 3.94$ 24 $\dfrac{0.628\ 3 \times 17.85}{8.347}$

Example 5 *Evaluate* $0.610\ 4^3$.

No.	Log.
$0.610\ 4^3$	$\bar{1}.785\ 6 \times 3$
$0.227\ 4$	$= \bar{1}.356\ 8$

Check $0.6^3 = 0.216$
Ans. $0.227\ 4$.

Example 6 *Evaluate* $\sqrt[3]{0.361\ 2}$.

No.	Log.
$\sqrt[3]{0.361\ 2}$	$\bar{1}.557\ 7 \div 3$
	$= (\bar{3} + 2.557\ 7) \div 3$
$0.712\ 2$	$= \bar{1}.852\ 6$

Check $0.7^3 = 0.343$
Ans. $0.712\ 2$.

Notice that in Ex. 6 it is simpler to check the cube of 0.7 than to guess the cube root of $0.361\ 2$.

Example 7 *Evaluate* $(5.375 \times 10^{-6})^3$.

No.	Log.
$(5.375 \times 10^{-6})^3$	$\bar{6}.730\ 4 \times 3$
1.553×10^{-16}	$= \bar{16}.191\ 2$

Check $(5 \times 10^{-6})^3 = 125 \times 10^{-18}$
$= 1.25 \times 10^{-16}$ *Ans.* 1.55×10^{-16}.

Example 8 *Evaluate* $\sqrt[3]{5{\cdot}629 \times 10^{-7}}$.

No.	Log.
$\sqrt[3]{5{\cdot}629 \times 10^{-7}}$	$\overline{7}{\cdot}750\ 4 \div 3$
	$= (\overline{9} + 2{\cdot}750\ 4) \div 3$
$8{\cdot}256 \times 10^{-3}$	$= \overline{3}{\cdot}916\ 8$

Check $(8 \times 10^{-3})^3 = 512 \times 10^{-9}$
$\qquad\qquad\qquad = 5{\cdot}12 \times 10^{-7}$ *Ans.* $8{\cdot}26 \times 10^{-3}$.

Exercise 7d

Evaluate the following, checking whenever it is reasonable to do so.

1 $0{\cdot}692\ 7^2$ **2** $0{\cdot}493\ 4^3$ **3** $0{\cdot}542\ 5^2$

4 $0{\cdot}215^4$ **5** $0{\cdot}672\ 5^3$ **6** $0{\cdot}294\ 5^4$

7 $\sqrt[3]{0{\cdot}388\ 7}$ **8** $\sqrt[3]{0{\cdot}038\ 87}$ **9** $\sqrt{0{\cdot}267\ 3}$

10 $\sqrt[4]{0{\cdot}063\ 57}$ **11** $\sqrt[4]{0{\cdot}061\ 3}$ **12** $\sqrt[10]{0{\cdot}065\ 68}$

13 $0{\cdot}926\ 7^3$ **14** $\sqrt[3]{0{\cdot}066\ 42}$ **15** $\sqrt[4]{0{\cdot}054\ 57}$

16 $0{\cdot}846\ 2^2$ **17** $\sqrt[5]{0{\cdot}008\ 91}$ **18** $0{\cdot}998\ 7^{10}$

19 $(0{\cdot}657 \times 0{\cdot}83)^4$ **20** $(0{\cdot}624 \div 0{\cdot}098\ 35)^2$

21 $(3{\cdot}47 \div 8{\cdot}74)^3$ **22** $\sqrt[3]{\frac{3\ 4\ 9}{2\ 6\ 0\ 8}}$ **23** $\sqrt[3]{0{\cdot}285\ 3^5}$

24 $0{\cdot}218\ 4^{0{\cdot}7}$ **25** $\sqrt[6]{0{\cdot}049\ 84^5}$

26 $(8{\cdot}462 \times 0{\cdot}086\ 77)^5$ **27** $\dfrac{0{\cdot}031\ 27 \times 0{\cdot}001\ 652}{0{\cdot}049\ 93}$

28 $\sqrt{0{\cdot}682\ 1 \times 0{\cdot}005\ 924}$ **29** $\sqrt[5]{\dfrac{26{\cdot}7}{9\ 562}}$

30 $\dfrac{1{\cdot}487^3 - 1}{1{\cdot}487^3 + 1}$ **31** $(4{\cdot}291 \times 10^5)^4$ **32** $(3{\cdot}172 \times 10^{-3})^6$

33 $\sqrt{6{\cdot}231 \times 10^{-5}}$ **34** $\sqrt[3]{3{\cdot}131 \times 10^{-2}}$ **35** $\sqrt[4]{2{\cdot}427 \times 10^{-15}}$

Further examples, including practical applications of the methods used here, will be found in Chap. 20.

Revision examples

I

1 Factorise   (i) $a^2 + 5a - 14$ (ii) $x^2 - 25y^2$
(iii) $ab + bm - an - mn$

2 Use logarithms to find the value of
(i) $35\cdot94 \div 5\cdot982$ (ii) $\sqrt[3]{65}$

3 A bankrupt pays his creditors at the rate of 56p in the £. How much does a creditor receive to whom £177·60 is owing?

4 ABC is a triangle in which AB = 8 cm, BC = 9 cm, and the length of the perpendicular from A to $\overline{BC}$ is 5 cm. Calculate the length of the perpendicular from C to $\overline{AB}$.

5 Solve the equation $\dfrac{a-8}{3} + \dfrac{a-3}{2} = 0$.

6 A cigarette manufacturer decides to make a smaller cigarette than his normal product. He reduces the diameter by $\frac{1}{4}$ of what it was, and the length by $\frac{1}{9}$. If the original product was sold at 28p for 20, what should be the price for 20 of the smaller cigarettes?

7 Solve the equations (i) $3x^2 - 13x + 10 = 0$
(ii) $3x^2 - 13x - 10 = 0$

8 Given a $\triangle$ as in Fig. 59, calculate the lengths of the two sides not given (in cm to 2 decimal places)

Fig. 59

9 The diagonals of the quad PQRS intersect at right angles. Prove that the difference of the squares on $\overline{PQ}$ and $\overline{PS}$ is equal to the difference of the squares on $\overline{RQ}$ and $\overline{RS}$.

10 Find the whole number such that three times its square subtracted from 85 is equal to twice the number.

II

1 Factorise (i) $m^2 - m - 42$ (ii) $9a^2 - 16c^2$
(iii) $2mn - un - 4mv + 2uv$

2 Use logarithms to find the value of
(i) $\dfrac{56 \cdot 24 \times 79 \cdot 6}{130 \cdot 5}$ (ii) $4 \cdot 992^3$

3 In one year the total catch of shellfish in thousands of tonnes was: cockles 15·2, crabs 4·4, lobsters 1·0, mussels 4·5, Norway lobsters 7·3, oysters 0·2, shrimps 1·4, whelks 2·0. Construct a pie-chart to show these figures.

4 ABCD is a parallelogram, and P, Q, R, S are the mid-points of its sides, taken in order. Prove that the area of ABCD is twice the area of PQRS.

5 Simplify $\dfrac{3m + 2}{4} - \dfrac{2m + 5}{3} + \dfrac{1}{6}$.

6 Find to the nearest penny the simple interest on £262·43 for 11 years at 2%.

7 Solve the equations
(i) $4x^2 - 2x + 3 = 0$
(ii) $\dfrac{5 - x}{4} = \dfrac{1}{x}$

Fig. 60

8 In Fig. 60 calculate a and b.

9 A ladder 10·6 m long leans against a wall, and touches it at a point 9 m from the ground. Find the distance of the foot of the ladder from the wall, and the angle which the ladder makes with the ground.

10 A rectangle has an area of 90 cm², and the length is 4 cm more than the width. Find the length in cm, correct to 3 sig. fig.

III

1 Factorise   (i) $a^2 - 2ab - 15b^2$ (ii) $49x^2 - 100$
  (iii) $ac - 2bc + 3ad - 6bd$

2 Use logarithms to find the value of $\sqrt[4]{10 + \sqrt[3]{10 + \sqrt{10}}}$.

3 Two bankrupts have debts of £2 754 and £1 782 respectively. The first has £816 and the second £529. Which pays the higher rate in the £?

4 Draw a △ with sides of 4·5 cm, 6 cm, 7·5 cm. Construct an isosceles △ of equal area on a base 6 cm long, and measure one of its equal sides.

5 Solve the simultaneous equations $2x + 3y = 4$,
$$3x - y = -5.$$

6 When a man's salary is increased by 4% it becomes £1 092. What was it originally?

7 Solve the equations   (i) $6x^2 + x - 3 = 0$
  (ii) $\frac{2}{3}x^2 + 4x - 9 = 0$

8 In Fig. 61 calculate AC in cm correct to 2 decimal places.

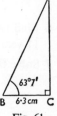

9 ABCD is a rectangle, and O is any point. Prove that the sum of the squares of the perpendiculars from O to the sides of the rectangle is equal to half the sum of the squares of the lines joining O to the corners of the rectangle.

Fig. 61

10 A man is now four times as old as his son, and in four years' time the product of their ages will be 520. Find their ages now.

IV

1 Factorise   (i) $m^2 - 2mn - 24n^2$ (ii) $16u^2 - 25v^2$
  (iii) $6mn + 3nu + 2mv + uv$

2 Use logarithms to find the value of $\pi r l$, where $r = 3·27$, $l = 7·35$ and $\log \pi = 0·497\ 1$.

3 Manganin is made up of 3 parts manganese, 1 part nickel and 21 parts copper. For how much manganin will 33 kg of manganese be needed?

4 $\overline{AL}$, $\overline{BM}$ are two altitudes of $\triangle ABC$. If $AL = 15$ cm, $BM = 12$ cm, $BC = 16$ cm, calculate AC.

5 Simplify (i) $3a - \{(2a - 5) + (3a + 2)\}$
(ii) $m - 2\{m - 2(m + n)\}$

6 Find the rate per cent at which £146·35 will earn £58·54 simple interest in 10 years.

7 Solve the equations (i) $10x^2 - 3x - 7 = 0$
(ii) $3x(x - 2) = 4x - 3$

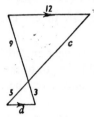

Fig. 62

8 In Fig. 62 calculate c and d.

9 PQRS is a quad in which $\hat{P}$ is a right angle, $PQ = 3·3$ cm, $QR = 3·9$ cm, $RS = 5·2$ cm, $SP = 5·6$ cm. Prove that $\hat{R}$ is also a right angle.

10 When an object is projected into the air its height h metres after t seconds is given by the formula $h = 35t - 5t^2$. How many seconds after being projected is it at a height of 50 m?

V

1 Factorise (i) $x^2 - 11xy + 30y^2$
(ii) $2ac - 2bc - 3ad + 3bd$
(iii) $3a(a + b) - (a + b)^2$

2 Use logarithms to find the value of

(i) $36·85 \times 2·564$ (ii) $\sqrt[3]{\dfrac{309·6}{25·7}}$

3 Divide £1·26 between two people so that their shares are in the ratio 9 : 5.

4 In $\triangle$PQR, S is a point in $\overline{QR}$ such that QS = 4SR, and T is the mid-point of $\overline{PS}$. Prove that $5\triangle PQT = 2\triangle PQR$.

5 Solve the equation $\dfrac{4x+1}{6} = \dfrac{5x-3}{4}$.

6 Two similarly shaped saucepans, formed from metal of the same gauge, hold 4·32 and 2·50 litres respectively. If the mass of the smaller one is 1·5 kg, what is the mass of the larger?

7 Solve the equations (i) $7x^2 - 12x = 1$
(ii) $(2x + 5)(x - 2) = (x + 3)^2 - 5$

8 In Fig. 63 calculate QR in cm correct to 2 decimal places.

9 Prove that a triangle is right-angled if its sides are respectively equal in length to the diagonals of the three squares drawn on the sides of a right-angled triangle.

10 The area of a triangle is 44 cm², and the height is 3 cm less than the base. Find the height.

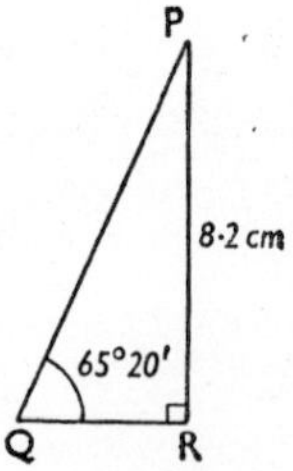

Fig. 63

VI

1 Factorise (i) $2a^2 + 5a - 12$ (ii) $(2m + n)^2 - (m + 2n)^2$
(iii) $2ab + 4bm - an - 2mn$

2 Use logarithms to find the value of

(i) $\dfrac{267\cdot5}{87\cdot9}$ (ii) $\sqrt[3]{72\cdot83 \times 1\cdot83}$

3 In a sale a shop reduces all prices by 35p in the £. Find the original price of an article which is sold for £1·82.

4 Draw a square ABCD with sides 6 cm long. On $\overline{BD}$ as base construct an isosceles $\triangle$EBD, equal in area to the square. Measure EB.

5 Simplify $\dfrac{7(3x-1)}{6} - \dfrac{3(2x-5)}{2} - \dfrac{25}{3}$.

6 A gas-holder is a cylinder 40 m long and 50 m in diameter. It is replaced by a cylinder 80 m long and 4 m in diameter which holds 40 000 m³ of compressed gas. (i) What is the ratio of the volumes of the two cylinders? (ii) What is the degree of compression of the gas in the second cylinder? Give both answers in the form $N:1$, where N is the nearest whole number.

7 Solve the equations (i) $10x^2 - 30x + 17 = 0$
(ii) $(3x - 1)(2x - 3) = 5x(x - 2)$

8 In Fig. 64 calculate AB and AC, all lengths being in cm.

9 In $\triangle$PQR, PQ = 17 cm, QR = 28 cm, and the altitude PM = 15 cm. Calculate PR and the altitude QN.

10 Find the number such that when it is added to 5 and the sum divided by 3, the result is the same as when 12 is divided by the number.

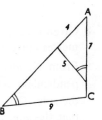

Fig. 64

VII

1 Factorise (i) $3u^2 + 2u - 5$ (ii) $(2a + b)^2 - (a - b)^2$
(iii) $(a + b)^2 - 3c(a + b)$

2 Use logarithms to find the value of πr^2, where $r = 2.73$ and $\log \pi = 0.497\ 1$.

3 In 1967 a census was taken of the ages of passenger ships being used: the figures are given below:

Age (years)	0–5	5–10	10–15	15–20	20–25
Number of ships	18	25	29	51	24

[Here 5–10 means 5 or more to under 10.]
Construct the cumulative-frequency ogive for this distribution: read from it the median value and also the mean age of the ships.

4 P, Q, R are three points of observation. Q is 1·8 km from P on a bearing S 32° W. R is 1·2 km from P on a bearing S 44° E. Find the area of $\triangle$PQR in km², correct to 3 sig. fig.

5 Solve the simultaneous equations $3a + 2b = 5$,
$$2a - 3b = 12.$$

6 Find the number of years in which £327·50 will earn £78·60 simple interest at 4% per annum.

7 Solve the equations (i) $5x^2 + 6 = 10x$

(ii) $\dfrac{6(x + 1)}{5} = \dfrac{4}{x} - \dfrac{1}{5}$

8 Given a $\triangle$ as in Fig. 65, calculate AC in metres correct to 3 sig. fig.

9 From X, any point inside $\triangle$PQR, perpendiculars $\overline{XL}$, $\overline{XM}$, $\overline{XN}$ are drawn to the sides $\overline{QR}$, $\overline{RP}$, $\overline{PQ}$ respectively. Prove that the sum of the squares on $\overline{PN}$, $\overline{QL}$, $\overline{RM}$ is equal to the sum of the squares on $\overline{PM}$, $\overline{RL}$, $\overline{QN}$.

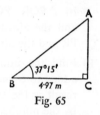

Fig. 65

10 A bookseller buys a number of copies of a book, and the price in pence that he pays per book is 4 more than the number of books. If he pays £6·72 altogether, how many books does he buy?

VIII

1 Factorise (i) $2a^2 + 3a - 54$ (ii) $(2c - 3d)^2 - (c - d)^2$
(iii) $2a(b - 2c) - (b - 2c)^2$

2 Use logarithms to find the value of

(i) $\left(\dfrac{28·67}{6·009}\right)^2$ (ii) $\sqrt[3]{28·5 \times 6·74 \times 10·83}$

3 Using a system of pulleys, the effort required to lift various loads is measured, and the results tabulated as given:

Load in kg	14	28	42	56	70	84	98	112
Effort in kg	6·6	7·7	8·8	9·8	10·7	11·8	12·9	13·7

Draw a graph connecting load with effort (this passes *approximately* through the plotted points). What effort is required to make the system move when there is no load to be lifted?

4 $\overline{\text{AOC}}$, $\overline{\text{BOD}}$ are two straight lines which intersect at O, and $\overline{\text{AB}}$ is parallel to $\overline{\text{DC}}$. If the parallelograms AODH, BOCK are completed, prove that they are equal in area.

5 Simplify (i) $a - \{2(a - b) - 3(a + b)\}$
(ii) $5x - 3\{(x - 2y) + (x - 3y)\}$

6 There were 21 boys in a form-room. 9 of them on one side of the room averaged 37% for an exam.; 12 on the other side averaged 51%. What was the average mark for the whole form?

7 Solve the equations
(i) $3x^2 - x + 2 = 0$
(ii) $(3x - 1)(x + 2) - (x - 1)(2x - 3) = 0$

8 In Fig. 66 calculate x and y.

9 An aircraft is heading due south at 300 km h^{-1}, but a wind blowing at 55 km h^{-1} from the west takes it off course. Find how far the aircraft travels in an hour relative to the ground, and in what direction.

10 A room is 5·5 m long, and the width is the same as the height. If the area of the walls is 63 m², find the height.

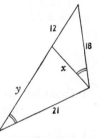

Fig. 66

IX

1 Factorise (i) $6m^2 - 13mu + 6u^2$ (ii) $9a^2 - (a - 2b)^2$
(iii) $2am - 6bm + an - 3bn$

2 Use logarithms to find the value of
(i) $3·886^3$ (ii) $\sqrt{9·231 \times 6·824}$

3 A starts a business with £840. Three months later B joins him with a capital of £560, and after another month C comes in with £1 120. A year after A started they share profits of £1 032. Find their shares.

4 ABC is a triangular field. B is 330 m from A on a bearing N 57° E. C is 220 m from A on a bearing S 69° E. Find the area of the field in hectares, correct to 3 sig. fig.

5 Solve the equation $\dfrac{3a-1}{2} - \dfrac{2a-5}{3} = 2$.

6 A man gains 5% by selling a tie for $73\frac{1}{2}$p. For how much should he have sold it to gain 10%?

7 Solve the equations (i) $10x^2 - 11x - 2 = 0$
(ii) $10x^2 + 11x - 3 = 0$

8 Given a $\triangle$ as in Fig. 67, calculate YZ in cm correct to 3 sig. fig.

9 In the equilateral $\triangle$PQR, X is a point in $\overline{QR}$ such that QX = 2XR. Prove that $PX^2 = \frac{7}{9}PQ^2$.

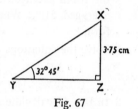

Fig. 67

10 The perimeter of a right-angled triangle is 90 cm, and the hypotenuse is 39 cm long. Find the lengths of the other two sides.

X

1 Factorise (i) $8a^2 - 2ab - 15b^2$ (ii) $16m^2 - (3m + n)^2$
(iii) $3a(m - 2n) - (a - b)(m - 2n)$

2 Use logarithms to find the value of $\dfrac{x^3 + 5}{x^3 - 5}$, where $x = 1\cdot934$.

3 Divide £11·05 between A, B and C so that C has $1\frac{1}{2}$ times as much as B, and B has 3 times as much as A.

4 O, Q are any two points inside an equilateral triangle, and perpendiculars are drawn from O, Q to the sides of the triangle. Prove that the sum of the lengths of the perpendiculars from O is equal to the sum of the lengths of the perpendiculars from Q.

5 Simplify $\dfrac{3a-1}{6} - \dfrac{3}{4} + \dfrac{3a-8}{4}$.

6 The weekly wage-packets of 150 workers in a small factory can be grouped as follows:

Wages (£)	15–19	20–24	25–29	30–34	35–39
Number of workers	30	61	33	18	8

Find the mean weekly wage and also the median of the distribution.

7 Solve the equations
      (i) $5x^2 = 20 - x$
      (ii) $9x + 40 = 4x^2$

8 In Fig. 68 calculate m and n.

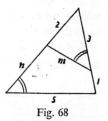

9 PQRS is a square, and X is any point in the side $\overline{RS}$. Prove that
      $QX^2 - SX^2 = 2SR \times XR$.

Fig. 68

10 A rectangular lawn, 30 m by 17 m, is surrounded by a path of uniform width. If the area of the path is 150 m², find its width.

107

Chapter 8

Flow charts

A flow chart is a diagram designed to show the successive steps necessary in carrying out a mathematical calculation. The object of this analysis is to break down the calculation into a series of elementary processes, each of which can be performed if required by a computer. This is what is meant by **programming** a computer, which can do only very simple things, but can do them very fast indeed once it is given the necessary programmed instructions.

For example a flow chart to calculate $2 \times (3 + 4)$ would be as follows:

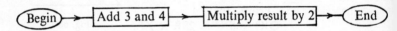

A more accurate flow chart to calculate $a(b + c)$ where a, b and c are numbers which have first to be read would be as follows:

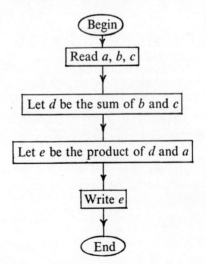

It is convenient to use a computer language symbol for 'let ... be'. The second step in the flow chart above can be written $d := b + c$ which is read as d becomes equal to b plus c.
The flow chart then becomes:

$$\boxed{\text{Begin}} \rightarrow \boxed{\text{Read } a, b, c} \rightarrow \boxed{d := b + c} \rightarrow \boxed{e := a \cdot \times d} \rightarrow \boxed{\text{Write } e} \rightarrow \boxed{\text{End}}$$

Example 1 *Draw a flow chart for adding fractions.*

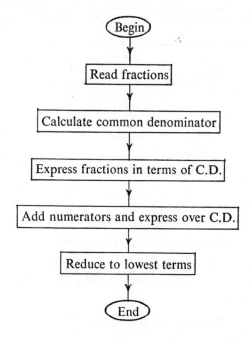

Notice in this example that 'calculate common denominator involves more than one step and a flow chart could be written for that part of the programme alone.

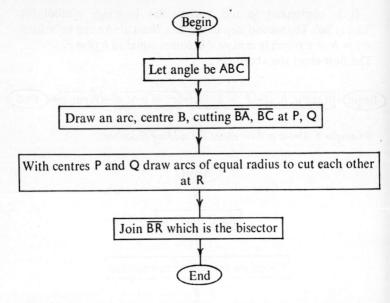

Example 2 *Draw a flow chart for the construction of the bisector of a given angle.*

Exercise 8a

Write flow charts for the following:

1 To find whether 2 is a factor of a number.

2 To find whether 3 is a factor of a number.

3 To convert a sum of money in £ and p into pence.

4 To multiply fractions.

5 To draw a triangle with given sides.

6 To multiply decimals.

7 To construct parallel lines with set square and ruler.

8 To subtract one directed number from another.

9 To bisect a given straight line.

10 To construct a perpendicular to a given straight line from a given point outside it.

11 To construct a perpendicular to a given straight line at a given point on it.

12 To construct an angle of 60°.

13 To construct an angle of 30°.

14 To construct an angle of 45°.

15 To calculate the simple interest from given values of principal, rate and time.

16 To add two vectors, each with three elements.

17 To find the co-ordinates of the vertices of a triangle displaced through a given vector.

18 To divide a given line into 5 equal parts.

19 To calculate the length of the adjacent side in a right-angled triangle given one angle and the length of the side opposite to this angle.

20 To multiply two 2 by 2 matrices.

New General Mathematics

In more complicated calculations it is sometimes necessary to have more than one route through a flow chart. Where a question is to be asked it is put into a diamond-shaped box and there must be two possible answers, namely yes or no.

Example 3 *Draw a flow chart to convert mass in grammes to kilogrammes and grammes.*

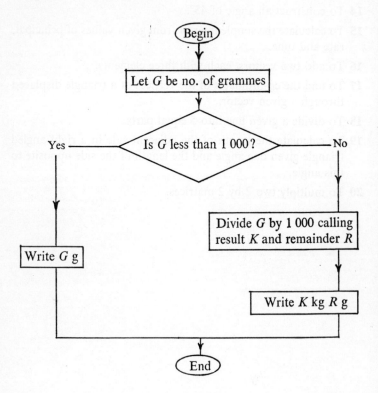

Other calculations involve repeated processes as in Example 4.

Example 4 *Draw a flow chart to find the prime factors of a number.*

The successive prime numbers (P), beginning with 2, are tried as divisors. After each factor has been tried once, it is tried again if it is a factor; if not the next prime factor is tried.

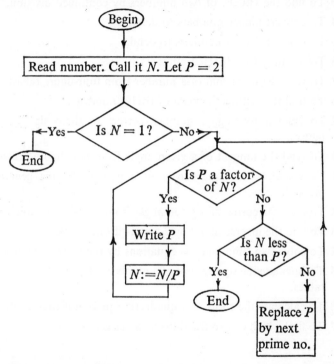

Note that $N:=N/P$ means that the new value of N is the old value of N divided by P.

113

Exercise 8b

Write flow charts for the following:

1 To find the H.C.F. of two numbers by factors.

2 To find the L.C.M. of two numbers by factors.

3 To find the H.C.F. of two numbers by continued division.

4 To convert binary numbers to denary.

5 To convert denary numbers to octal.

6 To multiply two directed numbers.

7 To read the logarithm of a number from four-figure tables.

8 To find the arithmetic mean of twelve numbers.

9 To state a four-figure number correct to three significant figures.

10 To read the tangent of a given angle from four-figure tables.

11 To calculate the square root of a number by the general method.

12 To read the cosine of a given angle from four-figure tables.

13 To find the inverse of a 2 by 2 matrix if one exists.

14 To solve two simultaneous equations by the matrix method.

15 To calculate the square root of a number using the square root tables.

16 To calculate the roots of a quadratic equation if they exist.

17 To find which of two fractions is the larger.

Chapter 9

The slide rule

If two rulers with the same scales are placed one on top of the other they can be used as a simple adding device. For example, to add 3 to 4 put the 0 of one ruler against the 3 of the other. Then against 4 on the first ruler, 7 will be seen on the second, as in Fig. 69.

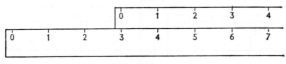

Fig. 69

Subtraction can be carried out in a similar way. To subtract 4 from 7, place 4 on one ruler against 7 on a second ruler, and read the answer (3) on the second ruler against 0 on the first.

In Chap. 1 it was shown that two numbers can be multiplied by adding their logarithms. Hence if two rulers are marked with the logarithms of numbers they can be used to multiply and divide. This is the principle of the slide rule.

Make a simple slide rule as follows. Draw a line 10 cm long across a piece of paper and mark the ends 1 and 10. The logarithm of 1 is 0 and the logarithm of 10 is 1, so that 10 cm represents 1 unit. The log of 2 is 0·301 0 so that 2 is marked on the scale 3·01 cm from the 1, the log of 3 is 0·477 1 so that 3 is marked on the scale 4·77 cm from the 1 and so on. The numbers should be marked on both sides of the line as in Fig. 70.

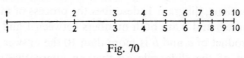

Fig. 70

Great care must be taken to mark the points as accurately as possible. Cut along the line, giving two identical scales. To multiply by 3, the 1 on the first scale is placed against the 3 on the second as in Fig. 71.

115

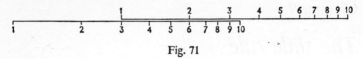

Fig. 71

Against the 2 on the first scale 6 will be found and against the 3 on the first scale 9 will be found.

The reason for this is that $\log 2 + \log 3 = \log 6$
and $\log 3 + \log 3 = \log 9$.

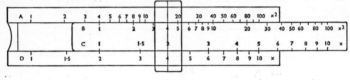

Fig. 72

Fig. 72 shows a slide rule. The scales already referred to are the C and D scales shown, and the transparent plate with a line down the middle on top of the scales is called the **cursor.** Most slide rules have markings on the C and D scales for 1, 1·5, 2, 3, 4, 5, 6, 7, 8, 9, 10 at least, but between the markings there are sub-divisions and one must examine one's own slide rule carefully to decide what each sub-division represents. For example between 1 and 1·5 there will be four clear markings for 1·1, 1·2, 1·3 and 1·4, and between each of these there will be either 4 markings giving 5 divisions representing 0·02 each or 9 representing 0·01 each.

Multiplication

The flow chart, diagram 1, describes the process of multiplying a by b, where a and b are both numbers between 1 and 10.

If the product of a and b is more than 10 the answer would be off the end of the slide rule, so that an alternative process is required. The right-hand end of the C scale, marked 10, is placed against the a on the D scale, and the number read opposite b on the D scale is one tenth of the product. Hence a flow chart for multiplying two numbers a and b where a and b are both between 1 and 10 is as shown in diagram 2.

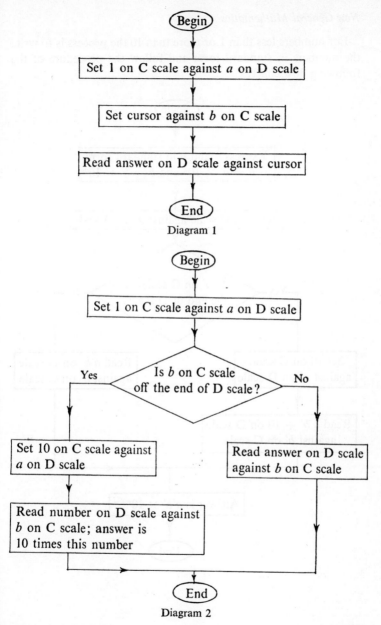

Begin

Set 1 on C scale against *a* on D scale

Set cursor against *b* on C scale

Read answer on D scale against cursor

End

Diagram 1

Begin

Set 1 on C scale against *a* on D scale

Is *b* on C scale off the end of D scale?

Yes

Set 10 on C scale against *a* on D scale

Read number on D scale against *b* on C scale; answer is 10 times this number

No

Read answer on D scale against *b* on C scale

End

Diagram 2

For numbers less than 1 or more than 10 the process is to write the numbers in standard form and follow the procedure of the following flow chart:

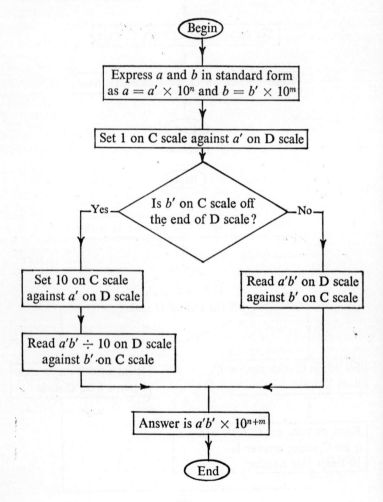

Begin

Express a and b in standard form as $a = a' \times 10^n$ and $b = b' \times 10^m$

Set 1 on C scale against a' on D scale

Is b' on C scale off the end of D scale?

Yes

No

Set 10 on C scale against a' on D scale

Read $a'b' \div 10$ on D scale against b' on C scale

Read $a'b'$ on D scale against b' on C scale

Answer is $a'b' \times 10^{n+m}$

End

Example 1 *Multiply* 0·33 *by* 432.

$$0.33 = 3.3 \times 10^{-1}$$
$$432 = 4.32 \times 10^2$$

1 on C scale against 3·3 on D scale puts 4·32 on C scale off the end of D scale: 10 on C scale against 3·3 on D scale gives 1·426 on D scale against 4·32 on C scale.

$$3.3 \times 4.32 = 1.426 \times 10 = 14.26$$
$$\therefore \ 0.33 \times 432 = 14.26 \times 10^{-1+2}$$
$$= 142.6$$

Note that the answer is stated only to the degree of accuracy to which it can reasonably be estimated from the slide rule.

Exercise 9a

Use a slide rule to perform the following multiplications:

1 1·7 × 2·5	**2** 1·95 × 3·21
3 2·12 × 4·03	**4** 6·2 × 1·3
5 7·56 × 1·04	**6** 2·3 × 4·8
7 3·21 × 3·92	**8** 4·31 × 6·02
9 1·09 × 9·9	**10** 2·21 × 8·43
11 23·1 × 14·2	**12** 31·2 × 45·3
13 520 × 321	**14** 62·1 × 0·13
15 23·1 × 0·003 4	**16** 0·012 × 0·34
17 97·3 × 6·29	**18** 0·94 × 86·2
19 6·73 × 0·83	**20** 0·005 3 × 0·856
21 5 670 × 632	**22** 5 934 × 4 786
23 21 780 × 3·45	**24** 76 849 × 3 685
25 425 × 87	**26** 0·000 58 × 0·764 9
27 0·649 × 6 947	**28** 3·142 × 2·718
29 3·16 × 1·414	**30** 981 × 2 378

New General Mathematics

Division

The process of division is the opposite to that of multiplication, and the following flow chart can be used for dividing *a* by *b* where *a* and *b* are both numbers between 1 and 10.

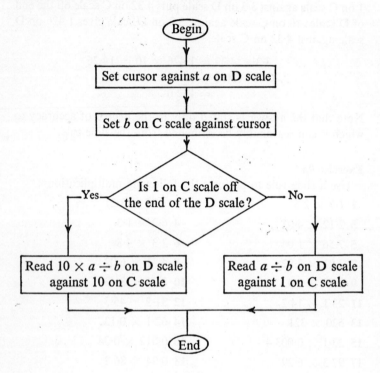

Begin

Set cursor against *a* on D scale

Set *b* on C scale against cursor

Is 1 on C scale off the end of the D scale?

Yes — No

Read 10 × *a* ÷ *b* on D scale against 10 on C scale

Read *a* ÷ *b* on D scale against 1 on C scale

End

120

For numbers less than 1 or more than 10 the following process is required.

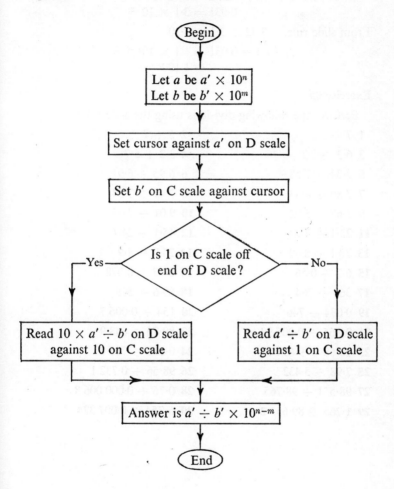

Example 2 *Divide* 34·2 *by* 0·031.

$$34 \cdot 2 = 3 \cdot 42 \times 10^1$$
$$0 \cdot 031 = 3 \cdot 1 \times 10^{-2}$$

From slide rule, $\quad 3 \cdot 42 \div 3 \cdot 1 = 1 \cdot 10$

$$\therefore \ 34 \cdot 2 \div 0 \cdot 031 = 1 \cdot 1 \times 10^{1 - (-2)}$$
$$= 1\ 100$$

Exercise 9b

Perform the following divisions using the slide rule:

1 $7 \div 5$	**2** $5 \div 7$
3 $6 \cdot 3 \div 2 \cdot 2$	**4** $3 \cdot 2 \div 5 \cdot 7$
5 $9 \cdot 34 \div 7 \cdot 58$	**6** $6 \cdot 93 \div 6 \cdot 91$
7 $7 \cdot 89 \div 6 \cdot 83$	**8** $7 \cdot 49 \div 7 \cdot 84$
9 $3 \cdot 67 \div 5 \cdot 92$	**10** $9 \cdot 01 \div 7 \cdot 05$
11 $23 \cdot 1 \div 21 \cdot 8$	**12** $45 \cdot 1 \div 24 \cdot 1$
13 $78 \cdot 1 \div 87 \cdot 9$	**14** $24 \cdot 9 \div 8 \cdot 9$
15 $6 \cdot 7 \div 0 \cdot 56$	**16** $0 \cdot 97 \div 0 \cdot 078$
17 $368 \div 764$	**18** $89 \cdot 6 \div 569$
19 $0 \cdot 074 \div 746$	**20** $154 \div 0 \cdot 006\ 7$
21 $0 \cdot 865 \div 0 \cdot 005\ 93$	**22** $89 \cdot 76 \div 648 \cdot 9$
23 $18 \cdot 68 \div 9 \cdot 654\ 3$	**24** $0 \cdot 178 \div 765 \cdot 8$
25 $7 \cdot 98 \div 5\ 432$	**26** $98 \cdot 56 \div 0 \cdot 732\ 1$
27 $98 \cdot 571 \div 98 \cdot 765$	**28** $0 \cdot 76 \div 0 \cdot 000\ 006\ 8$
29 $1 \cdot 765 \div 89 \cdot 653\ 2$	**30** $6\ 754 \div 0 \cdot 007\ 324$

Ratios

The slide rule is particularly suited to solving problems involving ratios. The following flow chart increases a in the ratio $b:c$ where a, b and c are numbers between 1 and 10, i.e. it calculates $a \times \dfrac{b}{c}$.

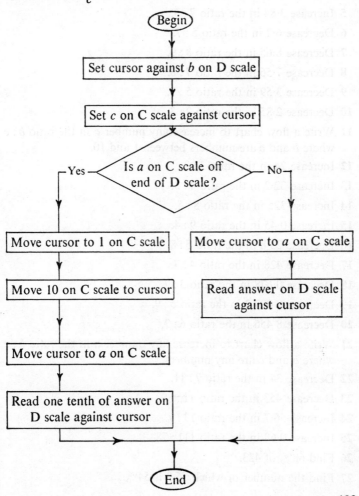

```
              ┌─────────┐
              │  Begin  │
              └─────────┘
                   │
    ┌──────────────────────────────┐
    │ Set cursor against b on D scale │
    └──────────────────────────────┘
                   │
    ┌──────────────────────────────┐
    │ Set c on C scale against cursor │
    └──────────────────────────────┘
                   │
           ◇ Is a on C scale off ◇
  ─Yes─    end of D scale ?    ─No─
```

Set cursor against b on D scale

Set c on C scale against cursor

Is a on C scale off end of D scale? — Yes / No —

Move cursor to 1 on C scale

Move 10 on C scale to cursor

Move cursor to a on C scale

Read one tenth of answer on D scale against cursor

Move cursor to a on C scale

Read answer on D scale against cursor

End

Exercise 9c

1 Increase 7 in the ratio 4 : 3.

2 Increase 5·4 in the ratio 7 : 2.

3 Increase 6·84 in the ratio 9 : 7.

4 Increase 4·72 in the ratio 5 : 4.

5 Increase 3·84 in the ratio 7 : 3.

6 Decrease 6·2 in the ratio 5 : 7.

7 Decrease 8·65 in the ratio 8 : 9.

8 Decrease 7·56 in the ratio 7 : 8.

9 Decrease 3·59 in the ratio 5 : 9.

10 Decrease 2·85 in the ratio 2 : 3.

11 Write a flow chart to increase any number a in the ratio $b : c$ where b and c are numbers between 1 and 10.

12 Increase 24 in the ratio 3 : 2.

13 Increase 32·2 in the ratio 4 : 3.

14 Increase 325 in the ratio 8 : 5.

15 Increase 0·45 in the ratio 9 : 4.

16 Decrease 23·8 in the ratio 5 : 8.

17 Decrease 428 in the ratio 4 : 7.

18 Decrease 0·678 in the ratio 3 : 7.

19 Decrease 0·007 3 in the ratio 5 : 9.

20 Decrease 8 456 in the ratio 6 : 7.

21 Write a flow chart to increase any number a in the ratio $b : c$ where b and c are any numbers.

22 Decrease 34 in the ratio 7 : 11.

23 Decrease 453 in the ratio 11 : 89.

24 Increase 56·7 in the ratio 13 : 7.

25 Increase 0·68 in the ratio 111 : 78.

26 Find 68% of 423.

27 Find the number of which 56·9 is 54%.

28 If a car is sold for £750 at a profit of 12% what did it cost?

29 If a boat is sold for £250 at a loss of 23% what did it cost?

30 Is $12\frac{1}{2}$% of £25 more than 15% of £23?

The exercises in Chapter 5 can be used for further examples.

Squares

The numbers on the A and B scales, see Fig. 72, are the squares of the numbers on the C and D scales, and run from 1 to 100. To find the square of a number between 1 and 10 the following flow chart can be used:

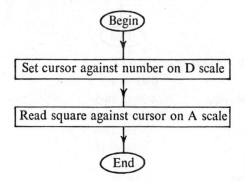

For numbers less than 1 or more than 10 the number is first expressed in standard form and the square of both parts of the number found as overleaf: i.e. $(a \times 10^n)^2 = a^2 \times 10^{2n}$.

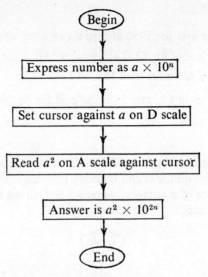

Example 3 *Find the square of* 0·43.

$$0·43 = 4·3 \times 10^{-1}$$

From slide rule,

$$4·3^2 = 18·5$$
$$\therefore 0·43^2 = 4·3^2 \times 10^{-2}$$
$$= 18·5 \times 10^{-2}$$
$$= 0·185$$

Square roots

To find the square root of a number between 1 and 100 the following flow chart is used:

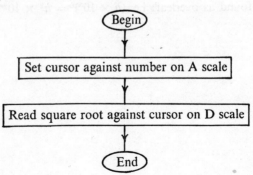

To find the square root of a number less than 1 or more than 100, the number is expressed in standard form and the process is as follows: i.e. $\sqrt{a \times 10^n} = \sqrt{a} \times 10^{\frac{n}{2}}$, but n must be even to make $\frac{n}{2}$ an integer.

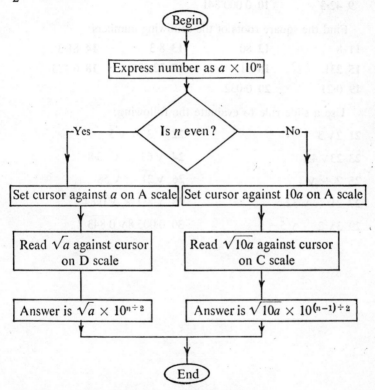

Example 4 *Find the square root of* 423 000.

$$423\,000 = 4 \cdot 23 \times 10^5 = 42 \cdot 3 \times 10^4$$

From slide rule, $\quad \sqrt{42 \cdot 3} = 6 \cdot 5$

$$\therefore \sqrt{423\,000} = 6 \cdot 5 \times 10^{(5-1) \div 2}$$
$$= 6 \cdot 5 \times 10^2$$
$$= 650$$

New General Mathematics

Exercise 9d

Find the squares of the following numbers:

1 2·47	**2** 7·81	**3** 21·4	**4** 32·1
5 0·723	**6** 0·41	**7** 0·032 3	**8** 234
9 42·3	**10** 0·000 341		

Find the square roots of the following numbers:

11 8	**12** 80	**13** 8·3	**14** 81·3
15 231	**16** 913	**17** 72 500	**18** 6 123
19 0·21	**20** 0·032		

Use a slide rule to evaluate the following:

21 $2\sqrt{3}$	**22** $\sqrt{3} \div \sqrt{5}$
23 $23\sqrt{43}$	**24** $\sqrt{63} \times \sqrt{75\cdot8}$
25 $2 \div \sqrt{3}$	**26** $\sqrt{21} \div \sqrt{58}$
27 $21 \div \sqrt{32}$	**28** $\sqrt{8\cdot7} \times \sqrt{0\cdot84}$
29 $3\sqrt{2} \div \sqrt{5}$	**30** $0\cdot005\ 8\sqrt{0\cdot843\ 7}$

Chapter 10

Further Trigonometry in a plane

Secant and cosecant

To find the hypotenuse of the triangle in Fig. 73.

Using sine, $\dfrac{10}{x} = \sin 38°$

$\therefore \dfrac{x}{10} = \dfrac{1}{\sin 38°}$

$\therefore x = \dfrac{10}{\sin 38°} = \dfrac{10}{0·615\ 7}.$

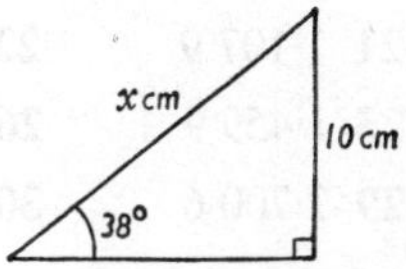

Fig. 73

At this point logarithms will have to be used (or tables of reciprocals) if a troublesome long division is to be avoided.

It is to overcome this difficulty that the two trigonometrical ratios given above are used.

Their definitions are

$$\mathbf{cosec\ \theta} = \dfrac{1}{\sin\ \theta} = \dfrac{\text{hyp.}}{\text{opp.}}$$

$$\mathbf{sec\ \theta} = \dfrac{1}{\cos\ \theta} = \dfrac{\text{hyp.}}{\text{adj.}}$$

The solution of the problem above now becomes

$$\dfrac{x}{10} = \dfrac{1}{\sin 38°} = \text{cosec } 38° = 1·624\ 3$$

$$\therefore x = 10 \times 1·624\ 3 = 16·243$$

$\therefore$ hypotenuse $= 16·24$ cm.

Note that, for all the ratios which begin with the letters *co-*, the number in the 'difference' columns of the tables must be subtracted.

Exercise 10a

From the tables write down the secant and cosecant of the following angles:

1 43° 24′	**2** 43° 26′	**3** 43° 22′	**4** 53° 13′
5 53° 17′	**6** 27° 10′	**7** 10° 50′	**8** 61° 31′
9 41° 56′	**10** 14° 23′	**11** 33° 45′	**12** 29° 32′
13 74° 7′	**14** 56° 25′	**15** 60° 44′	**16** 73° 5′
17 51° 49′	**18** 37° 13′	**19** 67° 32′	**20** 24° 38′

Write down the angle whose secant is:

21 1·107 9	**22** 1·108 7	**23** 3·137 9	**24** 1·287 4
25 1·459 9	**26** 4·085 5	**27** 1·011 2	**28** 1·188 1
29 2·700 6	**30** 1·123 6		

Write down the angle whose cosecant is:

31 1·571 0	**32** 1·399 2	**33** 2·079 0	**34** 3·233 4
35 1·024 8	**36** 2·005 1	**37** 1·140 8	**38** 1·075 3
39 2·334 3	**40** 4·924 1		

Exercise 10b

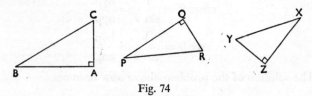

Fig. 74

1 Write down in terms of the sides of the triangles in Fig. 74 the ratios sec B, tan R, cosec X, cot Y, sin P, cos C.

2 Express the following ratios in trigonometrical form in two ways each (Fig. 74):

$$\frac{PQ}{PR}, \frac{XY}{YZ}, \frac{BA}{AC}, \frac{YZ}{XZ}, \frac{BC}{AC}, \frac{QR}{PQ}.$$

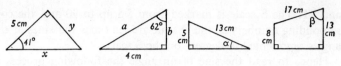

Fig. 75

3 Calculate x, y; a, b; α, β in Fig. 75.

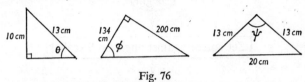

Fig. 76

4 Calculate θ, ϕ, ψ in Fig. 76.

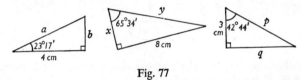

Fig. 77

5 Calculate a, b; x, y; p, q in Fig. 77.

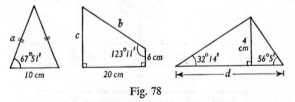

Fig. 78

6 Calculate a; b, c; d in Fig. 78.

Use of slide rule in trigonometric problems

Most slide rules have three trigonometric scales labelled S, T

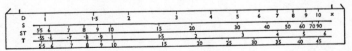

Fig. 79

131

and ST. The S scale is marked from 5·5 up to 90 and the corresponding numbers on the D scale are ten times the sines of the angles represented in degrees on the S scale.

Hence to read the sine of an angle the following process is required:

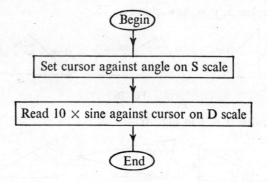

Similarly to find the angle whose sine is a number between 0·1 and 1 the following is required:

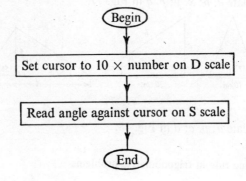

The T scale is marked from 5·5 up to 45 and the corresponding numbers on the D scale are ten times the tangents of the angles represented in degrees on the T scale. The use is consequently similar to that of the S scale. For small angles the sine and tangent are so nearly the same that one scale ST is suitable for sines and tangents of angles from 0·55 to 5·5 degrees. To read the sine or tangent of an angle in this range the following process is used:

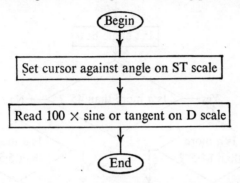

Note that the sub-divisions on the trigonometric scales are usually in tenths of a degree so that minutes have to be converted to degrees, remembering that there are 60 minutes in one degree.

Example 1 *Find the sine of* 4° 12′.

$$4° 12′ = 4·2°$$

Setting cursor against 4·2 on ST scale gives 7·32 on D scale

$$∴ \text{ sine } 4° 12′ = 0·073 2$$

To find the tangent of an angle greater than 45° one has to use the fact that the tangent of an angle is equal to the cotangent to its complement, and the cotangent of an angle is one divided by the tangent of that angle.

Hence
$$\tan a = \frac{1}{\tan (90° - a)}$$

A flow chart to find the tangent of any angle between 0·55° and 89·45° is as follows:

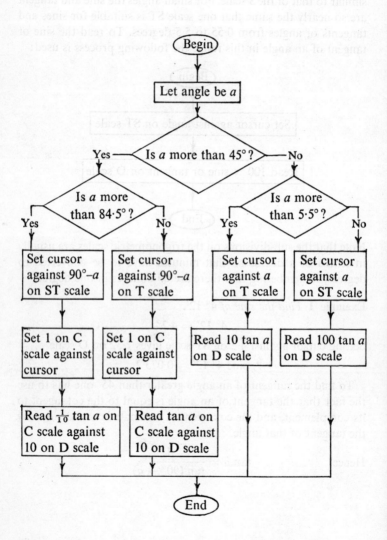

Example 2 *Find tan 72° 23'.*

$$72° \; 23' = 72·38°$$

Set cursor against $90° - 72·38° = 17·62°$ on T scale.
Set 1 on C scale against cursor.
Against 10 on D scale read 3·15 on C scale.

$$\tan 72° \; 23' = 3·15$$

Exercise 10c

Use a slide rule to read the sines of the following angles:

1 24°	**2** 32·2°	**3** 43·8°	**4** 5·2°	**5** 2·56°
6 34° 36'	**7** 67° 22'	**8** 82° 4'	**9** 4° 6'	**10** 3° 11'

Use a slide rule to read the tangents of the following angles:

11 32°	**12** 67·8°	**13** 43·13°	**14** 72·86°	**15** 54·63°
16 5°	**17** 4·3°	**18** 3·97°	**19** 2·78°	**20** 1·89°
21 42'	**22** 88·2°	**23** 10° 30'	**24** 53° 36'	**25** 72° 5'
26 2° 5'	**27** 87° 25'	**28** 86° 11'	**29** 36° 19'	**30** 2° 45'

$$\cos a = \sin (90° - a)$$

so that to find the cosine of an angle from a slide rule the sine of its complement is read.

The process of multiplying a number between 1 and 10 by the sine of an angle between 0·55° and 90° is as shown on page 136.

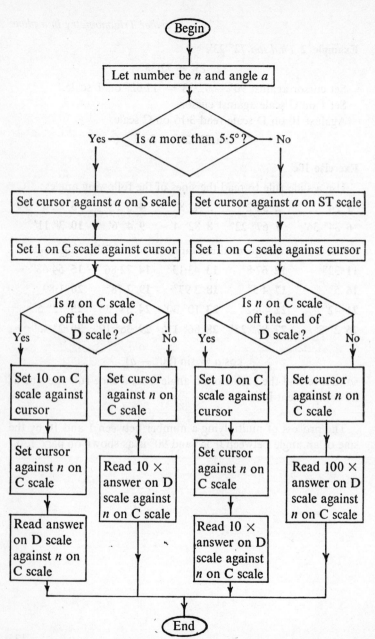

Example 3 In the given triangle find AB and BC.

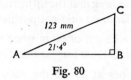

Fig. 80

$$BC = 123 \sin 21{\cdot}4° \text{ mm}$$
$$= 1{\cdot}23 \times 10^2 \sin 21{\cdot}4° \text{ mm}$$
$$1{\cdot}23 \sin 21{\cdot}4° = 4{\cdot}49 \div 10$$
$$\therefore \ 123 \sin 21{\cdot}4° = 4{\cdot}49 \div 10 \times 10^2$$
$$\therefore \ BC = 44{\cdot}9 \text{ mm}$$
$$AB = 123 \cos 21{\cdot}4° \text{ mm}$$
$$= 1{\cdot}23 \times 10^2 \sin (90° - 21{\cdot}4°) \text{ mm}$$
$$1{\cdot}23 \sin 68{\cdot}6° = 1{\cdot}145$$
$$\therefore \ 123 \sin 68{\cdot}6° = 1{\cdot}145 \times 10^2$$
$$\therefore \ AB = 114{\cdot}5 \text{ mm}$$
$$\therefore \ AB = 114{\cdot}5 \text{ mm and } BC = 44{\cdot}9 \text{ mm}$$

In examples like that at the beginning of this chapter the sine can be read and then the division performed in the usual manner. Many slide rules have the trigonometric scales on the sliding part, which makes this last calculation easier.

Exercise 10d

Miscellaneous examples on the six ratios

1 A mooring buoy is attached to the bed of an estuary by a chain 14·5 m long. At what angle is the chain inclined to the vertical when the river is 10 m deep?

2 From the top of a cliff 90 m high the angle of depression of a boat on the sea is 26° 14′. How far is the boat (i) from the foot of the cliff? (ii) from the observer?

3 A cylindrical sausage 5 cm in diameter, lying on a horizontal board, is sliced thinly so that the cut makes 40° with the horizontal. What is the length of each slice?

4 Through what angle has the minute-hand of a clock moved if the hand is 6·3 cm long and the tip has moved 3 cm (measured in a straight line) from its original position?

5 A kite is flying at a height of 90 m when the string is inclined at 15° to the vertical. How long is the string?

6 A ramp which slopes at 20° to the horizontal descends 5 m from the promenade to the beach below. How long is the ramp?

7 The chord $\overline{AB}$ of a circle whose centre is O is 10 cm long, and AÔB is 140°. What is the radius of the circle?

8 A roller 125 cm in diameter is about to be pulled over a kerbstone 15 cm high. What angle does the radius $\overline{OA}$ make with the vertical? (Fig. 81.)

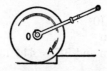

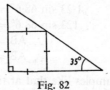

Fig. 81   Fig. 82

9 A man walks three km from A to B on a bearing of 20°, and then two km from B to C on a bearing of 110°. What is the distance and bearing of C from A?

10 The elevation of the top of a cliff from a point on the ground 120 m away from its base is 38° 17′. The elevation of the top of a flagstaff which stands on the edge of the cliff is 42° 26′ from the same point. How high is the flagstaff?

11 What is the elevation of the top of a tree 8 m high from a point on the ground 9·2 m away from the foot of the tree?

12 Find the sides of the right-angled triangle in Fig. 82, the sides of the square being 5 cm.

13 A flagstaff is held upright by three guy-ropes, each 6·9 m long, the peg in the ground to which a guy is attached being 3 m from the foot of the flagstaff. What angle does the guy make with the staff?

138

14 A roof slopes at 43° to the horizontal and its ridge is 2 m above the gutter. How long is the roof from ridge to gutter?

15 A street lamp hangs from the middle point of a wire, the ends of which are 3·6 m apart horizontally, so that the lamp is 1·5 m vertically below the two ends. How long is the wire, and what is the angle between the two halves of it?

16 Find the angles of the triangle ABC in Fig. 83, the quadrilateral circumscribing it being a rectangle.

17 To an observer on the ground the elevation of an aircraft flying at a height of 600 m is 33° 40′. How far is the aircraft from the observer?

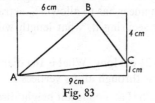
Fig. 83

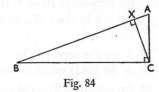
Fig. 84

18 What will be the elevation of the aircraft in no. 17 when its distance from the observer is exactly twice what it was when first seen?

19 To a boy scout standing 36 m from the base of a tree on level ground, and whose eye is 1·5 m from the ground, the elevation of the top of the tree is 19½°. What is the height of the tree, and what angle does it subtend at the scout's eye?

20 A straight tunnel is driven downwards so that, by the time it has descended 25 m vertically, it is 109·5 m long. At what angle to the horizontal is the tunnel descending?

21 A ridge-tent is made from a rectangular tarpaulin sheet 6 m long and 3·9 m wide so that it covers a floor space 6 m by 3 m, the centre of the sheet being supported by a horizontal pole. Calculate the angle the sides of the tent make with the horizontal, and the height of the ridge above the ground.

22 In Fig. 84, AB = 29 cm and AC = 10 cm. Calculate AX.

23 A yacht leaves a point A on a bearing of 61° 26′; sails on this bearing to a buoy B whose distance north of A is 2 km; then sails on a bearing of 123° 43′ until she reaches another buoy C which is due east of A. How far has the yacht sailed altogether?

24 How far is the yacht in no. 23 from the harbour when she is at the buoy C?

25 A survey-ship finds by echo-sounding that the depth at a certain point is 226 m; 440 m further on the depth is 116 m. If the sea bottom is rising steadily between these points, at what angle to the horizontal is it inclined?

26 A mining engineer has to erect a transporter cable between the top of a hill and an anchorage on the ground. The elevation of the top from the anchorage is 26° 19′, and its height above the anchorage 90 m. If the engineer has to allow 5% extra for the sag in the cable and for securing it, what length will he need?

27 A regular heptagon has sides 2½ cm long. What is the diameter of the circle which would pass through all its vertices?

28 An aircraft is flying at 600 km h⁻¹ at a constant height directly towards an observer at ground level. When first 'spotted' the aircraft was at an elevation of 11° 49′; twenty seconds later it was immediately overhead. At what height in metres is the aircraft flying?

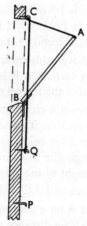

Fig. 85

29 A window $\overline{AB}$ 90 cm long, hinged about its lower edge **B** (Fig. 85), is opened and closed by means of a cord, attached to the top edge at **A**, which passes over a small pulley **C** in the top edge of the window frame. A loop in the lower end of the cord is then placed over one of a number of hooks in the wall under the window. If $A\hat{B}C = 35°$ when the loop is at **P**, through what further angle will the window open if the loop is placed over a hook **Q** 30 cm higher in the wall than **P**?

30 The captain of a ship steaming steadily at 8 km h⁻¹ on a bearing of 32° 18′ locates by radar another vessel at anchor on a bearing of 79° 50′. Twelve minutes later he estimates that he is as close to the second ship as he will be on the course that he is steering. How far was he from the anchored ship at first (in metres)?

Chapter 11

Everyday arithmetic

Rates

As soon as people congregate in communities instead of in single family groups, they find that life becomes simpler if certain services are provided centrally for the whole community instead of each man looking after his own family completely. For instance in a town or village it is essential that such services as water supply, drainage, libraries, police, education, etc. are provided by the town or county authorities, as there would be complete chaos if every man tried to provide them for himself without regard to his neighbour.

Such services have to be paid for.

The system is that a town or borough council first finds out how much money will be needed for all the services provided in a given year: this money will have to be found by the town or borough concerned. The council therefore **assesses** all the property in its area and calculates what this property should produce in the form of income or rent if it were let to householders, manufacturers and shopkeepers. The **rateable value** of the property is then fixed at a certain fraction of this theoretical rent, and this rateable value is the basis upon which the demands of the council are calculated as far as the individual is concerned.

The rate is always quoted as 'so much in the £', as in the following examples.

Example 1 *The rateable value of a house is £96 and the rate is 78p in the £. What rate is payable annually on the house?*

On £1 the rate is 78p

∴ „ £96 „ „ „ 96 × 78p = 7 488p

= £74·88

Example 2 *The total rateable value of Oakbridge is £238 869, and* *the amount raised by the rates is £124 243. What rate, to the nearest penny, is charged?*

On £238 869 the charge is £124 243

$$\therefore \quad ,, \quad £1 \quad ,, \quad ,, \quad ,, £\frac{124\ 243}{238\ 869}$$

$$= £0.519\ 8$$
$$\simeq 52p$$

$\therefore$ the rate charged is 52p in the £.

	No.	Log.
	124 200	5·094 1
	238 900	5·378 3
	0·519 8	1̄·715 8

Rates are generally payable in two equal half-yearly instalments, so that the householder of Example 1 would normally make two payments of £37·44 each, one at the beginning of and one half-way through the year in question.

The rate to be paid by a property owner includes payment for services rendered by the county authorities as well as by the local ones. For instance an Educational rate will be levied to cover the

BOROUGH OF ELMBRIDGE

Statement showing the rates levied for principal services in 1972

(a) BOROUGH PURPOSES	p	(b) COUNTY PURPOSES	p
Sewers & sewage disposal	2·7	Education	21·9
Refuse collection	2·9	Public assistance	6·7
Public health	0·9	Old people	2·5
Parks, recreation grounds	1·8	Deprived children	1·1
Public library	1·7	Mental deficiency	0·9
Highways	3·6	Highways	9·1
Administration	5·2	Police	4·2
Housing	2·7	Fire service	2·1
Fire Brigade	0·3	Public health	4·2
Isolation hospital	0·8	Other services	5·8
All other services	2·1		
	24·7		58·5
Deduct Exchequer Grant	6·7	Deduct Exchequer Grant	12·5
Net rate	18·0	Net rate	46·0

(c) TOTAL RATE 64p

cost of new schools, payment of salaries, etc.; also further rates for Police, Public Assistance, Roads, etc.

The table on page 143 shows the borough and county rates levied in Elmbridge for the year 1972.

The Exchequer Grants are contributions made by the Treasury to cover certain items of expenditure which are of national rather than of local concern, but which are more conveniently paid for by the local authority than by the national one.

Exercise 11a

1 In 1972 an Elmbridge householder owned a house whose rateable value was £90. What rate did he pay (i) to the Borough, (ii) to the County? (See table.)

2 What contribution did the householder in no. 1 make towards the cost of (i) the Public Library, (ii) Education, (iii) the Police, (iv) Housing?

3 If the rateable value in 1972 was £362 516, how much did a penny rate raise in that year?

4 What percentage of the total rate was applied to Education in 1972?

5 If a man paid £103·68 in rates, what was the rateable value of his house?

6 If the total rateable value is taken as £375 000 and it is proposed to build a new Town Hall at a cost of £110 000, the cost to be spread over 30 years, what additional burden would it put on the rates (per £, to the nearest penny)?

7 The rateable value in 1972 being £362 516, how much was earmarked by the Council for the upkeep of Parks and Recreation Grounds in that year?

In 1956 there was a revaluation of all rateable properties throughout the country. In one town this figure was increased from £394 681 to £670 451. Use these facts in the following questions.

8 If the rates were the equivalent of 124p in the £ in 1955, what

would they have become in 1956 in order to produce the same income (nearest penny)?

9 If a man paid £60 rates in 1955 and his property was not altered in rateable value during the revaluation, what rate would he have paid in 1956?

10 The rateable value of the premises of a small business in 1955 was £250. Under the new valuation this figure was increased to £400. How much more or less rates did the owner of the business have to pay in 1956 than in 1955, using the result of no. 8?

Gas and electricity

The consumption of gas is measured in cubic metres. The amount of heat that the gas produces is measured in megajoules, and the number of megajoules obtained from a cubic metre of gas depends on the **calorific value** of the gas. Manufactured gas has a calorific value of 19 megajoules per cubic metre, and for natural gas the figure is twice as great, i.e. 38 megajoules per cubic metre.

The customer is charged by a **unit of 100 megajoules**. In addition there is usually a quarterly 'standing charge', which is a minimum sum paid by every consumer, irrespective of the amount of gas he uses.

Example 3 *In one quarter a consumer uses* 102 *cubic metres of natural gas. Find the cost at* 7·8p *per unit if there is a standing charge of* 82p.

$$\text{No. of cubic metres used} = 102$$
$$\therefore \text{no. of megajoules} = 102 \times 38$$
$$= 3\,876$$
$$\therefore \text{no. of units} = 38\cdot76$$
$$\therefore \text{cost at } 7\cdot8\text{p per unit} = 38\cdot76 \times 7\cdot8\text{p}$$
$$= 302\cdot328\text{p}$$
$$= £3\cdot02 \text{ approx.}$$
$$\text{Standing charge} = £0\cdot82$$
$$\therefore \text{total cost} = £3\cdot84$$

145

New General Mathematics

The unit used for calculating the cost of electricity is the **kilowatt-hour**. There are various tariffs (i.e. methods of assessing the cost) such as the 'industrial tariff' and the 'farms tariff'. With the ordinary domestic tariff it is usual to charge for a certain number of units at a comparatively high rate, with a much lower rate for the remainder.

Example 4 *An electricity meter reading changes from* 48 446 *to* 53 700. *Calculate the cost if the first 72 units cost 3p each and the remainder* 0·715p *each.*

$$
\begin{array}{r}
53\ 700 \\
48\ 446 \\
\hline
\text{No. of units used} = \quad 5\ 254
\end{array}
$$

$$
\begin{array}{r}
72 \text{ at } 3\text{p each} \quad = \quad 216\text{p} \\
5\ 182 \text{ at } 0\cdot715\text{p each} = 3\ 705\cdot13\text{p} \\
\hline
3\ 921\cdot13\text{p}
\end{array}
$$

$$\therefore \text{ total cost} = £39\cdot21$$

Exercise 11b

1 Find the cost of 296 units of electricity if the first 72 units are charged at 2·95p each and the remainder at 0·75p each. If the consumer had used only half as many units, what would his bill have been?

2 Calculate the quarterly gas bill of a consumer who uses 93 units at 8·1p per unit, the standing charge being £1·05.

3 A family uses 1 833 units of electricity in a period of one quarter. The charge is 3·25p per unit for the first 75 units, and 0·725p per unit for the rest. Find the total cost.

4 The reading of an electricity meter changes from 10 819 to 14 027, and the charge is 3·15p for each of the first 72 units and 0·705p each for the remainder. Calculate the total cost.

5 A consumer uses 162 units of gas at 9·6p per unit, and the standing charge is £1·25. Calculate his gas bill.

6 The electricity bill for 588 units is £6·05. If the first 76 units

are charged at 3·75p each, find the charge per unit for the remainder.

7 The number of units of gas used in one quarter is 127. The charge is 13p per unit for the first 20 units, and 4·1p per unit for the rest. If there is no standing charge, calculate the total cost.

8 In one quarter a consumer uses 520 m³ of manufactured gas. Calculate the cost at 8·2p per unit, the standing charge being 76p.

9 Consecutive quarterly readings of an electricity meter are 39 125 and 45 223. If the first 80 units cost 2·95p each and the remainder 0·715p each, calculate the bill for the quarter.

10 Calculate the gas bill of a consumer who uses 471 m³ of natural gas, the price being 7·6p per unit and the standing charge 92p.

Insurance

Insurance is the means whereby a man protects himself against losses he may incur owing to damage to himself or to his property. The method is by paying an annual sum, called a **premium,** to his Insurance Company who, in return, guarantee to refund the amount lost or an agreed proportion of it.

It is possible to take out an **insurance policy** to cover almost any conceivable accident or risk, but the premium paid will vary with the degree of likelihood of the accident actually happening or the risk becoming a fact. For instance it is much more probable that a spark from the fire will burn a hole in a carpet or destroy the contents of a room than that the house will be burnt down: consequently the premium for Fire Insurance may be 25p per cent for furniture, and only 12½p per cent for buildings. (These are typical figures for a 'comprehensive' policy, covering risks by fire, burglary, floods, etc.) However, if the building is of timber and not brick the premium would probably be doubled, and a thatched roof would also attract a higher premium.

25p per cent means 25p for every £100 value of the property

insured. If a house is valued at £7 000 and its contents at £2 000, the annual premium would be calculated as follows:

£7 000 at 12½p per cent   12½p × 70 = £8·75
£2 000 at 25p per cent   25p × 20 = £5·00
                                           Total annual premium = £13·75

It is necessary by law to insure a car or motorcycle against 'third-party' risks; that is for injury the driver may cause to other people, but the driver would almost certainly also arrange with his insurance company to cover damage to himself and to his car or motorcycle.

The types of insurance so far dealt with are all concerned with something that may never happen. **Life Assurance,** on the other hand, deals with the inevitable and, whereas property can be insured only for its actual value, a life can be insured for any amount whatsoever.

Life Assurance is based upon experience because it can be estimated fairly accurately how long a person of any given age may be expected to live (some of course will live longer and some shorter than the estimated time, but on balance the 'expectation of life' tables are a reliable guide to the Assurance Company).

Generally speaking, a Life Assurance Policy is a means of saving money: in an **Endowment policy** the money is withdrawn when the policy has 'matured' (that is, has run for the number of years prearranged between the insurer and the company); but a **Whole Life policy** is paid up only upon the death of the insured person, so that a married man, for instance, can make certain that his wife and family have some security when he is no longer there to earn for them.

The amount of the premium payable depends upon the age of the person insuring, and the more years the policy has to run, the smaller will be the premium.

Table I gives a typical example of the premiums payable per £100 for a Whole Life Insurance; Table II gives similar figures for every £100 of an Endowment Insurance, maturing 30 years after it is taken out (or at previous death). These are both ex-

I		II	
Whole Life Assurance		**Endowment Assurance**	
Age next birthday	Premium (£)	Age next birthday	Premium (£)
20	2·030	20	3·400
21	2·070	21	3·405
22	2·115	22	3·410
23	2·160	23	3·415
24	2·210	24	3·420
25	2·260	25	3·430
26	2·315	26	3·440
27	2·370	27	3·450
28	2·430	28	3·460
29	2·490	29	3·475
30	2·555	30	3·490
31	2·620	31	3·510
32	2·690	32	3·530
33	2·765	33	3·550
34	2·840	34	3·575
35	2·920	35	3·605
36	3·000	36	3·635
37	3·085	37	3·670
38	3·170	38	3·705
39	3·260	39	3·745

amples of 'with profits' schemes, meaning that the person insured is entitled to a share of the profits earned by the company with which he is insured.

Pensions Schemes, Superannuation Schemes, etc. are all examples of life assurance policies.

Exercise 11c

1 Find the total annual premium payable on a house valued at £5 400 and its contents valued at £2 600 (12½p% for the building and 25p% for contents).

2 An amateur musician owns a £4 200 house with contents

149

valued at £3 800: he insures his musical instruments, which are worth £750, separately at £1%. What is his annual premium? (12½p% and 25p% as in no. 1.)

3 A lady insures her collection of furs (valued at £2 840) at 75p%; jewellery (valued at £4 700) at £1%; clothing (valued at £1 320) at £1·25%. What total premium does she pay?

4 A man about to go on a one month's journey by air insures himself against accident for £1·17, and his luggage, which includes some valuable samples and is worth £1 860, at 60p%. What premium does he pay?

5 A man insures his six-year-old car, valued at £470, for £17·85. His caravan, worth £450, is insured at £2% for the first £300 of its value and at 50p% thereafter. Its contents, valued at £110, are insured at £1%; and a £50 camera for 55p. What annual insurance does he pay?

6 If the motorist in no. 5 decided to insure his caravan and its contents for only three months of the year, for which the rate is 60% of the annual rate, what would his premium be? The camera is not to be included.

7 Use Table I to calculate the annual premiums payable for a £1 000 whole life policy when the age next birthday is 20, 25, 30, 35, 39. Represent these figures graphically.

8 What premium will a man pay for a £600 whole life policy if he will be 27 next birthday?

9 What premium will a man who is 35 next birthday pay for a £1 500 endowment policy?

10 A man who was 28 next birthday took out a £1 000 whole life policy and died after he had made 32 annual payments. How much had he paid in premiums during this time?

11 How much did the widow of the man in no. 10 actually receive after his death if the average profit made during the time that the policy was running was £2% per annum?

12 A man who was 30 next birthday took out a 30-year endowment policy (with profits) for £2 000. If the profits averaged

£2·5% over these thirty years, calculate how much he had paid in during this time, and also the value of the policy when it matured.

Taxation

Taxation is the means whereby the government makes the people pay for the items of national expenditure incurred on their behalf, just as rates look after the needs of the Town Council and the County Council: i.e. taxation is a national matter, while rates are local.

Income Tax, Purchase Tax, Motor Tax, etc. are all different methods of raising money, and it should be noticed that the Motor Tax is extracted only from those who use 'mechanically propelled vehicles' and not from other road users, whereas Income Tax is levied upon every member of the community who earns more than a certain minimum wage or salary, or who lives upon the profits from invested capital.

Income tax

The rates at which income tax is charged are apt to vary from year to year, and are announced by the Chancellor of the Exchequer in his annual Budget. Part of a person's income is free of tax, and the amount of tax is calculated on what is called the **taxable income.** This figure is arrived at by deducting from the gross income (i.e. the taxpayer's total income) various allowances. These again are apt to vary, and are sometimes complicated and arguable. A simplified version of the allowances for 1968–9 is:

(i) two-ninths of the income if earned (i.e. not interest or dividends from investments) up to an income of £4 005; for the next £5 940 only one-ninth is free of tax. For any further income there is no relief.
(ii) personal allowance of £220 for a single person, £340 for a married man.

   (iii) £115 or £140 or £165 for each child, depending on age (10 or under, 11 to 15, 16 or over if still receiving full-time education).

   (iv) part of the amount paid out by the taxpayer for life insurance premiums, superannuation, expenses unavoidably incurred by the taxpayer in doing his job, and so on.

For the examples which follow, the rates of tax are taken to be:

   (i) 20p in the £ for the first £100 of taxable income
  (ii) 30p in the £ for the next £200
 (iii) 42p in the £ (the **standard rate of tax**) for the remainder.

Surtax is levied on incomes which are sufficiently high; if the taxpayer's gross income does not exceed £5 000 he will generally not be liable. The rates of surtax vary from 10p to 50p in the £, and are in addition to the 42p in the £ already paid (1968–9 figures).

P.A.Y.E. is a method of collecting income tax whereby an employer is responsible for deducting tax from his employees' salaries or wages. He pays them what is left, and pays to the Inland Revenue the total tax deducted.

Example 5 *When a man has claimed all his allowances his resulting taxable income is £846. Calculate the income tax payable.*

$$\begin{array}{lr} & £ \\ \text{Tax on £100 at 20p in the £} = & 20 \cdot 00 \\ \text{,, ,, £200 ,, 30p ,, ,, ,,} = & 60 \cdot 00 \\ \text{,, ,, £546 ,, 42p ,, ,, ,,} = & 229 \cdot 32 \\ \hline \text{Total tax} = & 309 \cdot 32 \\ \hline \end{array}$$

Example 6 *A married man's annual salary is £2 367, and he has two children aged 10 and 13. He is entitled to allowances of £56 for life insurance premiums and £72 for business expenses. Calculate how much income tax he pays.*

		£	£
Gross income			2 367
Allowances (i) earned income		526	
(ii) man and wife		340	
(iii) children		115	
		140	
(iv) insurance		56	
(v) expenses		72	
Total		1 249	1 249
Taxable income			1 118

£

Tax on £100 at 20p in the £ = 20·00
„ „ £200 „ 30p „ „ „ = 60·00
„ „ £818 „ 42p „ „ „ = 343·56

Total tax = 423·56

Exercise 11d

Calculate the amount of income tax due in the following cases:

1 A bachelor earning £1 260 per annum.

2 A married man (no children) earning £2 250 per annum.

3 A married man with two children (ages 9 and 7) earning £1 539 per annum.

4 A married man with four children all at school (ages 17, 16, 14 and 10) earning £1 350 per annum.

5 A spinster with an income of £450 from investments (i.e. not earned).

6 A bachelor earning £828 per annum, whose allowance for life insurance premiums is £9.

7 A married man with no children, earning £4 500 per annum, with allowances of £85 for insurance policies and £160 for business expenses.

8 A married man with one child aged 14, if his salary is £1 449 a year and his allowance for life policies is £40.

9 A married man with three children (ages 14, 12 and 10) whose annual earnings are £1 647 and whose allowance for life policies is £35.

10 A widower with two children aged 17 and 15, both still at school, whose salary is £1 980 per annum and whose allowance for expenses is £23·50, if he has his elderly mother living with him, for whom he can claim an allowance of £60.

11 A single man with an income of £4 300 from investments and an allowance of £240 for life insurance premiums.

12 A married man with twins aged 8 earns £7 875 per annum, and also has an annual income of £360 from investments. His allowances are £95 for life policies and £135 for business expenses. Calculate his income tax for the year. (He would also pay some surtax.)

Chapter 12

Long multiplication and division. Cubic and other factors

Long multiplication

Example 1 *Multiply $4u^3 + 2 - 3u - u^2$ by $5u - 1 + 3u^2$.*
The working is simpler if the two expressions are arranged with the terms in order of powers, both in ascending order or both in descending order. The latter is used in this example.

$$
\begin{array}{r}
4u^3 - u^2 - 3u + 2 \\
3u^2 + 5u - 1 \\
\hline
12u^5 - 3u^4 - 9u^3 + 6u^2 \phantom{{}+10u} \\
+ 20u^4 - 5u^3 - 15u^2 + 10u \phantom{{}-2} \\
- 4u^3 + u^2 + 3u - 2 \\
\hline
12u^5 + 17u^4 - 18u^3 - 8u^2 + 13u - 2 \\
\end{array}
$$

Notice that in the partial products a separate column is kept for each power of u, just as in arithmetical long multiplication there is one column for units, one for tens, one for hundreds, and so on. (These are powers of ten.)

So long as the terms are in the right order, only the coefficients need to be written down. The working would then appear as follows:

$$
\begin{array}{r}
4 - 1 - 3 + 2 \\
3 + 5 - 1 \\
\hline
12 - 3 - 9 + 6 \phantom{{}+10} \\
+ 20 - 5 - 15 + 10 \phantom{{}-2} \\
- 4 + 1 + 3 - 2 \\
\hline
12 + 17 - 18 - 8 + 13 - 2 \\
\end{array}
$$

The term of highest degree is $12u^5$.

$\therefore$ the product is $12u^5 + 17u^4 - 18u^3 - 8u^2 + 13u - 2$.

This arrangement is known as the method of **detached co-efficients.**

Example 2 *Multiply* $a^3 - 4ab^2 - 2b^3$ *by* $6a - 3b$.

In the first expression a term containing a^2b might have been expected between a^3 and $-4ab^2$. This means that the coefficient of a^2b is 0, and that the expression might have been written as $a^3 + 0a^2b - 4ab^2 - 2b^3$. In practice a gap is left where this term would have appeared. As in Example 1, **separate columns** are kept for like terms.

$$
\begin{array}{l}
a^3 \qquad\quad\ - 4ab^2 - 2b^3 \\
6a - 3b \\
\hline
6a^4 \qquad\quad\ - 24a^2b^2 - 12ab^3 \\
\quad - 3a^3b \qquad\qquad\ + 12ab^3 + 6b^4 \\
\hline
6a^4 - 3a^3b - 24a^2b^2 \qquad\qquad\ + 6b^4 \\
\hline
\end{array}
$$

Example 3 *Multiply* $2a - b + 3c$ *by* $2b - c + a$.

$$
\begin{array}{l}
2a - \ \ b + 3c \\
\ \ a + 2b - \ \ c \\
\hline
2a^2 - \ ab + 3ac \\
\qquad + 4ab \qquad\quad - 2b^2 + 6bc \\
\qquad\qquad\quad\ - 2ac \qquad\quad + \ bc - 3c^2 \\
\hline
2a^2 + 3ab + \ ac - 2b^2 + 7bc - 3c^2 \\
\hline
\end{array}
$$

$\therefore$ the product is $2a^2 - 2b^2 - 3c^2 + 3ab + ac + 7bc$

Exercise 12a

Multiply

1 $x^2 - 3x + 1$	by	$2x + 3$
2 $2y^2 + y - 3$	„	$3y - 4$
3 $3z^2 - 5z - 2$	„	$3z + 5$
4 $a^2 + a - 3$	„	$2a + 6$
5 $2b^2 - 3b - 1$	„	$3b - 2$
6 $m^2 - mn + n^2$	„	$3m + 2n$

7 $3a^2 - ab - b^2$ „ $2a - 2b$

8 $x^2 - 2xy + 3y^2$ „ $2x - y$

9 $c^2 + 3cd - d^2$ „ $2c + d$

10 $2h^2 + 4hk - k^2$ „ $3h - 6k$

Multiply

11 $m + n + 1$ by $m - n - 1$

12 $u + v - 1$ „ $u + v + 1$

13 $2a - b + 3$ „ $2a + b - 3$

14 $2 + 3m - 2n$ „ $3 + 3m + 2n$

15 $m^3 + 2 + m - 3m^2$ „ $3m + 1$

16 $2n^2 - 1 + 3n + n^3$ „ $2n - 3$

17 $a^3 - 2a^2 - 2a + 5$ „ $a^2 - a + 2$

18 $b^2 - 2 + 2b^3 - b$ „ $b^2 + 2b - 4$

19 $3 + 3c^2 + 2c^3 - c$ „ $2c^2 - 3c - 9$

20 $d^3 + 3d^2 - 2$ „ $3d^2 + d + 2$

21 $2x^3 - 2x + 5$ „ $3x^2 + 3$

22 $a^3 + a^2m - 2m^3$ „ $2a + m$

23 $m^3 - 2mu^2 - 4u^3$ „ $m - 2u$

24 $2x^3 - 3x^2y - y^3$ „ $x - 3y$

25 $m^3 + 2n^3 - 3mn^2$ „ $2m - 3n$

26 $x^4 - 3x^2y^2 + y^4$ „ $2x - 3y$

27 $2u + v - 3w$ „ $u - 2v - 3w$

28 $c - 2d - 5e$ „ $c + 2d - 5e$

29 $a^3 + a^2d - d^3$ „ $a^2 - ad + d^2$

30 $p^2 + q^2 + r^2 - pq - qr - pr$ by $p + q + r$

Simplify

31 $(m^2 - 2m + 3)(2m - 1) - 2(m^3 - 3m^2 + 4m - 2)$

32 $(x - y + z)^2 + (x + y - z)^2$

33 $(2a - b + 1)^2 - (a - 2b - 1)^2$

34 $(a^2 - a - 3)(a - 3) - (a^2 + a + 2)(a - 2)$

35 $(u - v)^3 + (u + v)^3$

Long division

Example 4 *Divide* $6d^4 + 17d - 22d^3 - 11$ *by* $3d - 2$.

The expressions are first arranged so that the terms in each are in the same order of powers (both descending or both ascending) and gaps are left for missing terms.

$$
\begin{array}{r}
3d - 2) \; 6d^4 - 22d^3 \qquad\qquad + 17d - 11 \;(2d^3 - 6d^2 - 4d + 3 \\
\underline{6d^4 - 4d^3} \qquad\qquad\qquad\qquad\qquad \\
-18d^3 \qquad\qquad\qquad\qquad \\
\underline{-18d^3 + 12d^2} \qquad\qquad\qquad \\
-12d^2 + 17d \qquad\qquad \\
\underline{-12d^2 + 8d} \qquad\qquad \\
+9d - 11 \\
\underline{+9d - 6} \\
-5
\end{array}
$$

The quotient is $2d^3 - 6d^2 - 4d + 3$ and the remainder is -5.

The steps are closely related to those in arithmetical long division. It should however be noticed that each term in the quotient is obtained by making the first term in the divisor (i.e. $3d$) divide *exactly* each time, so that when the successive subtractions are done there is no remainder under $6d^4$, or under $-18d^3$, etc.

Detached coefficients may be used as follows:

$$
\begin{array}{r}
3 - 2) \; 6 - 22 + 0 + 17 - 11 \;(2 - 6 - 4 + 3 \\
\underline{6 - 4} \qquad\qquad\qquad\qquad \\
-18 + 0 \qquad\qquad\qquad \\
\underline{-18 + 12} \qquad\qquad \\
-12 + 17 \qquad \\
\underline{-12 + 8} \qquad \\
+9 - 11 \\
\underline{+9 - 6} \\
-5
\end{array}
$$

The first term in the quotient is $2d^3$ (i.e. $6d^4 \div 3d$).

$\therefore$ the quotient is

$2d^3 - 6d^2 - 4d + 3$ and the remainder is -5.

Example 5

Divide $5a^3 - 3b^3 + 19ab^2 - 21a^2b$ by $a^2 + 3b^2 - 4ab$.

$$a^2 - 4ab + 3b^2) \overline{5a^3 - 21a^2b + 19ab^2 - 3b^3} (5a - b$$
$$\underline{5a^3 - 20a^2b + 15ab^2}$$
$$- \quad a^2b + \quad 4ab^2 - 3b^3$$
$$\underline{- \quad a^2b + \quad 4ab^2 - 3b^3}$$

The quotient is $5a - b$ and there is no remainder.

Exercise 12b

Divide

1 $a^3 - a^2 - 3a + 2$	by	$a - 2$
2 $m^3 + 2m^2 - m + 6$	,,	$m + 3$
3 $2x^3 + 7x^2 - 2x - 10$	,,	$2x + 3$
4 $3u^3 - 7u^2 + 11u - 7$	,,	$3u - 1$
5 $2m^3 - 9m^2n + 5mn^2 + 6n^3$	,,	$2m - 3n$
6 $2x^3 + 3x^2y - 4xy^2 + y^3$	,,	$2x - y$
7 $2b^3 + 7b^2c - 6c^3$	,,	$2b + 3c$
8 $a^3 - 7ad^2 + 6d^3$	,,	$a + 3d$
9 $9x^3 - 16x - 10$	,,	$3x + 2$
10 $y^2 + 15 + 6y^3$	,,	$2y + 3$
11 $3a^3 - 7a^2b + 4b^3$	,,	$3a^2 - ab - 2b^2$
12 $4m^3 - 7mu^2 + 3u^3$	,,	$2m^2 + mu - 3u^2$
13 $9h^3 + 8k^3 - 22hk^2$	,,	$3h - 4k$
14 $31m^2n - 9n^3 + 10m^3$	,,	$5m + 3n$
15 $6b^2 + 1 - 11b + 9b^3$	,,	$3b^2 + 4b - 1$
16 $8 - 11a^2 + 6a^3 - 9a$	,,	$2a^2 - 3a - 4$

17 $m^3 - n^3$,, $m - n$

18 $m^3 + n^3$,, $m^2 - mn + n^2$

19 $6u^3 + 4v^3 - 23uv^2 + 7u^2v$,, $2u^2 - v^2 + 5uv$

20 $19mn^2 - 17m^2n + 4m^3 - 5n^3$,, $m^2 + n^2 - 3mn$

21 $8a^4 + 8 - 20a^2 - a$,, $2a + 3$

22 $2x^4 + 3 - 10x - 5x^3$,, $x - 3$

23 $m^4 - 1$,, $m - 1$

24 $y^4 - 1$,, $y + 1$

25 $a^4 - b^4$,, $a^3 - a^2b + ab^2 - b^3$

26 $m^4 - n^4$,, $m^3 + m^2n + mn^2 + n^3$

27 $12x - x^3 - 13 + 6x^4 - 13x^2$,, $2x^2 + x - 5$

28 $b^4 - b^2 + 2b - 1$,, $b^2 + b - 1$

29 $16u^4 - 12uv^3 + 5v^4 - 33u^2v^2$,, $4u^2 - 3uv - 5v^2$

30 $6y^4 - 9z^4 + y^2z^2 - 10y^3z$,, $3y^2 + 3z^2 - 2yz$

In the following examples, find the product of the first two expressions, and divide the result by the third.

31 $a^2 - 3a - 4, a^2 - a - 6, a^2 - 2a - 3$

32 $3x^2 + 7x - 6, 2x^2 - 3x - 2, 3x^2 - 8x + 4$

33 $m^2 - m - 12, 6m^2 + m - 2, 2m^2 + 5m - 3$

34 $3e^2 + ef - 4f^2, 4e^2 + ef - 3f^2, e^2 - f^2$

35 $6u^2 - uv - 2v^2, 4u^2 - 9v^2, 4u^2 - 4uv - 3v^2$

Cubic factors

Divide $a^3 + b^3$ by $a + b$.

$$
\begin{array}{r}
a^2 - ab + b^2 \\
a + b \overline{\smash{\big)}\ a^3 \qquad\qquad\ + b^3} \\
\underline{a^3 + a^2b} \\
- a^2b \\
\underline{- a^2b - ab^2} \\
+ ab^2 + b^3 \\
\underline{+ ab^2 + b^3} \\
\end{array}
$$

Divide $a^3 - b^3$ by $a - b$.

$$a - b) \overline{a^3 \qquad\qquad - b^3} \, (a^2 + ab + b^2$$
$$\underline{a^3 - a^2b}$$
$$+ a^2b$$
$$\underline{+ a^2b - ab^2}$$
$$+ ab^2 - b^3$$
$$\underline{+ ab^2 - b^3}$$

Hence $\qquad a^3 + b^3 = (a + b)(a^2 - ab + b^2)$

and $\qquad a^3 - b^3 = (a - b)(a^2 + ab + b^2)$

These results should be remembered, and quoted when factors are required of an expression consisting of the sum or difference of two cubes.

Example 6 *Factorise* $27u^3 - 1$.

$$27u^3 - 1 = (3u)^3 - 1^3$$
$$= [3u - 1][(3u)^2 + (3u) \times 1 + 1^2]$$
$$= (3u - 1)(9u^2 + 3u + 1).$$

Example 7 *Factorise* $125x^3y^9 + 8a^6$.

$$125x^3y^9 + 8a^6 = (5xy^3)^3 + (2a^2)^3$$
$$= [5xy^3 + 2a^2][(5xy^3)^2 - (5xy^3)(2a^2) + (2a^2)^2]$$
$$= (5xy^3 + 2a^2)(25x^2y^6 - 10a^2xy^3 + 4a^4).$$

Example 8 *Factorise* $(4m - 1)^3 - (m + 2)^3$.

$$(4m - 1)^3 - (m + 2)^3$$
$$= [(4m - 1) - (m + 2)][(4m - 1)^2 + (4m - 1)(m + 2) + (m + 2)^2]$$
$$= (4m - 1 - m - 2)(16m^2 - 8m + 1 + 4m^2 + 7m - 2 + m^2 + 4m + 4)$$
$$= (3m - 3)(21m^2 + 3m + 3)$$
$$= 3(m - 1) \times 3(7m^2 + m + 1)$$
$$= 9(m - 1)(7m^2 + m + 1).$$

Exercise 12c

Factorise

1 $x^3 + 1$ **2** $1 - y^3$ **3** $a^3 - 8$

4 $27 + b^3$ **5** $c^3 - 125$ **6** $d^3 + 64$

7 $u^3 + 27v^3$ **8** $8m^3 - n^3$ **9** $64a^3 + d^3$

10 $8c^3 + 27d^3$ **11** $27e^3 - 64f^3$ **12** $125x^3 - 8y^3$

13 $a^3m^3 + n^3$ **14** $x^3 - y^3z^3$ **15** $a^3 - 8d^3e^3$

16 $27m^3n^3 + u^3$ **17** $a^3 - 27b^3c^3$

18 $64m^3n^3 - 27u^3v^3$ **19** $x^3 + \dfrac{1}{64}$

20 $1 + a^6$ **21** $b^6 - 1$ **22** $\dfrac{m^3}{n^6} - 1$

23 $\dfrac{u^3}{8} + \dfrac{v^3}{27}$ **24** $3x^3 - 24y^3$ **25** $54m^3 - 2n^3$

26 $a^3 + b^6$ **27** $27x^3 - y^6$ **28** $m^6 + u^6$

29 $64h^6 - k^6$ **30** $27x^9 - 8y^9$

31 $(m + 2n)^3 - 8n^3$ **32** $(a + b)^3 + 27b^3$

33 $8u^3 + (2u - v)^3$ **34** $27x^3 - (3x - y)^3$

35 $(c + d)^3 - (c - d)^3$ **36** $(a - b)^3 + (a + b)^3$

37 $(2x - 1)^3 + (x + 1)^3$ **38** $(3m - n)^3 - (m + 2n)^3$

39 $27(a - b)^3 + 8a^3$ **40** $27a^3 - 8(a - b)^3$

Further factors

It was established in Book 2 that

$$a^2 + b^2 \text{ has no factors}$$

and that $a^2 - b^2 = (a + b)(a - b)$

Example 9 *Factorise* $16(u - 2v)^2 - (u + v)^2$.

$16(u - 2v)^2 - (u + v)^2$
$= 4^2(u - 2v)^2 - (u + v)^2$
$= [4(u - 2v) + (u + v)][4(u - 2v) - (u + v)]$

Long multiplication and division. Cubic and other factors

$$= (4u - 8v + u + v)(4u - 8v - u - v)$$
$$= (5u - 7v)(3u - 9v)$$
$$= (5u - 7v) \times 3(u - 3v)$$
$$= 3(5u - 7v)(u - 3v).$$

Example 10 *Factorise $9a^2 - m^2 + 10mn - 25n^2$.*

The last three terms, which contain m and n, naturally group themselves together. They are therefore put into a bracket preceded by a minus (since the squared terms are minus), and are then easily recognised as being the square of $(m - 5n)$.

$$9a^2 - m^2 + 10mn - 25n^2$$
$$= 9a^2 - (m^2 - 10mn + 25n^2)$$
$$= 9a^2 - (m - 5n)^2$$
$$= [3a + (m - 5n)][3a - (m - 5n)]$$
$$= (3a + m - 5n)(3a - m + 5n).$$

Example 11 *Factorise $(x - 4)^2 - 3(x - 4)(x + 1) - 10(x + 1)^2$.*

Let $x - 4 = $ A and $x + 1 = $ B.
Then $(x - 4)^2 - 3(x - 4)(x + 1) - 10(x + 1)^2$
$$= A^2 - 3AB - 10B^2$$
$$= (A + 2B)(A - 5B)$$
$$= [(x - 4) + 2(x + 1)][(x - 4) - 5(x + 1)]$$
$$= (x - 4 + 2x + 2)(x - 4 - 5x - 5)$$
$$= (3x - 2)-(4x - 9)$$
$$= -(3x - 2)(4x + 9).$$

Example 12 *Factorise $a^2 - 4b^2 - ac - 2bc$.*

$$a^2 - 4b^2 - ac - 2bc = (a - 2b)(a + 2b) - c(a + 2b)$$
$$= (a + 2b)(a - 2b - c).$$

Exercise 12d

Miscellaneous factors

Factorise

1 $h^2 - (u - v)^2$

2 $(3a - 2b)^2 - 4a^2$

3 $d^2 + 2d + 1 - e^2$

4 $h^2 + 6h + 9 - a^2$

163

5 $3(a + 1)^2 - 3$

6 $(x + 1)^2 - 2(x + 1) - 15$

7 $a^2 + 4ab + 4b^2 - x^2$ **8** $x^2 - y^2 - xz - yz$

9 $x^2 - 6xy + 9y^2 - a^2$ **10** $a^2 - x^2 - 2x - 1$

11 $b^2 - y^2 + 6y - 9$ **12** $9x^2 - (3x + 4y)^2$

13 $(5a + 2d)^2 - (3a - 2d)^2$ **14** $m^2 - n^2 + pm + pn$

15 $m^2 - 2mn + n^2 - 4p^2$ **16** $a^2 + 8ab + 16b^2 - 9m^2$

17 $u^2 - v^2 - 2mu + 2mv$ **18** $h^2 - x^2 + 2xy - y^2$

19 $k^2 - a^2 - 6ab - 9b^2$ **20** $16 + 8a + a^2 - b^2$

21 $3a(m + 2n) - 5b(m + 2n)$

22 $(4c - 3d)^2 + 3d(4c - 3d)$

23 $25 - 10b + b^2 - c^2$ **24** $9x^2 - a^2 + 4a - 4$

25 $l(l + m) - n(m + n)$ **26** $9x^2 - 4y^2 + 6x - 4y$

27 $(a - 2)^2 - 6(a - 2) + 5$

28 $6(m - 2)^2 - 5(m - 2) - 6$

29 $4a^2 - m^2 + 4mn - 4n^2$ **30** $9m^2 - 6mn + n^2 - h^2$

31 $4a^2 + 12am + 9m^2 - 4k^2$ **32** $m^4 - m^2 - 12$

33 $4x^4 - 37x^2y^2 + 9y^4$

34 $9b^2 - u^2 - 10uv - 25v^2$

35 $25x^2 + 20xy + 4y^2 - 9m^2$

36 $25d^2 - 9m^2 + 12mn - 4n^2$

37 $16a^2 - 9b^2 + 4ac + 3bc$

38 $4(3m - n)^2 - 9(m + n)^2$

39 $m^2 + 4mn + 4n^2 - u^2 - 4uv - 4v^2$

40 $a^2 + 2am + m^2 - b^2 + 6bn - 9n^2$

41 $a^2 + 2a - b^2 + 6b - 8$

42 $(n + 5)^2 + 7(n + 5)(n - 2) + 12(n - 2)^2$

43 $3(a + 2)^2 - 2(a + 2)(a - 1) - (a - 1)^2$

44 $16u^2 + 40uv + 25v^2 - 4m^2 + 12mn - 9n^2$

45 $20mn - 20ab + 4m^2 - 4a^2 + 25n^2 - 25b^2$

Chapter 13

H.C.F. and L.C.M. Fractions

The reasoning involved in finding the H.C.F. or L.C.M. of two or more expressions should be already familiar. The further complication introduced in this chapter is that the given expressions will usually have to be put into prime factors as a first step.

Example 1 *Find the H.C.F. and L.C.M. of $a^3 - ax^2$, $4a^2 - 4ax$ and $6a^2x - 6ax^2$.*

$$a^3 - ax^2 = a(a^2 - x^2) = a(a + x)(a - x)$$
$$4a^2 - 4ax = 4a(a - x)$$
$$6a^2x - 6ax^2 = 6ax(a - x).$$

All the expressions contain the factors a and $(a - x)$, and have no other factor in common.

$$\therefore \text{ H.C.F.} = a(a - x).$$

The L.C.M. is the smallest combination of factors that includes each of the three expressions.

$$\therefore \text{ L.C.M.} = 12ax(a + x)(a - x).$$

Example 2 *Find the H.C.F. and L.C.M. of $x^2 - 9$, $x^2 - 6x + 9$, $15 - 2x - x^2$ and $x^2 - 8x + 15$.*

$$x^2 - 9 = (x + 3)(x - 3)$$
$$x^2 - 6x + 9 = (x - 3)^2$$
$$15 - 2x - x^2 = (5 + x)(3 - x) = -(x + 5)(x - 3)$$
$$x^2 - 8x + 15 = (x - 5)(x - 3)$$
$$\therefore \text{ H.C.F.} = x - 3$$
$$\text{and L.C.M.} = (x + 3)(x - 3)^2(x + 5)(x - 5).$$

Notice that the minus sign preceding the factors in the third expression does not affect the answer; anything that is divisible by $x - 3$ is also divisible by $3 - x$ (just as 5 into 40 goes 8 times, and -5 into 40 goes -8 times).

New General Mathematics

Exercise 13a

Find the H.C.F. and L.C.M. of

1 $2a + 6, 3a + 9$ **2** $3b - 3, 4b - 4$

3 $4c - 8d, 6c - 12d$ **4** $9e + 6f, 18e + 12f$

5 $m^2 + mn, mn + n^2$ **6** $u^2 - uv, v^2 - uv$

7 $c^2 - e^2, c^2 - ce$ **8** $3x^2 - 6xy, 4y^2 - 2xy$

9 $3h^2 - 3k^2, h^2 + hk$ **10** $2m^2 - 8n^2, 4m^2 + 8mn$

11 $2a - 6b, a^2 - 9b^2$

12 $8a^3b - 12a^2b^2, 18ab^3 - 12a^2b^2$

13 $u^2 - 3uv + 2v^2, v^2 - u^2$

14 $x^2 - 5x + 6, x^2 - x - 6$

15 $a^2 - 3a - 10, a^2 - 6a + 5$

16 $16n^2 - 4m^2, 6m^2 - 6mn - 36n^2$

17 $3c^2 + 6cd + 3d^2, 2c^2 - 2d^2, 6c^2 - 6cd - 12d^2$

18 $a^2 + ad - 6d^2, 4a^3 - 4a^2d - 8ad^2, 2a^3 - 4a^2d$

19 $(a - 2b)(2a - b)(b - a), (2b - a)(2a + b)(a - b)$

20 $mn(m^2 - n^2), (m - n)^2(m^2 + mn)$

Simplification of fractions

Example 3 *Reduce* $\dfrac{6m^2u^2 - 4mu^3}{9m^3u - 4mu^3}$ *to its lowest terms.*

The rule is to **factorise fully first**; numerator and denominator may then be divided by any factors which they have in common.

$$\frac{6m^2u^2 - 4mu^3}{9m^3u - 4mu^3} = \frac{2mu^2(3m - 2u)}{mu(9m^2 - 4u^2)}$$

$$= \frac{2mu^2(3m - 2u)}{mu(3m + 2u)(3m - 2u)}$$

$$= \frac{2u}{3m + 2u}$$

dividing numerator and denominator by $mu(3m - 2u)$.

166

Example 4 *Simplify* $\dfrac{a^2 + ax - 6x^2}{2x^2 + ax - a^2}$.

$$\frac{a^2 + ax - 6x^2}{2x^2 + ax - a^2} = \frac{(a - 2x)(a + 3x)}{(2x - a)(x + a)}$$

$$= -\frac{a + 3x}{x + a}.$$

In this example, notice that

$$a - 2x = -(2x - a),$$

so that

$$\frac{a - 2x}{2x - a} = -1.$$

It should also be noticed that

$$\frac{c}{-d} = -\frac{c}{d} \quad \text{and} \quad \frac{-c}{d} = -\frac{c}{d}$$

so that

$$\frac{c}{-d} = \frac{-c}{d},$$

but $\dfrac{-c}{-d} = \dfrac{c}{d}$ since two minus signs make plus.

In the same way,

$$\frac{a - m}{2m - a} = \frac{a - m}{-(a - 2m)} = -\frac{a - m}{a - 2m}$$

$$\frac{a - m}{2m - a} = \frac{-(m - a)}{2m - a} = -\frac{m - a}{2m - a}$$

$$\frac{a - m}{2m - a} = \frac{-(m - a)}{-(a - 2m)} = \frac{m - a}{a - 2m}$$

Hence if the sign of the numerator or the denominator is changed, the sign of the fraction is changed and a minus sign must be placed before it; but if the signs of the numerator **and** the denominator are both changed, the sign of the fraction is unchanged.

Because of this there will sometimes be alternative answers to those given in the sets of examples in this chapter.

New General Mathematics

For example,

$$\frac{a^2 - 5ax + 6x^2}{2x^2 - 3ax + a^2} = \frac{(a-2x)(a-3x)}{(2x-a)(x-a)}$$

$$= -\frac{a-3x}{x-a} \text{ or } \frac{a-3x}{a-x} \text{ or } \frac{3x-a}{x-a}$$

$$\text{or } -\frac{3x-a}{a-x}$$

Exercise 13b

Simplify the following fractions. If there is no simpler form, say so.

1 $\dfrac{mnu}{nuv}$ **2** $\dfrac{8x^2z}{10xyz}$ **3** $\dfrac{u+m}{u+n}$ **4** $\dfrac{ab+ac}{ad+ae}$

5 $\dfrac{a^2+ab}{a^2+ac}$ **6** $\dfrac{a^2+b^2}{a+b}$ **7** $\dfrac{u^2+uv}{uv+v^2}$ **8** $\dfrac{h^2-hk}{hk}$

9 $\dfrac{5d^2nv^3}{15d^3n^2v^4}$ **10** $\dfrac{c^2-cd}{d^2-cd}$ **11** $\dfrac{a^2-b^2}{b^2-ab}$ **12** $\dfrac{x^2+xy}{x^2-y^2}$

13 $\dfrac{28c^2d^2e^2}{35ce^4}$ **14** $\dfrac{x^2-4x}{x^2-4}$ **15** $\dfrac{c^2-2cd+d^2}{c^2-cd}$

16 $\dfrac{m^2+2mn+n^2}{m^2-n^2}$ **17** $\dfrac{c^2-2c-15}{c^2-3c-10}$ **18** $\dfrac{d^2-9}{d^2-7d+12}$

19 $\dfrac{m^3n-2m^2n^2}{2mn^3-m^2n^2}$ **20** $\dfrac{xy-y^2}{(x-y)^2}$ **21** $\dfrac{xy-y^2}{(x+y)^2}$

22 $\dfrac{h^2+k^2}{(h+k)^2}$ **23** $\dfrac{h^2-k^2}{(h-k)^2}$ **24** $\dfrac{u^2-5uv+6v^2}{u^2+uv-12v^2}$

25 $\dfrac{x^2+xy-6y^2}{x^2-3xy+2y^2}$ **26** $\dfrac{a^3+b^3}{a^2+ab+ac+bc}$

27 $\dfrac{a^3-b^3}{a^2-b^2}$ **28** $\dfrac{15+2x-x^2}{x^2-25}$

29 $\dfrac{9a^2-m^2}{m^2-2am-3a^2}$ **30** $\dfrac{8-2a-a^2}{2a^2-3a-2}$

168

31 $\dfrac{a^2 - am - an + mn}{a^2 - am + an - mn}$ **32** $\dfrac{a^2 + am - an - mn}{a^2 + am + an + mn}$

33 $\dfrac{(u + w)^2 - v^2}{(v + w)^2 - u^2}$ **34** $\dfrac{a^2 - (b + c)^2}{c^2 - (a - b)^2}$

35 $\dfrac{(m - n)^2 + 3n^2}{m^3 + 8n^3}$ **36** $\dfrac{2a^2m - 3am^2 + m^3}{am^2 - a^2m - 2a^3}$

37 $\dfrac{(2m - u)^2 - (m - 2u)^2}{5m^2 - 5u^2}$ **38** $\dfrac{a(b + c) + (b + c)^2}{b^2 - c^2 + ab - ac}$

39 $\dfrac{x^2 - y^2 - ax + ay}{xy - x^2 + ax - ay}$ **40** $\dfrac{b^2 + ac - ab - bc}{c^2 - ac + ab - bc}$

Multiplication and division of fractions

Factorise fully first, before attempting to do any cancelling.

Example 5 *Simplify* $\dfrac{a^2 + 2a - 3}{a^2 - 16} \times \dfrac{a + 4}{a^2 + 8a + 15}.$

Given expression
$$= \frac{\cancel{(a + 3)}(a - 1)}{(a - 4)\cancel{(a + 4)}} \times \frac{\cancel{a + 4}}{(a + 5)\cancel{(a + 3)}}$$
$$= \frac{a - 1}{(a - 4)(a + 5)}.$$

The answer should be left in this form—the brackets should not be multiplied out.

Example 6 *Simplify* $\dfrac{m^3 + a^3}{m^2 + bm + cm + bc} \div \dfrac{m^2 - am + a^2}{cm + bc}.$

To divide by a fraction, multiply by its reciprocal.

$$\frac{m^3 + a^3}{m^2 + bm + cm + bc} \div \frac{m^2 - am + a^2}{cm + bc}$$
$$= \frac{(m + a)\cancel{(m^2 - am + a^2)}}{\cancel{(m + b)}(m + c)} \times \frac{c\cancel{(m + b)}}{\cancel{m^2 - am + a^2}}$$
$$= \frac{c(m + a)}{m + c}.$$

Example 7

$$Simplify \quad \frac{a^2 + ab}{a^2 - 2ab + b^2} \div \frac{a + 3b}{a + 2b} \times \frac{ab - a^2}{a^2 + 3ab + 2b^2}.$$

$$\frac{a^2 + ab}{a^2 - 2ab + b^2} \div \frac{a + 3b}{a + 2b} \times \frac{ab - a^2}{a^2 + 3ab + 2b^2}$$

$$= \frac{a\cancel{(a + b)}}{\cancel{(a - b)}(a - b)} \times \frac{\cancel{a + 2b}}{a + 3b} \times \frac{\overset{-1}{a\cancel{(b - a)}}}{\cancel{(a + b)}\cancel{(a + 2b)}}$$

$$= -\frac{a^2}{(a - b)(a + 3b)}.$$

Notice that $(a - b)$ cancels into $(b - a)$ and produces -1, because -1 times $(a - b)$ equals $(b - a)$.

Exercise 13c

Simplify

1 $\dfrac{18ab}{15bc} \times \dfrac{20cd}{24de}$

2 $\dfrac{12dn^3}{15cd^3} \div \dfrac{9c^3n}{10c^2d^2}$

3 $\dfrac{m + n}{m} \times \dfrac{mn}{3m + 3n}$

4 $\dfrac{uv}{3u - 6v} \times \dfrac{4u - 8v}{u^2v}$

5 $\dfrac{a^2 - b^2}{a^2 + ab} \div \dfrac{2a - 2b}{ab}$

6 $\dfrac{a^2 - 4}{a^2 - 3a + 2} \div \dfrac{a}{a - 1}$

7 $\dfrac{m^2 - 9}{m^2 - m - 6} \times \dfrac{m^2 + 2m}{m^2}$

8 $\dfrac{18m^2u}{16n^3v^2} \div \dfrac{24m}{15nu^3} \times \dfrac{8n^2v^3}{30m^3u}$

9 $\dfrac{a^2 - b^2}{ab + a^2} \times \dfrac{2a^3}{ab - a^2}$

10 $\dfrac{2a - 2b + 2c}{8bc} \times \dfrac{10abc}{5a - 5b + 5c}$

11 $\dfrac{n^2 - 9}{n^2 - n} \times \dfrac{n^2 - 3n + 2}{n^2 + n - 6}$

170

12 $\dfrac{m^2 - n^2}{m^2 - 2mn + n^2} \div \dfrac{m^2 + mn}{n^2 - mn}$

13 $\dfrac{a^2 - ab - 6b^2}{a^2 + ab - 6b^2} \times \dfrac{a^2 - ab - 2b^2}{a^2 - 2ab - 3b^2}$

14 $\dfrac{3d^2 - 12}{9d^2} \times \dfrac{6d^3}{4d + 8}$

15 $\dfrac{5abc^2 - 10abcd}{3b^2c^2 - 6b^2cd} \times \dfrac{12bc^2d}{10acd}$

16 $\dfrac{c^2 - cd}{d^2 - de} \div \dfrac{d^2 - cd}{cd - ce}$

17 $\dfrac{a^2 + au + av + uv}{a^3 + u^3} \times \dfrac{a^2 - au + u^2}{a + v}$

18 $\dfrac{e^2 - 5e + 6}{e^2 + 2e - 3} \div \dfrac{3e - 9}{2e^2 + 6e}$

19 $\dfrac{u^2 + 3u - 10}{3u^2 + 12u} \div \dfrac{u^2 - 25}{u^2 - u - 20}$

20 $\dfrac{x^2 - 3x - 4}{x^2 - 4x} \div \dfrac{x^2 - 4x + 4}{x^2 - 4}$

21 $\dfrac{a^3 - b^3}{a^3 + b^3} \times \dfrac{a^3 - a^2b + ab^2}{a^2b + ab^2 + b^3}$

22 $\dfrac{m^2 + 3m - 4}{m^2 - 2m + 4} \div \dfrac{m^2 + m - 2}{m^3 + 8}$

23 $\dfrac{a^2 + ab - 2b^2}{a^2 - 2ab - 3b^2} \times \dfrac{a^2 - b^2}{ab + 2b^2} \div \dfrac{a^2 - 2ab + b^2}{a^2 - 3ab}$

24 $\dfrac{m^2 - 4mn + 3n^2}{m^2 - mn - 2n^2} \div \dfrac{m^2 + mn - 2n^2}{m^2 + 3mn + 2n^2} \times \dfrac{m^2 - 2mn}{m^2 + mn}$

25 $\dfrac{m^2 - 4mn + 3n^2}{m^2 - mn - 2n^2} \div \left\{ \dfrac{m^2 + mn - 2n^2}{m^2 + 3mn + 2n^2} \times \dfrac{m^2 - 2mn}{m^2 + mn} \right\}$

Addition and subtraction of fractions

Example 8 *Simplify* $2 + \dfrac{6a^2 + 2b^2}{3ab} - \dfrac{4a - b}{2b}$.

The L.C.M. of $3ab$ and $2b$ is $6ab$.

∴ combine the parts of the expression with a common denominator of $6ab$.

$$2 + \frac{6a^2 + 2b^2}{3ab} - \frac{4a - b}{2b}$$

$$= \frac{2 \times 6ab}{6ab} + \frac{2(6a^2 + 2b^2)}{6ab} - \frac{3a(4a - b)}{6ab}$$

$$= \frac{12ab + 2(6a^2 + 2b^2) - 3a(4a - b)}{6ab}$$

$$= \frac{12ab + 12a^2 + 4b^2 - 12a^2 + 3ab}{6ab}$$

$$= \frac{15ab + 4b^2}{6ab}$$

$$= \frac{b(15a + 4b)}{6ab}$$

$$= \frac{15a + 4b}{6a}.$$

Example 9 *Simplify* $\dfrac{3}{m^2 + mn - 2n^2} - \dfrac{2}{m^2 - 4mn + 3n^2}$.

The denominators must be factorised fully first, so that their L.C.M. can be used as the common denominator.

$$\frac{3}{m^2 + mn - 2n^2} - \frac{2}{m^2 - 4mn + 3n^2}$$

$$= \frac{3}{(m - n)(m + 2n)} - \frac{2}{(m - n)(m - 3n)}$$

$$= \frac{3(m - 3n) - 2(m + 2n)}{(m - n)(m + 2n)(m - 3n)}$$

$$= \frac{3m - 9n - 2m - 4n}{(m - n)(m + 2n)(m - 3n)}$$

$$= \frac{m - 13n}{(m - n)(m + 2n)(m - 3n)}.$$

Example 10 *Simplify* $\dfrac{x + 4}{x^2 - 3x} - \dfrac{x - 1}{9 - x^2}.$

$$\frac{x + 4}{x^2 - 3x} - \frac{x - 1}{9 - x^2}$$

$$= \frac{x + 4}{x(x - 3)} - \frac{x - 1}{(3 - x)(3 + x)}$$

$$= \frac{x + 4}{x(x - 3)} + \frac{x - 1}{(x - 3)(3 + x)} \quad \text{since} \quad (3 - x) = -(x - 3)$$

$$= \frac{(x + 4)(x + 3) + x(x - 1)}{x(x - 3)(x + 3)}$$

$$= \frac{x^2 + 7x + 12 + x^2 - x}{x(x - 3)(x + 3)}$$

$$= \frac{2x^2 + 6x + 12}{x(x - 3)(x + 3)}$$

$$= \frac{2(x^2 + 3x + 6)}{x(x - 3)(x + 3)}.$$

Example 11 *Simplify* $\dfrac{3a - 5m}{a^2 - 5am + 6m^2} + \dfrac{1}{a - 2m} - \dfrac{2}{a - 3m}.$

$$\frac{3a - 5m}{a^2 - 5am + 6m^2} + \frac{1}{a - 2m} - \frac{2}{a - 3m}$$

$$= \frac{3a - 5m}{(a - 2m)(a - 3m)} + \frac{1}{a - 2m} - \frac{2}{a - 3m}$$

$$= \frac{3a - 5m + (a - 3m) - 2(a - 2m)}{(a - 2m)(a - 3m)}$$

$$= \frac{3a - 5m + a - 3m - 2a + 4m}{(a - 2m)(a - 3m)}$$

$$= \frac{2a - 4m}{(a - 2m)(a - 3m)}$$

$$= \frac{2(a - 2m)}{(a - 2m)(a - 3m)}$$

$$= \frac{2}{a - 3m}.$$

Example 12 *If* $x = \dfrac{2a + 3}{3a - 2}$, *express* $\dfrac{x - 1}{2x + 1}$ *in terms of a.*

$$\frac{x - 1}{2x + 1} = \frac{\dfrac{2a + 3}{3a - 2} - 1}{2 \times \dfrac{2a + 3}{3a - 2} + 1}$$

$$= \frac{(2a + 3) - (3a - 2)}{2(2a + 3) + (3a - 2)} \text{ multiplying num. and denom.}$$
$$\text{by } (3a - 2)$$

$$= \frac{2a + 3 - 3a + 2}{4a + 6 + 3a - 2}$$

$$= \frac{-a + 5}{7a + 4}.$$

Exercise 13d

Simplify

1 $\dfrac{3}{2ab} + \dfrac{4}{3bc}$

2 $5 - \dfrac{a - b}{c}$

3 $\dfrac{3a - b}{5ab} - \dfrac{2b + 3c}{6bc} + \dfrac{3c - 2a}{15ac}$

4 $\dfrac{3}{2(x + y)} - \dfrac{1}{3(x + y)}$

5 $\dfrac{6}{a - 2b} + \dfrac{4}{2b - a}$

6 $3 + \dfrac{2b}{a - b}$

7 $2 - \dfrac{x}{x + 2y}$

8 $\dfrac{1}{4(u-v)} - \dfrac{1}{5(v-u)}$

9 $\dfrac{7u}{2u+3v} - 3$

10 $\dfrac{3a}{2a+b} - \dfrac{b}{4a+2b}$

11 $\dfrac{3mn}{2m^2+2n^2} + \dfrac{5mn}{3m^2+3n^2}$

12 $\dfrac{1}{4x-2y} - \dfrac{1}{y-2x}$

13 $\dfrac{a+b}{ab} - \dfrac{b+c}{bc}$

14 $\dfrac{u^2-v^2}{uv} + \dfrac{v}{u} - \dfrac{3uv-u^2}{v^2}$

15 $\dfrac{d+1}{2d-8} - \dfrac{d+2}{12-3d}$

16 $\dfrac{2}{a+1} + \dfrac{3}{a+2}$

17 $\dfrac{3x}{x-1} - \dfrac{4}{x+2}$

18 $\dfrac{e-2}{e+2} - \dfrac{e-1}{e+3}$

19 $\dfrac{3}{m-n} + \dfrac{m+3n}{(m-n)^2}$

20 $\dfrac{7c+2d}{(2c+d)^2} - \dfrac{3}{2c+d}$

21 $\dfrac{a+b}{(a-2b)^2} - \dfrac{1}{2b-a}$

22 $\dfrac{3c}{c^2-d^2} - \dfrac{3d}{d^2-c^2}$

23 $\dfrac{4m-9n}{16m^2-9n^2} + \dfrac{1}{4m-3n}$

24 $\dfrac{(m+n)^2}{m^2-n^2} + \dfrac{m^2+mn}{n^2-mn}$

25 $\dfrac{1}{1-a} - \dfrac{1}{\dfrac{1}{a}-1}$

26 $\dfrac{c(3-c)}{c^2+3c-10} + \dfrac{c-1}{c+5}$

27 $\dfrac{5}{d^2-2d-8} + \dfrac{2}{d^2-6d+8}$

28 $\dfrac{4}{3a+3b} - \dfrac{3}{2a-2b} + \dfrac{b}{a^2-b^2}$

29 $\dfrac{5}{d^2-16} + \dfrac{2}{(d+4)^2}$

30 $\dfrac{4}{x-3} - \dfrac{1}{x+2} - \dfrac{x+7}{x^2-x-6}$

31 $\dfrac{1}{u+v} - \dfrac{3v^2}{u^3+v^3}$

32 $\dfrac{4}{a-m} - \dfrac{12am}{a^3 - m^3}$

33 $\dfrac{2a-1}{a^2 - 5a + 6} - \dfrac{a+3}{a^2 + 2a - 8}$

34 $\dfrac{1}{x^2 - x + 1} - \dfrac{3}{x^3 + 1} + \dfrac{1}{x+1}$

35 $\dfrac{1}{ab - ac - b^2 + bc} - \dfrac{1}{a^2 - ab - ac + bc}$

36 $\dfrac{2}{u^2 - 4uv + 3v^2} - \dfrac{3}{u^2 - 5uv + 4v^2} + \dfrac{1}{u^2 - 7uv + 12v^2}$

37 If $a = \dfrac{d+1}{d-1}$, express $\dfrac{a+1}{a-1}$ in terms of d.

38 ,, $x = \dfrac{a+3}{2a-1}$, ,, $\dfrac{2x+1}{3x+1}$,, ,, ,, a.

39 ,, $x = \dfrac{3m-5}{3m+5}$, ,, $\dfrac{x-1}{x+1}$,, ,, ,, m.

40 ,, $x = \dfrac{3w-1}{w+2}$, ,, $\dfrac{2x-3}{3x-1}$,, ,, ,, w.

Fractional equations

Example 13 *Solve the equation* $\dfrac{1}{3a-1} = \dfrac{2}{a+1} - \dfrac{3}{8}$.

The L.C.M. of the denominators is $8(3a-1)(a+1)$.

$\therefore$ the fractions will disappear if both sides of the equations are multiplied by $8(3a-1)(a+1)$.

$$\frac{1}{3a-1} = \frac{2}{a+1} - \frac{3}{8}$$

$$\therefore \frac{1}{3a-1} \times 8(3a-1)(a+1) \cdot$$

$$= \frac{2}{a+1} \times 8(3a-1)(a+1) - \frac{3}{8} \times 8(3a-1)(a+1)$$

$$\therefore\ 8(a+1) = 16(3a-1) - 3(3a-1)(a+1)$$
$$\therefore\ 8a+8\ = 48a - 16 - 3(3a^2 + 2a - 1)$$
$$\therefore\ 8a+8\ = 48a - 16 - 9a^2 - 6a + 3$$
$$\therefore\ 8a+8 - 48a + 16 + 9a^2 + 6a - 3 = 0$$
$$\therefore\ 9a^2 - 34a + 21 = 0$$
$$\therefore\ (a-3)(9a-7) = 0$$
$$\therefore\ a = 3\quad\text{or}\quad 9a = 7$$
$$\therefore\ a = 3\quad\text{or}\quad \frac{7}{9}.$$

Check If $a = 3$,

$$\frac{1}{3a-1} = \frac{1}{9-1} = \frac{1}{8}$$

and
$$\frac{2}{a+1} - \frac{3}{8} = \frac{2}{4} - \frac{3}{8} = \frac{1}{2} - \frac{3}{8} = \frac{1}{8}$$

If $a = \frac{7}{9}$,

$$\frac{1}{3a-1} = \frac{1}{\frac{7}{3}-1} = \frac{1}{\frac{4}{3}} = \frac{3}{4}$$

and
$$\frac{2}{a+1} - \frac{3}{8} = \frac{2}{1\frac{7}{9}} - \frac{3}{8} = \frac{18}{16} - \frac{3}{8} = \frac{9}{8} - \frac{3}{8} = \frac{3}{4}.$$

Example 14 *Solve the equation* $\dfrac{3}{x^2-5x+6} = \dfrac{2}{x^2-x-6}.$

$$\frac{3}{x^2-5x+6} = \frac{2}{x^2-x-6}$$
$$\therefore\ \frac{3}{(x-2)(x-3)} = \frac{2}{(x-3)(x+2)}$$

Multiply both sides by $(x-2)(x-3)(x+2)$.

Then
$$3(x+2) = 2(x-2)$$
$$\therefore\ 3x+6 = 2x-4$$
$$\therefore\ 3x-2x = -6-4$$
$$\therefore\ x = -10.$$

Check If $x = -10$,

$$\frac{3}{x^2 - 5x + 6} = \frac{3}{100 + 50 + 6} = \frac{3}{156} = \frac{1}{52}$$

and

$$\frac{2}{x^2 - x - 6} = \frac{2}{100 + 10 - 6} = \frac{2}{104} = \frac{1}{52}.$$

Exercise 13e

Solve the following equations.

1 $\dfrac{3}{a} = a - 2$

2 $5 - 2d = \dfrac{2}{d}$

3 $\dfrac{7}{3} + \dfrac{2}{e} = e$

4 $c = \dfrac{3}{c + 2}$

5 $m = \dfrac{8}{3m + 2}$

6 $a + 3 = \dfrac{6}{a + 4}$

7 $3x - 2 = \dfrac{4}{x - 1}$

8 $n - 3 = \dfrac{4}{n - 3}$

9 $\dfrac{x - 2}{x + 4} = x$

10 $\dfrac{3n}{2n - 1} = n$

11 $\dfrac{a - 4}{7} = \dfrac{2}{3a - 1}$

12 $\dfrac{4}{w + 3} - \dfrac{3}{w + 2} = 0$

13 $\dfrac{3}{2b - 5} - \dfrac{4}{b - 3} = 0$

14 $\dfrac{c}{c - 2} = \dfrac{3}{2c - 5}$

15 $\dfrac{2}{d - 2} = \dfrac{3d}{4d + 12}$

16 $\dfrac{4n - 3}{6n + 1} = \dfrac{2n - 1}{3n + 4}$

17 $\dfrac{2m + 3}{2m + 5} - \dfrac{m - 1}{m - 2} = 0$

18 $\dfrac{3}{c + 2} - \dfrac{2}{2c - 3} = \dfrac{1}{7}$

19 $\dfrac{3}{x - 4} = \dfrac{2}{x - 1} - 4$

20 $\dfrac{1}{2a - 5} + \dfrac{7}{9} = \dfrac{2}{a + 5}$

21 $\dfrac{2}{d + 3} = \dfrac{3}{2d - 1} - \dfrac{4}{15}$

22 $\dfrac{11}{m+3} = \dfrac{5}{2m} - \dfrac{1}{m-4}$

23 $\dfrac{1}{2n-3} + \dfrac{1}{2n+1} - \dfrac{1}{n-1} = 0$

24 $\dfrac{2}{u+2} = \dfrac{2}{u+1} - \dfrac{1}{u+4}$

25 $\dfrac{3}{2d+3} - \dfrac{1}{2d+1} = \dfrac{1}{d+1}$

26 $\dfrac{4a-1}{a+4} - 2 = \dfrac{2a-1}{a+2}$

27 $\dfrac{2}{x+3} - \dfrac{x-6}{x^2-9} = 0$

28 $\dfrac{4}{m^2+3m+2} - \dfrac{3}{m^2+5m+6} = 0$

29 $\dfrac{2}{u-2} = \dfrac{2u-1}{u^2+u-6} - \dfrac{3}{u+3}$

30 $\dfrac{3}{v-4} - \dfrac{v+2}{v^2-3v-4} = \dfrac{1}{2v+2}$

Compare Examples 15 and 16 which follow. Notice that in Example 15 both sides of the **equation** are multiplied by the L.C.M. of the denominators, thus causing the fractions to disappear; but that in Example 16 the common denominator is retained because the **expression** must remain the same size.

Example 15 *Solve the equation* $\dfrac{x}{x-3} - \dfrac{8}{x} = 2.$

$$\frac{x}{x-3} - \frac{8}{x} = 2$$

$$\therefore \frac{x}{x-3} \times x(x-3) - \frac{8}{x} \times x(x-3) = 2 \times x(x-3)$$

$$\therefore x^2 - 8(x-3) - 2x(x-3) = 0$$

$$\therefore x^2 - 8x + 24 - 2x^2 + 6x = 0$$

179

New General Mathematics

$$\therefore -x^2 - 2x + 24 = 0$$
$$\therefore x^2 + 2x - 24 = 0$$
$$\therefore (x - 4)(x + 6) = 0$$
$$\therefore x = 4 \quad \text{or} \quad -6.$$

Example 16 *Simplify the expression* $\dfrac{x}{x - 3} - \dfrac{8}{x} - 2.$

$$\frac{x}{x - 3} - \frac{8}{x} - 2 = \frac{x^2 - 8(x - 3) - 2x(x - 3)}{x(x - 3)}$$
$$= \frac{x^2 - 8x + 24 - 2x^2 + 6x}{x(x - 3)}$$
$$= \frac{-x^2 - 2x + 24}{x(x - 3)}$$
$$= -\frac{x^2 + 2x - 24}{x(x - 3)}$$
$$= -\frac{(x - 4)(x + 6)}{x(x - 3)}.$$

Exercise 13f

In this exercise solve the equations and simplify the expressions.

1 $\dfrac{5}{a + 4} - \dfrac{2}{a - 2} = 0$

2 $\dfrac{5}{a + 4} - \dfrac{2}{a - 2}$

3 $\dfrac{b - 15}{b^2 - 9} - \dfrac{2}{3 - b}$

4 $\dfrac{3}{c + 1} = \dfrac{2}{c^2 - 1}$

5 $\dfrac{3}{c + 1} - \dfrac{2}{c^2 - 1}$

6 $\dfrac{a}{a + 2} = \dfrac{a - 2}{a - 3}$

7 $\dfrac{a}{a + 2} - \dfrac{a - 2}{a - 3}$

8 $\dfrac{1}{n - 6} + \dfrac{1}{n - 4} - \dfrac{2}{n - 5}$

9 $\dfrac{5}{a - 1} - 3 = \dfrac{4}{a}$

10 $\dfrac{1}{3 + x} - \dfrac{3 - x}{(3 + x)^2}$

11 $\dfrac{1}{3 + x} = \dfrac{3 - x}{(3 + x)^2}$

12 $\dfrac{2}{m + 2} = \dfrac{3}{m + 3} - \dfrac{1}{m + 1}$

13 $\dfrac{2}{m+2} - \dfrac{3}{m+3} + \dfrac{1}{m+1}$ **14** $\dfrac{3}{2m-3} - \dfrac{2m+15}{4m^2-9}$

15 $\dfrac{e}{e+3} = 1\frac{2}{5} - \dfrac{2}{e}$

16 $\dfrac{3}{a^2-7a+10} = \dfrac{5}{a^2-2a-15}$

17 $\dfrac{3}{a^2-7a+10} - \dfrac{5}{a^2-2a-15}$

18 $\dfrac{5}{(m-3)^2} - \dfrac{3}{m^2-9} = 0$ **19** $\dfrac{2}{4n^2-25} - \dfrac{1}{(2n-5)^2}$

20 $\dfrac{b+2}{b^2-b-12} = \dfrac{b}{b^2+6b+9}$

21 $\dfrac{b+2}{b^2-b-12} - \dfrac{b}{b^2+6b+9}$

22 $\dfrac{2}{2t^2+3t-2} + \dfrac{1}{t+2} = \dfrac{5}{2t-1}$

23 $\dfrac{2}{2t^2+3t-2} + \dfrac{1}{t+2} - \dfrac{5}{2t-1}$

24 $\dfrac{5}{3d-1} - \dfrac{1}{2d+3} - \dfrac{d+7}{6d^2+7d-3}$

25 $\dfrac{5}{2b+2} - \dfrac{1}{3-b} - \dfrac{2b+1}{b^2-2b-3}$

26 $\dfrac{5}{2b+2} - \dfrac{2b+1}{b^2-2b-3} = \dfrac{1}{3-b}$

27 $\dfrac{1}{3h-2} - \dfrac{5h+1}{6h^2+5h-6} - \dfrac{2}{2h+3}$

28 $\dfrac{1}{m^2-4m+3} + \dfrac{1}{m^2-3m+2} = \dfrac{1}{m^2-5m+6}$

29 $\dfrac{1}{m^2-4m+3} + \dfrac{1}{m^2-3m+2} - \dfrac{1}{m^2-5m+6}$

30 $\dfrac{4}{x^2 - x - 2} + \dfrac{3}{x^2 - 4} = \dfrac{2}{x^2 + 3x + 2}$

31 $\dfrac{4}{x^2 - x - 2} + \dfrac{3}{x^2 - 4} - \dfrac{2}{x^2 + 3x + 2}$

32 $\dfrac{3}{4t^2 - 9} - \dfrac{1}{2t^2 + 5t + 3} = \dfrac{1}{2t^2 - t - 3}$

33 $\dfrac{3(5m - 2)}{6m^2 - 5m - 6} = \dfrac{3}{2m - 3} + \dfrac{2}{3m + 2}$

34 $\dfrac{3(5m - 2)}{6m^2 - 5m - 6} - \dfrac{3}{2m - 3} - \dfrac{2}{3m + 2}$

35 $\dfrac{1}{2d^2 + d - 1} - \dfrac{2}{3d^2 + 4d + 1} - \dfrac{3}{6d^2 - d - 1}$

36 $\dfrac{1}{2d^2 + d - 1} - \dfrac{2}{3d^2 + 4d + 1} = \dfrac{3}{6d^2 - d - 1}$

37 $\dfrac{2}{a^2 - 3a + 2} = \dfrac{3}{a^2 + a - 6} - \dfrac{4}{a^2 + 2a - 3}$

38 $\dfrac{2}{a^2 - 3a + 2} - \dfrac{3}{a^2 + a - 6} + \dfrac{4}{a^2 + 2a - 3}$

39 $\dfrac{2(5m + 2)}{6m^2 + 11m - 35} - \dfrac{2}{3m - 5} + \dfrac{1}{2m + 7}$

40 $\dfrac{2}{a^2 - 4} - \dfrac{1}{a^2 - 9} - \dfrac{1}{a^2 - a - 6}$

Problems involving fractions

Example 17 *A motorist drives from Rugby to Bristol, a distance of 156 km, at a certain average speed. On the return journey he increases his average speed by 4 km h⁻¹ and takes 15 minutes less. Find his average speed on the outward journey.*

Let speed on outward journey be v km h⁻¹.

$$\text{Then time taken} = \frac{156}{v} \text{ h.}$$

Speed on return journey is $(v + 4)$ km h^{-1}.

$$\therefore \text{ time taken to return} = \frac{156}{v + 4} \text{ h}.$$

Time to return is $\frac{1}{4}$ h less than outward time.

$$\therefore \frac{156}{v} - \frac{156}{v + 4} = \frac{1}{4}$$

Multiply both sides by $4v(v + 4)$,

$$\text{then } 156 \times 4(v + 4) - 156 \times 4v = v(v + 4)$$
$$\therefore 624v + 2\,496 - 624v = v^2 + 4v$$
$$\therefore v^2 + 4v - 2\,496 = 0$$
$$\therefore (v + 52)(v - 48) = 0$$
$$\therefore v = -52 \quad \text{or} \quad 48.$$

But -52 is an unsuitable result,

$\therefore$ average speed on outward journey is 48 km h^{-1}.

Check

$$\text{Time for outward journey} = \frac{156}{48} \text{ h} = 3\tfrac{1}{4} \text{ h} = 3 \text{ h } 15 \text{ min.}$$

$$\text{Time for return journey} \quad = \frac{156}{52} \text{ h} = 3 \text{ h.}$$

$$\text{Difference in times} = 15 \text{ min.}$$

Alternatively, the initial working may be arranged in tabulated form as follows:

	Av. speed (km h^{-1})	Distance (km)	Time (h)
Out	v	156	$\dfrac{156}{v}$
Back	$v + 4$	156	$\dfrac{156}{v + 4}$

Hence $\dfrac{156}{v} - \dfrac{156}{v + 4} = \dfrac{1}{4}$ etc. as before.

183

New General Mathematics

Example 18 *A man bought a certain number of tins of beans for £1·26. He kept 4 tins for his own use and sold the rest at 3p more per tin than he paid for them, making a total profit of 14p on the deal. How many tins did he buy?*

Suppose he bought x tins.

Then buying price $= \dfrac{126}{x}$p per tin.

He sold $(x - 4)$ tins for 140p.

$$\therefore \text{ selling price} = \frac{140}{x - 4}\text{p per tin.}$$

But profit is 3p per tin.

$$\therefore \frac{140}{x - 4} - \frac{126}{x} = 3$$

Multiply both sides by $x(x - 4)$,

then $140x - 126(x - 4) = 3x(x - 4)$
$$\therefore 140x - 126x + 504 = 3x^2 - 12x$$
$$\therefore 3x^2 - 26x - 504 = 0$$
$$\therefore (x - 18)(3x + 28) = 0$$
$$\therefore x = 18 \quad \text{or} \quad -9\tfrac{1}{3}.$$

But $-9\tfrac{1}{3}$ is unsuitable,

$$\therefore \text{ he bought 18 tins.}$$

Check

18 tins bought for 126p, i.e. 7p per tin
14 tins sold for 140p, i.e. 10p per tin

Profit $=$ 3p per tin.

Alternatively, the initial working may be arranged as follows:

	No. of tins	Total cash (p)	Price per tin (p)
Bought	x	126	$\dfrac{126}{x}$
Sold	$x - 4$	140	$\dfrac{140}{x - 4}$

184

Hence $\dfrac{140}{x-4} - \dfrac{126}{x} = 3$ etc. as before.

Example 19 *A boat goes 4 km upriver and 4 km back again in 50 minutes, the stream flowing at 2 km h^{-1}. What would be the speed of the boat in still water?*

Let the speed in still water be x km h^{-1}

	Speed (km h^{-1})	Distance (km)	Time (h)
Up	$x - 2$	4	$\dfrac{4}{x-2}$
Down	$x + 2$	4	$\dfrac{4}{x+2}$

Total time $= 50$ min $= \frac{5}{6}$ h.

$$\therefore \frac{4}{x-2} + \frac{4}{x+2} = \frac{5}{6}$$

Multiply both sides by $6(x-2)(x+2)$.
Then

$$24(x+2) + 24(x-2) = 5(x-2)(x+2)$$
$$\therefore 24x + 48 + 24x - 48 = 5x^2 - 20$$
$$\therefore 5x^2 - 48x - 20 = 0$$
$$\therefore (x - 10)(5x + 2) = 0$$
$$\therefore x = 10 \quad \text{or} \quad -\tfrac{2}{5}.$$

But $-\frac{2}{5}$ is unsuitable,

$$\therefore \text{ speed in still water} = 10 \text{ km h}^{-1}.$$

Check

4 km upstream at 8 km h^{-1} takes $\frac{1}{2}$ h $= 30$ min
4 km downstream at 12 km h^{-1} takes $\frac{1}{3}$ h $= 20$ min

Total time $= 50$ min.

New General Mathematics

Exercise 13g

1 A shopkeeper bought a certain number of clocks (all alike) for £60. The price then rose by £1 per clock, and three fewer clocks could be bought for the same money. What was the original price of each clock?

2 One day a postman had parcels with a total mass of 11 kg in his bag. On the next day his parcels again had a mass of 11 kg, but the number of parcels was one less, and their average mass $\frac{1}{10}$ kg more. How many parcels did he have on the first day?

3 Two kinds of ball-point pen are for sale, at prices which differ by a penny each. For 60p I can have two more of the cheaper kind than of the dearer. How many of the dearer kind can I buy?

4 A man travelled to a place 180 km away, and when he returned he took an hour longer than he did to go. Find his average speed on the outward journey, if it was 6 km h⁻¹ greater than on the return journey.

5 A vessel made a voyage of 120 kilometres. If its speed had been 1 km h⁻¹ greater, the voyage would have taken $\frac{1}{2}$ h less than it actually did. Find the vessel's speed.

6 A steamer travels 30 km upstream from **A** to **B**, and then back again, the stream running at 5 km h⁻¹. If the whole journey takes 8 hours, how fast would the steamer travel in still water?

7 A total of 120p is spent on cups. If the cost had been a penny more for each cup, there would have been 4 fewer of them. How many cups were bought?

8 A fisherman caught 20 kg of fish on Monday, and 20 kg again on Tuesday. On Tuesday there were four fish more than on Monday, but their average mass was $\frac{1}{4}$ kg less. How many fish did he catch on Monday?

9 A man paid £4·20 for some boxes of stationery. If each box had cost a penny less he could have had an extra two boxes for his £4·20. Find the price that he paid per box.

10 A man bought some copies of a magazine at a total cost of

£4·20. If they had cost a penny less per copy he could have bought an extra two copies for the same money. How many copies did he buy?

11 A farmer paid £200 for some sheep. Two died, but by selling each sheep for £1 more than he paid for it he made a profit on the whole of £40. What was the selling price of one sheep?

12 After a certain number of innings, a batsman has scored 240 runs. In his next two innings he scores 2 out and 5 not out, and his average drops by 1 run per innings. What is his new average?

13 A cyclist is due to reach his destination 30 kilometres away at a certain time. His start is delayed for 30 minutes, but he reaches his destination on time by riding 2 km h⁻¹ faster than he had intended. Find how long he actually takes.

14 A cyclist arranged to be at a place 27½ kilometres away at a certain time. He started 15 minutes later than he had intended, but by riding 1 km h⁻¹ faster than he had planned he reached his destination on time. At what speed did he ride?

15 An outfitter bought a number of jackets (all alike) for £154. He kept one for himself and one for his son, and sold the rest for £180, making a profit of £4 on each one. What did he pay for each jacket?

16 A river steamer goes to a place 6 kilometres downstream, and returns. If the speed of the current is 3 km h⁻¹ and the total travelling time is 1½ h, what would be the speed of the steamer in still water?

17 After a certain number of matches a bowler has had 200 runs knocked off him. In the next match he takes 2 wickets for 42 runs, and increases his average (runs per wicket) by 1. How many wickets has he now taken?

18 A motorist had timed his journey so as to arrive at a place 60 km away at noon, but owing to flooded roads he had to make a detour which increased the length of his journey by 12 km. However, by increasing his average speed by 10 km h⁻¹

G   187 he managed to reach his destination on time. At what time did he start?

19 A river steamer travels 20 km upstream and 20 km back again in 4 h 10 min. If the speed of the current is 2 km h⁻¹, what would be the speed of the steamer in still water?

20 A Christmas charity fund of £9 was to be divided among the deserving poor of a small parish. Immediately before the distribution it was discovered that two of the poor were not deserving at all, and consequently the others got 5p each more than they had expected. How many deserving poor were there?

21 A trader bought a number of baskets for £5. He sold all but 5 of them at a profit of 15p each, and these 5 (which were slightly damaged) at a loss of 5p each. Altogether he made a profit of £2. How many baskets did he buy?

22 On a river which runs at 3 km h⁻¹ a launch travels upstream to a certain place and then returns, the total travelling time being 2 h, and the total distance $22\frac{1}{2}$ km. Find what the speed of the launch would be in still water.

23 A number of pieces of rug wool of equal length are cut from a total length of 2 m. If each piece had been 2 cm longer, there would have been 5 fewer pieces. Find the length of each piece cut.

24 A manufacturer ordered a number of small castings from a foundry, the bill being £4. Five of the castings proved to be defective, but by selling the rest at a profit of 5p each he made a profit of £1·25 on his outlay. Find the selling price of a casting.

25 A trader bought a certain number of melons for £5·25. He kept six of them, and received £5·25 for the remainder by selling them at 10p each more than he had given for them. How many melons did he buy?

26 A certain number of people living together in a hostel decide to buy a television set between them, the cost of the set being £90. Before the set is bought three of the people move away, and the remainder have to pay £1·50 each more than they would have done. How many people were there originally living in the hostel?

27 A greengrocer bought a box of oranges for £2·40. Twenty of them were bad, but by selling the rest at a profit of 1p each he made 60p profit. How many oranges were there in the box at first?

28 A batsman had scored 340 runs after a certain number of innings. In his next two innings he made 6 (out) each time, and his average dropped by 1. What was his final average?

29 A confectioner reckoned to make £30 worth of cakes for Christmas. At the last minute another customer wanted a cake, and the confectioner found that by making the cakes smaller and charging 5p less for them, he could just make the number wanted and receive the same total payment. How many cakes were finally ordered?

30 A man intended to spend £18 in laying in a supply of his usual kind of tobacco. It was out of stock, and he was offered two other kinds, one costing 5p more and the other 5p less per tin than his usual kind. At the lower price he could have had 9 tins more than at the higher price. Find the price per tin of his usual kind.

Chapter 14

Locus

The simple idea of a **locus** (plural—**loci**) is that it is the path traced out by a point which moves so that it always obeys a certain law.

For example if a pencil point moves in a plane so that it is always at a constant distance from a fixed point in the plane, then the path that it traces out is a circle with the fixed point as centre. It is from this method of drawing a circle that the definition of a a circle is obtained.

Definition. A circle is the locus of a point which moves in a plane so that it is always at a constant distance from a fixed point.

However, it is not strictly correct to say that a locus is the *path traced out by a moving point*, as a point merely defines a certain position. A point has no size, and cannot really be said to move. In addition, a locus need not necessarily be a continuous line, curved or straight, but may consist of a number of disconnected parts. Hence, instead of describing it as the 'path traced out by a moving point', it is preferable to use a definition such as this:

Definition. A locus is the set of all the positions occupied by a point which varies its position according to a given law.

It should also be noticed that two conditions must be satisfied if the locus is to be complete:

(i) Every point on the locus must obey the given law.

(ii) Every point which obeys the given law must lie on the locus.

For example, in Fig. 86, $\overline{AB}$ is a line which is continued in-

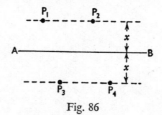

Fig. 86

definitely in both directions, and a point is such that it is always at a distance of x units from $\overline{AB}$. If the point is anywhere on the dotted line $\overline{P_1P_2}$ it is on the locus, since its distance from $\overline{AB}$ is always x units. But this is clearly not the complete locus, as any point on $\overline{P_3P_4}$ also obeys the law. Hence the complete locus consists of two straight lines parallel to, and on opposite sides of the line $\overline{AB}$, and at a distance of x units from it.

In Fig. 87 a loose length of thread has its ends attached to pins fixed at A and B. The thread is pulled taut by a pencil point which

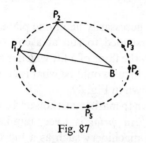

Fig. 87

is then moved round so that it describes the locus shown by the dotted line $P_1P_2P_3$ . . ., the thread being kept taut all the time. When the pencil point reaches the position P_4, in line with B and A, the thread must be lifted over the pin at B before the locus is continued. The curve so obtained is called an **ellipse**. Any point on it is such that the sum of its distances from the fixed points A and B is constant.

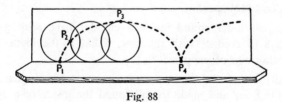

Fig. 88

Fig. 88 illustrates a locus which may be drawn with the aid of a simple working model.

New General Mathematics

A wheel is cut out of cardboard or thin wood and allowed to roll along a table, against a sheet of paper which is suitably supported. A point P is marked on the rim of the wheel, and successive positions of P are marked on the paper, starting at P_1. In this way the locus shown by the dotted line $P_1P_2P_3$ . . . is obtained. P returns to the table at P_4, where the distance P_1P_4, measured along the table, is equal to the circumference of the wheel.

As a matter of interest, the locus shown by the dotted line is called a **cycloid**, although this name is not important at the present stage.

A locus need not necessarily lie in one plane. For example, if a mouse could be persuaded to run at a constant speed round a circle marked out on the floor of a lift which is rising at a constant speed, its locus would be what is commonly called a spiral as shown in Fig. 89.

This curve is known to mathematicians and engineers as a **helix**, and a *helical spring* is a very familiar component of everyday machinery such as a bicycle or a car.

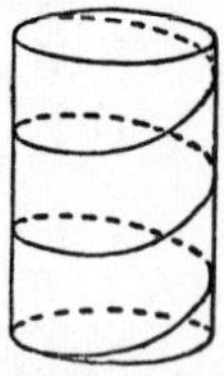

Fig. 89

Exercise 14a

1 Find the path traced out by the latch of a gate which swings on its hinges through 180°.

2 Find the locus of a small ball which rolls at a constant speed in a straight groove across the floor of a lift which is descending at a constant speed.

3 A pencil slides round inside a circular ring, with its ends always in contact with the ring. What is the locus of the middle point of the pencil?

4 Find the locus of the centre of a penny which is placed flat on the floor and made to roll round the inside of a circular ring which is also flat on the floor.

5 A thread equal in length to the perimeter of a square peg is wound round the peg, with one end attached to a corner of

192

the peg and the free end brought round to the same corner. Find the locus of the free end if it is now moved away, with the thread always taut, until the thread first becomes straight.

6 P may be anywhere on a straight line $\overline{AB}$, and Q is a fixed point 3 centimetres away from $\overline{AB}$. Find the locus of the mid-point of $\overline{PQ}$.

7 A pole stands vertically on horizontal ground, and a taut wire stretches from the top of the pole to a point on the ground some distance from the foot of the pole. Find the locus of the lower end of the wire.

8 A set-square lies flat on the table. It is then rotated about its hypotenuse until it is flat on the table again. What is the path traced out by its right-angled corner?

9 A goat is tethered by a chain $3\frac{1}{2}$ m long attached to its collar. At the other end of the chain is a ring which can slide along a straight wire fixed to pegs 10 m apart driven into the ground. Draw the locus of the goat's collar as the goat moves about, keeping as far as possible from the wire. Calculate the length of the locus. (Take π to be $\frac{22}{7}$.)

10 A, B are fixed points, and P is a variable point such that $A\hat{P}B = 30°$. Use a 30° set-square to plot a number of positions of P, and hence draw its locus.

11 Draw a circle of radius 4 cm, and mark a fixed point A on its circumference. If P is a variable point on the circumference and Q is the mid-point of $\overline{AP}$, plot a number of positions of Q and hence find its locus.

12 A bicycle wheel rolls across a flat road, over a kerb, and then across a flat pavement. Sketch the locus of the centre of the wheel.

13 A straight-edge consists of a piece of wood 30 cm long, its cross-section being an equilateral triangle of side 3 cm. The straight-edge is rolled along a drawing-board, with its length always in contact with the board. Sketch the locus of a point on one of its long edges.

14 A block of wood 30 cm long, 8 cm wide and 3 cm thick is rolled along a horizontal bench, with its length always in contact with the bench. Sketch the locus of the middle point of one of its 3-cm edges.

15 Find the locus of the centre of a variable circle which is drawn through two fixed points.

16 Find the locus of the centre of a variable circle which is drawn to touch two fixed intersecting lines.

17 A, B are fixed points, and P is a variable point such that the area of △APB is constant. Find the locus of P.

18 Draw two straight lines $\overline{AB}$, $\overline{AC}$ intersecting at an angle of 70°. Find the locus of a point which is such that its distance from $\overline{AB}$ is 1 cm more than its distance from $\overline{AC}$.

19 Draw a circle and mark a fixed point X on its circumference. Let Q be a variable point on the circumference, and produce $\overline{XQ}$ to P so that $\overline{PQ}$ is equal to the diameter of the circle. Plot a number of positions of P, and hence draw its locus.

20 C is a fixed point at a distance of 5 cm from a fixed straight line $\overline{AB}$. A point P is such that its perpendicular distance from $\overline{AB}$ is equal to PC. Plot a number of positions of P, and hence draw its locus. (*The curve thus obtained is called a* **parabola**, *and* C *is its* **focus**. *A parabolic reflector with a source of light concentrated at its focus gives a parallel beam.*)

21 A, B are two fixed points, and P is a point which is such that its distance from A is twice its distance from B. Plot the locus of P.

22 A cricket stump stands vertically against a wall with its lower end on the floor. The stump then slides so that its upper end describes a vertical straight line down the wall, and the lower end moves across the floor in a straight line at right-angles to the wall. Plot a number of positions of the middle point of the stump, and hence draw its locus.

23 In Fig. 90 a perambulator wheel of radius 14 cm starts with its centre in the position A, and rolls up two steps until its centre reaches the position B. Sketch the locus of the centre of the wheel. Calculate the length of the locus, taking π to be $\frac{22}{7}$.

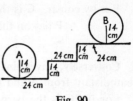

Fig. 90

Theorem 12

The locus of a point which is equidistant from two given fixed points is the perpendicular bisector of the straight line joining them.

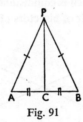

Fig. 91

Given two fixed points A, B, and P any point such that AP = BP.

To prove that P lies on the perpendicular bisector of $\overline{AB}$.

Construction Bisect $\overline{AB}$ at C, and join $\overline{PC}$.

Proof In △s APC, BPC

$$AP = BP \qquad \textit{given}$$
$$AC = BC \qquad \textit{constr.}$$
$$PC \text{ is common}$$

$\therefore \ \triangle APC \equiv \triangle BPC \qquad SSS$

$\triangle BPC$ is the reflection of $\triangle APC$ in $\overline{PC}$

$\therefore \ A\hat{C}P = B\hat{C}P.$

But these are adjacent angles,

$\therefore$ each is a right angle.

$\therefore \ \overline{PC} \perp \overline{AB}$

195

But by constr., C is the mid-pt. of $\overline{AB}$.

∴ P lies on the perpendicular bisector of $\overline{AB}$.

Q.E.D.

Conversely, any point on the perpendicular bisector of $\overline{AB}$ is equidistant from A and B.

For if $\overline{PC}$ is the perpendicular bisector of $\overline{AB}$, the △s APC, BPC may be proved congruent. (*SAS, or by reflection.*)

Hence   AP = BP

Theorem 13

The locus of a point which is equidistant from two given intersecting straight lines is the pair of bisectors of the angles between them.

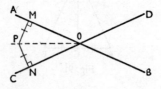

Fig. 92

Given two straight lines $\overline{AB}$, $\overline{CD}$ intersecting at O. P is a point such that its perpendicular distances PM, PN from $\overline{AB}$, $\overline{CD}$ are equal.

To prove that P lies on the bisector of one of the angles between $\overline{AB}$ and $\overline{CD}$.

Construction Join $\overline{OP}$.

Proof Suppose P lies within $A\hat{O}C$.

Then in △s POM, PON

$$P\hat{M}O = P\hat{N}O \qquad rt. \angle s$$

PO is common

$$PM = PN \qquad given$$

∴ △POM ≡ △PON   *RHS*

△PON is the reflection of △POM in $\overline{PO}$

∴ PÔM = PÔN

∴ P lies on the bisector of AÔC.

Similarly if P lies within any of the angles COB, BOD, DOA, it lies on the bisector of that angle.

Q.E.D.

Conversely, any point on either bisector of the angles between the lines $\overline{AOB}$, $\overline{COD}$ is equidistant from these lines.

For if $\overline{PO}$ bisects AÔC, and if $\overline{PM}$, $\overline{PN}$ are the perpendiculars from P to $\overline{AO}$, $\overline{CO}$, then the △s POM, PON may be proved congruent. (*AAS, or by reflection.*)

Hence   PM = PN.

Sometimes it is necessary to construct the position of a point as the intersection of loci, as in Construction 8, which follows.

Construction 8

To construct the circle passing through the vertices of a given triangle.

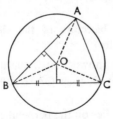

Fig. 93

Given any triangle ABC.

To construct the circle passing through A, B and C.

Construction Draw the perpendicular bisectors of $\overline{AB}$ and $\overline{BC}$, and let them meet at O.

Then the circle with centre O and radius OA is the required circle.

Proof O lies on the perpendicular bisector of $\overline{AB}$

$$\therefore \ OA = OB$$

Similarly $\quad OB = OC$

$$\therefore \ OA = OB = OC$$

$\therefore$ a circle with centre O and radius OA passes through A, B and C.

$$Q.E.F.$$

The circle is called the **circumcircle** of the triangle.

O is called the **circumcentre** of the triangle, and OA is the **circumradius**.

N.B. A circle can always be drawn through three given points which are not **collinear** (i.e. do not lie in the same straight line), and there is only one such circle.

Concurrency

Three or more lines are said to be **concurrent** if they all pass through the same point.

Three important examples of concurrency in connection with a triangle can now be stated.

(i) The perpendicular bisectors of the sides of a triangle are concurrent. (circumcentre)

It has already been shown that if the perpendicular bisectors of $\overline{AB}$ and $\overline{BC}$ meet at O, then $OA = OB = OC$ (Construction 8).

Since $OA = OC$, O lies on the perpendicular bisector of $\overline{AC}$.

$\therefore$ the perpendicular bisectors of the sides of a triangle are concurrent (at the circumcentre).

(ii) The altitudes of a triangle are concurrent. (orthocentre)

Let the altitudes of $\triangle ABC$ be $\overline{AD}$, $\overline{BE}$, $\overline{CF}$.

Through A, B, C draw lines parallel to $\overline{BC}$, $\overline{CA}$, $\overline{AB}$ respectively to make $\triangle PQR$.

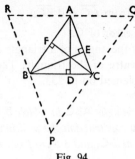

Fig. 94

Then since, by construction, RACB is a ‖gm,

$$RA = BC \qquad opp. \; sides$$

Similarly $\qquad AQ = BC$

$$\therefore \; RA = AQ.$$

But $\overline{AD} \perp \overline{RQ}$ since $\overline{RQ} \parallel \overline{BC}$ and $\overline{AD} \perp \overline{BC}$.

$$\therefore \; \overline{AD} \text{ is the perp. bisector of } \overline{RQ}.$$

Similarly, $\overline{BE}$, $\overline{CF}$ are the perp. bisectors of $\overline{PR}$, $\overline{PQ}$.
But the perp. bisectors of the sides of $\triangle PQR$ are concurrent.

$$\therefore \; \overline{AD}, \overline{BE}, \overline{CF} \text{ are concurrent.}$$

The point at which the three altitudes meet is called the **ortho-centre** of the triangle.

(iii) **The bisectors of the angles of a triangle are concurrent. (incentre)**

In $\triangle ABC$, let the bisectors of $\angle$s A, B meet at I.

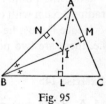

Draw $\overline{IL}$, $\overline{IM}$, $\overline{IN}$ perp. to $\overline{BC}$, $\overline{CA}$, $\overline{AB}$ respectively.

Then since I lies on the bisector of $\widehat{A}$, I is equidistant from $\overline{AB}$ and $\overline{AC}$.

Fig. 95

$$\therefore \; IN = IM$$

Similarly $\qquad IN = IL$

$$\therefore \; IM = IL.$$

∴ I is equidistant from $\overline{AC}$ and $\overline{BC}$.

∴ I lies on the bisector of $\hat{C}$.

∴ the bisectors of the angles of a triangle are concurrent.

I is called the **incentre** of the triangle. The properties of this point are further explained on p. 333.

Example *Given a triangle* ABC *in which* $\hat{B} = 70°$, AB = 5 *cm*, BC = 7·5 *cm, find by construction the positions of a point* P *which is equidistant from* B *and* C, *and* 3·5 *cm from* A.

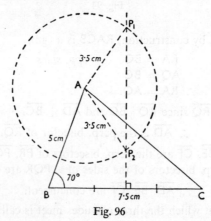

Fig. 96

Since the point P is equidistant from B and C, it must lie on the perpendicular bisector of $\overline{BC}$.

Since the point P is 3·5 cm from A, it must lie on a circle of radius 3·5 cm with centre A.

Hence P must lie at the points of intersection of these two loci, i.e. there are two possible positions for P, at P_1 and P_2.

Exercise 14b

1 A, B are two points which are 7 cm apart. Construct the position of a point P which is 4·2 cm from A, and 5·6 cm from B. How many possible positions for P are there? Measure the distance between them.

2 $\overline{AB}$, $\overline{CD}$ are two intersecting straight lines. Show how to construct the position of a point P which is 2 cm from $\overline{AB}$ and 3 cm from $\overline{CD}$. How many possible positions for P are there?

3 Given a $\triangle XYZ$, show how to construct a point P in $\overline{YZ}$ such that P is equidistant from $\overline{XY}$ and $\overline{XZ}$.

4 $\triangle ABC$ is isosceles, having $AB = AC = 6$ cm and $BC = 4$ cm. Construct points each of which is equidistant from B and C, and 3 cm from A. Measure their distances from $\overline{BC}$.

5 $\triangle ABC$ has a rt. $\angle$ at C, and $AC = BC = 4$ cm. Construct points each of which is equidistant from B and C, and 3 cm from A. Measure their distances from $\overline{BC}$.

6 An aircraft flies at a height of 1 000 m on a straight, level course, which passes directly over two points A and B which are 1 500 m apart on the horizontal ground. On a scale drawing construct two positions of the aircraft when its angle of elevation from A is 50°, and in each case measure its angle of elevation from B.

7 A is a fixed point 3 cm from a fixed straight line $\overline{BC}$. Construct points which are 1 cm from $\overline{BC}$ and 3·5 cm from A, and measure the distance between them.

8 O is a fixed point on a given straight line $\overline{AB}$. P is a point which is 4 cm from $\overline{AB}$ and 5 cm from O. Construct two positions of P on the same side of $\overline{AB}$, and measure the distance between them.

9 The lengths of the sides of a triangle are 8 cm, 7 cm, 5 cm. Construct the circumcircle and measure its radius.

10 In $\triangle ABC$, $AB = 10$ cm, $BC = 9$ cm, $CA = 11$ cm. Draw the three altitudes and measure the distance of the orthocentre from A.

11 Draw a $\triangle ABC$, and show how to construct the position of a point which is equidistant from $\overline{AC}$ and $\overline{BC}$, and also equidistant from A and B. How many possible positions of the point are there?

New General Mathematics

12 A buoy is moored 20 m from a straight river bank, and 29 m from a post on the edge of the bank. On a scale drawing construct two possible positions of the buoy, and measure the distance between them.

13 Draw $\triangle ABC$ in which $AB = 5.2$ cm, $BC = 9.2$ cm, $CA = 8$ cm. Show how to construct the possible positions of a point which is equidistant from $\overline{AB}$ and $\overline{AC}$, and 3.2 cm from $\overline{BC}$.

14 Draw two straight lines $\overline{AOB}$, $\overline{COD}$ intersecting at O. On $\overline{OA}$ mark a point Q such that $OQ = 2.5$ cm. Construct all the possible positions of a point which is equidistant from $\overline{AB}$ and $\overline{CD}$, and 4 cm from Q.

15 $\overline{AOB}$, $\overline{COD}$ are two straight lines which intersect at O. E is a given point on $\overline{OD}$. Show how to construct the positions of a point which is equidistant from the given straight lines, and also equidistant from O and E.

16 Show how to construct a quadrilateral PQRS in which $\hat{Q} = 90°$, $\hat{R} = 110°$, $QR = 4$ cm, $RS = 5$ cm, and $PQ = PS$.

17 A, B are two fixed points 6 cm apart, and a circle is drawn with centre B and radius 2 cm. Construct the positions of points which are equidistant from A and B, and 3 cm from the circumference of the circle. Measure the distance between them.

18 Two fixed points A and B are 7.5 cm apart. A circle is drawn with centre A and radius 2 cm, and another circle with centre B and radius 3.5 cm. Construct the points which are 2.5 cm away from the circumferences of both circles, and measure the distance between them.

19 Draw $\triangle ABC$ having $AB = 6$ cm, $BC = 9$ cm, $CA = 5$ cm. Construct a point P, equidistant from A and C, such that the area of $\triangle APB$ is 12 cm².

20 Draw $\triangle ABC$ having $\hat{A} = 75°$, $AB = 8$ cm, $AC = 7$ cm. Construct two positions of a point P, equidistant from $\overline{AC}$ and $\overline{BC}$, such that the area of $\triangle APB$ is 15.2 cm².

21 ABC is an acute-angled triangle, and H is its orthocentre. Prove that BÂC and BĤC are supplementary.

22 H is the orthocentre of △ABC, which is obtuse-angled at C. Prove that BÂC = BĤC.

23 A quadrilateral is divided by its diagonals into four triangles. Prove that the circumcentres of these triangles are the corners of a parallelogram.

24 The diagonals of a quadrilateral ABCD intersect at O. Prove that the incentres of △s AOB, BOC, COD, DOA are the corners of a quadrilateral whose diagonals intersect at right angles.

25 A parallelogram is divided by its diagonals into four triangles. Prove that the incentres of these triangles are the corners of a rhombus.

Revision examples

XI

1 (i) Multiply $n^2 - 5n - 3$ by $3n + 1$.

(ii) Divide $3m^3 - 11m^2 + 4$ by $3m - 2$.

2 Use logarithms to find the value of

(i) $0.037\,52 \div 0.692\,1$ (ii) $\sqrt[3]{0.065}$

3 Find the simple interest on £161·82 for 18 years at 5% (nearest penny).

4 Simplify   (i) $\dfrac{2b}{a^2 - b^2} + \dfrac{a}{b^2 - ab}$

(ii) $\dfrac{2a}{a^2 - b^2} + \dfrac{b}{b^2 - ab}$

5 The radius of a circle is 5·3 cm, and a chord is 2·8 cm from the centre. Calculate the length of the chord.

6 Find, correct to 2 decimal places, the square root of 12·315 7.

7 German silver contains 52% copper, 22% nickel, and the rest is zinc. Brass contains 67% copper, and the rest is zinc. If 10 kg of German silver and 20 kg of brass are melted together, what percentage of the mixture is zinc?

8 Two equal circles with centres O, Q intersect at A, B. When $\overline{OA}$ and $\overline{OQ}$ are produced they meet the circle with centre Q at C, D respectively. Prove that $C\hat{Q}D = 3\,A\hat{O}Q$.

9 A kite framework is of the shape given in Fig. 97, and AB = BC = 30 cm, BD = 75 cm. Calculate (i) $A\hat{D}C$, (ii) AC correct to the nearest cm.

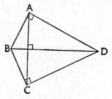

Fig. 97

10 A certain number of pencils are bought for £1·80. If each pencil had cost ½p less, an extra 18 could have been bought. Find the price paid per pencil.

XII

1 Factorise   (i) $24a^2 - 150b^2$ (ii) $6mx - 12ny - 9nx + 8my$
      (iii) $a^2 + 2ab + b^2 - c^2$

2 Use logarithms to find the value of
   (i) $0.072\,6 \div 0.293\,4$ (ii) $\sqrt[3]{0.8}$

3 Enough concrete is mixed to make a slab 84 cm square and $7\frac{1}{2}$ cm thick. It is laid in the form of a rectangular slab 105 cm long and 48 cm wide. Find its thickness.

4 Simplify $\dfrac{3}{2x - 4} + \dfrac{2}{6 - 3x}$.

5 Prove that equal chords of a circle subtend equal angles at the centre.

6 Solve $\dfrac{a - 4}{a^2 + 3a + 2} - \dfrac{2}{a + 2} = \dfrac{3}{a + 1}$.

7 22% of a man's income was taken by taxation and he had £936 left. What was his gross income?

8 Solve the equations   (i) $6x^2 + x - 15 = 0$
                    (ii) $4x^2 = 9x + 1$ (2 dec. pl.)

9 ABC is an equilateral $\triangle$ of side 5 cm, and D is a point on the median $\overline{\text{BM}}$ such that $\hat{\text{BAD}} = 25°$. Calculate AD and BD.

10 After a certain number of innings (never 'not out') a batsman had scored 120 runs. In the next innings he made 24 runs 'out', and so improved his average by 1. What was his final average?

XIII

1 (i) Multiply $2b^2 + 7b - 3$ by $2b - 5$.
(ii) Divide $3a^3 - 8a^2 + 13a - 6$ by $3a - 2$.

2 Use logarithms to calculate the area of a circle with diameter 1·7 cm, taking π to be 3·142.

New General Mathematics

3 Arthur can run 100 m in 12·5 s; Bill in 11·5 s. By how many metres does Bill beat Arthur in a 100-m race?

4 Simplify $\dfrac{1}{a+1} + \dfrac{2}{(a+1)^2} + \dfrac{3}{(a+1)^3}$.

5 A chord 40 cm long is 15 cm from the centre of the circle. Calculate the length of a chord which is 7 cm from the centre.

6 Solve $\dfrac{3}{2b+5} = \dfrac{2}{b+2}$.

7 Construct a flow-diagram to show how to find the square root of a number greater than one, using logarithms.

8 ABC is an isosceles triangle in which $AC = BC$, and $\overline{BC}$ is produced to Q so that $CQ = BC$. Prove that $\overline{AB}$ is perpendicular to $\overline{AQ}$.

9 A mine is anchored to the sea-bed 20 m below the surface by a chain 16 m long. When the tide is running the chain is inclined at 20° to the vertical. What is then the depth of the mine below the surface?

10 A man born in the 19th century was x years old in the year x^2. How old was he in 1875?

XIV

1 Factorise (i) $4a^2 - 2bc + a(c - 8b)$ (ii) $12x^2 + 7xy - 10y^2$
(iii) $x^2 - a^2 - 4am - 4m^2$

2 Use logarithms to find the value of
(i) $0.610\,2^3$ (ii) $\sqrt[3]{0.222\,2}$

3 Two circular lawns have diameters of 21 m and 20 m respectively. The turf is removed from these lawns and used to surface a single circular lawn. Find its diameter.

4 Simplify $\dfrac{a^2 + ab}{ab - b^2} - \dfrac{a^2 + 2ab + b^2}{a^2 - b^2}$.

5 In a circle with centre O, $\overline{AB}$ is a chord such that the radii $\overline{OA}$, $\overline{OB}$ are at right angles to each other. Prove that the square on $\overline{AB}$ is equal to half the square on the diameter.

6 Solve $\dfrac{1}{2-m} + \dfrac{3m}{m^2-4} = 0$.

7 A two-digit number 'xy' in the scale of 7 is equal to the denary number 'yx'. Form an equation connecting x and y. Show that there are two possible answers.

8 Solve the equations
$$\text{(i) } 10x^2 + 13x - 2 = 0$$
$$\text{(ii) } (x^2 + 6x + 15)^2 - (x^2 + 4x - 3)^2 = 0$$

9 What is the radius of the circle in which a chord of length 8 cm subtends an angle of 56° at the centre?

10 After a certain number of matches a bowler has had 400 runs knocked off him. In the next match he takes 3 wickets for 37 runs, and improves his average by 1. What is his new average?

XV

1 (i) Multiply $3c^2 - 4cd + 5d^2$ by $c + d$.
(ii) Divide $3x^3 + 14x^2 - 11x - 2$ by $3x - 1$.

2 Use logarithms to find the value of
(i) $0{\cdot}488\,2^3$ (ii) $\sqrt[3]{3\,176 \times 0{\cdot}088\,8}$

3 A floor measuring 6·5 m by 4 m is covered with carpet in strips 75 cm wide, laid lengthwise. Find the number of metres that must be bought, and the cost at £2·75 per metre.

4 Simplify $\dfrac{2}{m+2n} - \dfrac{m-6n}{m^2-4n^2}$.

5 A chord of length 4 cm is 3 cm from the centre of a circle. If another chord is 5 cm long, find, correct to 3 sig. fig., its distance from the centre.

6 Solve $\dfrac{1}{3-a} - \dfrac{1}{3} + \dfrac{4}{2a-5} = 0$.

7 Simplify $\dfrac{2\frac{4}{5} \times 1\frac{1}{7}}{3\frac{1}{9}} \div 3\frac{3}{5}$.

8 $\triangle$ ABC is right-angled at B. Squares ABLM, ACXY are drawn, lying outside $\triangle$ ABC. Prove that $\overline{BY} \perp \overline{CM}$.

9 A tall straight tree is leaning over at an angle of $12\frac{1}{4}°$ to the vertical, and its top is then projecting 3 m horizontally away from its base. If the tree falls, by what distance will it miss a house whose nearest point is 16 m from the base of the tree?

10 The residents in a boarding-house agreed to club together to buy a television set costing £96, but before it was bought three of the residents moved away, and those left had to pay an extra £1·60 each. How many of them were there originally?

XVI

1 Factorise (i) $3x^2 - 27y^4$ (ii) $9x^2 - 41xy - 20y^2$
(iii) $(u + 2v)^2 + 2(u + 2v) - 8$

2 Use logarithms to find the value of

(i) $\left(\dfrac{5·342}{8·966}\right)^2$ (ii) $\sqrt[4]{\dfrac{78·67}{317·2}}$

Fig. 98

3 A circular section of a tunnel is shown in Fig. 98, the height of the opening being 4 m and the chord of the circle also 4 m. Find the diameter of the tunnel.

4 Simplify $\dfrac{2}{a + 2} + \dfrac{1}{a + 1} - \dfrac{2a + 3}{a^2 + 3a + 2}$.

5 Show how to construct a circle with radius 6 cm, given a chord of length 9 cm.

6 Solve $\dfrac{b + 1}{2b - 3} = 2 - \dfrac{b + 3}{2b + 3}$.

7 Simplify $\dfrac{2}{3} \times \dfrac{4\frac{2}{3} \times \frac{5}{6}}{1\frac{1}{9} + 2\frac{7}{9}}$.

8 Solve the equations
(i) $5x^2 + 9x + 2 = 0$
(ii) $(x^2 + 3x - 4)^2 - (x^2 - 5x - 8)^2 = 0$

9 Calculate the radius of the circumcircle of a regular pentagon of side 6 cm.

10 A batsman's runs, just before the last match of the season, amount to 750. In his last two innings he scores only 6 runs, and his average drops by 2. Find his final average for the season.

XVII

1 (i) Multiply $4h^2 + 3hk + 2k^2$ by $h - k$.
(ii) Divide $4u^3 - 4u^2 - 21u - 4$ by $2u + 3$.

2 Use logarithms to find the value of

(i) $0.396\,4^3$ (ii) $\sqrt{\dfrac{27.49}{4.35 \times 9.73}}$

3 A rectangular box without a lid is 11 cm long, 7 cm wide and 9 cm high externally. If it is made of wood which is 5 mm thick, find the volume of the wood.

4 Simplify $\dfrac{2d}{d + 1} + \dfrac{2}{d^2 - 1} - \dfrac{1}{d - 1}$.

5 A chord of a circle is 4·8 cm long, and cuts a diameter at right angles. If the longer of the two parts into which the diameter is divided is 3·2 cm long, calculate the radius of the circle.

6 Solve $\dfrac{m + 3}{m^2 - 3m + 2} + \dfrac{7m + 5}{m^2 + m - 2} = 0$.

7 Find the square root of 2 945·232 9.

8 $\triangle$ABC is right-angled at A, and $\overline{\text{AD}}$ is an altitude. Prove that

$$\text{BC} = \frac{\text{AB} \times \text{AC}}{\text{AD}}.$$

9 Find the length of wire required to make an isosceles triangular framework of the dimensions given in Fig. 99.

Fig. 99

10 A cyclist has a choice of two routes for a short journey, one of 24 km and the other of 20 km. He can travel 4 km h^{-1} faster if he chooses the longer route, and this is 3 minutes shorter than the other. How long does this route take him?

XVIII

1 Factorise (i) $(x + 3y)^2 - 2(x + 3y) - 3$ (ii) $x^4 - 16$
(iii) $16 - c^2 + 6cd - 9d^2$

2 Use logarithms to find the value of

(i) $\left(\dfrac{28 \cdot 6}{39 \cdot 7}\right)^2$ (ii) $\sqrt[3]{0 \cdot 062\ 3}$

3 At what rate per cent does the simple interest on £42·80 amount to £6·42 in 6 years?

4 Simplify $\dfrac{5}{c^2 - 16} + \dfrac{2}{(c + 4)^2}$.

5 $\overline{AB}$ is the common chord of two intersecting circles, and $\overline{CD}$ is a chord of one of the circles. If $\overline{AB}$ is parallel to $\overline{CD}$, prove that the line joining the centres of the circles bisects $\overline{CD}$ at right angles.

6 Solve $\dfrac{1}{n + 2} = \dfrac{5}{n - 1} - \dfrac{2}{n + 1}$.

7 Simplify $\tfrac{7}{8}$ of $\dfrac{4\frac{4}{5}}{5\frac{3}{5} \times \frac{9}{34}}$.

8 If $h = \dfrac{m + 1}{m - 1}$, express $\dfrac{2h - 1}{2h + 1}$ in terms of m.

9 In Fig. 100, $\overline{AX}$ is the bisector of $B\hat{A}C$. Calculate AX correct to the nearest cm.

10 A wife has £3·60 to spend on cigars for her husband's birthday present. She hesitates between two brands, one costing 6p more per cigar than the other,

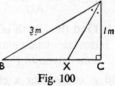

Fig. 100

but a box of the cheaper ones holds 5 more cigars than a box of the more expensive ones. If she finally decides on quality rather than quantity, how many cigars does her husband receive?

XIX

1 (i) Multiply $3u + v - 2$ by $3u - v + 2$.

(ii) Divide $15a^3 - 19a^2b + 4b^3$ by $5a + 2b$.

2 Use logarithms to find the value of

(i) $\sqrt[4]{0 \cdot 066}$ (ii) $6 \cdot 284 \times \sqrt{\dfrac{17 \cdot 6}{32 \cdot 2}}$

3 A floor 6·6 m long and 5·2 m wide is to be laid with carpet 70 cm wide, costing £2·25 per metre. If the carpet is laid lengthwise, find the total cost.

4 Simplify $\dfrac{3}{2d - n} - \dfrac{5(d + n)}{2d^2 + 3dn - 2n^2} - \dfrac{2}{d + 2n}$.

5 A chord of a circle is perpendicular to a diameter, and divides the diameter into two parts whose lengths are 4·9 cm and 2·5 cm. Calculate the length of the chord.

6 Solve $\dfrac{3}{e} - \dfrac{e}{e - 2} + 2 = 0$.

7 Find the square root of 723·518 61, correct to 2 decimal places.

8 $\overline{AB}$ is a straight line. P and Q are points on $\overline{AB}$ and $\overline{AB}$ produced such that $BP = BQ$. Prove that

$$AP^2 + AQ^2 = 2(AB^2 + BQ^2).$$

9 A cone of base diameter 6 cm and vertical angle 30° has to be packed in a rectangular box, as in Fig. 101. Calculate the inside dimensions of the smallest box that will do.

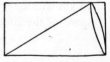

Fig. 101

10 After a certain number of matches a bowler has had 200 runs knocked off him. In the next match he takes 3 wickets for 52 runs, and his average goes up by 1. What is it now?

XX

1 Factorise   (i) $\pi R^2 - 4\pi r^2$ (ii) $15a^2 - 2ab - 24b^2$

(iii) $(2a + d)^2 - 3(2a + d)(a - d) - 4(a - d)^2$

2 Use logarithms to calculate the value of r if $\frac{4}{3}\pi r^3 = 250$, taking π to be 3·142.

3 The average age of 15 boys is 8 yr 1 mth, and of 5 others 8 yr 9 mth. Find the average age of the 20 boys.

4 Simplify $\dfrac{3}{2a^2 - 3ab - 2b^2} - \dfrac{2}{2a^2 - 5ab + 2b^2}$.

5 $\overline{AP}$, $\overline{PB}$ are chords of a circle, and $\overline{AB}$ is a diameter. Prove that $\widehat{P} = \widehat{A} + \widehat{B}$, and hence prove that $\widehat{P}$ is a right angle.

6 Solve $\dfrac{3}{c+1} = \dfrac{5}{2(c-1)} - \dfrac{1}{3}$.

7 Simplify $\dfrac{8\frac{3}{8} - 3\frac{1}{2}}{3\frac{1}{4} - 2\frac{1}{6} \text{ of } 1\frac{1}{5}}$.

8 If $a = \dfrac{2m+1}{2m-1}$, express $\dfrac{2a+1}{2a-1}$ in terms of m.

9 A mast 16 m high was originally secured by guy-wires from its top to pegs 4 m from its base on the horizontal ground. Later, more guy wires were added, attached to the same pegs and to a point in the mast such that the line of each new wire bisected the angle between the original wire and the ground. Find the lengths of (i) the original wires, (ii) the new wires.

10 A launch takes 2 h 8 min to travel 16 km upstream and 16 km back again. If the current runs at 4 km h⁻¹, what is the speed of the launch in still water?

Chapter 15

Chords of a circle

A **chord** of a circle is a straight line joining any two points on the circumference.

If $\overline{AB}$ is a chord of a circle with centre O, then OA = OB (*radii*),

i.e. O is equidistant from A and B.

∴ O lies on the perpendicular bisector of $\overline{AB}$.

Hence **the perpendicular bisector of a chord passes through the centre of the circle.**

Also **the perpendicular to a chord from the centre of the circle bisects the chord.**

Fig. 102

This statement may be proved by congruent triangles.

In Fig. 102, $\overline{OD}$ is the perp. from the centre O to the chord $\overline{AB}$.

△s ADO, BDO may be proved congruent   *RHS*

△BDO is the reflection of △ADO in $\overline{OD}$.

Hence   AD = BD.

Conversely, **the line joining the centre of a circle to the mid-point of a chord is perpendicular to the chord.**

In Fig. 103, M is the mid-point of the chord $\overline{AB}$, and O is the centre of the circle.

△s AMO, BMO are congruent   *SSS*

△BMO is the reflection of △AMO in $\overline{OM}$.

∴ $A\hat{M}O = B\hat{M}O$, and since these are adjacent supplementary angles, each is a right angle.

Fig. 103

Chords are called equal if their lengths are equal.

Equal chords are equidistant from the centre of the circle.

In Fig. 104, O is the centre of the circle. $\overline{AB}$, $\overline{CD}$ are equal chords, and $\overline{OP}$, $\overline{OQ}$ are the perpendiculars to them from O.

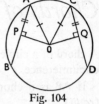

Fig. 104

Perpendiculars from the centre bisect the chords; and since the chords are equal, their halves are equal.

∴ AP = CQ

∴ △s APO, CQO may be proved congruent

RHS

△CQO is the reflection of △APO in the line through O bisecting AÔC.

$$\therefore OP = OQ.$$

Conversely, **chords which are equidistant from the centre of a circle are equal to each other.**

In Fig. 105, O is the centre of the circle. $\overline{OP}$, $\overline{OQ}$ are the perpendiculars from O to the chords $\overline{AB}$, $\overline{CD}$, and OP = OQ.

△s APO, CQO may be proved congruent

RHS

△CQO is the reflection of △APO in the line through O bisecting AÔC.

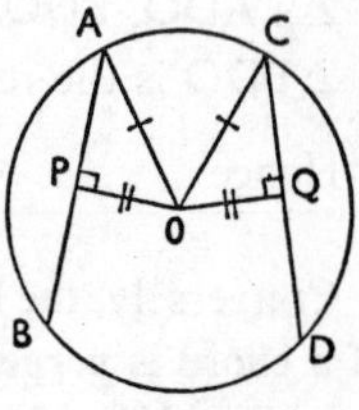

Fig. 105

∴ AP = CQ
∴ 2AP = 2CQ
i.e. AB = CD   *since the perps. bisect the chords.*

It can similarly be proved that:
(i) **Equal chords of equal circles are equidistant from the centres of the circles.**
(ii) **In equal circles, chords which are equidistant from the centres are equal to each other.**

Example *A chord 6·6 cm long is 5·6 cm from the centre of the circle. Find the radius of the circle. Find also the length of a chord which is 6·3 cm from the centre of the circle.*

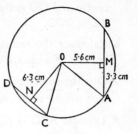

Fig. 106

In Fig. 106, $\overline{AB}$ is the chord of length 6·6 cm, and $\overline{OM}$ the perpendicular to it from the centre.

Then M is the mid-point of $\overline{AB}$, and AM = 3·3 cm.

$$\therefore \text{ in rt.-}\angle\text{d} \quad \triangle\text{AMO},$$
$$AO^2 = 5\cdot6^2 + 3\cdot3^2 = 31\cdot36 + 10\cdot89 = 42\cdot25$$
$$\therefore AO = \sqrt{42\cdot25} \text{ cm} = 6\cdot5 \text{ cm}.$$

$\overline{ON}$, of length 6·3 cm, is the perpendicular from O to the chord $\overline{CD}$, N is the mid-point of $\overline{CD}$, and OC = OA = 6·5 cm.

Then in rt.-$\angle$d $\quad \triangle$CNO,
$$CN^2 = 6\cdot5^2 - 6\cdot3^2 = 42\cdot25 - 39\cdot69 = 2\cdot56$$
$$\text{(or } CN^2 = 6\cdot5^2 - 6\cdot3^2 = (6\cdot5 + 6\cdot3)(6\cdot5 - 6\cdot3)$$
$$= 12\cdot8 \times 0\cdot2 = 2\cdot56)$$
$$\therefore CN = \sqrt{2\cdot56} \text{ cm} = 1\cdot6 \text{ cm}$$
$$\therefore CD = 2CN = 3\cdot2 \text{ cm}.$$

Exercise 15

1 A chord 4·2 cm long is 2·8 cm from the centre of a circle. Calculate the radius of the circle.

2 A chord 7 cm long is drawn in a circle of radius 3·7 cm. Calculate the distance of the chord from the centre of the circle.

3 The radius of a circle is 3·9 cm, and a chord is 1·5 cm from the centre. Calculate the length of the chord.

4 In a circle, centre C, if the chords $\overline{XY}$, $\overline{YZ}$ are equal, prove that $\overline{CY}$ bisects $X\hat{Y}Z$.

5 $\overline{XY}$ is a diameter of a circle, and $\overline{XZ}$ is a chord. If O is the

215

centre and $\overline{OD}$ is the perpendicular from O to $\overline{XZ}$, prove that
YZ = 2OD.

6 Calculate the radius of the circle which passes through the corners of a square whose sides are each 8 cm long. (3 sig. fig.)

7 O is the centre of a circle of radius 37 cm, and the length of a chord $\overline{AB}$ is 24 cm. Find the area of △OAB.

8 Triangle ABC is right-angled at B, and E is the centre of a circle passing through A and B. Prove that the line through E parallel to $\overline{BC}$ bisects $\overline{AC}$.

9 Two equal chords intersect inside a circle. Prove that the line joining their point of intersection to the centre of the circle bisects the angle between the chords.

10 Two circles with centres A, B intersect at P, Q. Prove that $\overline{AB}$ bisects $\overline{PQ}$ at right angles.

11 Two circles with centres O, Q intersect at A, B, and $\overline{AOX}$, $\overline{AQY}$ are diameters. Assuming the result of no. 10, prove that the straight line $\overline{XY}$ passes through B, and that XY = 2OQ.

12 Calculate the distance between a pair of opposite sides of a regular hexagon with sides each 6 cm long. (3 sig. fig.)

13 A chord 30 cm long is 20 cm from the centre of a circle. Calculate the length of a chord which is 24 cm from the centre.

14 In a circle of radius 2·5 cm the lengths of two parallel chords are 1·4 cm and 3 cm. Find the distance between the chords (i) if they are on opposite sides of the centre, (ii) if they are on the same side of the centre.

15 Prove that if two chords of a circle subtend equal angles at the centre, then the chords are equal.

16 In a given circle, $\overline{AB}$, $\overline{CD}$ are two equal chords which intersect at Q (inside the circle), and $\overline{QB}$, $\overline{QC}$ are the shorter of the parts into which the chords are divided. Use the result of no. 15 to prove that AC = BD.

17 Two equal circles intersect, and the length of their common

216

chord is 5·6 cm. If the centres of the circles are 9 cm apart, calculate their radii.

18 Two equal chords of a circle intersect at right angles. Prove that their point of intersection, their mid-points, and the centre of the circle are the four corners of a square.

19 Prove that if two chords drawn from a point on a circle are equally inclined to the radius from that point, then the chords are equal.

20 Calculate, in centimetres correct to 2 decimal places, the radius of the circumcircle of an isosceles triangle with sides of length 13 cm, 13 cm, 10 cm.

21 Calculate the radius of the circumcircle of an equilateral triangle with sides each 15 cm long. (3 sig. fig.)

22 A chord of length 16 cm is 5 cm from the centre of a circle. If another chord is 8 cm long, calculate its distance from the centre. (3 sig. fig.)

23 The straight lines $\overline{PQX}$, $\overline{SRX}$ are such that $\overline{PQ}$ and $\overline{SR}$ are equal chords of a circle. Prove that QX = RX.

24 Two circles with centres A, B intersect at C, D. A line through C parallel to $\overline{AB}$ meets one circle at P and the other at Q. Prove that $AB = \frac{1}{2}PQ$.

25 A straight line $\overline{AXYB}$ cuts two concentric circles in A, B and X, Y respectively. Prove that AX = BY.

26 XYZ is an isosceles triangle in which the equal sides are $\overline{XZ}$, $\overline{YZ}$. A circle with centre Z cuts $\overline{XY}$ at A, B. Prove that AX = BY.

27 The radius of a circle is 5·3 cm, and a chord of length 9 cm cuts a diameter at right angles. Find the lengths of the two parts into which the diameter is divided.

28 A chord of length c cm is drawn in a circle of radius r cm. Find the distance of the chord from the centre of the circle.

29 The centre of a circle is O, and two chords $\overline{AB}$, $\overline{CD}$ when produced meet at Q. If $\overline{OQ}$ bisects $\hat{BQD}$, prove that AB = CD.

30 $\overline{AB}$ is a chord of a circle, and lines $\overline{AM}$, $\overline{BN}$, at right angles to

217

$\overline{AB}$, meet a diameter at M, N. Prove that M, N are equidistant from the centre of the circle.

31 In a circle with centre O, equal chords $\overline{AB}$, $\overline{CD}$ intersect inside the circle at a point Q, so that O lies within $A\hat{Q}C$. Prove that $AQ = CQ$.

32 A chord of a circle is at right angles to a diameter, and divides the diameter into two parts whose lengths are 25 cm and 9 cm respectively. Calculate the length of the chord.

33 Two circles intersect at X, Y. Parallel lines $\overline{AXB}$, $\overline{CYD}$ cut the circles at A, B, C, D. Prove that $AB = CD$.

34 Given a circle and two fixed points X, Y on its circumference, show how to construct a circle passing through X and Y, and having its centre on the circumference of the given circle. How many such circles are there?

35 A hemispherical bowl is placed so that its rim is uppermost and forms a horizontal circle of diameter 74 cm. Water is poured in until its surface is a circle of diameter 70 cm. Calculate the depth of the water.

36 In no. 35, if the depth of the water is 5 cm and the radius of its surface is 9 cm, calculate the radius of the bowl.

37 Two equal circles are such that each passes through the centre of the other. Prove that the square on the common chord is three times the square on a radius.

38 O is the centre of a circle, and the radii $\overline{OX}$, $\overline{OY}$ are at right angles to each other. If $\overline{OM}$ is the perpendicular from O to the chord $\overline{XY}$, prove that eight times the square on $\overline{OM}$ is equal to the square on a diameter.

39 Two circles intersect at P, Q. A line $\overline{ACDB}$ parallel to $\overline{PQ}$ meets one circle at A, B and the other at C, D. Prove that $AC = DB$.

40 A chord of a circle is 24 cm long, and cuts a diameter at right angles. If the shorter of the two parts into which the diameter is divided is 8 cm long, calculate the length of the longer part.

41 P, Q are any two points on a circle, and $\overline{AB}$ is a diameter. If $\overline{AX}$, $\overline{BY}$ are the perpendiculars from A, B to $\overline{PQ}$ (produced each way if necessary), prove that PX = QY.

42 In a circle with radius 1·7 cm a chord $\overline{AB}$ of length 3 cm is drawn at right angles to a diameter $\overline{PQ}$. Calculate AP and AQ, correct to 3 significant figures.

43 $\overline{AB}$, $\overline{CD}$ are parallel chords of a circle, and $\overline{OM}$, $\overline{ON}$ are the perpendiculars from the centre to $\overline{AB}$, $\overline{CD}$ respectively. Prove that $AB^2 - CD^2 = 4MN(ON - OM)$.

Chapter 16

Literal equations. Change of subject. Formula for quadratics

A literal equation is one in which letters as well as numbers are used as coefficients. For example, the following are three equations in x:

$$\text{(i)} \quad ax - a^2 = bx - b^2$$

$$\text{(ii)} \qquad a = \frac{b + x}{b - x}$$

$$\text{(iii)} \qquad 2b = \sqrt{a^2 - x^2}$$

The solutions of these equations are as follows:

(i)
$$ax - a^2 = bx - b^2$$
$$\therefore \ ax - bx = a^2 - b^2$$
$$\therefore \ x(a - b) = a^2 - b^2$$
$$\therefore \ x = \frac{a^2 - b^2}{a - b}$$
$$= a + b.$$

(ii)
$$a = \frac{b + x}{b - x}$$
$$\therefore \ a(b - x) = b + x$$
$$\therefore \ ab - ax = b + x$$
$$\therefore \ ab - b = ax + x$$
$$= x(a + 1)$$
$$\therefore \ x = \frac{ab - b}{a + 1}$$
$$= \frac{b(a - 1)}{a + 1}.$$

Literal equations. Change of subject. Formula for quadratics

(iii)
$$2b = \sqrt{a^2 - x^2}$$
$$\therefore\ 4b^2 = a^2 - x^2$$
$$\therefore\ x^2 = a^2 - 4b^2$$
$$\therefore\ x = \pm\sqrt{a^2 - 4b^2}.$$

It will be seen from the above examples that it is impossible to lay down any general rules for solving such equations, but the following points should be remembered:

(1) Begin by clearing fractions, brackets and root signs.

(2) Rearrange the equation so that all the terms which contain x are on one side and the rest on the other. There is no virtue in placing x on the left-hand side if it comes more naturally on the right, as was the case in Ex. 2.

(3) Take x outside a bracket if there is more than one term which involves x.

(4) Divide both sides by the bracket, and simplify as far as possible.

Exercise 16a

Solve for x the following equations:

1 $x + a = b$ **2** $a - x = b$ **3** $ax = b$

4 $ax + bx = c$ **5** $ax + b = x$ **6** $\dfrac{a}{x} = b$

7 $\dfrac{a}{x} + b = c$ **8** $\dfrac{x}{a} + b = c$ **9** $\dfrac{x}{a} + \dfrac{x}{b} = 1$

10 $\dfrac{a}{x} + \dfrac{b}{x} = 1$ **11** $a(x + b) = c$ **12** $ax = b(c + x)$

13 $a(b - x) = cx$ **14** $\dfrac{x}{2a} + \dfrac{x}{3a} = b$

15 $x(a - b) = b(c - x)$ **16** $\dfrac{a}{b - x} = c$

17 $a = \dfrac{2b + 3x}{3b - 2x}$ **18** $\sqrt{x} = a$ **19** $\sqrt{2x} = a$

221

20 $2\sqrt{x} = a$ **21** $\sqrt{\dfrac{x}{2}} = a$ **22** $\dfrac{\sqrt{x}}{2} = a$

23 $a\sqrt{x} = b$ **24** $\sqrt{ax} = b$ **25** $\sqrt[3]{\dfrac{x}{a}} = b$

26 $x^2 = a^4$ **27** $x^2 = a$ **28** $\sqrt{x + a} = b$

29 $\sqrt{x} + a = b$ **30** $\sqrt{x^2 + a^2} = b$

31 $\sqrt{x^2 + a^2} = 3a$ **32** $\dfrac{a}{x} - 1 = \dfrac{b}{2x}$

33 $a\sqrt{x - 1} = b$ **34** $a\sqrt{x} - 1 = b$

35 $(ax - b)(bx + a) = (bx^2 + a)a$

36 $\dfrac{a}{a - x} = \dfrac{b}{b + x}$ **37** $\dfrac{a}{b - x} = \dfrac{b}{a + x}$

38 $a(a^2 - x) = b(b^2 - x)$ **39** $\dfrac{x}{x + a} - \dfrac{a}{x + b} = 1$

40 $\dfrac{x^2}{a^2} + \dfrac{y^2}{b^2} = 1$ **41** $\sqrt{a^2 + bx} = a + b$

42 $\sqrt{b^2 + 2ax} = x + a$ **43** $2\sqrt{x^2 + b^2} = 2x + b$

44 $\sqrt{x^2 - a^2} + a = x$ **45** $\sqrt{x^2 - a^2} - x = a$

46 $\dfrac{x + a}{a} - \dfrac{x - b}{b} = \dfrac{x}{b}$ **47** $\dfrac{x - a}{x - b} - \dfrac{x}{x - b} = \dfrac{a}{x}$

48 $\dfrac{1}{x + a} = \dfrac{2}{x + b} - \dfrac{1}{x - a}$ **49** $\dfrac{2}{x} - \dfrac{1}{x + a} = \dfrac{2}{2x - a}$

50 $x = a + \sqrt{b(x - a)}$

Formulae: change of subject

It is often necessary to 'change the subject' of a formula; that is to rearrange the order of the letters, regarding the formula as a literal equation which is solved for the letter which is to be made the 'subject'.

Literal equations. Change of subject. Formula for quadratics

Example 1 *The time of oscillation of a simple pendulum is given by the formula* $T = 2\pi\sqrt{\dfrac{l}{g}}$, *where l is the length of the pendulum and g the constant of gravitation. Make l the subject of the formula.*
(T is the subject of the formula as given.)

$$T = 2\pi\sqrt{\frac{l}{g}}$$

$$\therefore\ T^2 = 4\pi^2\frac{l}{g}$$

$$\therefore\ gT^2 = 4\pi^2 l$$

$$\therefore\ l = \frac{gT^2}{4\pi^2}.$$

Example 2 *Make W the subject of the formula* $T = W + \dfrac{Wv^2}{gx}$.

$$T = W + \frac{Wv^2}{gx}$$

$$\therefore\ gxT = gxW + Wv^2$$

$$= W(gx + v^2)$$

$$\therefore\ W = \frac{gxT}{gx + v^2}.$$

Exercise 16b

Rearrange the following formulae, taking as 'subject' the letter printed in heavy type after each one: if there are two letters, make each in turn the subject.

1 $P = \dfrac{N + 2}{D}$ **N**   **2** $k = \dfrac{brt}{v - b}$ ***b***

3 $c = 2\pi r$ ***r***   **4** $P = aW + b$ **W**

5 $s = \dfrac{n}{2}(a + l)$ ***n, l***   **6** $A = P + \dfrac{PRT}{100}$ **P, T**

7 $S = 2\pi r(r + h)$ ***h***   **8** $v^2 = u^2 + 2as$ ***s, u***

9 $L = \dfrac{Wh}{a(W + P)}$ **W**   **10** $\dfrac{L}{E} = \dfrac{2a}{R - r}$ **R**

11 $R = \sqrt{\dfrac{ax - P}{Q + bx}}$ **x**   **12** $D = \sqrt{\dfrac{3h}{2}}$ **h**

13 $S = 4\pi r^2$ **r**   **14** $T = 2\pi\sqrt{\dfrac{I}{MH}}$ **M**

15 $A = \frac{1}{2}m(v^2 - u^2)$ **u**   **16** $d = a\sqrt[3]{\dfrac{H}{N}}$ **H**

17 $M = \dfrac{wd}{4}\left(l - \dfrac{d}{2}\right)$ **l**   **18** $S = \dfrac{wd}{l}\left(l - \dfrac{d}{2}\right)$ **l**

19 $H = \dfrac{(T - t)\pi Rn}{275}$ **t**   **20** $H = \dfrac{w^2}{2g}(R^2 - r^2)$ **r**

21 $T = \sqrt{\dfrac{Pbh}{4 + a^2}}$ **b, a**   **22** $x = \dfrac{a + 2b}{3(a + b)}h$ **a**

23 $v = w\sqrt{a^2 - x^2}$ **x**   **24** $A = \pi r\sqrt{h^2 + r^2}$ **h**

25 $T = \sqrt{H + \dfrac{w^2 l^2}{4}}$ **H, l**   **26** $\dfrac{1}{u} + \dfrac{1}{v} = \dfrac{2}{f}$ **u**

27 $V = \dfrac{1}{3}\sqrt{\dfrac{s^3}{8\pi}}$ **s**   **28** $A = \sqrt{\dfrac{P^2 - 2Q^2}{2P^2 + Q^2}}$ **P**

29 $A = \pi r\sqrt{h^2 + r^2} + \pi r^2$ **h**

30 $r = \dfrac{f}{2} + \sqrt{\dfrac{f^2}{4} + q^2}$ **q**

31 The simple interest £I on a sum of money £P after T years at R% is given by the formula $I = \dfrac{PRT}{100}$. Make T the subject of the formula. Find T if $I = 51$, $P = 340$, $R = 2\frac{1}{2}$.

32 The total resistance, R ohms, of two resistances, respectively x and y ohms, in parallel is given by the formula $\dfrac{1}{R} = \dfrac{1}{x} + \dfrac{1}{y}$.

Obtain a formula for y in terms of R and x, and find y if $x = 2\frac{2}{3}$, R $= 2\frac{1}{4}$.

33 The area A of a circle is given by the formula A $= \pi r^2$, where r is the radius of the circle. Obtain a formula for r, and find the radius of a circle of area 38·5 cm², taking $\pi = \frac{22}{7}$.

34 The volume V of a solid consisting of a cone of height h and base-radius r attached to a hemisphere of the same radius is $\frac{2}{3}\pi r^3 + \frac{1}{3}\pi r^2 h$. Change the subject of the formula to h. What is the height of the cone if the radius is $2\frac{1}{2}$ cm, the volume 55 cm³, and $\pi = \frac{22}{7}$?

35 If a tight wire L metres long is stretched between two points at the same level and l metres apart, the sag in the middle of the wire is s metres, where $s = \sqrt{\dfrac{3l(\text{L} - l)}{8}}$. Change the subject of the formula to L. What is the length of the wire if the points are 16 m apart and the sag is 0·6 m?

36 The tonnage T of a ship l metres long and b metres wide is $\dfrac{4b^2}{21}(l - \frac{3}{5}b)$. Make l the subject of the formula and find the length of a 4 500-tonne ship if it is 20 m wide.

37 The energy E possessed by an object of mass m kilogrammes travelling at a height of h metres with velocity v ms⁻¹ is $\left(\dfrac{mv^2}{2} + mgh\right)$ joules. Find v in terms of the other letters. If the energy of a 20-kg mass at a height of 15 m is 4 900 joules and $g = 9·8$, how fast is the mass moving?

38 The sum S of n terms of a series in which each term is d more than the one before, and of which a is the first term, is given by the formula S $= \dfrac{n}{2}\{2a + (n - 1)d\}$. Obtain a formula for d in terms of the other letters and find the value of d if the sum of 32 terms of a series, whose first term is 25, is 56.

39 The volume V of a cone of height h and base radius r is $\frac{1}{3}\pi r^2 h$. Obtain a formula for r. What is the base-radius of a cone of height 14 cm and volume $91\frac{2}{3}$ cm³ if $\pi = \frac{22}{7}$?

225

40 The curved surface area A of a cone of height h and base-radius r is $\pi r \sqrt{h^2 + r^2}$. Make h the subject of the formula. Calculate the height of a cone of area 550 cm² and base-radius 7 cm, taking $\pi = \frac{22}{7}$.

The formula for solving quadratic equations

The general form of a quadratic equation is $ax^2 + bx + c = 0$, and its roots are found by the method of 'completing the square', as already explained on page 54.

$$ax^2 + bx + c = 0$$

$$\therefore x^2 + \frac{b}{a}x + \frac{c}{a} = 0$$

$$\therefore x^2 + \frac{b}{a}x = -\frac{c}{a}$$

$$\therefore x^2 + \frac{b}{a}x + \left(\frac{b}{2a}\right)^2 = -\frac{c}{a} + \left(\frac{b}{2a}\right)^2$$

$$= -\frac{c}{a} + \frac{b^2}{4a^2}$$

$$\therefore \left(x + \frac{b}{2a}\right)^2 = \frac{b^2 - 4ac}{4a^2}$$

$$\therefore x + \frac{b}{2a} = \pm \sqrt{\frac{b^2 - 4ac}{4a^2}}$$

$$= \pm \frac{\sqrt{b^2 - 4ac}}{2a}$$

$$\therefore x = -\frac{b}{2a} \pm \frac{\sqrt{b^2 - 4ac}}{2a}$$

$$\therefore x = \frac{-b \pm \sqrt{b^2 - 4ac}}{2a}$$

Example 3 *Find, correct to 2 decimal places, the roots of the equation* $3x^2 - 5x - 7 = 0$.

Comparing $3x^2 - 5x - 7 = 0$ with $ax^2 + bx + c = 0$; $a = 3$, $b = -5$, $c = -7$.

$$\therefore x = \frac{-(-5) \pm \sqrt{(-5)^2 - 4 \times 3 \times (-7)}}{2 \times 3}$$

$$= \frac{5 \pm \sqrt{25 + 84}}{6}$$

$$= \frac{5 \pm \sqrt{109}}{6}$$

$$= \frac{5 \pm 10\cdot44}{6}$$

$$= \frac{15\cdot44}{6} \quad \text{or} \quad \frac{-5\cdot44}{6}$$

$$\simeq 2\cdot57 \quad \text{or} \quad -0\cdot91.$$

Exercise 16c

Use the formula to solve the following equations, giving the roots correct to 2 decimal places, except in the first ten, which should be checked by using factors.

1 $x^2 + 5x + 6 = 0$	**2** $x^2 - 5x + 4 = 0$
3 $x^2 - 4x - 5 = 0$	**4** $2x^2 + 5x + 3 = 0$
5 $3x^2 - 4x + 1 = 0$	**6** $3x^2 - 5x - 2 = 0$
7 $5x^2 - 3x - 2 = 0$	**8** $4x^2 + 7x - 2 = 0$
9 $6x^2 + 13x + 6 = 0$	**10** $3x^2 - 13x - 10 = 0$
11 $x^2 + 3x + 1 = 0$	**12** $x^2 - 2x - 4 = 0$
13 $2x^2 + 7x - 3 = 0$	**14** $3x^2 - 5x - 3 = 0$
15 $5x^2 - 6x - 3 = 0$	**16** $5x^2 + 8x - 2 = 0$
17 $3x^2 + 7x + 3 = 0$	**18** $3x^2 - 12x + 10 = 0$
19 $3x^2 - 8x + 2 = 0$	**20** $5x^2 + 3x - 3 = 0$
21 $4x^2 - 16x + 3 = 0$	**22** $2x^2 - 7x - 3 = 0$

23 $3x - 2 = \dfrac{4}{x}$

24 $2(2x + 1)^2 + 5(2x + 1) = 1$

25 $3(x + 1) = \dfrac{5}{x + 1}$

26 $\dfrac{2}{x} - \dfrac{1}{x + 1} = 3$

27 $\dfrac{x}{x - 2} - 3 = 2x$

28 $3 - \dfrac{5}{x + 2} = \dfrac{1}{2x - 1}$

29 $\dfrac{2}{x - 3} - \dfrac{3}{x - 2} = \dfrac{1}{x}$

30 $\dfrac{2}{2x - 1} - \dfrac{1}{2x + 1} = 5$

Chapter 17

Circle theorems

If P, Q, R, . . . are points on the circumference of a segment of a
circle (major or minor segment), then
$A\hat{P}B$, $A\hat{Q}B$, $A\hat{R}B$, . . . are said to be angles
subtended at the circumference of the circle
by the arc AB, or by the chord $\overline{AB}$, and
$A\hat{P}B$, $A\hat{Q}B$, $A\hat{R}B$, . . . are all **angles in the
same segment** APQR . . . B of the circle.

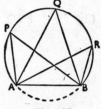

Fig. 107

Theorem 14

**The angle which an arc of a circle subtends at the centre of the
circle is twice that which it subtends at any point on the remaining
part of the circumference.**

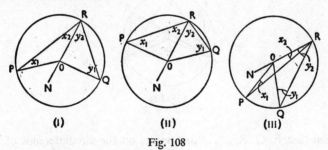

(i) (ii) (iii)

Fig. 108

Given a circle PQR with centre O.

To prove that $P\hat{O}Q = 2\,P\hat{R}Q$.

Construction Join $\overline{RO}$ and produce to any point N.

Proof

$$OP = OR \qquad radii$$
$$\therefore\ x_1 = x_2 \qquad base\ \angle s\ of\ isos.\ \triangle POR$$
$$\therefore\ P\hat{O}N = x_1 + x_2 = 2x_2 \qquad ext.\ \angle\ of\ \triangle POR$$

229

Similarly $\quad$ $Q\hat{O}N = y_1 + y_2 = 2y_2$ $\quad$,, $\quad$,, $\quad$ $\triangle QOR$

(i) $P\hat{O}Q$
(ii) reflex $P\hat{O}Q$ $\Big\} = P\hat{O}N + Q\hat{O}N$

$$= 2x_2 + 2y_2$$
$$= 2(x_2 + y_2)$$
$$= 2\,P\hat{R}Q.$$

(iii) $\quad$ $P\hat{O}Q = Q\hat{O}N - P\hat{O}N$
$$= 2y_2 - 2x_2$$
$$= 2(y_2 - x_2)$$
$$= 2\,P\hat{R}Q. \qquad \text{Q.E.D.}$$

Theorem 15

Angles in the same segment of a circle are equal.

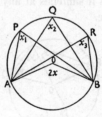

Fig. 109

Given that P, Q, R, . . . are points on the circumference of a circle APQR . . . B.

To prove $A\hat{P}B = A\hat{Q}B = A\hat{R}B = \ldots$

Construction Join A and B to the centre O of the circle.

Proof $\quad A\hat{O}B = 2x_1 \qquad\qquad \angle$ *at centre* $= 2 \times \angle$ *at O*^{ce}
$\qquad\qquad\quad = 2x_2 \qquad\qquad$,, $\quad$,, $\quad$,, $\quad$,,
$\qquad\qquad\quad = 2x_3,$ etc. $\qquad$,, $\quad$,, $\quad$,, $\quad$,,

230

$$\therefore \ x_1 = x_2 = x_3 = \ldots$$
$$\therefore \ A\hat{P}B = A\hat{Q}B = A\hat{R}B = \ldots$$
Q.E.D.

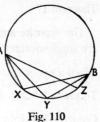

Notice that the theorem is also true for angles in the minor segment AB

(i.e. $A\hat{X}B = A\hat{Y}B = A\hat{Z}B = \ldots$)

Fig. 110

Theorem 16

The angle in a semicircle is a right angle.

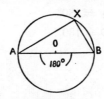

Fig. 111

Given that $\overline{AB}$ is a diameter of a circle centre O. X is any point on the circumference of the circle.

To prove $A\hat{X}B = 90°$

Proof $A\hat{O}B = 2 \ A\hat{X}B$ $\angle$ *at centre* $= 2 \times \angle$ *at* O^{ce}
But $A\hat{O}B = 180°$ *straight line*
$\therefore \ 2A\hat{X}B = 180°$
$\therefore \ A\hat{X}B = 90°.$

Q.E.D.

A **cyclic quadrilateral** is a quadrilateral whose vertices lie on a circle.

231

New General Mathematics

Theorem 17

The opposite angles of a cyclic quadrilateral are supplementary.

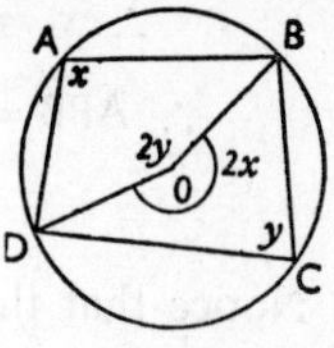

Given a cyclic quadrilateral ABCD.

To prove $\hat{\text{BAD}} + \hat{\text{BCD}} = 180°$.

Fig. 112

Construction Join B and D to the centre O of the circle ABCD.

Proof

$$\hat{\text{BOD}} = 2y \qquad \angle \text{ at centre} = 2 \times \angle \text{ at O}^{ce}$$
$$\text{reflex } \hat{\text{BOD}} = 2x \qquad " \qquad " \qquad " \qquad "$$
$$\therefore 2x + 2y = 360° \qquad \angle s \text{ at a point}$$
$$\therefore x + y = 180°$$
$$\therefore \hat{\text{BAD}} + \hat{\text{BCD}} = 180°.$$

Q.E.D.

Corollary

If one side of a cyclic quadrilateral is produced, the exterior angle so formed is equal to the interior opposite angle.

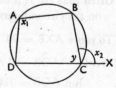

$$x_1 + y = 180° \qquad opp. \angle s \text{ cycl. quad.}$$
$$x_2 + y = 180° \qquad adj. \angle s$$
$$\therefore x_2 = x_1$$
$$\therefore \hat{\text{BCX}} = \hat{\text{BAD}}.$$

Fig. 113

Exercise 17a

1 (Fig. 114.)

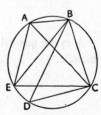

By what arc is $\hat{\text{ABE}}$ subtended?

Write down (i) an angle equal to $\hat{\text{ABE}}$,

(ii) two angles equal to $\hat{\text{BEC}}$,

(iii) an angle equal to $\hat{\text{EAC}}$.

Fig. 114

2 Sketch Fig. 115.

By marking equal angles with the same letter show that

(i) △s ABY and CDY are similar,

(ii) △s BCX and DAX are similar.

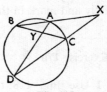

Fig. 115

3 Sketch Fig. 116.

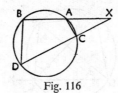

Fig. 116

As in no. 2, show that △s XAC and XDB are similar.

In each of the following figures (in which O is always the centre of the circle) find the marked angle: some construction may be

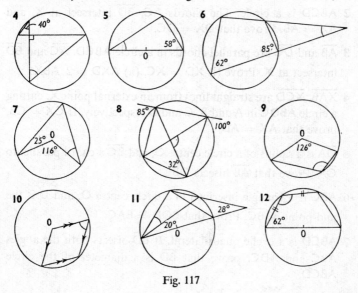

Fig. 117

necessary. No formal proofs are required. Draw the figures carefully and mark in the angles as they are found.

Exercise 17b

1 Use Fig. 118 to prove that $B\hat{C}X = B\hat{A}D$ and also that $B\hat{A}D + B\hat{C}D = 180°$.

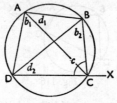

Fig. 118

(This is an alternative proof of Theorem 17 and its corollary.)

2 ABCD is a circle. The chords $\overline{AC}$, $\overline{BD}$ intersect at X, and $AX = AB$. Prove that $DX = DC$.

3 $\overline{AB}$ and $\overline{DC}$ are parallel chords in a circle ABCD. $\overline{AC}$ and $\overline{BD}$ intersect at X. Prove (i) $XD = XC$, (ii) $A\hat{X}D = 2\ A\hat{B}X$.

4 $\overline{XAB}$, $\overline{XCD}$ are straight lines from an external point X, cutting a circle ABDC in A and B, C and D respectively. If $CX = CB$, prove that $AX = AD$.

5 $\overline{OA}$ is a radius of a circle centre O, and $\overline{BC}$ a chord parallel to $\overline{OA}$. Prove that $\overline{AB}$ bisects $O\hat{B}C$.

6 ABC is a triangle inscribed in a circle centre O, and D is the mid-point of $\overline{BC}$. Prove that $B\hat{O}D = B\hat{A}C$.

7 ABCD is a cyclic quadrilateral. If $\overline{BD}$ bisects both the angles ABC and ADC, prove that $\overline{BD}$ is a diameter of the circle ABCD.

8 ABCD is a rhombus and its diagonals intersect at X. Prove that the circles on the sides as diameters all pass through X.

9 If, in a circle ABC centre O, OABC is a parallelogram, prove that $\overline{OB}$ is perpendicular to $\overline{AC}$.

10 In a circle ABCD with centre O, $\overline{AD}$ is a diameter and AB = BC. Prove that $\overline{BO}$ is parallel to $\overline{CD}$.

11 $\overline{OA}$ is a radius of a circle centre O, and $\overline{AB}$ any chord. Prove that the circle on $\overline{OA}$ as diameter bisects $\overline{AB}$.

12 Two circles PABR and SABQ intersect at A and B. $\overline{PAQ}$ and $\overline{RAS}$ are straight lines. Prove $P\hat{B}R = S\hat{B}Q$.

13 ABC is a triangle in which AB = AC. Any circle through A and B cuts $\overline{AC}$ at X and $\overline{BC}$ at Y. Prove YX = YC.

14 In a circle ABCDE, centre O, AB = BC = CD. Prove $A\hat{O}B = B\hat{E}D$.

15 Two circles cut at A and B. $\overline{AC}$ is a diameter of one circle and $\overline{CB}$ produced cuts the other at D. Prove that $\overline{AD}$ is a diameter of the second circle.

16 ABC is a triangle in which AB = AC. The circle on $\overline{AC}$ as diameter cuts $\overline{BC}$ at M. Prove that M is the mid-point of $\overline{BC}$.

17 Two circles PABR, QABS cut at A and B. $\overline{PAQ}$ and $\overline{RBS}$ are straight lines. Prove that $\overline{PR}$ is parallel to $\overline{QS}$.

18 ABC is a triangle and the bisector of $A\hat{B}C$ cuts $\overline{AC}$ at D. The circle BCD cuts $\overline{AB}$ at E. Prove that DE = DC.

19 Any circle through A and B cuts at D the side $\overline{BC}$ produced of an isosceles triangle ABC, in which AB = AC. A line through A parallel to $\overline{BC}$ cuts the circle at E. Prove that $\overline{ED}$ is parallel to $\overline{AC}$.

20 $\overline{BC}$ is a diameter of a circle ABC centre O. $\overline{CA}$ produced cuts at D the circle through B, O, A. Prove DB = DC.

21 Two equal circles intersect at A and B. A straight line through A cuts one circle at X and the other at Y. Prove BX = BY.

22 APQRB is a semicircle with diameter $\overline{AB}$. Prove that $\hat{APQ} + \hat{QRB} = 270°$.

23 O is any point on a circle S_1: S_2 is a circle with centre O which cuts S_1 at A and B. R is a point on S_1 between A and O, and $\overline{AR}$ produced cuts S_2 at P (Fig. 119). Prove that RB = RP.

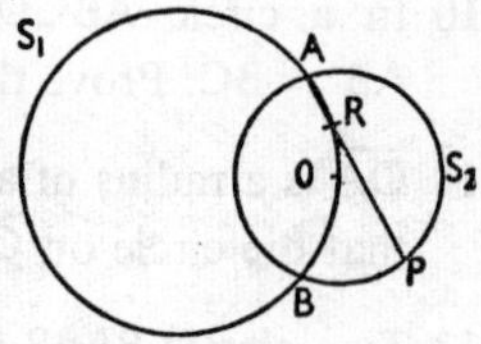

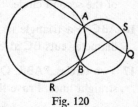

Fig. 119

24 Two circles CABD and PAQB cut at A and B. $\overline{CAP}$ is a straight line and $\overline{CD}$ a diameter. $\overline{AD}$ cuts the second circle at Q. Prove that $\overline{PQ}$ is a diameter of the second circle.

25 Two chords $\overline{AB}$, $\overline{CD}$ of a circle meet outside the circle at X. $\overline{AD}$ and $\overline{BC}$ intersect at Y. If the points X, B, Y, D lie on a circle, prove that $\overline{AC}$ is a diameter of the circle ABDC.

26 ABCD is a parallelogram. The circle through A, D and C cuts $\overline{AB}$ at X. Prove that CX = CB.

27 In Fig. 120 prove that $\overline{PR}$ is parallel to $\overline{SQ}$.

28 BAC is a triangle right-angled at A, and P is any point inside the triangle. The circles ABP, ACP cut $\overline{BC}$ at X, Y respectively. Prove that $\hat{XPY} = 90°$.

Fig. 120

29 ABCDEF is a hexagon (not regular) inscribed in a circle. Prove that $\hat{A} + \hat{E} + \hat{C} = 360°$.

30 Two circles AQPB, AYXB cut at A and B. A straight line $\overline{APX}$ through A cuts one circle at P and the other at X; another straight line $\overline{BQY}$ through B cuts the first circle at Q and the other at Y. Prove that $\overline{XY}$ is parallel to $\overline{PQ}$.

31 D is any point on the side $\overline{BC}$ of a triangle ABC. The circle

ABD cuts $\overline{AC}$ at Y, and the circle ACD cuts $\overline{AB}$ at X. Prove that $X\hat{D}B = Y\hat{D}C$.

32 In Fig. 121 $\overline{PXQ}$, $\overline{PYR}$ are straight lines. Prove that $\overline{QZR}$ is also a straight line.

33 ABDE is a circle. $\overline{AB}$ is produced to C so that BC = BD, and $\overline{CD}$ cuts the circle at E. Prove that EA = EC.

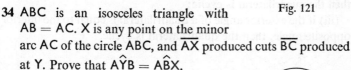

Fig. 121

34 ABC is an isosceles triangle with AB = AC. X is any point on the minor arc AC of the circle ABC, and $\overline{AX}$ produced cuts $\overline{BC}$ produced at Y. Prove that $A\hat{Y}B = A\hat{B}X$.

35 ABCD is a semicircle on diameter $\overline{AB}$. $\overline{DC}$ is produced to E. Prove that the angles ABD and BCE are complementary.

36 In Fig. 122 prove that $\overline{AX}$ is parallel to $\overline{YB}$.

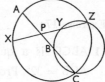

Fig. 122

37 O is a point on a circle S_1, and a second circle S_2 with centre O cuts S_1 at A and B. R is a point on the arc AOB of S_1, and P a point on the minor arc AB of S_2. Prove that $A\hat{P}B = P\hat{A}R + P\hat{B}R$.

38 $\overline{AB}$ and $\overline{CD}$ are two chords of a circle centre O which intersect at right angles at a point inside the circle. Prove that $A\hat{O}D + B\hat{O}C = 180°$.

39 $\overline{AB}$ and $\overline{DC}$ are parallel chords in a circle ABCD. P is any point on the minor arc AB, and $\overline{PD}$ cuts $\overline{AB}$ at X. Prove that (i) $A\hat{P}C = B\hat{P}D$,
 (ii) $P\hat{A}C = P\hat{X}B$.

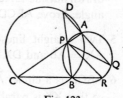

Fig. 123

40 In Fig. 123 prove that PQ = PR.

New General Mathematics

Concyclic points and cyclic quadrilaterals

If the four points A, B, C, D lie on a circle they are said to be **concyclic.**

The converses of the theorems given at the beginning of this Chapter are all true: in particular

(i) if the angles APB, AQB, ARB, . . . are equal, then B, A, P, Q, R, . . . are concyclic points;

(ii) **if the opposite angles of a quadrilateral are supplementary, then the quadrilateral is cyclic;**

(iii) if the exterior angle of a quadrilateral is equal to the interior opposite angle, then the quadrilateral is cyclic.

Exercise 17c

1 ABCD is a quadrilateral in which $\hat{B} = 95°$, $B\hat{A}C = 53°$, $A\hat{D}B = 32°$. Prove that ABCD is a cyclic quadrilateral.

2 ABCD is a quadrilateral with $\hat{C} = 96°$. O is a point inside ABCD such that, in quadrilateral BODC, $B\hat{O}D = 168°$, and OB = OA = OD. Prove ABCD a cyclic quadrilateral.

3 PQRS is a trapezium having $\overline{PQ}$ parallel to $\overline{SR}$, and $P\hat{S}R = Q\hat{R}S = 73°$. Prove PQRS a cyclic quadrilateral.

4 ABC is an equilateral triangle, and ACD an isosceles triangle drawn outside △ABC such that DA = DC and $D\hat{C}B$ is a right angle. Prove ABCD cyclic.

5 Two straight lines $\overline{AXC}$ and $\overline{BXD}$ intersect at X so that AX = AB and DX = DC. Prove ABCD cyclic.

6 ABCD is a circle. $\overline{AB}$, $\overline{DC}$ are produced to X, Y respectively so that $\overline{XY}$ is parallel to $\overline{AD}$. Prove BXYC cyclic.

7 ABCD is a parallelogram. X is a point on $\overline{AB}$ such that CX = CB. Prove AXCD cyclic.

8 XYZ is a triangle and B any point on $\overline{XY}$. A circle through X and B cuts $\overline{XZ}$ at P, and another circle through Y and B cuts $\overline{YZ}$ at Q. If the circles cut again at A, prove that ZPAQ is a cyclic quadrilateral.

9 ABCD is a parallelogram. Any circle through A and D cuts $\overline{AB}$ at X and $\overline{DC}$ at Y. Prove XBCY cyclic.

10 ABCD is a circle and the chords $\overline{AC}$, $\overline{BD}$ cut at X. P and Q are points on $\overline{XC}$, $\overline{XD}$ respectively such that $\overline{PQ}$ is parallel to $\overline{CD}$. Prove ABPQ cyclic.

11 ABC is an isosceles triangle, obtuse-angled at B, and D is any point on $\overline{CB}$ produced. The perpendicular bisector of $\overline{CD}$ cuts $\overline{AC}$ at E. Prove AEBD cyclic.

12 $\overline{BE}$ and $\overline{CF}$ are altitudes of any triangle ABC, and intersect at H. Prove that

    (i) AEHF is a cyclic quadrilateral,
    (ii) BFEC is a cyclic quadrilateral,
    (iii) if $\overline{AH}$ is produced to cut $\overline{BC}$ at D, ADC is a right angle,
    (iv) $\overline{BE}$ bisects $D\hat{E}F$,
    (v) H is the incentre of the triangle DEF,
    (vi) if X is the mid-point of $\overline{BC}$, then X is the centre of the circle BFEC, and also XDEF is cyclic.

13 Prove that the bisectors of the exterior angles of any quadrilateral form a cyclic quadrilateral.

14 Prove that the bisectors of the interior angles of any quadrilateral form a cyclic quadrilateral.

15 ABCD is a square inscribed in a circle, and P is any point on the minor arc CD. The diagonals of the square cut at O, and $\overline{PA}$, $\overline{PB}$ cut $\overline{BD}$, $\overline{AC}$ respectively at Q and R. Prove OCPQ and ODPR cyclic quadrilaterals.

Equal arcs and chords

It follows from Theorems 14 and 15 that, in the same circle or in equal circles,

equal arcs subtend equal angles at the centre,
equal arcs subtend equal angles at the circumference,
equal chords cut off equal arcs,

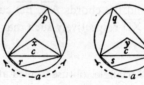

Fig. 124

e.g. in Fig. 124, if the circles are equal and the chords c are equal, then arcs a are equal, and

$$\angle x = \angle y$$
$$\angle p = \angle q$$
$$\angle r = \angle s$$

Length of an arc of a circle

If a circular cake is cut into slices in the usual way and the 'angle at the centre' in each slice is 10°, there will be 36 slices, since the whole angle at the centre is 360°, and the lengths of the arcs of the slices will be equal. Similarly the arc of a slice of angle 20° will be twice that of a slice of angle 10°. The conclusion is that the length of the arc of a circle is proportional to the angle which that arc subtends at the centre.

Further, since the angle at the centre is twice the angle at the circumference, the length of the arc is also proportional to the angle it subtends at the circumference.

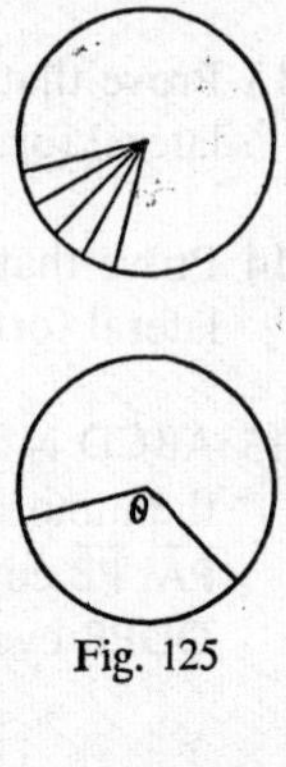

Fig. 125

Circle theorems

In particular, the length of the arc of a sector of angle θ degrees $= \dfrac{\theta}{360}$ of the circumference.

N.B. If an arc BC of a circle is twice another arc AB of the same circle, the chord $\overline{BC}$ is *not* equal to twice the chord $\overline{AB}$.

Example 1 *The angles of a triangle inscribed in a circle are 45°, 60°, 75°. Find the ratio of the minor arcs cut off by the sides of the triangle on the circle.*

Fig. 126

$$\text{Ratio } a:b:c = 45:60:75$$
$$= 3:4:5$$

Example 2 *The angle at the centre in a sector of a circle of radius 3 cm is 150°. Find the lengths of the two arcs of the circle (without substituting for π).*

$$\text{Arc } a = \frac{150}{360} \times 2\pi 3 \text{ cm} = \frac{5\pi}{2} \text{ cm}$$

$$\text{Arc } b = \frac{210}{360} \times 2\pi 3 \text{ cm} = \frac{7\pi}{2} \text{ cm}$$

N.B. $a:b = 150:210 = 5:7$.

Fig. 127

Exercise 17d

1

Fig. 128

Find the ratios of (i) $a:b:c$, (ii) $x:y$, (iii) $p:q:r$ in Fig. 128.

2 Find, in terms of π, the lengths of the arcs in Fig. 128, taking the radii of all three circles as 6 cm.

3

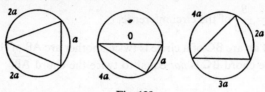

Fig. 129

Find the angles of the triangles in Fig. 129.

4 In Fig. 130 calculate (i) AD̂B, (ii) AĈD, (iii) BĈD. (iv) Find the angle between $\overline{AC}$ and $\overline{BD}$. (v) If $\overline{AC}$ cuts $\overline{BD}$ at X, prove that $DX = DC$.

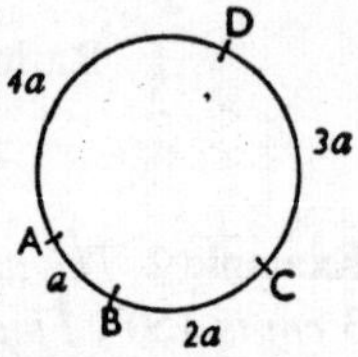

Fig. 130

5 Sketch the face of a clock. Calculate the angles between the lines (i) VI–IX and III–VIII, (ii) VI–X and V–VIII.

What is the angle between the hands at (iii) 12.24, (iv) 2.30, (v) 7.45?

6 ABCDE is a regular pentagon inscribed in a circle centre O. Calculate AÔB, AÊB, AÊC, AÊD, AD̂B.

7 In the figure for no. 6 a rectangle CDXY is inscribed in the circle. Prove that X is the mid-point of the arc AE.

8 ABCD is a square inscribed in a circle and AXY is an equilateral triangle in the same circle, having X the vertex nearest to D. Prove (i) arc $CX = 2$ arc DX, (ii) arc $DX = \frac{1}{12}$ of circumference of circle.

9 $\overline{AB}$, $\overline{CD}$ are equal chords of a circle ABCD. Prove that $\overline{AD}$ is parallel to $\overline{BC}$.

10 In a circle ABCD, $DA = DC$. Prove that $\overline{BD}$ bisects AB̂C.

11 Two equal circles ABX and ABY intersect at A and B, and $\overline{XBY}$ is a straight line. Prove that $AX = AY$.

12 $\overline{AB}$ and $\overline{CD}$ are equal chords of a circle ABDC which, when produced, meet outside the circle at X. Prove that $XB = XD$.

13 ABCD is a rectangle inscribed in a circle, and $\overline{AX}$ is a chord equal to $\overline{AD}$. Prove that CX = CD.

14 Three equal circles all pass through the point O, and intersect again in pairs at A, B, C. $\overline{CO}$ produced cuts the circle AOB again at X. Prove that $\overline{AB}$ bisects $\overline{CX}$ at right angles.

15 $\overline{AB}$, $\overline{AC}$ are two chords of a circle, and L, M the mid-points of the arcs AB, AC respectively. If $\overline{LM}$ cuts $\overline{AB}$, $\overline{AC}$ in X, Y respectively, prove that AX = AY.

16 $\overline{AB}$, $\overline{BC}$, $\overline{CD}$ are equal chords of a circle ABCD. $\overline{AC}$ and $\overline{BD}$ intersect in X, and the bisector of $A\hat{X}B$ cuts $\overline{AB}$ in Y. Prove that $\overline{XY}$ is parallel to $\overline{DA}$.

17 ABC is a triangle in a circle, and AB = AC. X, Y are the mid-points of the arcs AB, BC respectively. $\overline{AY}$ and $\overline{CX}$ intersect at Z. Prove that YZ = YC.

18 A, B, C, D are points on a circle ABCD; arc BC = 2 arc AB; also $\overline{AC}$ is perpendicular to $\overline{BD}$. Prove that DC = DB.

19 In Fig. 131 the circles are equal, and $\overline{XPR}$, $\overline{XAB}$, $\overline{XSQ}$, $\overline{PAQ}$, $\overline{RAS}$ are all straight lines. Prove that $\overline{AX}$ bisects $P\hat{X}S$.

20 ABC is any triangle in any circle. L, M, N are the mid-points of the arcs BC, CA, AB respectively. I is the incentre of △ABC. Prove that the triangles IBC and MAN are similar.

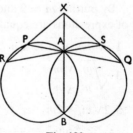

Fig. 131

Chapter 18

Surds

If the $\pm$ sign is disregarded, $\sqrt{4} = 2$, $\sqrt{49} = 7$, $\sqrt[3]{27} = 3$. These are **rational numbers**, and their values can be written down exactly.

Numbers which cannot be written down exactly are called **irrational numbers**, an example of which is π. The value of π can be found to any desired degree of accuracy, e.g. 3·14, 3·142, 3·1416 etc., but these are only approximations. Further values sometimes taken for π are $\frac{22}{7}$, $\frac{333}{106}$ and $\frac{355}{113}$, but these again are approximations.

Other examples of irrational numbers are $\sqrt{3} = 1\cdot732\ldots$ and $\sqrt{28} = 5\cdot291\ldots$ Irrational numbers of this kind are called **surds**.

Exercise 18a

By putting $m = 9$ and $n = 4$, find which of the following pairs of expressions are equal.

1 $\sqrt{mn}$, $\sqrt{m} \times \sqrt{n}$ **2** $\sqrt{m + n}$, $\sqrt{m} + \sqrt{n}$

3 $\sqrt{\dfrac{m}{n}}$, $\dfrac{\sqrt{m}}{\sqrt{n}}$ **4** $\sqrt{m - n}$, $\sqrt{m} - \sqrt{n}$

5 $2\sqrt{m}$, $\sqrt{2m}$ **6** $3\sqrt{n}$, $\sqrt{9n}$

As a result of experimenting with numbers as in Ex. 18a it appears to be true that $\sqrt{mn} = \sqrt{m} \times \sqrt{n}$, and $\sqrt{\dfrac{m}{n}} = \dfrac{\sqrt{m}}{\sqrt{n}}$. These statements are, in fact, true and can be used when simplifying surds.

For example,

$$\sqrt{x^2y} = \sqrt{x^2} \times \sqrt{y} = x\sqrt{y}$$
$$\sqrt{a^2b^4c^3} = \sqrt{a^2} \times \sqrt{b^4} \times \sqrt{c^2} \times \sqrt{c} = ab^2c\sqrt{c}$$

$$\sqrt{45} = \sqrt{9 \times 5} = \sqrt{9} \times \sqrt{5} = 3\sqrt{5}$$
$$\sqrt{162} = \sqrt{81 \times 2} = \sqrt{81} \times \sqrt{2} = 9\sqrt{2}.$$

Notice also the reverse process. For example,

$$2\sqrt{5} = \sqrt{4} \times \sqrt{5} = \sqrt{4 \times 5} = \sqrt{20}$$
$$7\sqrt{3} = \sqrt{49} \times \sqrt{3} = \sqrt{49 \times 3} = \sqrt{147}.$$

Multiplication of surds

When two or more surds have to be multiplied together, they should first be simplified if possible. Then whole numbers should be taken with whole numbers, and surds with surds.

For example,

$$\sqrt{27} \times \sqrt{50} = \sqrt{9 \times 3} \times \sqrt{25 \times 2}$$
$$= 3\sqrt{3} \times 5\sqrt{2}$$
$$= 15\sqrt{6}$$
$$\sqrt{12} \times 3\sqrt{60} \times \sqrt{45} = \sqrt{4 \times 3} \times 3\sqrt{4 \times 15} \times \sqrt{9 \times 5}$$
$$= 2\sqrt{3} \times 3 \times 2\sqrt{15} \times 3\sqrt{5}$$
$$= 36\sqrt{3 \times 15 \times 5}$$
$$= 36\sqrt{15 \times 15}$$
$$= 36 \times 15$$
$$= 540$$
$$(2\sqrt{5})^2 = 2\sqrt{5} \times 2\sqrt{5} = 4 \times 5 = 20$$
$$[\text{i.e. } (2\sqrt{5})^2 = 2^2 \times (\sqrt{5})^2 = 4 \times 5 = 20].$$

It is sometimes possible to pair off the surds to give a simpler result, for example,

$$\sqrt{2} \times \sqrt{3} \times \sqrt{5} \times \sqrt{12} \times \sqrt{45} \times \sqrt{50}$$
$$= \sqrt{2 \times 3 \times 5 \times 12 \times 45 \times 50}$$
$$= \sqrt{(2 \times 50) \times (3 \times 12) \times (5 \times 45)}$$

$$= \sqrt{100 \times 36 \times 225}$$
$$= 10 \times 6 \times 15$$
$$= 900$$

$$\sqrt{3} \times \sqrt{6} = \sqrt{3 \times 6} = \sqrt{18} = \sqrt{9 \times 2} = 3\sqrt{2}$$

or $\sqrt{3} \times \sqrt{6} = \sqrt{3} \times \sqrt{3 \times 2} = \sqrt{3} \times \sqrt{3} \times \sqrt{2} = 3\sqrt{2}$.

Division of surds

When a surd occurs in the denominator of a fraction it is usually best to **rationalise the denominator.** This is done by multiplying the numerator and denominator of the fraction by a surd which will make the denominator rational.

For example,

$$\frac{6}{\sqrt{3}} = \frac{6 \times \sqrt{3}}{\sqrt{3} \times \sqrt{3}} = \frac{6\sqrt{3}}{3} = 2\sqrt{3}$$

$$\frac{7}{\sqrt{18}} = \frac{7}{3\sqrt{2}} = \frac{7 \times \sqrt{2}}{3\sqrt{2} \times \sqrt{2}} = \frac{7\sqrt{2}}{3 \times 2} = \frac{7\sqrt{2}}{6}$$

$$\frac{5}{\sqrt{5}} = \frac{\sqrt{5} \times \sqrt{5}}{\sqrt{5}} = \sqrt{5}$$

Notice also, since $\dfrac{\sqrt{m}}{\sqrt{n}} = \sqrt{\dfrac{m}{n}}$,

$$\frac{\sqrt{18}}{\sqrt{2}} = \sqrt{\frac{18}{2}} = \sqrt{9} = 3$$

$$\frac{\sqrt{5}}{\sqrt{2}} = \sqrt{\frac{5}{2}} = \sqrt{2\tfrac{1}{2}} \text{ or } \sqrt{2 \cdot 5} \text{ or } \tfrac{1}{2}\sqrt{10}$$

The advisability of having a rational denominator is emphasised when a fraction is to be expressed approximately as a decimal.

For example, $\dfrac{2}{\sqrt{3}} = \dfrac{2}{1 \cdot 732}$ approx. $= 1 \cdot 154 \ldots$ The final step involves division by $1 \cdot 732$.

It is clearly simpler to rationalise the denominator before dividing, as follows:

$$\frac{2}{\sqrt{3}} = \frac{2\sqrt{3}}{3} = \frac{2 \times 1 \cdot 732}{3} \text{ approx.} = \frac{3 \cdot 464}{3} \text{ approx.}$$

$$= 1 \cdot 154 \ldots$$

Example 1 *Simplify* $3\sqrt{50} - 5\sqrt{32} + 4\sqrt{8}$.

$$3\sqrt{50} - 5\sqrt{32} + 4\sqrt{8} = 3\sqrt{25 \times 2} - 5\sqrt{16 \times 2} + 4\sqrt{4 \times 2}$$
$$= 3 \times 5\sqrt{2} - 5 \times 4\sqrt{2} + 4 \times 2\sqrt{2}$$
$$= 15\sqrt{2} - 20\sqrt{2} + 8\sqrt{2}$$
$$= 3\sqrt{2}.$$

Example 2 *Simplify* $\dfrac{5\sqrt{7} \times 2\sqrt{3}}{\sqrt{45} \times \sqrt{21}}$.

$$\frac{5\sqrt{7} \times 2\sqrt{3}}{\sqrt{45} \times \sqrt{21}} = \frac{5\sqrt{7} \times 2\sqrt{3}}{3\sqrt{5} \times \sqrt{3} \times \sqrt{7}}$$
$$= \frac{5 \times 2}{3\sqrt{5}}$$
$$= \frac{2\sqrt{5}}{3}.$$

Exercise 18b

Express each of the following as the square root of a single number:

1 $2\sqrt{3}$	**2** $3\sqrt{2}$	**3** $2\sqrt{2}$	**4** $3\sqrt{3}$	**5** $5\sqrt{2}$
6 $3\sqrt{5}$	**7** $2\sqrt{7}$	**8** $4\sqrt{6}$	**9** $6\sqrt{3}$	**10** $5\sqrt{5}$
11 $10\sqrt{3}$	**12** $3\sqrt{10}$	**13** $2\sqrt{11}$	**14** $3\sqrt{8}$	**15** $5\sqrt{7}$

Simplify the following by making the number under the square root sign as small as possible:

16 $\sqrt{20}$	**17** $\sqrt{32}$	**18** $\sqrt{48}$	**19** $\sqrt{75}$	**20** $\sqrt{72}$

21 $\sqrt{24}$ **22** $\sqrt{63}$ **23** $\sqrt{54}$ **24** $\sqrt{200}$ **25** $\sqrt{84}$

26 $\sqrt{99}$ **27** $\sqrt{150}$ **28** $\sqrt{98}$ **29** $\sqrt{288}$ **30** $\sqrt{147}$

Simplify the following:

31 $\sqrt{5} \times \sqrt{10}$ **32** $\sqrt{8} \times \sqrt{2}$ **33** $\sqrt{2} \times \sqrt{6} \times \sqrt{3}$

34 $\sqrt{30} \times \sqrt{5}$ **35** $\sqrt{12} \times \sqrt{3}$ **36** $\left(4\sqrt{3}\right)^2$

37 $\left(\sqrt{2}\right)^3$ **38** $\sqrt{15} \times \sqrt{12}$ **39** $\sqrt{32} \times \sqrt{12}$

40 $\left(\sqrt{3}\right)^5$ **41** $\left(2\sqrt{7}\right)^2$ **42** $\sqrt{10} \times 3\sqrt{2} \times \sqrt{20}$

43 $\sqrt{5} \times \sqrt{24} \times \sqrt{30}$ **44** $(2\sqrt{3})^3$

45 $\sqrt{6} \times \sqrt{8} \times \sqrt{10} \times \sqrt{12}$

Simplify the following by rationalising the denominators:

46 $\dfrac{2}{\sqrt{2}}$ **47** $\dfrac{6}{\sqrt{2}}$ **48** $\dfrac{10}{\sqrt{5}}$ **49** $\dfrac{4}{\sqrt{8}}$ **50** $\dfrac{21}{\sqrt{6}}$

51 $\dfrac{15}{\sqrt{3}}$ **52** $\sqrt{\dfrac{4}{5}}$ **53** $\sqrt{\dfrac{9}{7}}$ **54** $\dfrac{21}{\sqrt{7}}$ **55** $\dfrac{2\sqrt{3}}{\sqrt{6}}$

56 $\dfrac{8}{\sqrt{18}}$ **57** $\sqrt{\dfrac{12}{50}}$ **58** $\dfrac{3\sqrt{2}}{\sqrt{10}}$ **59** $\dfrac{30}{\sqrt{75}}$ **60** $\dfrac{30}{\sqrt{72}}$

Simplify the following:

61 $\sqrt{12} + \sqrt{3}$ **62** $3\sqrt{2} - \sqrt{18}$ **63** $\sqrt{175} - 4\sqrt{7}$

64 $\sqrt{45} + 3\sqrt{20} - 8\sqrt{5}$ **65** $\sqrt{99} - \sqrt{44} - \sqrt{11}$

66 $2\sqrt{8} - 3\sqrt{32} + 4\sqrt{50}$ **67** $2\sqrt{150} - \sqrt{96} - 2\sqrt{24}$

68 $2\sqrt{54} + \sqrt{24} - \sqrt{216}$ **69** $3\sqrt{28} - 5\sqrt{63} + 4\sqrt{112}$

70 $\dfrac{\sqrt{18} \times \sqrt{20} \times \sqrt{24}}{\sqrt{8} \times \sqrt{30}}$ **71** $\dfrac{\sqrt{3} \times \sqrt{8} \times \sqrt{39}}{\sqrt{24} \times \sqrt{26}}$

72 $\sqrt{3} + \dfrac{1}{\sqrt{3}} - \dfrac{1}{\sqrt{27}}$ **73** $2\sqrt{2} - \dfrac{3}{\sqrt{2}} + \dfrac{4}{\sqrt{8}}$

74 $\dfrac{12}{\sqrt{24} - \sqrt{6}}$ **75** $\dfrac{4}{\sqrt{18} + \sqrt{2}}$

Chapter 19

Angles of 45°, 60°, 30°, 0°, 90°

45° If a square ABCD is drawn with sides each 1 unit in length, then since △BCD has a rt. ∠ at C,

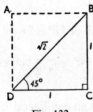

Fig. 132

$$BD^2 = BC^2 + CD^2 = 1^2 + 1^2 = 2$$

$$\therefore\ BD = \sqrt{2}\ \text{units}.$$

Also △BCD is isosceles, having BC = CD.

$$\therefore\ B\hat{D}C = D\hat{B}C.$$

But $B\hat{D}C + D\hat{B}C = 90°$, since the sum of the angles of a △ is 180°, and $B\hat{C}D = 90°$.

$$\therefore\ B\hat{D}C = 45°$$

$$\therefore\ \sin 45° = \frac{BC}{BD} = \frac{1}{\sqrt{2}}$$

$$\cos 45° = \frac{CD}{BD} = \frac{1}{\sqrt{2}}$$

$$\text{and}\quad \tan 45° = \frac{BC}{CD} = \frac{1}{1} = 1$$

249

Further, any triangle which is similar to △BCD, with angles of 45°, 45°, 90° will have sides whose lengths are in the ratio $1 : 1 : \sqrt{2}$.

For example in Fig. 133, if JK = 5 cm, then KL is also 5 cm, and JL is found by multiplying JK by $\sqrt{2}$,

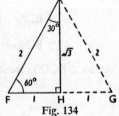

i.e. JL = $5\sqrt{2}$ cm.

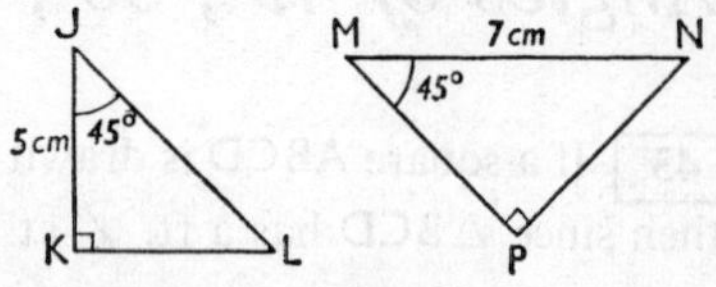

Fig. 133

Also if MN = 7 cm, MP or NP is found by *dividing* MN by $\sqrt{2}$,

$$\text{i.e. MP} = \text{NP} = \frac{7}{\sqrt{2}} \text{ cm} = \frac{7\sqrt{2}}{2} \text{ cm.}$$

60° In Fig. 134, EFG is an equilateral △ with sides each 2 units in length, and $\overline{EH}$ is an altitude.

Then since △EFG is isosceles, with EF = EG, the perpendicular from the vertex bisects the base,

i.e. H is the mid-point of $\overline{FG}$, and FH = 1 unit.

Hence by Pythagoras, in the rt.-∠d △EFH,

Fig. 134

$$EH^2 = EF^2 - FH^2 = 2^2 - 1^2 = 4 - 1 = 3$$

$$\therefore EH = \sqrt{3} \text{ units.}$$

Hence, since $\hat{F} = 60°$ (angle of an equilat. △),

$$\sin 60° = \frac{EH}{EF} = \frac{\sqrt{3}}{2}$$

$$\cos 60° = \frac{HF}{EF} = \frac{1}{2}$$

and $$\tan 60° = \frac{EH}{HF} = \frac{\sqrt{3}}{1} = \sqrt{3}$$

30° Fig. 135 is merely Fig. 134 repeated in a different position.

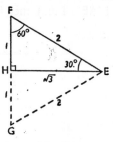

$$\widehat{FEH} = 180° - 90° - 60° = 30°.$$

Hence $\sin 30° = \dfrac{FH}{FE} = \dfrac{1}{2}$

$\cos 30° = \dfrac{HE}{FE} = \dfrac{\sqrt{3}}{2}$

and $\tan 30° = \dfrac{FH}{HE} = \dfrac{1}{\sqrt{3}}$

Fig. 135

Notice that any triangle which is similar to △EFH, with angles of 30°, 60°, 90° will have sides whose lengths are in the ratio $1 : \sqrt{3} : 2$.

EF is twice FH   EH = FH times $\sqrt{3}$

FH is half EF   FH = EH $\div \sqrt{3}$

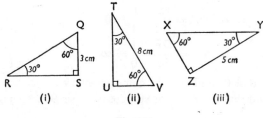

Fig. 136

For example in Fig. 136,

(i) if QS = 3 cm, then QR = 6 cm and RS = $3\sqrt{3}$ cm,

(ii) if TV = 8 cm, then UV = 4 cm and TU = $4\sqrt{3}$ cm,

(iii) if YZ = 5 cm, then XZ = $\dfrac{5}{\sqrt{3}}$ cm and XY = $\dfrac{10}{\sqrt{3}}$ cm.

ɪ

251

New General Mathematics

0° In the rt.-∠d △ in Fig. 137, the angle B is nearly 0°.

If AB is 1 unit, then BC is very nearly 1 unit, and AC is nearly 0.

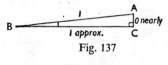
Fig. 137

Hence $\sin 0° = \dfrac{AC}{AB} = \dfrac{0}{1} = 0$

$\cos 0° = \dfrac{CB}{AB} = \dfrac{1}{1} = 1$

$\tan 0° = \dfrac{AC}{CB} = \dfrac{0}{1} = 0$

90° In the rt.-∠d △ in Fig. 138, the angle E is nearly 90°.

If DE is 1 unit, then DF is very nearly 1 unit, and EF is nearly 0.

Hence $\sin 90° = \dfrac{DF}{DE} = \dfrac{1}{1} = 1$

$\cos 90° = \dfrac{FE}{DE} = \dfrac{0}{1} = 0$

$\tan 90° = \dfrac{DF}{FE} = \dfrac{1}{0} = \infty$

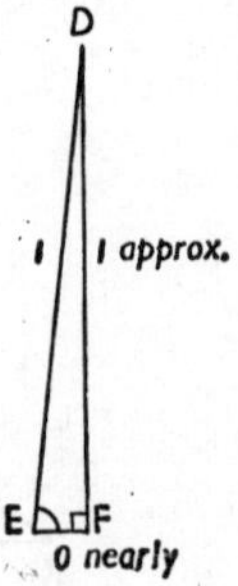

Notice that 0° and 90° are complementary angles, and that sin 0° = cos 90°, cos 0° = sin 90°.

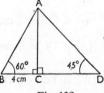
Fig. 138

Example 1 *In Fig. 139, if BC = 4 cm, find AD.*

In △ABC, with angles 30°, 60°, 90°,

$BC = 4$ cm,

∴ $AC = 4\sqrt{3}$ cm.

In △ACD, with angles of 45°, 45°, 90°,

$AC = 4\sqrt{3}$ cm

∴ $AD = 4\sqrt{3} \times \sqrt{2}$ cm

$= 4\sqrt{6}$ cm.

Fig. 139

252

Example 2 P *and* Q *are two pegs in the level ground, and both lie due west of a flagstaff. The angle of elevation of the top of the flagstaff is 45° from* P, *and* 60° *from* Q. *If* P *is 24 m from the foot of the flagstaff, find* PQ.

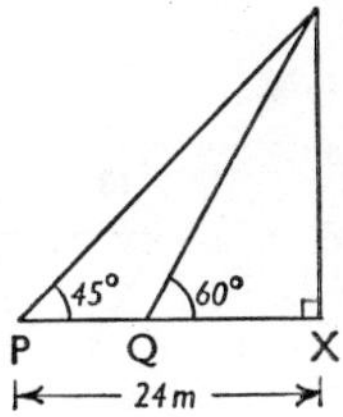

Let the flagstaff be $\overline{XY}$ as in Fig. 140.
The angles of $\triangle PXY$ are 45°, 45°, 90°,

$$\therefore \ XY = PX = 24 \text{ m}$$

The angles of $\triangle QXY$ are 30°, 60°, 90°,

$$\therefore \ QX = \frac{XY}{\sqrt{3}} = \frac{24}{\sqrt{3}} \text{ m} = \frac{24\sqrt{3}}{3} \text{ m} = 8\sqrt{3} \text{ m}$$

$$\therefore \ PQ = 24 \text{ m} - 8\sqrt{3} \text{ m}$$
$$= 8(3 - \sqrt{3}) \text{ m}.$$

Fig. 140

Exercise 19

No tables or decimals should be used in this exercise. Answers which are not rational numbers should be given in surd form. Denominators of fractions should be rationalised where necessary.

In nos. 1–15 the length of one side of a triangle is given in centimetres. Find the lengths of the other two sides.

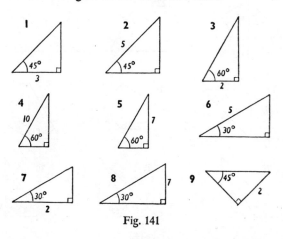

Fig. 141

253

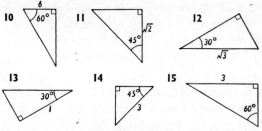

Fig. 141 continued

In nos. 16–30, find the lengths marked *x*. (All lengths are in cm.)

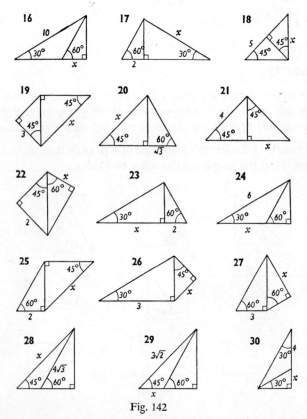

Fig. 142

31 From a point P on the level ground the angle of elevation of the top of a flagstaff is 60°. If the height of the flagstaff is 39 metres, how far from its base is the point P?

32 A regular hexagon has sides each 8 cm long. Find the perpendicular distance between two opposite sides.

33 The length of a diagonal of a square field is 220 metres. Find the length of a side in metres, and the area of the field in hectares.

34 A cone has a circular base, a perpendicular height of 21 cm, and a semi-vertical angle of 30°. Find the slant height of the cone, and the area of its base. (Take $\pi = \frac{22}{7}$)

35 In the isosceles triangle ABC, AB = AC = 4 cm, $\hat{BAC} = 30°$, and $\overline{CN}$ is an altitude. Find BN.

36 A pendulum consists of a bob hanging at the end of a string which is 18 cm long. Find the vertical height through which the bob rises and falls as the pendulum swings through 30° on each side of the vertical.

37 The shadow of a post is 6 m longer when the altitude of the sun is 30° than it is when the altitude is 60°. Find the height of the post.

38 From the top of a cliff 80 m high two boats are seen in a direction due west. Find the distance between the boats if their angles of depression from the cliff top are 45° and 30°. Find also the actual distance of the further boat from the top of the cliff.

39 The angle of elevation of the top of a church spire from a point due east of it and 96 m away from its base is 30°. From another point due west of the spire the angle of elevation of the top is 60°. Find the distance of the latter point from the base of the spire.

40 The angle of elevation of the top of a building 24 m high is observed from the top and from the bottom of a vertical ladder, and found to be 45° and 60° respectively. Find the height of the ladder.

Chapter 20

Logarithms (3)

Theory of logarithms

It was shown in Chap. 1 that logarithms depend upon indices, and that the statements

$$10^2 = 100, \quad \log 100 = 2$$

express the same fact in different terms.

The second statement is written in full as $\log_{10} 100 = 2$, and in words 'the logarithm of 100 to the base 10 is 2'. The reason for choosing 10 as base is the fact that, by so doing, the characteristic can be written down by inspection, since all normal numerical calculations are worked on the denary system. However, in the binary system $2^2 = 4$ and $\log_2 4 = 2$.

The general statements which correspond to the two above are

$$a^x = N, \quad \log_a N = x$$

which again express the same fact in different ways.

In general the logarithm of a number to a given base is the power to which that base must be raised in order to make the given number.

Example 1 *Find* (*i*) $\log_2 8$, (*ii*) $\log_9 27$, (*iii*) $\log_5 0.04$.

$$
\begin{array}{lll}
\text{(i)} & \text{Let} & \log_2 8 = N \\
& \text{Then} & 2^N = 8 = 2^3 \\
& & \therefore N = 3.
\end{array}
$$

$$
\begin{array}{lll}
\text{(ii)} & \text{Let} & \log_9 27 = N \\
& \text{Then} & 9^N = 27 \\
& & \therefore 3^{2N} = 3^3 \\
& & \therefore 2N = 3 \\
& & \therefore N = 1\tfrac{1}{2}.
\end{array}
$$

$$
\begin{array}{lll}
\text{(iii)} & \text{Let} & \log_5 0.04 = N \\
& \text{Then} & 5^N = 0.04 = \tfrac{1}{25} = 5^{-2} \\
& & \therefore N = -2.
\end{array}
$$

Exercise 20a

Evaluate the following logarithms:

1 $\log_2 4$ **2** $\log_{10} 1\,000$ **3** $\log_5 25$ **4** $\log_3 81$

5 $\log_{12} 144$ **6** $\log_6 216$ **7** $\log_7 \frac{1}{7}$ **8** $\log_4 64$

9 $\log_4 8$ **10** $\log_8 4$ **11** $\log_{25} 0{\cdot}2$ **12** $\log_{49} 7$

13 $\log_{1\,000} 10$ **14** $\log_4 \frac{1}{8}$ **15** $\log_{16} 0{\cdot}25$

16 $\log_{100} 0{\cdot}001$ **17** $\log_9 \frac{1}{27}$ **18** $\log_8 0{\cdot}062\,5$

19 $\log_{1{\cdot}2} 1{\cdot}728$ **20** $\log_{0{\cdot}2} 25$

The three fundamental laws of indices can now be restated in their logarithmic form:

1   $a^x \times a^y = a^{x+y}$ $\log (MN) = \log M + \log N$

2   $a^x \div a^y = a^{x-y}$ $\log \left(\dfrac{M}{N}\right) = \log M - \log N$

3     $(a^x)^p = a^{xp}$ $\log (M^p) = p \, \log M$

To prove $\log (MN) = \log M + \log N$.

     Let $\log_a M = x, \quad \log_a N = y$
     Then $a^x = M, \quad a^y = N$
     $\therefore \; MN = a^x \times a^y$
              $= a^{x+y}$
   $\therefore \; \log_a (MN) = x + y = \log_a M + \log_a N.$

The proof of rules 2 and 3 are left to be done as examples in Exercise 20b.

It will be noticed that, in the proof above, logarithms to the base a have been used, whereas the base is not specified in the original statement. In fact the statement is true for any base whatever, as can be seen immediately if the first words of the proof had been 'Let $\log_b M = x$, $\log_b N = y$', etc.

Example 2 *Assuming only that* $\log_{10} 2 = 0{\cdot}301\,0$, $\log_{10} 3 = 0{\cdot}477\,1$, *evaluate (i)* $\log_{10} 6$, *(ii)* $\log_{10} 9$, *(iii)* $\log_{10} 15$.

(i) $\log_{10} 6 = \log_{10} (2 \times 3) = \log_{10} 2 + \log_{10} 3$
$$= 0.301\ 0 + 0.477\ 1 = 0.778\ 1$$

(ii) $\log_{10} 9 = \log_{10} (3^2) = 2\ \log_{10} 3 = 2 \times 0.477\ 1 = 0.954\ 2$

(iii) $\log_{10} 15 = \log_{10} (\frac{30}{2}) = \log_{10} 10 + \log_{10} 3 - \log_{10} 2$
$$= 1 + 0.477\ 1 - 0.301\ 0 = 1.176\ 1$$

Example 3 *Evaluate to 2 places of decimals* $\log_3 6.84$.

	No.	Log.
	8.351	0.921 8
	4.771	0.678 6
	1.751	0.243 2

Let $\quad \log_3 6.84 = x$

Then $\qquad 3^x = 6.84$

$\therefore \ \log_{10} (3^x) = \log_{10} 6.84$

$\therefore \ x \log_{10} 3 = \log_{10} 6.84$

$$\therefore \ x = \frac{\log_{10} 6.84}{\log_{10} 3} = \frac{0.835\ 1}{0.477\ 1} = \frac{8.351}{4.771}$$

$$\eqsim 1.75$$

Exercise 20b

1 Prove (i) $\log \left(\dfrac{M}{N} \right) = \log M - \log N$

(ii) $\log (M^p) = p \log M$

2 Assuming only that $\log_{10} 2 = 0.301\ 0$, $\log_{10} 3 = 0.477\ 1$, $\log_{10} 7 = 0.845\ 1$, evaluate

(i) $\log_{10} 5$, (ii) $\log_{10} 8$, (iii) $\log_{10} 49$, (iv) $\log_{10} 14$,

(v) $\log_{10} 35$, (vi) $\log_{10} 42$, (vii) $\log_{10} 3.75$.

3 Use logarithm tables to evaluate (i) $\log_2 6$, (ii) $\log_7 6$, (iii) $\log_5 12.64$, (iv) $\log_{12} 0.862\ 1$, giving answers to two decimal places.

4 Express as logarithms of single numbers (or fractions), all the logarithms being to base 10:

(i) $\log 3 + \log 4$ (ii) $\log 4 - \log 3$

(iii) $3 \log 5$ (iv) $\frac{1}{2} \log 25$

(v) $- \log 3$ (vi) $1 + \log 3$

(vii) $1 - \log 5$ (viii) $2 \log 3 + \log 2$

(ix) $2 - 2 \log 2$ (x) $\frac{3}{4} \log 16$

5 Solve for x
  (i) $\log_{10} x = 3$ (ii) $\log_{10} x = -2$
  (iii) $\log_x 81 = 4$ (iv) $2\log_x (3\frac{3}{8}) = 6$

6 Simplify without using tables
  (i) $\dfrac{\log 4}{\log 2}$ (ii) $\dfrac{\log 16}{\log 8}$ (iii) $\dfrac{\log \sqrt{3}}{\log 9}$ (iv) $\dfrac{\log 0\cdot2}{\log 25}$

7 Express in index form the equations
  (i) $\log_a x = b$ (ii) $\log_a x + \log_a y = 1$
  (iii) $\log_a x + 1 = 0$ (iv) $\log_a x + 2\log_a y = 3$
  (v) $\log_a x - \log_a y = \log_a z$

8 Simplify (i) $\log 8 - \log 4$ (ii) $\log 8 \div \log 4$
  (iii) $\log 8 + \log 4$ (iv) $\dfrac{\log 8 - \log 4}{\log 4 - \log 2}$

9 Solve the equations
  (i) $2^{2x} - 3 \times 2^x + 2 = 0$ (put $2^x = y$)
  (ii) $4^x - 10 \times 2^x + 16 = 0$
  (iii) $3^{2x+1} - 10 \times 3^x + 3 = 0$

10 Solve the equation $x + \dfrac{1}{x} = 2\frac{1}{2}$. Hence find y, correct to two places of decimals, if $e^y + e^{-y} = 2\frac{1}{2}$ and $e = 2\cdot718$.

Exercise 20c (Revision)

Evaluate the following, checking answers whenever it is reasonable to do so:

1 $5\cdot024^3$ **2** $\sqrt[3]{26\cdot71}$ **3** $\sqrt[4]{82\cdot64 \times 137\cdot5}$

4 $\sqrt[3]{0\cdot056\,78}$ **5** $16\cdot84^{\frac{3}{8}}$ **6** $0\cdot076\,38^{\frac{3}{4}}$

7 $\sqrt[100]{0\cdot000\,006\,658}$ **8** $\dfrac{0\cdot062\,95}{0\cdot081\,83}$

9 $\sqrt[3]{2\cdot93 \times 0\cdot825 \times 0\cdot000\,362}$ **10** $(0\cdot267 \times 0\cdot934)^3$

11 $\left(\dfrac{0\cdot009\,213}{0\cdot076\,46}\right)^2$ **12** $\dfrac{0\cdot387\,2 \times 0\cdot092\,16}{0\cdot056\,57}$

13 $\dfrac{0{\cdot}678\,4^2}{0{\cdot}921\,6^3}$

14 $\dfrac{0{\cdot}358\,1 \times 0{\cdot}028\,47}{0{\cdot}009\,418 \times 3{\cdot}219}$

15 $\sqrt[3]{69{\cdot}5^2 - 30{\cdot}5^2}$

16 $0{\cdot}003\,872^{0{\cdot}6}$

17 $\sqrt[3]{8{\cdot}3^3 + 1{\cdot}7^3}$

18 $\sqrt[5]{\dfrac{0{\cdot}076\,4}{0{\cdot}000\,921}}$

19 $0{\cdot}239\,4^{1{\cdot}4}$

20 $\{\sqrt[3]{0{\cdot}834} + \sqrt[3]{0{\cdot}716}\}^3$

21 $6{\cdot}28 \times \sqrt{\frac{3\,0\,4}{9\,8\,1}}$

22 $\dfrac{13{\cdot}87^2 \times 2{\cdot}95}{4\,009}$

23 $\sqrt{22{\cdot}1 \times 13{\cdot}9 \times 29{\cdot}2 \times 47{\cdot}4}$

24 $\sqrt[5]{100 + \sqrt[4]{100 + \sqrt[3]{100}}}$

25 $\dfrac{3{\cdot}87^3 + 20}{3{\cdot}87^3 - 20}$

26 $\sqrt[4]{\dfrac{0{\cdot}076\,3}{309 \times 0{\cdot}008\,465}}$

27 $\sqrt{785{\cdot}6 + 37\sqrt{23{\cdot}14}}$

28 $0{\cdot}925^3 \div \sqrt{0{\cdot}673}$

29 $\sqrt{\dfrac{14{\cdot}25 \times 2{\cdot}87}{3{\cdot}869 \times 29{\cdot}45}}$

30 $\dfrac{0{\cdot}382\,6^2}{0{\cdot}598\,5^3}$

---

31 $10^{-\frac{2}{3}}$ **32** $3{\cdot}54^{-0{\cdot}6}$ **33** $\dfrac{1}{\sqrt[3]{10}}$ **34** $\dfrac{1}{0{\cdot}1^{0{\cdot}2}}$

35 $0{\cdot}924^{-2{\cdot}5}$ **36** $\sqrt[4]{0{\cdot}562\,4^{-3}}$ **37** $4{\cdot}27^{-0{\cdot}4}$

38 $0{\cdot}5^{0{\cdot}6}$ **39** $86{\cdot}43^{-1{\cdot}5}$ **40** $0{\cdot}83^{-0{\cdot}3}$

Solve for x the equations

41 $10^x = 3$ **42** $3^x = 10$ **43** $5^x = 100$

44 $6^x = 120$ **45** $4^x = 0{\cdot}88$ **46** $0{\cdot}2^x = 0{\cdot}8$

47 $2^{-x} = 5$ **48** $3^{-2x} = 0{\cdot}7$ **49** $\dfrac{2}{x} = \dfrac{1}{10{\cdot}3} + \dfrac{1}{15{\cdot}4}$

50 $\dfrac{1}{x} = \dfrac{1}{2{\cdot}62} - \dfrac{1}{2{\cdot}73}$

Exercise 20d

Miscellaneous questions involving logarithms or slide rule

Unless otherwise instructed take $\pi = 3.142$ or $\log \pi = 0.497\ 1$. The volume of a sphere is $\frac{4}{3} \pi r^3$.

1 Find x when $\dfrac{1}{x} = \dfrac{1}{8.63} + \dfrac{1}{5.41}$.

2 Evaluate $\dfrac{a + b}{ab}$ when $a = 21.56$ and $b = 9.84$.

3 Evaluate $\sqrt{a^2 - b^2}$ when $a = 2.736$ and $b = 1.364$.

4 Two lead cubes of edges 0·7 cm and 0·3 cm are melted together and recast into another cube. What is the length of an edge of this cube?

5 Evaluate $\dfrac{x^3 - 1}{x^3 + 1}$ when $x = 1.254$.

6 Find the radius of a circle of area 2 square centimetres.

7 If $s = \frac{1}{2}(a + b + c)$, evaluate $\sqrt{s(s - a)(s - b)(s - c)}$ when
    (i) $a = 25.7$, $b = 33.5$, $c = 30.4$
    (ii) $a = 5.93$, $b = 6.47$, $c = 11.36$

Evaluate also for the values of a, b, c given in (ii)

    (iii) $\sqrt{\dfrac{s(s - a)}{bc}}$ (iv) $\sqrt{\dfrac{(s - a)(s - b)}{s(s - c)}}$

8 Solve for x the equation $13x = \dfrac{343}{51.2} - \dfrac{1}{9} \log 0.426$.

9 Calculate the volumes of spheres of radius (i) 2·85 cm, (ii) 6·95 cm, (iii) 0·962 m.

10 How many lead balls, each $\frac{1}{2}$ cm in diameter, could be cast from 1 000 cm³ of lead?

11 The time of swing of a pendulum of length l cm is t s, where $t = 2\pi\sqrt{\dfrac{l}{g}}$ and $g = 981$. What is the time of swing of a pendulum of length 800 cm?

12 Using the formula in no. 11, find what length of pendulum, to the nearest millimetre, will swing in exactly one second.

13 Find the diameter of a ball-bearing of volume half a cubic centimetre.

14 What is the mass in kg of a solid steel ball of diameter 6·8 cm if the mass of 1 cm³ of steel is 7·76 g?

15 The capacity V cm³ of a test-tube of diameter d cm and overall length l cm is given by the formula

$$V = \frac{\pi d^2}{24}(6l - d).$$

Find the capacity of a test-tube of diameter 1·9 cm and length 15·4 cm.

Chapter 21

Inequalities (1).
Linear programming

Equations and inequalities

Consider a field of area 3 hectares which has a number of sheep (say x) in it.

(i) If there are 50 sheep, then $x = 50$.
This is an **equation.**
(ii) If there are fewer than 20 sheep to the hectare, then $x < 60$.
This is an **inequality.**

Notice that the equation has only one answer, but in the inequality (where $<$ stands for 'is less than' and $>$ for 'is greater than') x can take any numerical value from 0 to 59 inclusive, negative values for x having no real meaning in this case.

Inequalities are solved in much the same way as equations, but certain precautions have to be taken, e.g.

(i) $x + 4 < 6$	$\therefore x < 2$	subtracting 4 from both sides
(ii) $4 - x > 3$	$\therefore 4 > 3 + x$	adding x to both sides
	$\therefore 1 > x$	subtracting 3 from both sides
	$\therefore x < 1$	
or $4 - x > 3$	$\therefore -x > -1$	subtracting 4 from both sides
	$\therefore x < 1$	multiplying both sides by -1 and at the same time changing $>$ into $<$.

The reason for changing $>$ into $<$ in (ii) becomes clearer if the position of points on the x-axis is considered, the numerical value of x becoming

Fig. 143

greater as the point moves from left to right: e.g. $6 > 4$, but $-6 < -4 \ (-6 = -4 - 2)$ (Fig. 143).

New General Mathematics

It is convenient to represent the solution of the inequality $x < 2$ by a line as in Fig. 144, where the ○ shows that the value 2 is not included as a possible answer, but any other value to the left of 2 is correct.

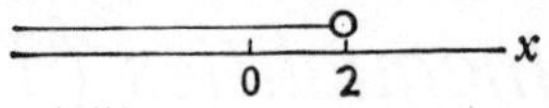

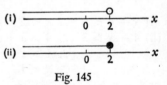

Fig. 144

Exercise 21a

Solve the following inequalities, showing the solutions by a line as in Fig. 144:

1 $x - 2 < 3$ **2** $x + 3 > 6$ **3** $3 - x < 1$

4 $2 > x - 4$ **5** $2x < 6$ **6** $-2x < -6$

7 $3x + 4 < 1$ **8** $5 - 2x > 1$ **9** $5x - 2 > 19 - 2x$

10 $2(x + 3) > 3(2 - x)$ **11** $\frac{1}{4}(x - 3) < \frac{1}{3}x$

12 $-2(x - 3) > -3(x + 2)$

It is very important to distinguish between the two statements (i) x is less than 2, (ii) x is not greater than 2. In the first x can take any value from $-\infty$ up to but not including 2: in the second the value 2 is included.

These two cases are shown in Fig. 145, ○ meaning that 2 is *not* included, and ● meaning that 2 *is* included in the set of possible solutions.

Fig. 145

The inequalities $x \leqslant 2$ and $x \ngtr 2$ are equivalent, the symbol $\leqslant$ meaning 'is less than or equal to', and $\ngtr$ meaning 'not greater than'. Similarly $x \geqslant 2$ and $x \nless 2$ are equivalent.

Exercise 21b

Solve the following inequalities, illustrating solution-sets as in Fig. 145:

1 $x - 3 \leqslant 5$ **2** $x + 1 \geqslant 3$ **3** $2 - x \ngtr 3$

4 $2x \not< 6$ **5** $3x - 1 \leqslant 2$ **6** $1 - 3x \not< 4$

7 $5x + 6 \geqslant 3 + 2x$ **8** $5 - 5x \not> x - 4$

9 $2(x - 3) \geqslant 5$ **10** $2(x - 3) \geqslant 5x$

11 $\frac{1}{2}(3x - 2) \not> \frac{1}{3}(x + 4)$ **12** $\dfrac{x}{3} + \dfrac{1}{4} \leqslant \dfrac{x}{5} - \dfrac{1}{2}$

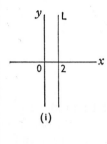 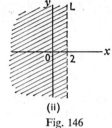 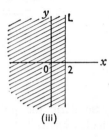

(i)   (ii)   (iii)

Fig. 146

In Fig. 146

(i) $x = 2$ is the set of all points *on* the line L,

(ii) $x < 2$ is the set of all points in the shaded area to the left of the line L (but *not* including points on the line),

(iii) $x \leqslant 2$ is the set of all points in the shaded area, together with the set of all points on the line L itself.

In the drawings the boundary for $x < 2$ is shown as a broken line, and for $x \leqslant 2$ as a solid line.

Example 1 *Show on a graph the area giving the solution-set of the inequalities* $2x + 3y < 6$, $y - 2x < 2$.

Consider first $2x + 3y < 6$.

This may be written $3y < 6 - 2x$

$$\therefore \ y < \tfrac{1}{3}(6 - 2x)$$

if $x = 0$ $y < 2$
       $x = 1\tfrac{1}{2}$ $y < 1$
       $x = 3$ $y < 0$
       $x = 4\tfrac{1}{2}$ $y < -1$

The points $(0,2)$, $(1\tfrac{1}{2},1)$, $(3,0)$, $(4\tfrac{1}{2},-1)$, ... lie on the line $2x + 3y = 6$ (the line P in the diagram).

$\therefore$ points satisfying $2x + 3y < 6$ lie to the left of the line P in the area shaded horizontally.

265

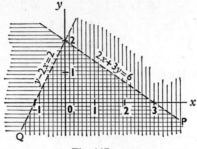

Fig. 147

Similarly the points satisfying $y - 2x < 2$ lie in the area shaded vertically to the right of the line $y - 2x = 2$ (the line Q).

Hence the solution-set lies in the cross-hatched area between P and Q, which extends downwards indefinitely.

Example 2 *Solve graphically* $4x + 3y \leqslant 12$, $y < 3$, $y > 0$, $x > 0$ *for integral (i.e. whole number) values of x and y.*

The solution-set consists of all points in the shaded area, including points on the boundary line L ($4x + 3y = 12$), but not including points on the other three boundary lines.

Solutions are (1,1), (2,1), (1,2).

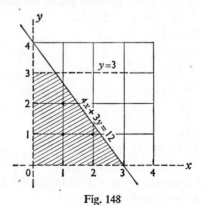

Fig. 148

Exercise 21c

Draw diagrams on squared paper and shade in the areas giving solution-sets for the following (use solid and broken lines as above):

1 $x + y < 6$, $y - x < 2$, $x \geqslant 0$, $y \geqslant 0$

2 $x - y > 1$, $3x + 4y < 12$, $x \geqslant 0$, $y \geqslant 0$

3 $4x + 3y > 0$, $5x + 2y < 10$, $y \leqslant 4$, $y \geqslant 0$

4 $2x - 3y \leqslant 6$, $3x + 2y + 4 \geqslant 0$, $y < 3$, $x < 6$

5 $y - x \geqslant 3$, $2x + y \leqslant 4$, $y > -2$, $x > 0$

6 $x + y \leqslant 2$, $x - y \leqslant 2$, $2x + y \geqslant 2$

7 $4y - 3x > 12$, $2x + y < 0$, $y \leqslant 1$

8 $x - y > 3$, $y - 3x < 0$, $x + y \geqslant 4$

8 $3x + 5y < 15$, $x - y < 2$, $y \leqslant 2$, $x \geqslant -3$

10 $2x - 3y \leqslant 6$, $4x + 3y \geqslant 12$, $y \leqslant 5$, $x \geqslant 0$

Linear programming

Problems involving inequalities frequently occur in industry and in ordinary life. Many of these problems can be solved graphically, and solutions reached in this way are examples of linear programming, so called because lines are used in finding the answers.

Example 3 *A caterer has £1 to spend on prizes for a choir-treat: she can buy bags of toffees (6p each) and bags of chocolates (8p each) and there must not be less than 6 of either sort. There are 13 children to be catered for, each of whom must get at least one prize. How can the money be spent?*

Suppose she buys x bags of toffees and y bags of chocolates. She has 100p to spend, $\therefore 6x + 8y \leqslant 100$.

As there must be at least 6 of each sort,

$$x \geqslant 6 \quad \text{and} \quad y \geqslant 6.$$

There are 13 children, so that there must be at least 13 prizes, $\therefore x + y \geqslant 13$.

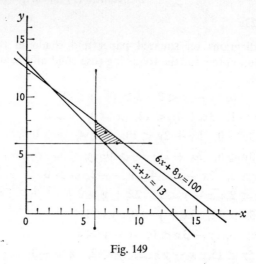

Fig. 149

The shaded area in Fig. 149 shows all the possible solutions, and it will be noticed that there are 5 points inside the area and on its boundaries which represent possible solutions to the problem. These points are shown as heavy dots in Fig. 149, and they are (6, 7), (6, 8), (7, 6), (7, 7), (8, 6).

∴ she can buy

6 bags of toffees and 7 of chocolates
or 6 ,, ,, ,, ,, 8 ,, ,,
or 7 ,, ,, ,, ,, 6 ,, ,,
or 7 ,, ,, ,, ,, 7 ,, ,,
or 8 ,, ,, ,, ,, 6 ,, ,, .

Now suppose that there had been an additional question: *what is the largest number of bags she can buy?* This can be solved in the following way.

The number of bags bought is $x + y$.

If this number is called n, then $x + y = n$, which is represented by a family of parallel lines in the graph as n takes different values (the line $x + y = 13$ is already there).

Inequalities (1) Linear programming

As n increases the line moves further to right, as can be seen in Fig. 150, which shows the lines $x + y = 5$, $x + y = 10$, $x + y = 15$.

The largest possible value of n occurs when the line is as far as possible to the right, but still goes through the shaded area.

In this particular case the line required is the line $x + y = 14$, which goes through the points (6,8), (7,7), (8,6), and therefore the largest possible number of

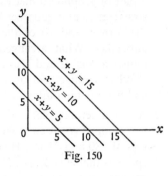

Fig. 150

bags of sweets that can be bought is 14, and there are three possible ways in which this can be done.

Exercise 21d

1 Draw Fig. 149 to as large a scale as possible, showing the shaded area and adding the lines $x + y = 14$, $x + y = 15$.

2 At a fair a ride on the bumper-cars costs 5p and on the galloping horses 3p. A boy has 30p to spend and wants to have at least three rides on each. How can he do it if he decides to spend as much as possible of his 30p? There are in fact only two ways of doing it: does either of these give him any change out of his money?

3 A man setting up a shop dealing in small components needs a large number of handles for small drawers: two types of handle are required, one costing 3p each and the other 4p. He has budgeted for £3 on handles and needs at least twice as many of the cheap ones as of the more expensive. There must be at least 50 cheap and 20 expensive handles.

What is the largest number of handles he can buy, and in what way? If he decides to get as many of the expensive ones as his money will allow, how many of each sort can he get?

4 Strawberries occupy half a square metre per plant and cost

269

5p each; gooseberries $1\frac{1}{2}$ m² and 30p each. A smallholder has a plot of ground 10 metres square and wants to plant it with strawberries and gooseberries, planning to have at least 50 of the former and 20 of the latter. He can spend up to £15 altogether. What arrangement allows him to spend all the money available and also to use as much space as possible?

What arrangement uses all the space for the least outlay, and what is the outlay in this case?

5 A manufacturer plans to install some new machines in his workshop. Type A costs £60 and occupies 3 m² of floor space; type B £80 and $2\frac{1}{2}$ m². He can spend £720 altogether and the space available is 27 m². Machine A turns out 10 components per hour and type B 15 per hour, but trade restrictions compel him to have at least 3 of A and 4 of B.

What is the maximum number of machines he can install?
Which arrangement gives him the biggest output?

6 A heavy smoker decides to ration himself to a maximum of four packets of tobacco a week at 45p per packet and two cigars a day at 10p each. He also decides that he will not spend more than £3 a week, and that he cannot spend less than £2.

Is there any way in which he can spend exactly (i) his maximum? (ii) his minimum?

If a packet is of mass 30 g and a cigar of mass 6 g, and the doctor says he ought not to smoke more than 150 g per week, in how many different ways can he conform to the doctor's recommendation?

Revision examples

XXI

1 Simplify (i) $2a^3 \times 3a^{-2}$ (ii) $2a^3 \times (3a)^{-2}$ (iii) $(2a^{-2})^{-2}$
(iv) $0{\cdot}008^{-\frac{2}{3}}$ (v) $2^x \times 4^x$ (vi) $3^{x+y} \times 3^{x-y} \times 9^{-x}$.

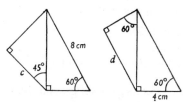

Fig. 151

2 In Fig. 151 calculate the lengths marked c and d. Do not use tables or decimals.

3 PQRS is a cyclic quadrilateral: $\overline{PQ}$ and $\overline{SR}$ produced meet at X. If $R\hat{Q}X = 61°$ and $\hat{X} = 32°$, calculate $\hat{P}$.

4 Solve the equation $\dfrac{2x-5}{5} - \dfrac{x-4}{4} = \dfrac{x+14}{30}$. Check the answer.

5 $a = 3{\cdot}65 \times 10^3$, $b = 5{\cdot}28 \times 10^{-4}$. Evaluate (i) a^2, (ii) b^3, (iii) $\dfrac{a}{b}$.

6 ABC is a triangle right-angled at B: AB $= 10$ cm, BC $= 7$ cm, and M is the mid-point of $\overline{BC}$. Calculate $C\hat{A}M$.

7 Express l as the subject of the formula $e = \dfrac{kl}{l+a}$.

8 Solve, correct to 2 dec. places, $x^2 - 4x + 1 = 0$.

9 (i) Simplify $\sqrt{288} \div \sqrt{8}$, $(3\sqrt{5})^2$, $5\sqrt{27} - 3\sqrt{75}$.

    (ii) Express with rational denominators $\dfrac{5\sqrt{2}}{\sqrt{10}}$, $\dfrac{2\sqrt{5}}{5\sqrt{10}}$.

10 Evaluate (i) $\log_8 16$, (ii) $\log_{25} 125$, (iii) $\log_2 (\frac{1}{4})$.

XXII

1 Express *r* as the subject of the formula

$$V = \pi h^2 \left(r - \frac{h}{3} \right).$$

Calculate *r* if V = 138·6 cm³, *h* = 4·2 cm, and $\pi = \frac{22}{7}$.

2 Find the length *x* in Fig. 152.

3 Factorise (i) $3p^2 - 75q^2$
        (ii) $17xy - 4x^2 - 4y^2$
        (iii) $a^2 - 2bc - a(2b - c)$.

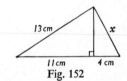
Fig. 152

4 A and B are two points on level ground, both due south of a flagstaff. The angle of elevation of the top of the flagstaff is 60° from A and 45° from B. If A is 20 m from the foot of the flagstaff, find AB. (Leave the answer in surd form.)

5 After 10 innings a batsman who had never been 'not out' had an average of 8·4. In the next match he batted twice, being out both times, and improved his average to 9·5. If he made 7 runs in the first of these innings, how many did he make in the second?

6 (i) Simplify $(3\sqrt{3})^3$, $\sqrt{8} \times \sqrt{6} \times \sqrt{4}$, $\sqrt{176} - \sqrt{99}$.

(ii) Express with rational denominators $\dfrac{10}{\sqrt{18}}$, $\dfrac{9}{\sqrt{162}}$.

7 Solve, correct to 2 dec. places, $2x^2 + 3x - 6 = 0$.

8 In Fig. 153 find the marked angle by calculation. O is the centre of the circle.

9 ABCD is a circle. $\overline{BA}$ produced and $\overline{CD}$ produced meet at X; $\overline{AD}$ produced and $\overline{BC}$ produced at Z. $\overline{BD}$ produced cuts $\overline{XZ}$ at Y. Prove that, if ABZY is a cyclic quadrilateral, then so also is BCYX.

Fig. 153

10 Draw the graph of $y = 2x^2 - 4x - 3$ for values of *x* between −2 and +4. Find from the graph the minimum value of *y* and also the solutions of the equation $2x^2 - 4x = 3$.

XXIII

1 Factorise (i) $2x^2 - 5x + 2$ (ii) $9a^3 - a$
(iii) $6ax - 6y - 9ay + 4x$ (iv) $10 - 7r - 12r^2$.

2 Evaluate, using logarithms,

(i) $\sqrt[3]{210}$ (ii) $0.792\ 1^3$ (iii) $\dfrac{1.69^2 - 1}{1.69^2 + 1}$.

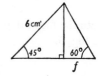

Fig. 154

3 In Fig. 154 calculate the lengths marked e and f. Do not use tables or decimals.

4 Solve the equation $\dfrac{1}{x - 1} + \dfrac{2}{2x - 1} = \dfrac{6}{3x - 1}$.

5 $\overline{AB}$ is a diameter of a circle of radius 3 cm, and $\overline{AC}$ is a chord of length 4 cm. $\overline{AC}$ is produced to D so that CD = CB. Calculate (to 2 dec. pl.) BD.

6 Change the subject of the following formula to L:

$$e = \frac{L - l}{LT - lt}.$$

7 ABC is a triangle right-angled at C. BC = 10 cm, AC = 12 cm. The bisector of $\widehat{B}$ cuts $\overline{AC}$ at X. Calculate AX and BX.

8 (i) Simplify $\sqrt{147} \div 14$, $\sqrt{32} \times \sqrt{2}$, $\sqrt{32} + \sqrt{2}$.

(ii) Express with rational denominators $\dfrac{15}{\sqrt{45}}$, $\sqrt{\dfrac{63}{75}}$.

9 The depth of water in a reservoir is taken at equal intervals along a straight line down the middle of it, with the following results:

Depth (m)	1–5	6–10	11–15	16–20	21–25
Frequency	5	4	3	1	3

Depth (m)	26–30	31–35	36–40	41–45	46–50
Frequency	6	2	3	8	15

Calculate the mean depth along this line.

10 Calculate $\log_2 3$.

XXIV

1 Calculate CD and BD in Fig. 155.

2 Express H as the subject of the formula

$$E = \frac{2Hg - V^2}{2Hg}.$$

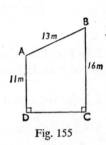

Fig. 155

3 (i) Simplify $\sqrt{84} \times \sqrt{14}$, $(5\sqrt{2})^3$,
$5\sqrt{32} + 2\sqrt{50}$.

(ii) Express with rational denominators

$$\frac{\sqrt{24}}{\sqrt{50}}, \frac{16\sqrt{5}}{\sqrt{10}}.$$

4 ABCD is a cyclic quadrilateral, and $\overline{AB}$ is produced to E.
$\overline{BC}$ bisects $D\hat{B}E$. Prove that CA = CD.

5 Solve to 2 dec. pl. the equation $3x^2 + 12x + 11 = 0$.

6 A man sells a chair for £5·15, making a profit of 3%. What
profit % would he have made if he had sold it for £5·85?

7 Solve the equation $\dfrac{10}{x-2} - \dfrac{10}{x+3} = 1$. Check the result.

8 $\overline{AD}$ is an altitude of a triangle ABC in which AB = 6 cm,
$\hat{A} = 90°$, $\hat{B} = 30°$. Find CD, expressing the answer in surd
form.

274

9 A farmer makes a rectangular sheepfold, using hurdles for three sides and a wall for the fourth. He uses 27 metres of hurdles altogether and the area enclosed is 90 m². Find the length and breadth of the fold.

10 Show graphically the area defined by the inequalities $2x + y \leqslant 10$, $x + 3y \leqslant 9$ for positive values of x and y. If the numerical values of x and y may include $\frac{1}{2}$ but no other fraction, what solution-sets (x,y) will give $x + y$ its maximum value, and what is that value?

XXV

1 $v = \sqrt{gd\left(1 + \dfrac{3h}{d}\right)}$. Rearrange the formula with d as subject.

2 Solve the equations

(i) $\frac{1}{10}\left(\dfrac{7x}{2} + 8\right) - \dfrac{4x - 5}{3} = \frac{1}{2}$

(ii) $2x = 3y + 4$, $x - 2y + 3 = 0$.

3 (i) Simplify $(3\sqrt{2})^2$, $\sqrt{21} \times \sqrt{3}$, $2\sqrt{2} + 3\sqrt{18}$.

(ii) Rearrange with rational denominators $\dfrac{20}{\sqrt{50}}$, $\dfrac{18}{\sqrt{3}}$.

4 $\overline{AB}$ is the diameter of a circle ACBD. AC = 2·5 cm, BC = 1·5 cm and DA = DB. Calculate $C\hat{B}D$ and the radius of the circle.

5 A motorist has a journey of 96 km to make. A second motorist whose average speed is 8 km h⁻¹ more than the first, takes 24 minutes less time on the journey. What are the speeds of the two drivers?

6 ABC is an equilateral triangle inscribed in a circle. Any line through A cuts $\overline{BC}$ at Y and the circle at X.

Prove that $A\hat{Y}B = A\hat{B}X$.

7 Use logarithms to evaluate (i) $\dfrac{0·835 \times 0·076\ 2}{0·324\ 6}$

(ii) $\sqrt[3]{0·783^3 - 0·594^3}$

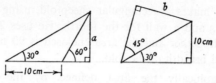

Fig. 156

8 In Fig. 156, calculate the lengths marked a and b, leaving the answers in surd form.

9 Solve the equation $2x^2 - 5x + 1 = 0$, giving the answers correct to two dec. pl.

10 Solve the equation $5^x = 8$, giving the answer correct to three sig. fig.

XXVI

1 Solve the equations

  (i) $(x - 1)^2 = 0$ (ii) $(x - 1)^2 = 1$
  (iii) $(x - 1)^2 = x^2$ (iv) $(x - 1)^2 = x - 1$

2 $\overline{AB}$ is a chord 26 cm long in a circle centre O. $\overline{PQ}$ is another chord of the circle, and the distances of $\overline{AB}$ and $\overline{PQ}$ from O are respectively 4 cm and 8 cm. Find (i) the radius of the circle, (ii) PQ.

3 Solve, to two dec. pl., the equation $3x^2 - 5x + 1 = 0$.

4 A year-book for 1969 records the number of deaths of distinguished people in different age-groups during the year as follows:

Age	36–40	41–45	46–50	51–55	56–60	61–65
Frequency	1	4	8	5	15	25

Age	66–70	71–75	76–80	81–85	86–90	91–95	96–100
Frequency	23	32	40	31	19	6	1

Calculate the mean of this distribution. Draw the cumulative-frequency ogive and read from it the median and the inter-quartile range.

5 Express k as the subject of the formula

$$T = 2\pi\sqrt{\dfrac{h^2 + k^2}{2gh}}.$$

6 A circle is inscribed in a 60° sector of a larger circle (Fig. 157). Prove that the ratio of the radii of the circles is $1:3$, and find the ratio of the areas of the circle and the sector.

Fig. 157

7 (i) Simplify $\sqrt{45} \times \sqrt{15}$, $\sqrt{63} \times \sqrt{28}$, $3\sqrt{54} - 4\sqrt{24}$.

  (ii) Express with rational denominators $\dfrac{15}{\sqrt{5}}$, $\dfrac{3\sqrt{2}}{\sqrt{12}}$.

8 PQRS is a cyclic quadrilateral drawn in a circle with centre O. If $\overline{PR}$ is perpendicular to $\overline{QS}$, prove that $P\hat{O}Q$ and $R\hat{O}S$ are supplementary.

9 Evaluate $\log_e 3{\cdot}8$, when $e = 2{\cdot}718$.

10 x km at y km h^{-1} takes $4\frac{1}{2}$ hours; x km at $(y - 1)$ km h^{-1} takes 5 hours. Find x and y.

XXVII

1 (i) Simplify $2\sqrt{12} \times 2\sqrt{15}$, $(5\sqrt{3})^2$, $2\sqrt{27} - \sqrt{48}$.

  (ii) Express with rational denominators $\dfrac{15}{\sqrt{75}}$, $\dfrac{4\sqrt{18}}{\sqrt{12}}$.

2 $c = \dfrac{ab\sqrt{2g}}{\sqrt{a^2 - b^2}}$. Express a as the subject of the formula.

3 Simplify $\dfrac{4}{x^2 - 2xy - 3y^2} + \dfrac{1}{x^2 + 3xy + 2y^2}$.

4 Fig. 158 shows a heavy roller, used for a school cricket field, and the shafts are 120 cm from the ground when they are horizontal, as shown. The diameter of the roller is 150 cm. What angle do the shafts make with the ground when their ends are on the ground?

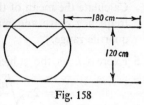

Fig. 158

5 When the sun's altitude is 30° the shadow thrown by a vertical mast is 20 m longer than it is when the sun's altitude is 60°. Find the height of the mast, without using tables or decimals.

6 $a = 2 \cdot 9$, $b = 4 \cdot 7$, $c = 5 \cdot 4$ and $s = \frac{1}{2}(a + b + c)$.

Evaluate (i) $\sqrt{s(s - a)(s - b)(s - c)}$ (ii) $\sqrt{\dfrac{s(s - c)}{ab}}$

7 Solve the equation $3x^2 - 7x - 2 = 0$, giving the answers to 2 dec. pl.

8 For £2·10 I can buy either new golf-balls or repaints, the latter being 5p each cheaper than the former, and of which I get one more. How much do new balls cost?

9 In Fig. 159, $\overline{PAQ}$ and $\overline{BXY}$ are straight lines. Prove that $\overline{PX}$ is parallel to $\overline{QY}$.

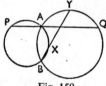

Fig. 159

10 Find x if $5^x = 0 \cdot 68$.

XXVIII

1 Solve the equations

(i) $x(x - 1) = 6$

(ii) $(x - 2)(x - 3) = 2$

(iii) $10\left(3 + \dfrac{1}{x}\right) = 29$

(iv) $10\left(x + \dfrac{1}{x}\right) = 29$

2 Express u as the subject of the formula $E = \dfrac{m}{2g}(v^2 - u^2)$.

3 (i) Simplify $\sqrt{32} \div \sqrt{12}$, $(2\sqrt{7})^2$, $2\sqrt{175} - \sqrt{567}$.

(ii) Express with rational denominators $\dfrac{35}{\sqrt{7}}$, $\sqrt{\dfrac{9}{5}}$.

4 Draw a triangle XYZ such that $\hat{Y}$ is a right angle, YZ $= 12$ cm, and the area of the triangle is 24 cm². Construct $\triangle$AYZ equal in area to $\triangle$XYZ and having $\hat{A} = 90°$. Measure AY and AZ.

5 $y = \dfrac{1 + 3x}{x - 3}$. Express $x + y$ as a fraction

(i) in terms of x only

(ii) ,,   ,,   ,, y ,,.

6 From the top of an aerial mast 150 m high two huts are observed on the level ground, one due east and the other due west of the mast, their angles of depression being respectively 60° and 45°. Find the distance between the huts, leaving the answer in surd form.

7 Solve the equation $2x^2 - 4x - 3 = 0$, giving answers to 2 dec. pl.

8 An open rectangular tank made of thin metal sheet is 3 m long, 2·5 m wide and 2 m deep. Find (i) the cost of galvanising the tank inside and out at 54p per m²; (ii) the capacity of the tank in litres; (iii) the depth to which 3 000 litres would fill the tank.

9 A stick 15 cm long rests in a thin hemispherical bowl of diameter 10 cm in such a way that the lower end of the stick is 2 cm above the bottom of the bowl. Find (i) the angle that the stick makes with the horizontal; (ii) the length of stick outside the bowl.

10 Solve the equation $9^x - 4 \times 3^x + 3 = 0$.

XXIX

1 (i) Simplify $\sqrt{30} \times 2\sqrt{5}$, $(7\sqrt{3})^2$, $3\sqrt{2} - \dfrac{5}{\sqrt{2}}$.

(ii) Express with rational denominators $\dfrac{6\sqrt{5}}{\sqrt{10}}, \dfrac{8\sqrt{3}}{\sqrt{6}}$.

2 $E = 2c\left(1 + \dfrac{1}{m}\right) = 3k\left(1 - \dfrac{2}{m}\right)$. Eliminate E, and express m in terms of the other letters.

3 Use the formula $V = \frac{4}{3}\pi r^3$ to find
  (i) V when $r = 2\cdot53$,
  (ii) r when $V = 2$.   (Take $\pi = 3\cdot142$.)

4 Solve the equation $\dfrac{10x + 1}{2x - 1} - \dfrac{3x + 8}{x + 1} = 2$.

5 Without using a protractor, construct a parallelogram ABCD in which $AB = DC = 6$ cm, $BD = 10$ cm and $\hat{A} = 120°$. Measure AD and AC.

6 Ashton and Barton are 24 km apart. Smith leaves Ashton at 10.00 and cycles to Barton at a steady 12 km h^{-1}: his business there takes him exactly one hour, and he then returns to Ashton at 15 km h^{-1}. Jones leaves Barton at 11.45 and pedals his tricycle straight to Ashton, which he reaches 9 minutes after Smith.
  (i) When did Smith reach Ashton?
  (ii) How fast did Jones ride?
  (iii) At what times did Smith and Jones pass one another?

7 ABC is a triangle inscribed in a circle whose centre is O: $\overline{AD}$ is an altitude of this triangle. Prove that $C\hat{A}D = O\hat{A}B$.

8 Find x if $\log_x 1\,000 = 6\cdot908$.

9 Fig. 160 shows three 2-cm diameter pulleys centred at the corners of a triangular framework with sides 10, 24 and 26 cm. If a piece of string is tied tightly round the three pulleys, what is its length?

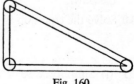

Fig. 160

10 Draw the graph of $y = 3x^2 - 7x - 2$ for values of x from -2 to $+4$. Hence solve the equation $3x^2 - 7x - 2 = 0$, and find also the minimum value of y.

XXX

1 (i) Simplify $2\sqrt{5} \div \sqrt{30}$, $\sqrt{5} - \dfrac{1}{\sqrt{5}}$, $\dfrac{18}{2\sqrt{24} - 3\sqrt{6}}$.

(ii) Express with rational denominators $\dfrac{30}{\sqrt{45}}$, $\dfrac{5\sqrt{2}}{\sqrt{10}}$.

2 Two places are 144 km apart by rail and 150 km by road. A car averages 15 km h^{-1} less than a train for a journey between the two places, and takes 24 minutes longer than the train does. What are the speeds of the car and of the train?

3 Three cylinders are packed into a rectangular box, as shown in Fig. 161. If the radii of the cylinders are 9 cm, 4 cm and 4 cm, what are the interior dimensions of the box?

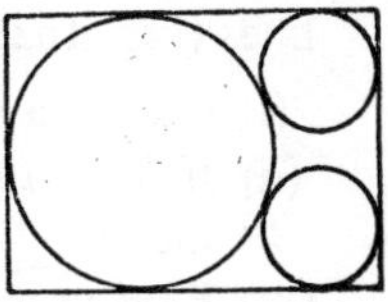

Fig. 161

4 ABC is a △ in which AB = 9 cm, BC = 8 cm and CA = 7 cm. Find by construction a point P inside the △ which is equidistant from A and B, and is also 2 cm from $\overline{BC}$. Measure PA.

5 If T minutes is the time occupied for a meeting when N people are present, then $T = a + bN^2$, when a and b are numbers. When 5 people are present the meeting takes 62 minutes; for 8 people 140 minutes. How long does the meeting take if 7 people are present? How many are present if the meeting lasts for 5 hours?

6 Two circles PARB, SAQB intersect at A and B, and $\overline{AP}$, $\overline{AS}$ are equal chords. $\overline{PQRS}$ is a straight line. Prove that $\overline{AB}$ bisects $Q\hat{B}R$.

281

7 Express d as the subject of the formula

$$D = \sqrt{\frac{2v^2d}{g} + \frac{d^2}{4}} - \frac{d}{2}.$$

8 A locomotive approaching an observer at 50 km h⁻¹ whistles at one-kilometre intervals. If sound travels at 335 m s⁻¹, what is the time-interval between the successive whistles heard by the observer?

9 Solve the equation

$$2^{2x} - 5 \times 2^{x-1} + 1 = 0.$$

10 An open box is bent up from a sheet of thin metal $(x + 2)$ cm long and $(x - 1)$ cm wide by cutting out a square of side 1 cm at each corner, and then folding along the dotted lines (Fig. 162).

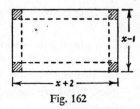

Fig. 162

  (i) Obtain a formula for the volume (V cm³) of the box.

 (ii) If $V = 70$, find the dimensions of the original sheet of metal.

(iii) Find graphically the value of x for which $V = 50$.

Chapter 22

Harder mensuration

A **right circular cone** is a solid whose base is a circle, and whose vertex is vertically above the centre of the base (Fig. 163 (i)).

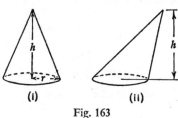

(i)   **(ii)**

Fig. 163

The word 'right' here means 'upright': the solid shown in Fig. 163 (ii) is a cone, but not a right cone.

The volume of any solid which rises to a point, whatever the shape of the base, is one-third of the product of the base-area and the perpendicular height. In particular, the volumes of the cones in Fig. 163 are both $\frac{1}{3}\pi r^2 h$.

If a piece of paper in the shape of a sector of a circle centre O and radius l, bounded by the radii $\overline{OA}$ and $\overline{OB}$ (Fig. 164), is bent

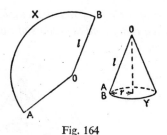

Fig. 164

so that the radii $\overline{OA}$ and $\overline{OB}$ coincide, the distance of O from the circumference of the base is always l and the hollow figure thus formed is a right circular cone, where l is the slant height.

Since the circumference of the base of this cone is simply the arc of the sector bent into a complete circle of smaller radius, this circumference is equal in length to the arc.

If $A\hat{O}B$ is $\theta°$, arc $AXB = \dfrac{\theta}{360}$ of $2\pi l$.

But the circumference of the circle $AYB = 2\pi r$, where r is the radius of the base of the cone,

$$\therefore \frac{\theta}{360} \times 2\pi l = 2\pi r$$

$$\therefore \frac{\theta}{360} = \frac{2\pi r}{2\pi l} = \frac{r}{l}$$

$\therefore$ area of curved surface of cone = area of sector

$$= \frac{\theta}{360} \text{ of } \pi l^2$$

$$= \frac{r}{l} \times \pi l^2$$

$$= \pi r l.$$

Fig. 165

Summary

Volume $= \frac{1}{3}\pi r^2 h$

Curved surface area $= \pi r l.$

Example 1 *A sector of a circle of radius 5 cm, having an angle of 216°, is bent to form a cone. Find the radius of the base of the cone and its vertical angle.*

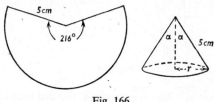

Fig. 166

Let radius of base of cone be r cm, and vertical angle 2α.

284

Then, since circumference of base of cone = length of arc of sector,

$$2\pi r = \tfrac{216}{360} \times 2\pi 5$$
$$\therefore\ r = \tfrac{216}{360} \times 5 = 3$$
$$\sin \alpha = \tfrac{3}{5} = 0{\cdot}6$$
$$\therefore\ \alpha = 36° \ 52'$$
$$\therefore\ 2\alpha = 73° \ 44'.$$

Ans.   Radius of base = 3 cm
Vertical angle = 73° 44'.

If a cone (or pyramid) standing on a horizontal table is sliced through parallel to the table, the top part is a smaller cone (or pyramid) and the other part is called a **frustum.**

In problems which involve frusta it is always necessary to consider the frustum as a complete cone minus a smaller similar one, as in the following example.

Example 2 *Find the capacity in litres of a bucket 24 cm in diameter at the top, 16 cm in diameter at the bottom, and 20 cm deep.*

Complete the cone of which the bucket is a frustum by adding a cone of height x cm and base diameter 16 cm.

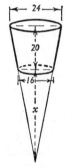

Then, from similar triangles, $\dfrac{x}{8} = \dfrac{x + 20}{12}$

$$\therefore\ x = 40$$

$\therefore$ volume of bucket

$$= (\tfrac{1}{3}\pi 12^2 \times 60 - \tfrac{1}{3}\pi 8^2 \times 40) \text{ cm}^3$$
$$= \tfrac{1}{3}\pi(8\ 640 - 2\ 560) \text{ cm}^3$$
$$= \tfrac{1}{3}\pi 6\ 080 \text{ cm}^3$$
$$= 6\ 366 \text{ cm}^3$$

$\therefore$ capacity of bucket $\simeq 6{\cdot}37$ litres

Fig. 167

The surface area of a frustum may be found in the same way, by completing the cone and using $\pi r l$ instead of $\tfrac{1}{3}\pi r^2 h$, as in Example 3, overleaf.

Example 3 *Find in cm² the area of fabric required for a lampshade in the form of a frustum of a right circular cone, of which the top and bottom diameters are respectively 20 cm and 30 cm, and the vertical height 12 cm.*

Complete the cone of which the lampshade is a frustum by adding a cone of height x cm and base 20 cm in diameter.

By similar triangles,

$$\frac{x}{10} = \frac{12}{5}$$

$$\therefore x = 24$$

By Pythagoras, $y = 26$ and $z = 13$

$\therefore$ surface area of frustum

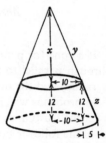

$$= (\pi 15 \times 39 - \pi 10 \times 26) \text{ cm}^2$$

$$= 13\pi(45 - 20) \text{ cm}^2$$

$$= 13\pi \times 25 \text{ cm}^2$$

$$\simeq 1\ 021 \text{ cm}^2.$$

Fig. 168

Exercise 22a

From no. 2 onwards leave the answers in terms of π if π is involved—e.g. 317π cm².

1 Find the base-radii and vertical angles of cones formed from
   (i) a semicircle of radius 12 cm,
   (ii) a sector of a circle of radius 10 cm and angle 144°,
   (iii) a sector of a circle of radius 6 cm and angle 300°,
   (iv) a quadrant of radius 8 cm.

2 Find the areas of the curved surfaces of the cones in no. 1.

3 If a cone of base-diameter 8 cm and height 3 cm is slit and opened out into a sector of a circle, what is the angle of the sector?

4 What is the volume and the curved surface area of the cone in no. 3?

5 In a cone of height 9 cm the number of cm³ in the volume is equal to the number of cm² in the curved surface area. Find the vertical angle of the cone.

6 A right pyramid 6 cm high stands on a rectangular base 6 cm by 4 cm. What is the volume of the pyramid? Use the Theorem of Pythagoras to find the length of one of the sloping edges of the pyramid, and hence draw full size the shape of the single piece of paper from which the sides of the pyramid could be developed (corresponding to the sector for the development of a cone).

7 A lampshade is in the form of a frustum of a cone, the upper and lower diameters being respectively 10 cm and 20 cm, and the height 12 cm. What area of material is required to cover the lampshade, top and bottom being left open? What is the volume of the frustum?

8 A flower-pot is in the form of a frustum of a cone, its top and bottom diameters being 14 cm and 10 cm respectively, and its depth 6 cm. Find the volume of the pot.

9 A right pyramid on a base 10 m square is 15 m high. What is its volume? If the top six metres of the pyramid are removed, what is the volume of the remaining frustum?

10 A frustum of a pyramid is 16 cm square at the bottom, 6 cm square at the top, and 12 cm high. Find the volume of the frustum and the area of one of its sloping faces.

The solids shown below and overleaf are those most commonly met. When problems arise dealing with hollow figures, the volume is found by subtracting the volume of the space inside from the volume of the figure if it were solid, as was done for boxes in Bk. 2, Chap. 23, and in the following examples.

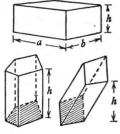

Rectangular block or cuboid

Volume $= abh$
Surface area $= 2ab + 2ah + 2bh$

Prism

Volume $=$ base area $\times$ perpendicular height

Fig. 169

Pyramid

Volume = $\frac{1}{3}$ base area × perpendicular height

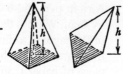

Cone

Volume = $\frac{1}{3}\pi r^2 h$
Curved surface area = $\pi r l$

Right circular cylinder

Volume = $\pi r^2 h$
Curved surface area = $2\pi r h$
Total surface area = $2\pi r h + 2\pi r^2$
$\qquad\qquad\qquad\quad = 2\pi r(h + r)$

Sphere

Volume = $\frac{4}{3}\pi r^3$
Surface area = $4\pi r^2$

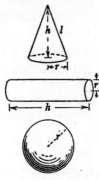

Fig. 169 (cont.)

Example 4 *Find the mass of a cylindrical iron pipe 2·1 m long and 12 cm in external diameter, the metal being 1 cm thick and of density 7·8 g cm⁻³. (Take $\pi = \frac{22}{7}$.)*

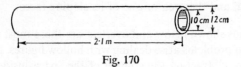

Fig. 170

Volume of outside cylinder = $\pi 6^2 \times 210$ cm³
,, ,, inside ,, = $\pi 5^2 \times 210$ cm³
∴ volume of iron = $(\pi 6^2 \times 210 - \pi 5^2 \times 210)$ cm³
$\qquad\qquad\qquad\quad = \pi 210(6^2 - 5^2)$ cm³
$\qquad\qquad\qquad\quad = \pi 210 \times 11$ cm³
∴ mass of iron = $\pi 210 \times 11 \times 7\cdot8$ g
$\qquad\qquad\qquad = \frac{22}{7} \times 210 \times 11 \times 7\cdot8$ g
$\qquad\qquad\qquad = 56\ 628$ g
$\qquad\qquad\qquad = 56\cdot628$ kg
$\qquad\qquad\qquad \simeq 56\cdot6$ kg.

Example 5 *Find, to one place of decimals, the volume in cm³ of the metal in a hollow sphere 10 cm in external diameter, the metal being 1 mm thick. Take log π = 0·497 1.*

		No.	Log.
Outer radius $= 5$ cm			
Inner radius $= 4·9$ cm		$4·9^3$	$0·690\ 2 \times 3$
$\therefore$ volume $= (\frac{4}{3}\pi 5^3 - \frac{4}{3}\pi 4·9^3)$ cm³		$117·7$	$2·070\ 6$
$= \frac{4}{3}\pi(125 - 117·7)$ cm³		$29·2$	$1·465\ 4$
$= \frac{4}{3}\pi \times 7·3$ cm³		π	$0·497\ 1$
			$1·962\ 5$
$= \dfrac{29·2\pi}{3}$ cm³		3	$0·477\ 1$
$\simeq 30·6$ cm³.		$30·58$	$1·485\ 4$

Exercise 22b

In the first five examples leave the answers in terms of π if π is involved.

1 Find the volumes of the following solids, all lengths given being in cm.

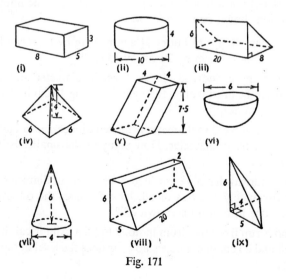

Fig. 171

2 Find the total surface areas of the solids shown in Fig. 171, parts (i), (ii), (iii), (iv) and (vi).

3 A hopper in a granary is in the form of a frustum of a right pyramid 4 m square at the top, 2·5 m square at the bottom and 3 m deep. What is the capacity of the hopper?

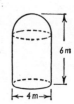

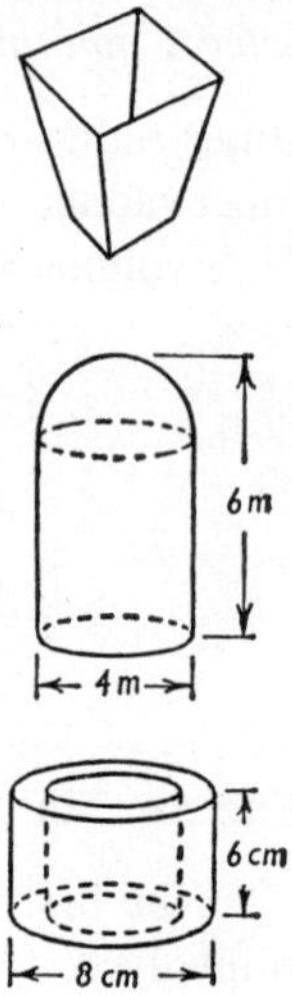

4 A storage tank is in the form of a cylinder with one hemispherical end, the other end being flat. The diameter of the cylinder is 4 m and the overall length of the tank 6 m. What is the capacity of the tank?

5 A small container is made from a length of metal piping 8 cm in external diameter, the metal being $\frac{1}{2}$ cm thick, by welding on to one end a flat disc of the same metal $\frac{1}{2}$ cm thick and 8 cm in diameter. The length of the completed container is $6\frac{1}{2}$ cm. What is the volume of metal in it?

Fig. 172

In nos. 6–17, π will be found to cancel if it occurs: no numerical substitution should be made for π.

6 How many lumps of butter $2\frac{1}{2}$ cm by 2 cm by 1 cm can be cut from a block 25 cm by 20 cm by 15 cm?

7 How many cylindrical glasses 6 cm in diameter and 10 cm deep can be filled from a full cylindrical jug 10 cm in diameter and 18 cm deep?

8 A lead ball 6 cm in diameter is melted and cast into balls half a centimetre in diameter. How many of the smaller balls will there be?

9 A cylindrical drum 42 cm high and 30 cm in diameter holds approximately 30 litres of oil. How far does the oil-level fall when one litre of oil is drawn off?

10 If oil is run from the drum in no. 9 to fill a cylindrical tin 8 cm high and 24 cm in diameter, how far does the level in the drum fall?

11 A conical funnel 12 cm deep and 15 cm in diameter is full of liquid. If it is emptied into a cylindrical tin 10 cm in diameter, what is the least possible height of the tin if it is to contain all the liquid?

12 A spherical retort 15 cm in diameter is half full of acid, which is run off into a tall cylindrical beaker of diameter 6 cm. How deep is the liquid in the beaker?

13 A cylindrical tin of internal diameter 8 cm contains 6 cm of water. How far does the water-level rise when a heavy 6 cm diameter ball is placed in the tin?

14 A bucket is 20 cm in diameter at the open end, 12 cm diameter at the bottom, and 16 cm deep. How deep would the bucket fill a cylindrical drum 28 cm in diameter?

15 A cone is 12 cm in base-diameter and 16 cm high internally. If the cone is exactly half full of water by volume, how deep is the water in the cone? (vertex down)

16 An iron ball 6 cm in diameter is placed in a cylindrical tin 12 cm in diameter, and water is poured into the tin until its depth is 8 cm. If the ball is now removed, how far does the water-level drop?

17 If, instead of the ball in no. 16, an iron rod 8 cm long and 6 cm in diameter had been placed flat in the tin, the other circumstances remaining the same, how far would the level have dropped when the rod was removed?

In the following examples take $\pi = \frac{22}{7}$ or $\log \pi = 0.497\,1$, using whichever value is the more convenient for the problem being solved.

18 What are the volume and curved-surface area of a cone 14 cm in base-diameter and 24 cm high?

19 If the cone in no. 18 is made of paper, and the paper is flattened into a sector of a circle, what is the angle of the sector?

20 A cylindrical rain-water butt is 1·05 m in diameter and 1·2 m deep. How many litres of water can it hold?

21 A telegraph pole is 8 m high and its average diameter 25 cm. What is the mass of the pole if the density of the timber is 0·7 g cm^{-3}?

22 During a war cylinders of solid concrete were used as tank-traps. If they were 1 m long and 60 cm in diameter, and the density of concrete is approximately 2·3 g cm^{-3}, what was the approximate mass of a cylinder?

23 What is the volume in cubic centimetres of the material in a drainpipe 1·8 m long, the internal and external diameters being respectively 16 cm and 18 cm?

24 If water flows through the pipe in no. 23 at the rate of 5 metres per second, the pipe being only half full, how many litres of water are discharged per hour?

25 How far does the water-level drop in a cylindrical tank of internal diameter 35 cm if 11 litres are drawn off?

26 The cross section of a trench is a trapezium 1·8 m wide at the top, 1·2 m wide at the bottom and 1·5 m deep. How many cubic metres of earth are removed in making a trench of this section 100 m long?

27 A roll of paper, as delivered to the printer, is 60 cm in diameter, and the paper is wound on to a wooden cylinder 8 cm in diameter. The paper is 0·005 cm thick. What length of paper is there in the roll in kilometres?

28 A tight roll of 'gumstrip' adhesive paper is 20 cm in diameter, and is stated to contain half a kilometre of paper. If the statement is true, how thick is the paper, to 2 sig. fig.?

29 Find the approximate mass in kilogrammes of a two-metre length of clay drainpipe 15 cm in external diameter, with a 12-cm diameter bore, the density of clay being 1·3 g cm^{-3}.

30 What is the diameter of an iron ball used in 'putting the shot' if its mass is 7·3 kg and the density of the metal is 7·8 g cm^{-3}? Give the answer to the nearest millimetre.

31 A solid aluminium alloy casting for a pulley consists of three discs, each $1\frac{1}{2}$ cm thick, of diameters 4 cm, 6 cm and 8 cm, with a central hole 2 cm in diameter. If the density of the alloy is 2·8 g cm⁻³ what is the mass of the casting?

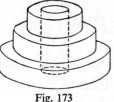

Fig. 173

32 An open cylindrical acid-bath is made from sheet lead one centimetre thick: its external dimensions are 24 cm diameter and 20 cm depth. What is the mass of the bath if the density of lead is 11·45 g cm⁻³?

Chapter 23

Plans and elevations (2)

Exercise 23a (Revision)

Describe the solids shown in elevation and in plan in Figs. 174 and 175.

1

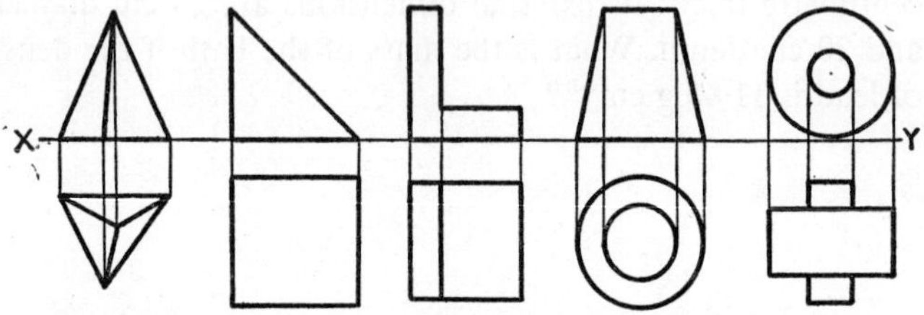

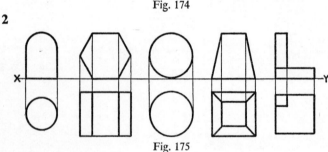

Fig. 174

2

Fig. 175

In the following questions, drawings should be full size unless other directions are given.

3 A brick 22 cm long, 11 cm wide and 7 cm thick is placed flat on a horizontal plane with one of its long edges making 20° with $\overline{XY}$. Draw (half size) the plan, and the elevation on a vertical plane parallel to $\overline{XY}$.

4 A right pyramid is 7 cm high and stands on a base 7 cm square, with one of the edges of the base inclined at 25° to $\overline{XY}$. Draw the plan of the pyramid, and elevations on vertical planes (i) parallel to $\overline{XY}$, (ii) perpendicular to $\overline{XY}$.

5 A pyramid 8 cm high stands on a base which is a regular hexagon ABCDEF of side 5 cm. Draw the plan of the pyramid, and an elevation on a vertical plane parallel to the line joining A to the mid-point of $\overline{\text{EF}}$.

6 A wooden tray consists of a rectangular base 13 cm by 8 cm and 0·8 cm thick, with a rim made of the same wood in a strip 3 cm wide glued on to the outside of the base. The tray is placed on a desk with a slope of 20° so that both the short edges are horizontal. Draw the side elevation of the tray in this position, and its plan.

7 A waste-paper basket (Fig. 176) is 25 cm square at the top, 20 cm square at the bottom, and 22·5 cm deep. Draw the plan of the basket, and also its elevation on a vertical plane making an angle of 30° with one of the sides of the base. (Scale: $\frac{2}{5}$ full size.)

Fig. 176

8 A dog-kennel (Fig. 177) is 90 cm long and 75 cm wide: the walls are 60 cm high, and the ridge is 75 cm above the ground. The entrance is 45 cm square. If the kennel is placed north and south, as shown, draw its plan, and also its elevation from the S.E. (Scale: $\frac{1}{10}$ full size.)

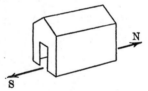

Fig. 177

9 A barn is 10 m square and has walls 7 m high: the roof rises to a point 10 m above the ground (Fig. 178). Draw a plan, and an elevation on a vertical plane making an angle of 15° with one of the sides. (Scale: 1 cm to 1 m.)

Fig. 178

10 A hexagonal prism of side 5 cm, which is 8 cm long, rests with two of its rectangular faces horizontal and with the horizontal edges inclined at 25° to $\overline{\text{XY}}$. Draw the plan of the prism, and an elevation on a vertical plane parallel to $\overline{\text{XY}}$, showing one of the end faces.

In all the drawings so far considered, enough dimensions have been given to allow the plan and elevation to be drawn immediately. In many problems this is not the case, and subsidiary drawings have to be made in order to arrive at the dimensions necessary for the completion of the drawing.

Example 1 *Draw the plan, and front and side elevations of a pyramid* VABCD *standing on a base* ABCD *6 cm square, and having slant edges* 10·5 *cm long, if two edges of the base make an angle of* 20° *with* $\overline{XY}$.

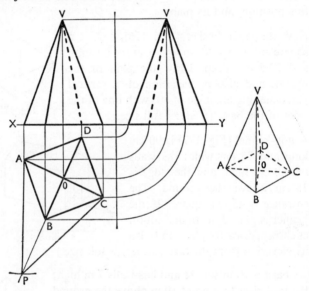

Fig. 179

1 Draw the plan ABCD full size.

2 The elevation cannot be drawn until the height of V above the base is known. This height can be found from the triangle VAC, in which VA = VC = 10·5 cm and $\overline{AC}$ has already been drawn.

On the plan draw an arc with centre A and radius 10·5 cm to cut $\overline{DB}$ produced at P. Then △PAC is congruent to △VAC, and $\overline{PO}$ is the height required.

3 Mark this height above $\overline{XY}$ in the elevation to give V on the projection of O.

4 Complete the elevations, as shown in Fig. 179.

In effect, when drawing PAC, the △VAC has been rotated about $\overline{AC}$ until V lies at P in the horizontal plane. This process is known as **rabatment**.

Notice particularly the value of the rough drawing, which is sketched in order to show what has to be done.

Example 2 *A house roof is shown in Fig.* 180, *the slope of the roof at the sides being* 35°, *and at the ends* 40°, *to the horizontal. Draw the plan.*

In order to obtain the plan, end and side elevations must first be drawn (in that order). The end elevation shows the height of the ridge: the side elevation then shows its length. Once these details are known, the plan can be completed.

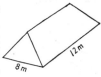

Fig. 180

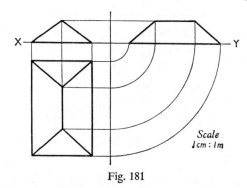

Scale
1 cm : 1 m

Fig. 181

Example 3 VABC *is a tetrahedron, the base* ABC *being horizontal*: AB = AC = 10 *cm*, BC = 8 *cm*, VA = VB = VC = 12 *cm. Draw the plan of the tetrahedron, and the elevation on a vertical plane making* 10° *with* $\overline{AB}$.

(A **tetrahedron** is a pyramid on a triangular base.)

By symmetry, V is seen to be vertically above the median through A of △ABC.

1 Draw △ABC so that $\overline{AB}$ makes 10° with $\overline{XY}$.

2 Draw the median $\overline{AM}$.

3 In order to find VO, the triangle VAM must first be drawn. To draw this triangle VM must be found:

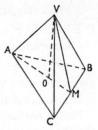

Fig. 182

(*a*) with centre C and radius 12 cm draw an arc to cut $\overline{AM}$ produced in *v*: then △BC*v* is a rabatment of △BCV, establishing VM.

(*b*) draw △AM*v'* a rabatment of △AMV (A*v'* = 12 cm, M*v'* = M*v*).

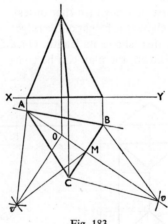

Fig. 183

4 Draw $\overline{v'O} \perp \overline{AM}$.

5 Project a line from O $\perp$ to $\overline{XY}$, and produce it above $\overline{XY}$ a distance equal to *v'*O.

6 Complete the elevation.

Exercise 23b

1 A pyramid has a base 9 cm square, and the slant edges are

298

Plans and elevations (2)

all 12 cm long. Draw the plan and elevation when two sides of the base are parallel to $\overline{XY}$.

2 A pyramid on a base 6 cm square has slant edges 9 cm long. Two edges of the base are inclined at 20° to $\overline{XY}$. Draw the plan and elevation of the pyramid.

3 All the edges of a regular tetrahedron are 8 cm long. Draw its plan, and also the elevation on a vertical plane making an angle of 15° with one of the edges of the triangular base.

4 The base of a tetrahedron is an equilateral triangle of side 7 cm, and the slant edges are 11 cm long. Draw the plan of the tetrahedron, and its elevation on a vertical plane making 45° with one edge of the base.

5 A pyramid having the dimensions given in no. 1 is placed with one of its triangular faces on the horizontal plane, the 9-cm side of this face being inclined at 70° to $\overline{XY}$. Draw the plan and elevation of the pyramid in this position.

6 Fig. 184 shows a small building: the roof-slopes are 45° at the ends and 35° at the sides. Draw the plan of the building, and also its side and end elevations, on a scale of 1 cm to 1 m.

7 The plan of the roof of an L-shaped building is shown roughly in Fig. 185. The roof slopes at 40° to the horizontal. Draw the plan of the roof and its elevation on a vertical plane parallel to $\overline{AB}$.

8 A lamp is suspended from a ceiling by six chains, each 1·2 m long, the upper ends of the chains being at the vertices of a regular hexagon ABCDEF of side 80 cm (Fig. 186). Draw the plan of the figure thus formed, and its elevation on a vertical plane parallel to the line joining A to the mid-point of $\overline{CD}$.

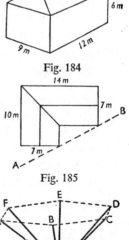

Fig. 184

Fig. 185

Fig. 186

299

9 A lampshade is of the form shown in Fig. 187, the top being 10 cm square, the bottom 17·5 cm square, and all four slant-edges 20 cm long. Draw the plan of the lampshade half-size, and also the elevation on a vertical plane making an angle of 25° with one of the edges of the base.

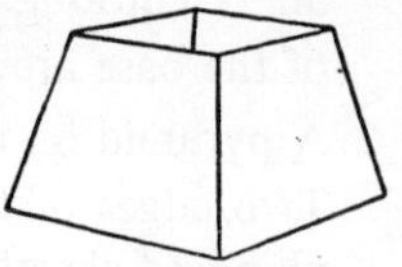

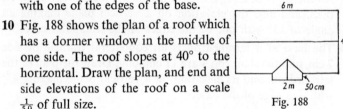

Fig. 187

10 Fig. 188 shows the plan of a roof which has a dormer window in the middle of one side. The roof slopes at 40° to the horizontal. Draw the plan, and end and side elevations of the roof on a scale $\frac{1}{50}$ of full size.

Fig. 188

11 An obelisk (Fig. 189) consists of a tapered column, square in section, 35 cm square at the bottom, 15 cm square at the top, surmounted by a pyramid 15 cm high: the column is mounted on a base 60 cm square and 30 cm high. Draw to a suitable scale the elevation of the obelisk on a vertical plane parallel to $\overline{AB}$, the overall height being 2·4 m.

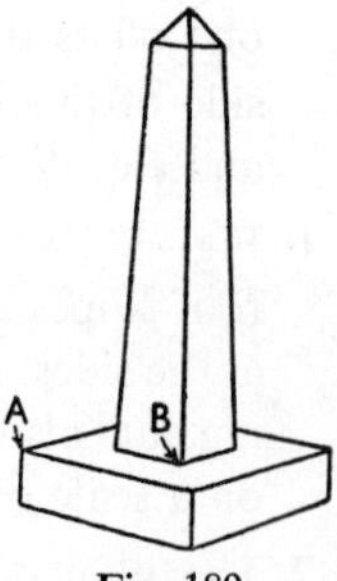

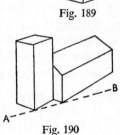

Fig. 189

12 Fig. 190 is a sketch of a small church with a square tower at the middle of one end. The tower is 5 m square and 10 m high: the church itself is 14 m long, 9 m wide, 5 m from the ground to the eaves, and 7 m from the ground to the ridge, which is also 14 m long. Draw the elevation on a vertical plane parallel to $\overline{AB}$, to a scale of 1 cm to 1 m.

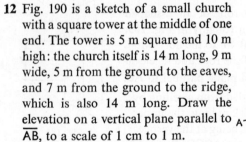

Fig. 190

13 A triangular piece of cardboard ABC has sides 8 cm, 10 cm and 12 cm long. X, Y and Z are the mid-points of $\overline{BC}$, $\overline{CA}$ and $\overline{AB}$ respectively, and a tetrahedron on XYZ as base is formed by bending the three corners round the lines $\overline{YZ}$, $\overline{ZX}$ and $\overline{XY}$ so that A, B and C come together at the vertex of the

300

tetrahedron. Draw the plan of the tetrahedron, and its elevation on a vertical plane parallel to $\overline{BY}$.

14 The plan of a three-legged stool is shown in Fig. 191. The diameter of the top is 30 cm; the legs are 25 cm long and are inclined at 75° to the horizontal, their tops being symmetrically disposed on a 25-cm diameter circle. Draw a plan of the stool (one quarter linear size), and its elevation on a vertical plane parallel to $\overline{PQ}$.

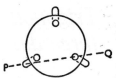

Fig. 191

15 Two corners of a 9-centimetre cube are sliced off by a cut through the mid-points of four edges, as shown in Fig. 192. The cube is placed with the cut face horizontal, and with the two vertical faces making an angle of 20° with $\overline{XY}$. Draw, full-size, the plan and elevation of the cube.

Fig. 192

16 A grain hopper is 50 cm square at the top, 20 cm square at the bottom and 60 cm deep. The face shown shaded in Fig. 193 is vertical. Draw the plan of the hopper, and its elevation on a vertical plane making an angle of 25° with the vertical face. (Top and bottom squares are horizontal.)

Fig. 193

Chapter 24

Trigonometrical problems in three dimensions

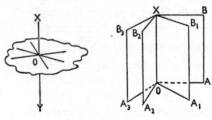

Fig. 194

1 A line $\overline{XY}$ which cuts a **plane** (i.e. a flat surface) at O is at right angles to the plane if it is perpendicular to every line in the plane drawn through O.

If, for instance, $\overline{XO}$ is the line of the hinges in a door, and $\overline{OA}$ is the bottom edge of the door, the various positions $\overline{OA}$, $\overline{OA_1}$, $\overline{OA_2}$, ... of $\overline{OA}$ as the door opens all lie in the plane which is the floor of the room, and all the lines $\overline{OA}$, $\overline{OA_1}$, $\overline{OA_2}$, ... are at right angles to $\overline{XO}$.

2 If a line $\overline{XY}$ cuts a plane obliquely at O, the angle between the line and the plane is found by drawing a perpendicular $\overline{XP}$ from X to the plane, when the required angle is XOP.

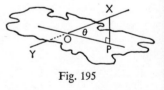

Fig. 195

3 The angle between two planes is the angle between lines in the planes which are both at right angles to the line of intersection of the planes (often more easily thought of as the 'hinge' between the planes as the angle between them varies).

In Fig. 194 the angle between the planes XOA_1B_1 and XOA_2B_2

302

is clearly $A_1\hat{O}A_2$ (or $B_1\hat{X}B_2$): in Fig. 196, which represents a rectangular trap-door ABCD propped open by means of a vertical stick $\overline{BP}$, the angle between the planes ABCD and XYCD is $B\hat{C}Y$ or $A\hat{D}X$. Since the plane XYCD is horizontal the 'slope' of the plane ABCD is $B\hat{C}Y$ (or $A\hat{D}X$), but the slope of the diagonal $\overline{BD}$ is $B\hat{D}P$, which is a smaller angle than $B\hat{C}Y$.

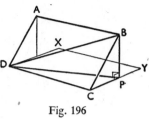
Fig. 196

Notice that, since $\overline{BP}$ is vertical and the plane XYCD is horizontal, $\overline{BP}$ is at right angles to every line on the plane XYCD, and in particular to $\overline{CY}$ and $\overline{DP}$.

When the angle between a line and a horizontal plane is required it is often easier to think of it as the angle between the line and its 'shadow' on the plane (called the projection of the line on the plane), imagining the sun to be vertically above the plane. Similarly, when finding the angle between a line and a vertical plane, what is required is the angle between the line and its

Fig. 197

projection on that plane: e.g. in Fig. 197 the angle between $\overline{XO}$ and its projection $\overline{PO}$ is $X\hat{O}P$, and this is therefore the angle between $\overline{XO}$ and the plane.

Example 1 *A pyramid with a vertex O and edges $\overline{OA}$, $\overline{OB}$, $\overline{OC}$, $\overline{OD}$ each 13 cm long stands on a rectangular base ABCD, where AB = CD = 8 cm and AD = BC = 6 cm. Find*

(i) *the height OP of the pyramid,*
(ii) *the angle between the base and an edge,*
(iii) ,, ,, ,, ,, ,, ,, △OBC,
(iv) ,, ,, ,, ,, ,, ,, △OCD.

(*N.B.* Since the pyramid is symmetrical, the point P vertically below O is at the centre of the rectangle ABCD.)

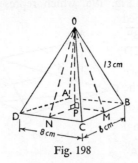

Fig. 198

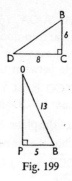

Fig. 199

(i) $BD^2 = 6^2 + 8^2 = 36 + 64 = 100$ *Pythagoras*

$\therefore$ $BD = 10$ cm

$\therefore$ $BP = \frac{1}{2}BD = 5$ cm

$\therefore$ $OP^2 = 13^2 - 5^2 = 169 - 25 = 144$ *Pythagoras*

$\therefore$ $OP = 12$ cm.

(ii) Since $\overline{OP}$ is $\perp$ to the base, the $\angle$ between $\overline{OB}$ and the base $= O\hat{B}P$.

$$\tan O\hat{B}P = \frac{12}{5} = 2\cdot4$$
$$\therefore \ O\hat{B}P = 67° \ 23'.$$

(iii) The $\angle$ between $\triangle OBC$ and the base $= O\hat{M}P$, since $\overline{OM}$ and $\overline{PM}$ are both $\perp$ to the 'hinge' $\overline{BC}$, of which M is the mid-point.

$$\tan O\hat{M}P = \frac{12}{4} = 3$$
$$\therefore \ O\hat{M}P = 71° \ 34'.$$

(iv) The $\angle$ between $\triangle OCD$ and the base $= O\hat{N}P$.

$$\tan O\hat{N}P = \frac{12}{3} = 4$$
$$\therefore \ O\hat{N}P = 75° \ 58'.$$

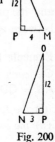

Fig. 200

Example 2 *A rectangular lid 25 cm by 20 cm is propped open at an angle of 65° to the horizontal, the hinges being in one of the long sides. Find the slope of the diagonal $\overline{BD}$.*

$$BP = 20 \sin 65°$$
$$BD^2 = 20^2 + 25^2 = 1\,025$$
$$\therefore \ BD = 32 \cdot 02 \text{ cm}$$

$$\therefore \ \sin B\widehat{D}P = \frac{20 \sin 65°}{32 \cdot 02}$$

$$\therefore \ B\widehat{D}P = 34° \ 29'.$$

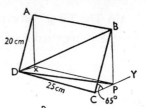

20	1·301 0
*sin 65°	$\overline{1}$·957 3
	1·258 3
32·02	1·505 4
*sin 34° 29'	$\overline{1}$·752 9

(*N.B.* *—Tables of 'log-sines' are used here, which obviate the need to use natural sines first and then logarithms.)

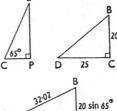

Fig. 201

Example 3 *The hall shown in Fig. 202 is 28 m long, 21 m wide and 12 m high. Find the angles between*

(i) *$\overline{PC}$ and the plane CDSR,*

(ii) *the planes PBCS and QBCR.*

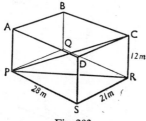

Fig. 202

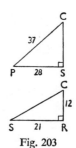

Fig. 203

(i) The projection of $\overline{PC}$ on the plane CDSR is $\overline{SC}$,

$\therefore$ the $\angle$ required is $P\widehat{C}S$.

$$PC^2 = 12^2 + 21^2 + 28^2$$
$$\therefore \ PC = 37 \text{ m}$$
$$\operatorname{cosec} P\widehat{C}S = \tfrac{37}{28} = 1 \cdot 321\,4$$
$$\therefore \ P\widehat{C}S = 49° \ 11'.$$

305

(ii) The 'hinge' between the planes PBCS and QBCR is $\overline{BC}$,
∴ the $\angle$ required is $S\hat{C}R$ (or $P\hat{B}Q$).

$$\tan S\hat{C}R = \tfrac{21}{12} = 1{\cdot}75$$
$$\therefore\ S\hat{C}R = 60°\ 15'.$$

(*N.B.* In (i) cosec is used rather than sine, because 28 is an easier divisor than 37.)

Example 4 *A hillside slopes at 27° to the horizontal, and a path runs up it at 50° to the line of greatest slope. Find the inclination of the path to the horizontal. If a man using the path rises 1 m vertically for every d m he travels on the path, find the value of d.*

Let $\quad AB = x$ m
Then $\quad AC = x \sec 50°$
and $\quad CY = BX = x \sin 27°$

$$\therefore\ \sin C\hat{A}Y = \frac{CY}{AC} = \frac{x \sin 27°}{x \sec 50°}$$
$$= \sin 27° \times \cos 50°$$
$$\therefore\ C\hat{A}Y = 16°\ 58'$$

In $\triangle$ CAY, $\dfrac{d}{1} = \text{cosec } C\hat{A}Y$

$$= 3{\cdot}426\,4$$
$$\therefore\ d \simeq 3{\cdot}4$$

No.	Log.
sin 27°	$\bar{1}{\cdot}657\,0$
cos 50°	$\bar{1}{\cdot}808\,1$
sin 16° 58′	$\bar{1}{\cdot}465\,1$

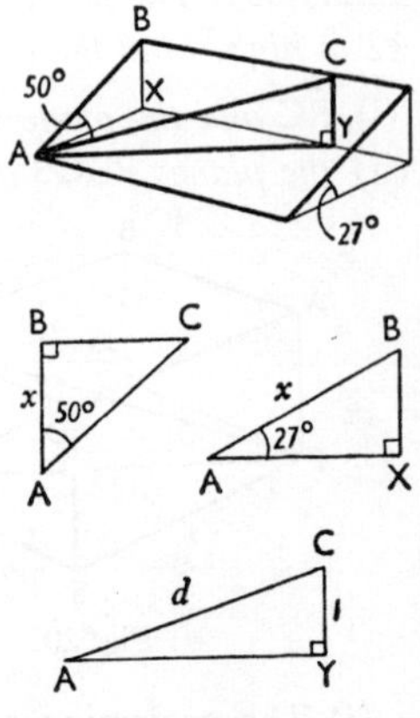

Fig. 204

Notice particularly in these worked examples, the value of 'thumbnail' sketches of the various triangles as they are solved. If this is done it will be found simpler to place the right angles correctly than if they are taken directly from the perspective drawing.

Exercise 24

1 A stick is propped up in the angle of a room so that its foot is 30 cm from one wall and 40 cm from the other, and its top is 120 cm above the floor. Find the length of the stick and the angle it makes with the floor.

2 A 50-cm stick is propped up, as in no. 1, so that its foot is 10 cm from one wall and 20 cm from the other. How high is its top above the floor (3 sig. fig.), and at what angle to the floor is it leaning?

3 A pyramid on a base 8 cm square has sloping edges 9 cm long. Find (i) the height of the pyramid, (ii) the slope of an edge, (iii) the slope of a triangular face.

4 A pyramid 12 cm high stands on a rectangular base 8 cm by 12 cm. Find (i) the length of an edge of the pyramid, (ii) the angles the triangular faces make with the base.

5 A pyramid is 4 cm high and stands on a base which is a regular hexagon of side 3 cm. Find (i) the length of an edge of the pyramid, (ii) the slope of an edge, (iii) the slope of one of the triangular faces.

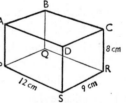

Fig. 205

6 For the box shown in Fig. 205 calculate

    (i) PR,
    (ii) PC,
    (iii) the angle between $\overline{PC}$ and PQRS,
    (iv) ,, ,, ,, $\overline{PC}$ and DCRS,
    (v) ,, ,, ,, $\overline{PC}$ and BCRQ,
    (vi) ,, ,, ,, ABCD and PBCS,
    (vii) ,, ,, ,, PQCD and ABQP.

7 If in Fig. 205 a point X is taken on $\overline{PQ}$ so that PX = 5 cm, calculate

    (i) the angle between $\overline{DX}$ and PQRS,

    (ii)   ,,   ,,   ,, $\overline{DX}$ and ABQP,

    (iii) ,,   ,,   ,,   the planes DSX and ADSP,

    (iv) ,,   ,,   ,,   ,,   ,,   DSX and CRX.

8 A rectangle 3 cm by 4 cm is propped up so that the four-cm sides are horizontal, and the slope of the rectangle is 40°. Find the slope of a diagonal of the rectangle.

9 Fig. 206 shows a reading-slope, where M is the mid-point of $\overline{AD}$. Find the slopes of $\overline{BM}$ and of $\overline{BD}$.

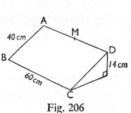

Fig. 206

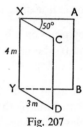

Fig. 207

10 A door 4 m high and 3 m wide is opened to an angle of 50°, as shown in Fig. 207. Calculate (i) BD, (ii) $B\hat{X}D$, (iii) the slope of $\overline{BC}$, (iv) the slope of the plane BXD.

11 Using the same lettering as for the door in Fig. 207, but considering a door 2·8 m high and 1·6 m wide, opened to an angle of 60°, find (i) the slope of $\overline{BC}$, (ii) the slope of the plane BXD.

12 A hillside slopes upwards at an angle of 30° to the horizontal, and a path runs up it at an angle of 45° to the line of greatest slope. Find the inclination of the path to the horizontal, and also the gradient of this path, in the form '1 in d', as in worked Example 4.

13 A rectangular trapdoor ABCD is propped open by means of a stick $\overline{BX}$ 30 cm long, so that BXC is an isosceles triangle with CB = CX. Find (i) the slope of the door, (ii) the slope of a diagonal of the door (Fig. 208).

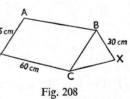

Fig. 208

14 A rectangular mirror 30 cm by 40 cm is hung against a vertical wall with its long edges horizontal, in such a way that the top edge is 18 cm away from the wall. Find (i) the angle between the mirror and the wall, (ii) the angle between a diagonal of the mirror and the wall.

15 If the mirror in no. 14 were hung with the two short edges horizontal and the top edge still 18 cm from the wall, what would now be the answers to (i) and (ii)?

16 A cardboard clock-face is placed on a desk sloping at 35° to the horizontal in such a way that the line from VI to XII is along a line of greatest slope of the desk. What angle does the minute hand make with the horizontal when it is pointing at (i) III? (ii) II? (iii) V?

17 All four faces of a pyramid on a base 6 cm square slope at an angle of 70° to the horizontal. Find (i) the height of the pyramid, (ii) the angle between the sloping edges and the base.

18 In the diagram of a roof given in Fig. 209 the slopes of both sides and ends are 40° to the horizontal. Find the slope of an edge.

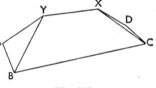

19 A vertical flagstaff is secured by five equal guy-lines attached to a point P on the flagstaff 8 m

Fig. 209

above the ground, and the ends of the lines are tied to pegs which form a regular pentagon ABCDE of side 8 m centred at the foot of the flagstaff. Find the slope of △PAB.

20 A slice is cut from the centre of a large cylindrical cheese, as shown in Fig. 210. $A\hat{O}X = 45°$, the diameter of the cheese is 40 cm and its height 45 cm. Find (i) the slope of $\overline{AY}$, (ii) the slope of △BOY.

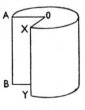

21 A blackboard standing on an easel makes an angle of 70° with the horizontal. What is the slope of a line drawn on the board which makes an angle of 20° with the line of greatest slope?

Fig. 210

22 If a line drawn on the board in no. 21 is inclined at 25° to the horizontal, what is the angle this line makes with a line of greatest slope on the board?

23 For the roof illustrated in Fig. 209, AB = 12 m and XY = 18 m, the roof-slopes being 40° at both sides and ends. Find (i) BC, (ii) the slope of △BAX.

24 ABCD is the rectangular cover of a thin book which opens about the line $\overline{\text{CD}}$. CD = 28 cm, BC = 21 cm. If the book is opened to an angle of (i) 30°, (ii) 130°, through what angle has a diagonal of the cover moved?

25 A triangular set-square with sides 15 cm, 20 cm and 25 cm is placed on a horizontal table and is rotated about its hypotenuse through an angle of 65°. How high is the vertex of the triangle now above the table, and through what angle has the 20-cm side turned?

Chapter 25

Harder graphs

Note.—In drawing graphs of functions it is correct practice to mark a point with a small cross, since the position of a point is most accurately defined by the intersection of two lines. However, because of the difficulty of showing this on the comparatively small figures in this book, dots have been used instead of crosses for the sake of neatness.

Example 1 *Draw the graph of $y = \frac{1}{5}x(x - 2)(x + 2)$ for values of x from -3 to $+3$. What are the values of x at the points in which the graph is cut by the line $5y = x + 2$?*

x		-3	-2	-1	0	1	2	3	$2\frac{1}{2}$	$\frac{1}{2}$
$x - 2$		-5	-4	-3	-2	-1	0	1	$\frac{1}{2}$	$-1\frac{1}{2}$
$x + 2$		-1	0	1	2	3	4	5	$4\frac{1}{2}$	$2\frac{1}{2}$
$x(x - 2)(x + 2)$		-15	0	3	0	-3	0	15	$\frac{45}{8}$	$-\frac{15}{8}$
$y = \frac{1}{5}x(x - 2)(x + 2)$		-3	0	0.6	0	-0.6	0	3	1.125	-0.375

The values of y for the integral values of x are first plotted: it can then be seen that additional values of y for $x = \pm\frac{1}{2}$, $\pm2\frac{1}{2}$ will be helpful in establishing the precise curves of the graph. These additional points are plotted and the graph is drawn (Fig. 211). Then the line $5y = x + 2$ is drawn by plotting the values:

x	-2	0	3
y	0	0.4	1

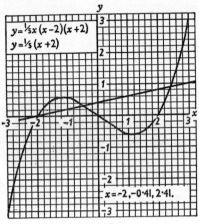

Fig. 211

The values of x at the intersections are read off. They are $x = -2, -0.41, 2.41$.

Example 2 *Solve for x the equations $xy = 6$, $y = 2x + 3$, taking values of x from -4 to $+2$. Of what equation in x are the solutions the roots?*

(i) $y = \dfrac{6}{x}$

(ii) $y = 2x + 3$

x	-4	-3	-2	-1	0	1	2	$\pm 1\frac{1}{2}$
y	-1.5	-2	-3	-6	∞	6	3	± 4
y	-5				3		7	

Notice particularly that (*a*) there is a break in the continuity of the first graph, which has two branches separated by the axes of x and y. As x decreases from 1 to 0 through the values $\frac{1}{2}$, $\frac{1}{3}$, $\frac{1}{4}$, $\frac{1}{5}$, ... y has the values 12, 18, 24, 30, ... and approaches an infinite value as x approaches zero. The same occurs on the negative side of the origin.

(This curve is called a **hyperbola**.)

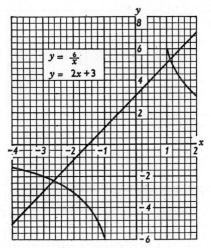

Fig. 212

(*b*) After the values of y for the integral values of x have been plotted, the extra values for $x = \pm 1\frac{1}{2}$ are added, as in Ex. 1.

Where the curves intersect (and at no other points) y simultaneously equals $\dfrac{6}{x}$ and $2x + 3$. Hence, at the intersections,

$$\frac{6}{x} = 2x + 3$$

i.e. $\qquad 2x^2 + 3x - 6 = 0$

which is the equation required.

The roots are $-2\cdot64$, $1\cdot14$.

Example 3 *The area (S cm²) of tin in a hollow metal cylinder of internal volume 100 cm³, closed at both ends, is $6\cdot28r^2 + \dfrac{200}{r}$, where r is the radius of the base in centimetres. Draw the graph of*

$$S = 6\cdot28r^2 + \frac{200}{r}$$

for values of r between 1 and 5. Deduce from the graph the smallest area of tin which can be used to contain this volume.

r	1	2	3	4	5	$2\frac{1}{2}$	$1\frac{1}{2}$
$6\cdot28r^2$	6·28	25·12	56·52	100·48	157	39·25	14·13
$\dfrac{200}{r}$	200	100	66·67	50	40	80	133·33
$S = 6\cdot28r^2 + \dfrac{200}{r}$	206	125	123	150	197	119	147

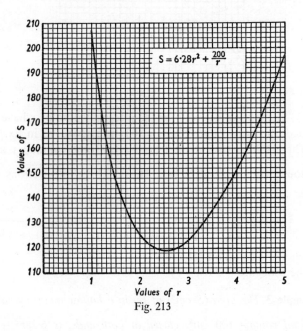

Fig. 213

As in Exs. 1 and 2, extra values $2\frac{1}{2}$, $1\frac{1}{2}$ are plotted for r after the integral values have been plotted, in order to determine the shape of the curve accurately, especially as regards its lowest point.

The smallest area of tin is given by the value of S at the lowest point of the curve; i.e. the smallest value is 119 cm².

Exercise 25

1 Draw the graphs of $y = x(x - 1)$ and $xy = 5$ from $x = \frac{1}{2}$ to $x = 5$. Read off the value of x at the intersection. Of what equation in x is this value a real root?

2 Solve the equation $x^3 = 5x + 2$ by drawing graphs of $y = x^3$ and $y = 5x + 2$ for values of x between -3 and $+3$, and reading off the values of x at the intersections of the graphs.

Solve graphically the following equations: the range of values for x is given in brackets.

3 $x^3 + 3x - 7 = 0$ (0 to 4)

4 $x^3 = 5x - 3$ (-3 to $+3$)

5 $7 - x^2 = \dfrac{7}{x}$ (-4 to $+2$)

6 $2x^2 - 3 = \dfrac{6}{x}$ ($\frac{1}{2}$ to 4)

7 $x(x + 2)(x - 2) = 3x + 1$ (-3 to $+3$)

8 $\dfrac{3x^2 + 1}{x + 1} = 5$ (0 to 4)

9 $x - \dfrac{5}{x} = 2$ (-2 to 4)

10 Draw the graphs of $y = \dfrac{x^2}{x + 2}$ and $y = 3x - 1$ for values of x between -4 and $+2$. Read off the values of x at the intersections, and find the equation in x of which these values are roots.

11 Draw the graph of $y = x + \dfrac{1}{x}$ for values of x from 0·1 to 10.

Use the graph to find approximately the roots of the equation $2x^2 - 9x + 2 = 0$.

12 Complete the following table, which gives corresponding values of x and y for which $y = 30 - 3x - \dfrac{60}{x}$.

x	2	$2\frac{1}{2}$	3	4	5	6	7	8	9	10
y	-6	$-1\frac{1}{2}$		3			0·43		$-3·67$	

Hence draw the graph of $y = 30 - 3x - \dfrac{60}{x}$. Read off the greatest value of y.

To what value of x does this value of y correspond?

13 The cost £C of a ship's voyage at V km h⁻¹ is given by the formula

$$C = \frac{9900}{V} + \frac{V^2}{2}.$$

Plot the C–V curve for values of V from 10 to 30, and deduce the most economical speed for the voyage, and also the total cost at that speed.

14 Plot the graph of $y = \dfrac{3x^2 - 8}{3x + 8}$ for values of x from -2 to $+3$.

Draw on the same diagram the graph of $y = -\frac{1}{3}x$, and read off the values of x at the intersections of the two graphs. Of what equation in x are these values the roots?

15 Draw the graphs of $y = x + \dfrac{4}{x}$ and $y = x^2 - x$ for values of x equal to 1, $1\frac{1}{2}$, 2, $2\frac{1}{2}$, 3.

Show that the intersections of these graphs satisfy the equation $x^3 - 2x^2 - 4 = 0$, and use the graph to find the real root of this equation.

16 A rectangular sheet of metal 20 cm by 30 cm has a square of side x cm removed from each corner. The edges of the sheet are then bent up to make an open tray of depth x cm.

Prove that the volume of the tray is $4x(10 - x)(15 - x)$ cm³, and find graphically the value of x which results in the largest possible tray from this piece of metal.

17 A particle is projected against a spring on a horizontal table in such a way that the distance d cm it has travelled after t seconds is given by the formula $d = 12t - \frac{1}{4}t^3$. By plotting d against t, find out how far the particle travels before it begins to come back again, and after what time it returns to the point of projection.

18 The height above the water of the arch of a bridge is given by the formula $h = \frac{5}{2}d\left(1 - \frac{d}{50}\right)$, where h m is the height at a distance d m from the bank. By plotting h against d find the greatest height of the bridge and also what width of water is available to a ship if the tip of its mast is 25 m above the water.

19 A skeleton box on a square base of side x cm is made from a 36-cm length of wire, and the height of the box is y cm. Show that the volume of the box is $(6x^2 - \frac{3}{2}x^3)$ cm³. Find graphically the maximum volume of the box, and its dimensions when the volume is a maximum. (Fig. 214.)

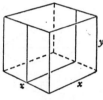

Fig. 214

20 The largest rectangular package that a firm of road carriers will accept is of volume $\frac{1}{16}x(6 - x)^2$ cubic metres, where x metres is the length of the package, which is square in section. Draw a graph showing the volume for values of x from 0 to 6.

Deduce the length of the largest package which can be sent.

Chapter 26

Tangents. Contact of circles. Alternate segment

In Fig. 215 a circle, centre O, is cut by the straight line $\overline{MN}$ in two points X, Y. The distance from O of every point on the line which lies between X and Y is less than the radius of the circle. Also if $\overline{OX}$, $\overline{OY}$ are joined, $\triangle OXY$ is isosceles and $O\hat{X}Y = O\hat{Y}X$. Hence $O\hat{X}M = O\hat{Y}N$.

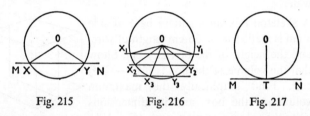

Fig. 215   Fig. 216   Fig. 217

If the line is allowed to move so that X and Y occupy successively positions such as X_1 and Y_1, X_2 and Y_2, etc., then X and Y become closer and closer to each other as in Fig. 216. Ultimately the points X and Y will coincide in the single point T (Fig. 217), and the lines $\overline{OX}$ and $\overline{OY}$ will coincide in the line $\overline{OT}$.

Since the angles OXM and OYN are equal, it follows that in the final position $O\hat{T}M = O\hat{T}N$, and since these angles are supplementary, each is a right angle. Hence $\overline{OT} \perp \overline{MN}$.

In this final position the line $\overline{MN}$ is said to be a **tangent** to the circle. It does not *cut* the circle, but *touches* it at T (*cf.*—the tangent to a parabola—Book 2, p. 280). Since no part of the line lies within the circle, there is no point on the line whose distance from O is less than the radius.

The following statements should be noticed:

A tangent to a circle is perpendicular to the radius drawn to its point of contact.

318

The perpendicular to a tangent at its point of contact passes through the centre of the circle.

Tangents from an external point

Let Q be a point outside a circle whose centre is O. Two tangents to the circle are drawn from Q (Fig. 218). Let the tangents touch the circle at A and B, and join $\overline{OA}$, $\overline{OB}$, $\overline{OQ}$.

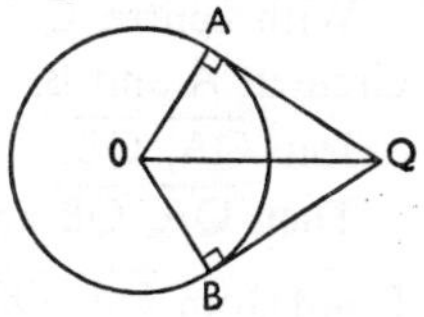

Fig. 218

Triangles OAQ, OBQ are right-angled at A and B respectively, have OQ in common, and have OA = OB.

Hence △s OAQ, OBQ are congruent. *RHS*
△ OBQ is the reflection of △OAQ in $\overline{OQ}$.

Hence AQ = BQ, the angles at Q are equal, and the angles at O are equal.

Hence

(i) **the tangents to a circle from an external point are equal.**

(ii) **the line joining the external point to the centre of the circle bisects the angle between the tangents.**

(iii) **the line joining the external point to the centre of the circle bisects angle between the radii drawn to the points of contact of the tangents.**

In Fig. 218, since the angles at A and B are right angles, it follows that a circle drawn on $\overline{OQ}$ as diameter passes through A and B. This suggests a method for constructing the tangents to a circle from an external point.

Construction 9

To construct the tangents to a given circle from a given external point.

Given a circle centre O and a point Q lying outside it.

To construct the tangents to the circle from Q.

319

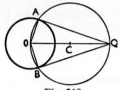

Fig. 219

Construction Join $\overline{OQ}$ and bisect it at C.

With centre C and radius CO draw a circle to cut the given circle at A and B.

Join $\overline{QA}$, $\overline{QB}$.

Then $\overline{QA}$, $\overline{QB}$ are the required tangents from Q.

Proof Join $\overline{OA}$, $\overline{OB}$.

Since C is the mid-point of $\overline{OQ}$, the circle centre C has $\overline{OQ}$ as diameter.

$$\therefore \ O\hat{A}Q = 90° = O\hat{B}Q. \qquad \angle \ in \ semicircle$$

But $\overline{OA}$, $\overline{OB}$ are radii of the given circle.

$$\therefore \ \overline{QA}, \ \overline{QB} \text{ are tangents to the given circle.} \qquad rad. \perp tan.$$
$$\text{Q.E.F.}$$

Contact of circles

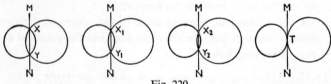

Fig. 220

Consider two circles with a common chord $\overline{XY}$. If the circles move away from each other so that X and Y occupy successively positions such as X_1 and Y_1, X_2 and Y_2, etc., then X and Y become closer and closer to each other as in Fig. 220. Ultimately the points X and Y will coincide in the single point T, and the line $\overline{MN}$ through X and Y becomes a tangent at T to both circles.

Two circles are said to touch each other if they both touch the same straight line at the same point. Hence if two circles touch each other, then through their point of contact a line can be drawn which is a tangent to both circles at that point.

320

Tangents. Contact of circles. Alternate segment

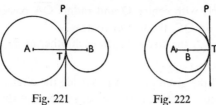

Fig. 221   Fig. 222

In Fig. 221 the two circles touch each other **externally,** and in Fig. 222 **internally,** at T.

Let their centres be A, B, and let the common tangent at T be $\overline{PT}$.

Then in Fig. 221, since $A\hat{T}P = 90° = B\hat{T}P$, $\overline{ATB}$ is a straight line, since adjacent angles are supplementary.

Also in Fig. 222, since $A\hat{T}P = 90° = B\hat{T}P$, $\overline{AT}$ and $\overline{BT}$ are both at right angles to $\overline{TP}$ and therefore coincide with each other.

Hence in either case, **if two circles touch each other, the line joining their centres passes through their point of contact.**

The distance between their centres is the **sum** of their radii if the circles touch externally, and the **difference** if they touch internally.

Example 1 *Show how to construct a circle to pass through a given point, and to touch a given circle at a given point.*

Given a point A, and a point B on the circumference of a circle with centre C.

To construct a circle to pass through A, and to touch the given circle at B.

Construction Draw the perpendicular bisector of $\overline{AB}$, and let it meet $\overline{CB}$ produced at Q. Then the circle with centre Q and radius $\overline{QA}$ is the required circle.

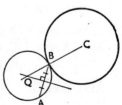

Fig. 223

Proof Q lies on the perpendicular bisector of $\overline{AB}$.

$$\therefore \ QA = QB.$$

321

New General Mathematics

∴ the circle with centre Q and radius $\overline{QA}$ passes through B.
But B lies on $\overline{QC}$, the line of centres,
  ∴ the circles touch each other at B.

Q.E.F.

In Fig. 223 the given point A is outside the circle. If A is inside the circle the construction is the same, except that the perpendicular bisector of $\overline{AB}$ meets $\overline{CB}$, and not $\overline{CB}$ produced.

Example 2 *Show how to construct a circle to touch a given circle, and to touch a given straight line at a given point.*

Given a circle with centre C, and a point A on a straight line $\overline{HK}$.
To construct a circle to touch the given circle, and to touch $\overline{HK}$ at A.

Construction Draw the perpendicular $\overline{CD}$ from C to $\overline{HK}$, and let $\overline{DC}$ produced cut the circle at E.
Let $\overline{EA}$ cut the circle at B.
At A draw a perpendicular to $\overline{HK}$, and let it meet $\overline{CB}$ produced at Q.
Then the circle with centre Q and radius QA is the required circle.

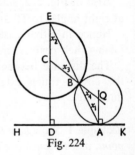
Fig. 224

Proof $x_1 = x_2$ *alt.*
    $= x_3$ $CB = CE$
    $= x_4$ *vert. opp.*
∴ $QA = QB$

∴ the circle with centre Q and radius QA passes through B.
But B lies on $\overline{QC}$, the line of centres,
  ∴ the circles touch each other at B.
Also, since $\overline{QA} \perp \overline{HK}$, the constructed circle touches $\overline{HK}$ at A.

Q.E.F.

The construction can easily be modified to suit the case in which A lies inside the given circle.

322

Tangents. Contact of circles. Alternate segment

Exercise 26a

In Fig. 225, O is the centre of the circle, and $\overline{TA}$, $\overline{TB}$ are tangents. Nos. 1–5 refer to this figure.

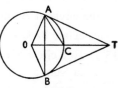

Fig. 225

1 If $A\widehat{T}O = 36°$, calculate $A\widehat{C}O$.

2 „ $A\widehat{B}T = 57°$, „ $A\widehat{O}T$.

3 „ $O\widehat{A}C = 69°$, „ $A\widehat{T}B$.

4 „ $A\widehat{C}T = 122°$, „ $C\widehat{A}T$.

5 „ $B\widehat{T}C = 44°$, „ $B\widehat{A}C$.

6 The tangent from a point T touches a circle at R. If the radius of the circle is 2·8 cm, and T is 5·3 cm from the centre, calculate the length of the tangent $\overline{TR}$.

7 A point P is 6·5 cm from the centre of a circle, and the length of the tangent from P is 5·6 cm. Calculate the radius of the circle.

8 $\overline{AB}$ is a chord and O is the centre of a circle. If $A\widehat{O}B = 78°$, calculate the obtuse angle between $\overline{AB}$ and the tangent at B.

9 Three circles are such that each touches the other two externally, and their centres form a triangle with sides of length 9 cm, 7 cm, 6 cm. Calculate the radii of the circles.

10 A, B are the centres of two circles which touch each other externally. Both circles lie inside a third circle, centre C, and touch it internally. If AB = 11 cm, BC = 8 cm, CA = 9 cm, calculate the radii of the circles.

11 Two circles have the same centre, and their radii are 15 cm and 17 cm. A tangent to the inner circle cuts the outer circle at P, Q. Calculate PQ.

12 Draw a circle of radius 3 cm, and mark its centre O. Mark a point A on the circumference and construct $A\widehat{O}B = 40°$, making OB = 8 cm. Construct a circle to pass through B and to touch the given circle at A, and measure its radius.

13 Two circles, centres X and Y, touch externally at T, and A is

323

a point on their common tangent at T such that AT = 12 cm. If AX = 13 cm, AY = 15 cm, find XY. If the circles touch internally instead of externally, what is XY?

14 O is the centre of a circle, the tangents from a point X touch the circle at A and B, and $\overline{AC}$ is a diameter. If $A\hat{O}X = 47°$, calculate $B\hat{A}C$.

15 Draw a circle of radius 3 cm, with its centre O at a distance of 7 cm from a straight line $\overline{AB}$. On $\overline{AB}$ mark points M, N such that $O\hat{M}N = 90°$ and MN = 5 cm. Construct a circle to touch the given circle, and to touch AB at N. Measure its radius.

16 $\overline{AD}$ is a diameter of a circle, and $\overline{AT}$ is a tangent. P is a point on the circle such that $P\hat{A}T = 35°$. Calculate $A\hat{D}P$. Hence calculate $A\hat{Q}P$, where Q is any other point on the circle.

17 A, B, C are three points on a circle, and $B\hat{A}C = 37°$. If the tangents at B and C meet at T, calculate $B\hat{T}C$.

18 P, Q, R are three points on a circle, and the tangents at P and Q meet at T. If $P\hat{T}Q = 62°$, calculate $P\hat{R}Q$.

19 The vertical height of a cone is 24 cm, and the radius of its base is 10 cm. A sphere of radius 5 cm rests inside the cone, which stands with its vertex downwards and axis vertical. Find the distance of the lowest point of the sphere from the vertex of the cone. (*Use similar triangles.*)

20 In no. 19, if the radius of the sphere is 6 cm, what is the distance of its lowest point from the vertex?

Exercise 26b

1 A, B, C are three points on a circle. The tangents at A, B meet at T, and $\overline{BC}$ is parallel to $\overline{TA}$. Prove that $\overline{AB}$ bisects $T\hat{B}C$.

2 Two circles touch externally, and a line through their point of contact cuts one circle at A and the other at B. Prove that the radii to A and B are parallel.

3 Two circles touch externally or internally at A, and T is any point on their common tangent at A. Tangents from T touch one of the circles at P and the other at Q. Prove that TP = TQ.

4 $\overline{AD}$ is a diameter of a circle, $\overline{AB}$ is a chord, and $\overline{AT}$ is a tangent, $B\hat{A}T$ being acute. Prove that $B\hat{A}T = A\hat{D}B$.

5 C is the centre of a circle, $\overline{AB}$ is a chord, $\overline{AD}$ is a diameter, and $\overline{BT}$ is a tangent, $D\hat{B}T$ being acute. Prove that $A\hat{B}C = D\hat{B}T$.

6 C is the centre of a circle, $\overline{AB}$ is a chord, and $\overline{BD}$ is the perpendicular from B to the tangent at A. Prove that $A\hat{B}C = A\hat{B}D$.

7 $\overline{AB}$ is a diameter of a circle and $\overline{AC}$ is a chord. The tangents at A and C meet at T. Prove that $A\hat{T}C = 2B\hat{A}C$.

8 The centre of a circle is O, and the tangents from T touch the circle at A, B. If $\overline{AD}$ is a diameter, prove that $\overline{BD}$ is parallel to $\overline{TO}$.

9 The quadrilateral PQRS is such that a circle can be drawn inside it to touch all four sides. Prove that PQ + RS = PS + QR.

10 Two circles with radii 2 cm, 3 cm touch each other externally. Show how to construct a circle with radius 4 cm to touch externally the two given circles.

11 A circle with radius 2 cm lies inside a circle with radius 7 cm, and touches it. Find a construction for drawing a circle with radius 3 cm to touch the smaller of the given circles externally and the greater internally.

12 O is the centre of a circle, and the tangents from a point T touch the circle at A, B. If $\overline{BT}$ is produced to C, prove that $A\hat{T}C = 2A\hat{O}T$.

13 X is a fixed point 5 cm from a given straight line $\overline{YZ}$, and a circle is drawn with centre X and radius 2 cm. Show how to construct a circle with radius 2·5 cm to touch the given circle externally, and also to touch $\overline{YZ}$.

14 Two circles touch each other at T, and a straight line touches one circle at A and the other at B. Prove that AT̂B is a right angle.

15 $\overline{CD}$ is a diameter of a circle, centre O. $\overline{CA}$, $\overline{DB}$ are tangents, and the straight line $\overline{AB}$ is also a tangent. Prove that AÔB is a right angle.

16 Given two fixed points X and Y, 9 cm apart, show how to construct a line through X such that its perpendicular distance from Y is 4 cm.

17 Two circles touch internally, and a line through their point of contact cuts one circle at A and the other at B. Prove that the tangents at A and B are parallel.

18 T is any point on a circle, and $\overline{CD}$ is a diameter. If $\overline{CM}$, $\overline{DN}$ are the perpendiculars from C, D to the tangent at T, prove that TM = TN.

19 Given two fixed points H and K, 8·4 cm apart, show how to construct a circle with centre H, such that the tangents to it from K are of length 7·6 cm.

20 $\overline{AD}$ is a diameter of a circle, and $\overline{AB}$, $\overline{CD}$ are parallel chords. Prove that the tangents at B, C are parallel to each other.

Alternate segment

In Fig. 226, the chord $\overline{AB}$ divides the circle into two segments APB and AQB.

Let $\overline{SAT}$ be the tangent at A.

Then the segment APB is said to be **alternate** to TÂB, since it is on the *other* side of $\overline{AB}$ from TÂB. Similarly the segment AQB is alternate to SÂB.

(Sometimes the word 'opposite' is used instead of alternate.)

Fig. 226

326

Theorem 18

The angles between a tangent to a circle and a chord through the point of contact are equal respectively to the angles in the alternate segments.

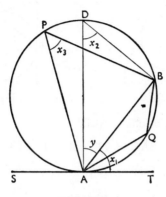

Fig. 227

Given a circle, with $\overline{SAT}$ a tangent at A, and a chord $\overline{AB}$ dividing the circle into two segments APB and AQB, segment APB being alternate to $T\hat{A}B$.

To prove $T\hat{A}B = A\hat{P}B$ and $S\hat{A}B = A\hat{Q}B$.

Construction Draw the diameter $\overline{AD}$. Join $\overline{BD}$.

Proof		
	$x_1 + y = 90°$	*tan.* $\perp$ *rad.*
Also	$A\hat{B}D = 90°$	$\angle$ *in semi*$\odot$
	$\therefore x_2 + y = 90°$	$\angle s$ *of* $\triangle$ *add to* $180°$
	$\therefore x_1 = x_2$	
	$= x_3$	*same seg.*
	$\therefore T\hat{A}B = A\hat{P}B.$	
Also	$S\hat{A}B = 180° - x_1$	*adj.* $\angle s$ *on a str. line*
	$= 180° - x_3$	
	$= A\hat{Q}B.$	*opp.* $\angle s$ *of cyclic quad.*

Q.E.D.

327

Exercise 26c (*numerical*)

In Fig. 228, $\overline{TAX}$ and $\overline{TBY}$ are tangents to the circle, and C is a point on the major arc AB. Nos. 1–5 refer to this figure.

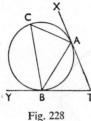

Fig. 228

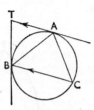

Fig. 229

1 If $A\hat{T}B = 68°$, calculate $A\hat{C}B$.

2 „ $A\hat{B}C = 43°$, $B\hat{A}C = 73°$, calculate $A\hat{T}B$.

3 „ $A\hat{C}B = 59°$, $C\hat{B}Y = 78°$, „ $C\hat{A}X$.

4 „ $C\hat{A}X = 65°$, $C\hat{B}Y = 76°$, „ $A\hat{T}B$.

5 „ $A\hat{B}C = 48°$, $A\hat{T}B = 72°$, „ $B\hat{A}C$.

6 In Fig. 229, if $A\hat{T}B = 82°$, calculate the angles of $\triangle ABC$.

7 The tangents from T touch a circle at A, B, and the chord $\overline{BC}$ is parallel to $\overline{TA}$. If $B\hat{A}T = 54°$, calculate $B\hat{A}C$.

8 $\overline{AB}$ is a chord of a circle, ACB is the minor arc, and the tangents at A, B meet at T. If $A\hat{T}B = 54°$ and $C\hat{B}T = 23°$, calculate $C\hat{A}T$.

9 In Fig. 230, if $A\hat{C}B = 37°$ and $A\hat{T}B = 42°$, calculate $A\hat{B}T$ and $A\hat{E}B$.

10 A, B, C are three points on a circle. The tangent at C meets

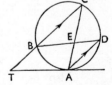

Fig. 230

$\overline{AB}$ produced at T. If $A\hat{C}T = 103°$, $A\hat{T}C = 43°$, calculate the angles of $\triangle ABC$.

Tangents. Contact of circles. Alternate segment

11 The angles of a triangle are 40°, 60°, 80°, and a circle touches the sides at P, Q, R. Calculate the angles of △PQR.

12 $\overline{AT}$ is a tangent to the circle ABCD. $B\hat{A}C = 64°$ and $C\hat{A}T = 72°$. Calculate $B\hat{C}A$ and $C\hat{D}A$.

Exercise 26d

1 $\overline{AB}$, $\overline{BC}$, $\overline{CA}$ are three equal chords of a circle, and the tangents at B and C meet at T. Prove that △BCT is equilateral.

2 A, B, C are three points on a circle such that $\overline{BC}$ is parallel to the tangent at A. Prove that △ABC is isosceles.

3 A, B, C are three points on a circle, centre O. Prove that $A\hat{B}C$ and $O\hat{C}A$ are complementary, $A\hat{B}C$ being acute.

4 P, Q, R are three points on a circle. If the tangent at P meets $\overline{QR}$ produced at S, prove that $P\hat{R}S = Q\hat{P}S$.

5 C is the mid-point of the arc cut off by a chord $\overline{AB}$. Prove that the perpendiculars from C to $\overline{AB}$ and to the tangent at A are equal.

6 $\overline{BC}$ is a diameter of a circle, and $\overline{BD}$ is the perpendicular from B to the tangent at any point A on the circle. Prove that $\overline{AB}$ bisects $C\hat{B}D$.

7 Two circles intersect at P and Q. The chord $\overline{PX}$ of one circle is a tangent to the second circle. The chord $\overline{QY}$ of the second circle is a tangent to the first. Prove that $\overline{PY}$ is parallel to $\overline{XQ}$.

8 Two circles intersect at X, Y. The chord $\overline{AX}$ of one circle is a tangent to the second circle, and the chord $\overline{BX}$ of the second circle is a tangent to the first. Prove that $A\hat{Y}X = B\hat{Y}X$.

9 With the figure of no. 8 prove that if $\overline{AX}$ and $\overline{BX}$ are at right angles, then Y lies on the straight line $\overline{AB}$.

10 Two circles intersect at X, Y, and a common tangent touches the circles at P, T. Prove that $T\hat{X}P$ and $T\hat{Y}P$ are supplementary.

329

11 A, B are the points of intersection of two circles. The chords
$\overline{CA}$, $\overline{CB}$ of one circle are produced to cut the other circle at
P, Q. Prove that $\overline{PQ}$ is parallel to the tangent at C.

12 Two circles intersect at A and B, and a straight line through A
cuts one circle at P and the other at Q. If the tangents at P and
Q meet at T, prove that PBQT is a cyclic quadrilateral.

13 $\overline{CD}$ is a diameter of a circle, and P is any point on the circumference. $\overline{DP}$ is produced to B so that BP = PD. Prove that
the tangent to the circle at P is perpendicular to $\overline{BC}$.

14 P, Q, R are three points on a circle. The tangents at P, Q meet
at X, and $\overline{RQ}$ is parallel to $\overline{PX}$. Prove that $Q\hat{P}R = P\hat{X}Q$.

15 Two circles touch internally at T. Straight lines $\overline{TAC}$, $\overline{TBD}$
cut one circle at A, B, and the other at C, D. Prove that $\overline{AB}$ is
parallel to $\overline{CD}$.

16 The tangent at any point A of a circle cuts the diameter $\overline{CD}$
produced in T. Prove that $A\hat{T}D$ is the complement of twice
$T\hat{A}D$.

17 The tangents from a point X to a circle touch it at P,Q. $\overline{QR}$
is a diameter, and $\overline{XN}$ is the perpendicular from X to $\overline{PQ}$.
Prove that $P\hat{X}N = P\hat{Q}R$.

18 Two circles intersect at A, B. P is a point on the first circle such
that $\overline{PA}$ produced and $\overline{PB}$ produced cut the second circle at
C and D respectively. If $\overline{CD}$ is a diameter of the second circle
and O is its centre, prove that $\overline{OA}$ is a tangent to the first
circle.

19 Two circles touch internally at T, and the tangent at any
point X on the inner circle cuts the outer circle at A, B. Prove
that $A\hat{T}X = B\hat{T}X$.

20 $\overline{BAC}$ is the tangent to a circle at A, and $\overline{AD}$ is a diameter.
$\overline{BD}$, $\overline{CD}$ cut the circle at E, F. Prove that B, E, F, C are concyclic.

21 $\overline{AB}$, $\overline{AC}$ are equal chords of a circle, centre O, and $\overline{AD}$ is a diameter. Prove that $\overline{BD}$ is a tangent to the circle through C, D, O.

22 Two circles touch internally at T, and the tangent at any point X on the inner circle cuts the outer circle at A, B. The chords $\overline{AT}$, $\overline{BT}$ of the outer circle cut the inner circle at P, Q respectively. Prove that $A\hat{X}P = B\hat{X}Q$.

23 Two circles touch externally at T. A chord $\overline{AB}$ of one of them, when produced, touches the other at C. The chord $\overline{CT}$ of the second, when produced, cuts the first at D. Prove that $A\hat{T}D = B\hat{T}C$.

24 Two circles touch externally at T. A, B are points on one circle such that $\overline{AB}$ produced touches the second circle at P. $\overline{AT}$ produced, $\overline{BT}$ produced cut the second circle at Q, R. Prove that PQ = PR.

Common tangents

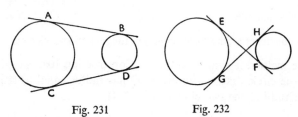

Fig. 231   Fig. 232

Fig. 231 shows two circles with their **direct** (or **exterior**) common tangents $\overline{AB}$ and $\overline{CD}$.

Fig. 232 shows two circles with their **transverse** (or **interior**) common tangents $\overline{EF}$ and $\overline{GH}$.

331

Construction 10a

To construct a direct common tangent to two circles.

Given two circles, centres O and Q.

To construct the direct common tangents to the circles.

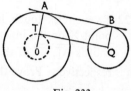

Fig. 233

Construction O being the centre of the larger circle, draw a circle with centre O and radius equal to the *difference* between the radii of the two circles.

Construct the tangent $\overline{QT}$ to this circle (Construction 9).

Join $\overline{OT}$ and produce to cut the circle centre O at A.

Draw $\overline{QB}$ parallel to $\overline{OA}$ to cut the circle centre Q at B.

Join $\overline{AB}$, which is the required tangent.

Proof $O\hat{T}Q = 90°$ and $\overline{AT}$, $\overline{BQ}$ are equal and parallel

∴ ABQT is a rectangle

∴ $O\hat{A}B$ and $Q\hat{B}A$ are right angles

∴ $\overline{AB}$ is a tangent to both circles.

Q.E.F.

Construction 10b

To construct a transverse common tangent to two circles.

The method is similar to that in Construction 10a, except that here the circle drawn with centre O has radius equal to the *sum* of the radii of the two circles. (Fig. 234)

N.B. No common tangents can be drawn if the smaller circle lies entirely within the larger.

Only direct common tangents can be drawn if the circles intersect.

Both direct and transverse common tangents can be drawn if the circles lie entirely outside one another.

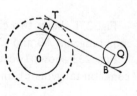

Fig. 234

Construction 11

To construct the incircle of a given triangle.

Given any triangle ABC.

To construct the circle touching the sides of the triangle.

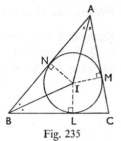

Fig. 235

Construction Bisect the angles A and B of the triangle, and let these bisectors meet at I.

Draw $\overline{IL}$ perpendicular to $\overline{BC}$ to cut $\overline{BC}$ at L.

Then the circle with centre I and radius IL is the required circle.

Proof Draw $\overline{IN}$, $\overline{IM}$ perpendicular to $\overline{AB}$, $\overline{AC}$ respectively.

Since the bisectors of the angles of a triangle are concurrent (*see* p. 199 (iii)) IM = IN = IL.

∴ the circle with centre I and radius IL will pass through L, M and N.

But $\overline{IL} \perp \overline{BC}$.

∴ the circle touches $\overline{BC}$ at L, and similarly $\overline{CA}$ at M and $\overline{AB}$ at N.

∴ the circle centre I and radius IL is the required circle.

I is called the **incentre** of the triangle and the circle is the **incircle** (or **inscribed circle**).

Construction 12

To construct the three e–circles of a given triangle.

Fig. 236 shows one of the required circles, which touches $\overline{BC}$, $\overline{AB}$ produced and $\overline{AC}$ produced.

The method of construction is similar to that of Construction 11 and should be obvious from the figure.

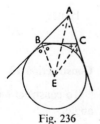

Fig. 236

333

There are three such circles, called the **e-circles** (or **escribed circles**), and their centres are the **e-centres**.

Example 3 *The inscribed circle of* $\triangle ABC$ *touches* $\overline{BC}$, $\overline{CA}$, $\overline{AB}$ *at* P, Q, R *respectively. If* AB $= 11$ *cm,* BC $= 10$ *cm,* CA $= 8$ *cm, calculate* AR, BP, CQ.

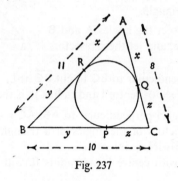

Fig. 237

The tangents from a point are equal.

Let $\qquad$ AQ $=$ AR $= x$ cm,
$\qquad\qquad$ BR $=$ BP $= y$ cm,
$\qquad\qquad$ CP $=$ CQ $= z$ cm.

Then $\qquad\qquad$ $x + y = 11 \qquad$ (i)
$\qquad\qquad\qquad$ $y + z = 10 \qquad$ (ii)
$\qquad\qquad\qquad$ $x + z = \;\; 8 \qquad$ (iii)

(i)$-$(ii) $\qquad\qquad$ $x - z = \;\; 1$

Add $\qquad\qquad\qquad$ $2x = \;\; 9$
$\qquad\qquad\qquad$ $\therefore x = \;\; 4\tfrac{1}{2}$

Hence $\qquad\qquad$ $y = 6\tfrac{1}{2}$ and $z = 3\tfrac{1}{2}$.
$\qquad$ $\therefore$ AR $= 4\tfrac{1}{2}$ cm, BP $= 6\tfrac{1}{2}$ cm, CQ $= 3\tfrac{1}{2}$ cm.

Construction 13

To construct on a given line an arc of a circle containing a given angle.

It is convenient here to give a numerical example.

Tangents. Contact of circles. Alternate segment

Example 4 *On a line* $\overline{BC}$, *6 cm long, construct an arc of a circle to contain an angle of* 50°.

Method 1. Since the angle at the circumference is 50°, the angle at the centre is 100°.

∴ if O is the centre of the circle, the angles of △OBC are 100°, 40°, 40°.

Construct △OBC.

With centre O and radius OB draw a circle.

$\overline{BC}$ then divides this circle into two segments, one of which contains an angle of 50°, and the other an angle of 130°.

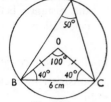

Fig. 238

Method 2. Draw $\overline{BT}$ so that $\hat{CBT} = 50°$.

At B draw a line perpendicular to $\overline{BT}$, to meet the perpendicular bisector of $\overline{BC}$ at O.

Then the circle with centre O and radius OB is the required circle.

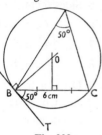

Fig. 239

Method 1 depends on the theorem that the angle at the centre is twice the angle at the circumference.

Method 2 depends on the 'alternate segment' theorem.

Exercise 26e

Common tangents

1 Draw two circles with radii 5 cm and 3 cm, their centres being 9 cm apart. Construct a direct common tangent and measure the distance between the points of contact. Check by calculation.

2 Using the same dimensions as for no. 1 construct a transverse common tangent. Measure the distance between the points of contact, and check by calculation.

3 Draw a circle of radius 5 cm and, with centre on its circumference, another circle of radius 3 cm. Construct a direct common tangent: measure the distance between the points of contact, and check by calculation.

335

4 Draw two circles with radii 2 cm and 3 cm, their centres being 8 cm apart. Construct a transverse common tangent: measure the distance between the points of contact, and check by calculation.

In-circle and e-circle

Construct in-circles to the following triangles: measure their radii.

5 Sides 6 cm, 7 cm, 9 cm.

6 „ 7 cm, 8 cm, 10 cm.

7 „ 4·5 cm, 6 cm, 8·5 cm.

8 „ 6 cm, 8 cm, included angle 70°.

9 Draw a triangle ABC in which AC = 2 cm, BA = BC = 3 cm. Construct the e-circle opposite A (i.e. touching $\overline{BC}$, $\overline{AB}$ produced and $\overline{AC}$ produced). Measure the radius of the circle.

10 Draw a triangle with sides 2 cm, 3 cm, 4 cm and construct the e-circle which touches the shortest side. Measure its radius.

11 Draw a triangle with sides 2 cm, 3 cm, 3·5 cm. Construct all three e-circles and measure their radii.

12 In △ABC, AB = 6 cm, BC = 7 cm, CA = 8 cm, and the inscribed circle touches $\overline{BC}$, $\overline{CA}$, $\overline{AB}$ at P, Q, R respectively. Calculate AR, BP, CQ.

13 One of the escribed circles of △ABC touches $\overline{BC}$ at P, $\overline{AC}$ produced at Q, and $\overline{AB}$ produced at R. If AB = 10 cm, BC = 7 cm, CA = 9 cm, calculate BP and CP.

14 The inscribed circle of △ABC touches $\overline{BC}$, $\overline{CA}$, $\overline{AB}$ at P, Q, R respectively, and the incentre is X. If $P\hat{X}Q = 110°$ and $P\hat{X}R = 130°$, calculate the angles of △ABC and also the angles of △PQR.

15 In △ABC, $\hat{A} = 60°$, $\hat{B} = 40°$, $\hat{C} = 80°$. An escribed circle touches $\overline{BC}$, $\overline{AC}$ produced, $\overline{AB}$ produced at P, Q, R respectively. Calculate the angles of △PQR.

16 The tangents to a circle at A, B meet at T. C is the mid-point of the minor arc AB. Prove that C is the incentre of △ABT.

17 The inscribed circle of △ABC touches $\overline{AB}$ at D, and $\overline{AC}$ at E. If I is the incentre, prove that $\hat{A} = 2D\hat{E}I$.

18 The inscribed circle of △ABC touches $\overline{BC}$, $\overline{CA}$, $\overline{AB}$ at P, Q, R respectively. Prove that $2P\hat{Q}R$ is the supplement of B.

In many of the following examples it will be found helpful to draw a rough figure first.

19 Draw a quadrant of a circle of radius 6 cm. Construct a circle to touch the radii bounding the quadrant and also to touch the arc. Measure the radius of this circle.

20 Draw a semicircle of radius 5 cm. Construct two circles of radius 2 cm to touch both the semicircle and its diameter.

21 Draw a quad. ABCD with AB = 6 cm, BC = 5 cm, CD = 3 cm, DA = 4 cm, $A\hat{D}C = 100°$. Construct a circle to touch $\overline{BA}$, $\overline{AD}$ and $\overline{DC}$, and measure its radius. Does this circle also touch $\overline{BC}$?

22 Draw a circle with centre O and radius 3 cm. Mark a point P such that OP = 7 cm. Construct two tangents from P to the circle, and measure their lengths.

23 Show how to construct a trapezium ABCD in which $\overline{AB} \parallel \overline{DC}$, AB = 4 cm, BC = 8 cm, CD = 11 cm, DA = 6 cm. (*Hint—in the rough figure, divide the trapezium into a ∥gm and a* △.)

24 Construct a trapezium ABCD in which $\overline{AB} \parallel \overline{DC}$, AB = 4 cm, BC = 6 cm, CD = 9 cm, DA = 5 cm. Measure AC and $\hat{D}$.

25 On a base $\overline{AB}$, 6 cm long, construct an arc of a circle containing an angle of 40°. Find a point C on this arc such that AC = 8 cm. Measure BC.

26 On a base $\overline{BC}$, 6 cm long, construct a △ABC of area 12 cm² with $\hat{A} = 65°$. Measure AB and AC.

New General Mathematics

27 On a base $\overline{XY}$, 8 cm long, construct an arc of a circle containing an angle of 100°. Find a point Z on this arc such that $Z\hat{X}Y = 50°$. Measure ZX, ZY and the radius of the circle.

28 Draw a circle of radius 4 cm. Draw a radius and produce it outside the circle. Construct two circles of radius 2 cm which touch this line and the circle, and are outside the circle.

29 Draw a circle centre O and radius 3 cm. Mark a point P such that OP = 5 cm. Draw two circles to pass through P and to touch the original circle.

30 Draw two circles of radii 2 cm and 1·5 cm, with their centres 4 cm apart. Construct a circle of radius 3 cm to touch both circles.

31 Draw $\triangle ABC$ in which AB = 5 cm, BC = 8 cm, $\hat{B} = 70°$. Construct a circle to touch $\overline{BC}$ at B, and to pass through A. Measure its radius.

32 Draw a circle of radius 4 cm. Construct a triangle with angles of 50°, 60°, 70°, whose vertices are on the circle. Measure the longest side.

33 Draw a circle of radius 4 cm, and a tangent to it at any point. Construct as many circles as possible of radius 2 cm which touch both the tangent and the circle.

Chapter 27

Miscellaneous arithmetical problems

Speed, time and distance

$$\textbf{Distance} = \textbf{Speed} \times \textbf{Time}$$
$$\text{Speed} = \text{Distance} \div \text{Time}$$
$$\text{Time} = \text{Distance} \div \text{Speed}$$

Relative speed

If a car and a motorcycle are travelling at 50 km h^{-1} and 70 km h^{-1} respectively on a motorway, and the cyclist is behind the motorist, he is overtaking at the rate of 20 km h^{-1}, which is called the **relative speed** of the two vehicles.

Similarly, if they are travelling in opposite directions, the relative speed (i.e. the speed at which they are approaching one another) is 120 km h^{-1}.

In general the relative speed of two moving objects is the rate at which the distance between them is increasing or decreasing.

Example 1 *A car and a motorcycle are travelling at 50 km h^{-1} and 70 km h^{-1} respectively on a straight road and are 500 m apart. After what times will the car and the motorcycle be level with one another if (i) the motorcycle is overtaking the car? (ii) they are approaching one another?*

(i)   Relative speed = 20 km h^{-1}
       Distance to be covered = 500 m = $\frac{1}{2}$ km
   $\therefore$ time taken to overtake = $\frac{1}{2} \div 20$ h = $\frac{1}{40}$ h
                                       = $1\frac{1}{2}$ minutes.

(ii)   Relative speed = 120 km h^{-1}
       Distance to be covered = $\frac{1}{2}$ km
   $\therefore$ time taken to meet = $\frac{1}{2} \div 120$ h = $\frac{1}{240}$ h
                                   = 15 seconds.

N.B. The work is shortened if it is realised that 120 km h⁻¹ is six times 20 km h⁻¹. Therefore the time taken in (ii) is one-sixth of that taken in (i): therefore the time taken in (ii) is one-sixth of $1\frac{1}{2}$ minutes = 15 seconds.

Example 2 *A goods train leaves Euston at* 10.00, *travelling at* 48 *km h⁻¹. At* 11.15 *an express follows, travelling at* 80 *km h⁻¹. When does the express catch up with the goods train, and how far from Euston?*

At 11.15 the goods train has travelled at 48 km h⁻¹ for $1\frac{1}{4}$ hours
∴ the distance it has gone = $48 \times 1\frac{1}{4}$ km = 60 km
∴ the express has to catch up 60 km at (80 − 48) km h⁻¹
            i.e. at 32 km h⁻¹
∴ the time taken to overtake = $60 \div 32$ hours = $1\frac{7}{8}$ hours
   = 1 h $52\frac{1}{2}$ min
∴ the express catches up with the goods train 1 h $52\frac{1}{2}$ min after
   11.15; i.e. at $13.07\frac{1}{2}$.

The distance travelled by the goods train in the time between 10.00 and $13.07\frac{1}{2}$ (i.e. $3\frac{1}{8}$ hours) = $48 \times 3\frac{1}{8}$ km = 150 km.

The trains are level 150 km from Euston at $13.07\frac{1}{2}$.

If a train of length l passes through a station with a platform of length L, the time taken for the train to clear the platform completely lasts from the moment that the engine is level with the near end of the platform until the tail lamp of the train is level with the far end.

The time taken is therefore $(l + L) \div v$.

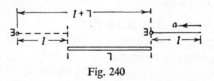

Fig. 240

Similarly, if two trains are passing one another, the time taken for one to pass the other is equal to the sum of the lengths of the trains divided by their relative speed.

N.B. 36 km h^{-1} = 36 000 m in 3 600 seconds = 10 m s^{-1}.

The use of this relationship between km h^{-1} and m s^{-1} often saves a great deal of labour when problems involving speed, time and distance are being worked, as will be seen in Example 3.

Example 3 *Two trains 246 m and 304 m long are travelling towards one another at 114 km h^{-1} and 66 km h^{-1} respectively. How long do the trains take to pass one another?*

Relative speed = (114 + 66) km h^{-1} = 180 km h^{-1}
$$= 180 \times \tfrac{10}{36} \text{ m s}^{-1} = 50 \text{ m s}^{-1}$$
Distance to be covered = (246 + 304) m = 550 m

∴ time taken to pass = 550 ÷ 50 seconds
$$= 11 \text{ seconds.}$$

Exercise 27a

1 Express as speeds in km h^{-1}: (i) 25 m s^{-1}, (ii) 1 cm s^{-1},
(iii) 56 km in 35 minutes, (iv) 5 063 km in 2 days 13 hours,
(v) 42 m in 1·4 s.

2 Express as speeds in m s^{-1}: (i) 90 km h^{-1}, (ii) 1 km in 25 s,
(iii) 56 km in 35 minutes, (iv) 10 cm in 0·04 s,
(v) 1 500 m in 4 minutes.

3 How long does it take a train travelling at 56 km h^{-1} to cover 3 080 m?

4 If successive telegraph posts are 20 m apart along a straight road, and a car passes from the first to the thirteenth post in 16 seconds, how fast is the car travelling in km h^{-1}?

5 Two cars travelling towards one another at 53 km h^{-1} and 91 km h^{-1} respectively are half a kilometre apart. In how many seconds will the cars be level with one another?

6 A car travelling at 80 km h^{-1} is 187 m behind another car travelling in the same direction at 46 km h^{-1}. How long will it take the faster car to catch the slower one?

7 Two trains, each travelling at 80 km h^{-1}, start towards one another from stations 424 km apart at 10.30. When will the trains meet?

8 A man starts at 9.00 and walks steadily along the main road at 6 km h^{-1}. At 10.30 a car leaves the same place and follows the same road at 51 km h^{-1}. When and where does the car overtake the man?

9 How long does it take a train 150 m long to pass a stationary observer if the train is travelling at 72 km h^{-1}?

10 How long is a train if it is travelling at 48 km h^{-1} and passes a signal in 18 seconds?

11 How fast is a train 375 m long moving if it passes a point in 25 seconds?

12 How long will it take a train 218 m long to pass completely through a station 132 m long if it is travelling at 112 km h^{-1}?

13 How fast is a train 106 m long travelling if it passes a stationary train 139 m long in 14 seconds?

14 A car overtakes and passes a column of troops 300 m long, marching at 5 km h^{-1}, in half a minute exactly. How fast is the car travelling?

15 How long does it take a column of troops one kilometre long to pass completely over a bridge 200 m long if the troops are marching at 6 km h^{-1}?

16 How long will it take a motor-boat which can travel at 20 km h^{-1} in still water to go (i) 24 km upstream, (ii) 15 km downstream, on a river flowing at 5 km h^{-1}?

17 How long will a man take to row 10 km upstream and back again if the water is moving at 3 km h^{-1} and he can row at 9 km h^{-1} on still water?

18 How fast does a man row on still water if he goes 15 km downstream in 1 h 15 min when the speed of the current is $3\frac{1}{2}$ km h^{-1}?

19 What is the speed of the current if a man can swim 2 km upstream in 40 minutes and $3\frac{1}{2}$ km downstream in 30 minutes?

20 A man can bicycle at 30 km h^{-1} with the wind and at 24 km h^{-1} against it. How much longer does it take him to ride to a station 18 km away and back again if the wind is blowing straight down the road than it would take him if there were no wind?

Mixtures

Example 4 *In what proportion must teas costing 76p and 84p per kilo be mixed in order to produce a blend worth 81p per kilo?*

On each kilo at 76p there is a gain of 5p

,, ,, ,, ,, 84p ,, ,, ,, loss ,, 3p

∴ 3 kilo of the first tea must be taken with 5 kilo of the second so that the gain on the first is exactly balanced by the loss on the second.

∴ required proportion is 3 : 5.

Example 5 *A tobacconist makes a profit of* 20% *by selling his 'special mixture' at 54p for a 30 g packet. The mixture is blended from two tobaccos which cost him respectively £12 and £16 per kilo. In what proportion does the tobacconist mix the two tobaccos?*

Selling price of mixture per kilo $= \frac{1\,000}{30} \times 54p = 1\,800p$

∴ cost ,, ,, ,, ,, ,, $= \frac{100}{120} \times 1\,800p = 1\,500p$

$= £15$

∴ gain on first tobacco $= £3$ per kilo

and loss on second ,, $= £1$,, ,,

∴ required proportion $= 1 : 3$.

Exercise 27b

1 In what proportion should teas at 78p and 84p per kilo be mixed to obtain a blend worth 82p per kilo?

2 In what proportion should coffee at 88p per kilo and chicory at 22p per kilo be mixed in order to obtain a blend worth $82\frac{1}{2}$p per kilo?

3 How must two sorts of sugar, costing respectively 13p and $10\frac{1}{2}$p per kilo be mixed in order to produce a mixture worth $11\frac{1}{2}$p per kilo?

4 How must two sorts of wine at 11F and 7·50F per litre be mixed to obtain a wine worth 10·50F per litre?

5 Equal quantities of sweets at two a penny and six a penny are mixed together. How many of the mixed sweets do you get for a penny?

6 Five cases of apples at £2·28 per case are mixed with four cases at £1·50 and three cases at £2. What is the resulting mixture worth per case?

7 Two sorts of oranges are bought, one at six for 10p and the other at twopence each. The oranges are mixed in such a way that there are three of the first kind to every two of the second, and they are then sold at five for 13½p. What is the profit per cent?

8 Three grades of tea, costing respectively 61p, 71p and 75p per kilo, are mixed together, taking equal amounts of the first two, to produce a blend worth 72p per kilo. What is the ratio in which the three teas are mixed?

9 Three teas at 58p, 73p and 77p per kilo are blended in the ratio 2 : 3 : 5. What is the blend worth per kilo?

10 Wines at £0·94 and £1·10 per litre are mixed with a third wine in the ratio 1 : 1 : 2. What is the price of the third wine per litre if the blend is worth £1·21 per litre?

11 Acid costing £1·08 per litre is diluted with water in the ratio of eight parts of acid to one of water. The diluted acid is sold at £1·20 per litre. What is the profit per cent?

12 A certain cocktail is made up of gin, Italian Martini and French Martini, mixed in the proportion 2 : 1 : 1. The respective costs of litre bottles of each of the three components are £4·60, £1·10 and £1·20. What is the cost of one glass of the cocktail if there are approximately 25 glasses to the bottle?

Work, pipes, etc.

Example 6 *A can finish a piece of work in 6 hours and B can do the same work in 7½ hours. How long will they take over it if both work together?*

In 1 hour A does $\frac{1}{6}$ of the work.

In 1 hour B does $\frac{2}{15}$ of the work.

$\therefore$ in 1 hour A and B together do $\frac{1}{6} + \frac{2}{15} = \frac{9}{30} = \frac{3}{10}$ of the work.

$\frac{3}{10}$ of the work is done in 1 hour

$\therefore \frac{10}{10}$,, ,, ,, ,, ,, ,, $\frac{10}{3}$ hours.

$\therefore$ A and B together do the work in $\frac{10}{3}$ hours

$\qquad\qquad\qquad\qquad = 3$ hours 20 minutes.

N.B. First find out the fraction of the work that each does in 1 hour; then the fraction of the work that they do together in 1 hour. Turn this fraction upside down, and the result is the number of hours they take when working together.

All problems of this type are done in this way.

Example 7 *One pipe can fill a bath in 5 minutes, and another can empty the bath in 10 minutes. Both pipes are opened at the same time and, after 5 minutes, the second pipe is turned off. What fraction of the bath is then full, and how long will it take for the first pipe to fill the bath completely from then?*

In 1 minute the first pipe fills $\frac{1}{5}$ of the bath.

In 1 minute the second pipe empties $\frac{1}{10}$ of the bath.

$\therefore$ in 1 minute both pipes together fill $\frac{1}{5} - \frac{1}{10} = \frac{1}{10}$ of the bath

$\therefore$ in 5 minutes both pipes together fill $5 \times \frac{1}{10} = \frac{1}{2}$ of the bath

$\therefore$ the first pipe completes the filling in $\frac{1}{2} \times 5 = 2\frac{1}{2}$ minutes.

Exercise 27c

1 If one tap can fill a bath in 6 min and another in 12, how long will they take when both are turned on together?

2 If tap A can fill a cistern in 5 min and tap B in 20, how long will they take together?

3 A can do a job of work in $4\frac{1}{2}$ days, and B in 9 days. How long will the job take A and B working together?

4 The hot-water tap fills a bath in $7\frac{1}{2}$ min, and the cold-water tap in 5 min. How long will it take to fill the bath when both taps are turned on together?

5 A tap fills a bath in 8 min, and the waste-pipe can empty the bath in 10 min. How long will it take the bath to fill if the waste-pipe is left open when the tap is turned on?

6 Tap A fills a tank in 9 h and tap B empties it in 12 h. How long does it take the tank to fill if both taps are open together?

7 A can fill a bath in 2 min, B in 3, and C in 6. If all three are on together, how long will it take to fill the bath?

8 A can do a job in $4\frac{1}{2}$ days, B in 5 days, and C in $7\frac{1}{2}$ days. How long will the job take if A, B and C work at it together?

9 A and B working together can do a job in 1 day, and A working alone can do it in 3 days. How long would it take B alone?

10 A, B and C together dig a ditch in 2 days; A and B together could do the same amount of work in 4 days, and B and C together in 3 days. How long would each take by himself?

11 Smith can do a piece of work in 6 days and Jones in 9 days. Smith starts alone, and is joined by Jones after 1 day. How long do they take to finish the work together?

12 The cold tap can fill a bath in 5 min, the hot tap in 15, and the waste-pipe empty the full bath in 10 minutes. All three are fully open for 2 min, after which the waste-pipe is closed. How much longer will it take to fill the bath?

13 Arthur and Bates start on a job of work which Arthur could complete alone in 6 days, and Bates alone in 8 days. After 2 days Bates falls ill. How long does it take Arthur to finish off the job by himself?

14 Fred and Bert can build a certain length of wall in 10 h, Bert and Sid can do the same amount in 9 h, and Fred and Sid in $7\frac{1}{2}$ h. Which of them, working alone, would complete the job most quickly and how long would it take him?

15 A contractor had allowed 20 days in which to complete a certain job. After 12 days it was only half done, but by getting sixteen more men to work, it was finished at the right time. How many men were on the job to begin with?

Races, games of skill, etc.

Example 8 *A can give B 20 m start and C 29 m start in a 200-metre race. How many metres start could B give C in the same distance?*

A runs 200 m while B runs 180 m and C runs 171 m

∴ B „ 180 m „ C „ 171 m

∴ B „ 200 m „ C „ $171 \times \frac{200}{180}$ m = 190 m

∴ B can give C 10 m start in 200 m.

Example 9 *In 'a hundred up' at billiards A beats B by 10 points and B beats C by 10 points. How many points should A give C in a hundred up?*

B scores 90 while A scores 100 (× 10)

∴ B „ 900 „ A „ 1 000

B scores 100 while C scores 90 (× 9)

∴ B „ 900 „ C „ 810

∴ A scores 1 000 while C scores 810 (÷ 10)

∴ A „ 100 „ C „ 81

∴ A can give C 19 points in a hundred up.

N.B. First put down statements showing the actual scores made (or distances run, or whatever it may be), putting down first the score of the man mentioned twice. Then, by multiplication (or by division if that is simpler), make the scores of this man the same in both statements; this gives a connection between the scores of the other two players, from which the required result may be obtained.

The same method can be applied to more complicated problems, but the one used in the following example is sometimes useful. This is known as the **Chain Rule**.

Example 10 *In a 1 500-m race A can give B 100 m, B can give C 60 m, and C can give D 125 m. How many metres can A give D in a race over the same distance?*

A runs 1 500 m while B runs 1 400 m

B „ 1 500 m „ C „ 1 440 m

C „ 1 500 m „ D „ 1 375 m

M

347

New General Mathematics

$\therefore$ in a given time C runs $\dfrac{1\,440}{1\,500}$ of the distance B runs, while

D runs $\dfrac{1\,375}{1\,500}$ of the distance C runs

$\therefore$ while A runs 1 500 m, B runs 1 400 m

$$\text{C } \,, \quad 1\,400 \times \dfrac{1\,440}{1\,500}\text{ m}$$

$$\text{D } \,, \quad 1\,400 \times \dfrac{1\,440}{1\,500} \times \dfrac{1\,375}{1\,500}\text{ m}$$

$$= 1\,232\text{ m}$$

$\therefore$ A can give D 268 m in a 1 500-m race.

Exercise 27d

1 In a 100-metre race A can beat B by 10 m and C by 19 m. By how many metres can B beat C in a hundred?

2 In a 200-metre race A can give B 10 m start and C 29 m start. How much start should B allow C in a 200-metre race?

3 In a 100-metre race A gives B 5 m start and beats him by 7 m. A can just give C 1 m start. How much start should C allow B in a 100-metre race?

4 A can beat B by 10 points in a hundred up at billiards, and B can give C 10 points in fifty up. How many points can A give C in a hundred up?

5 A can give B 50 m start in 200 m, and B can give C 8 m start over the same distance. How much can A give C in 100 m?

6 In a game of squash (9 points) A can give B 3 points and, in three games, A beats C 9–8, 9–4, 9–4. How many points can B give C in a game?

7 At squash A can give B 4 points per game and, in three games with C, B scores only 10 points altogether. How many points per game should C give A?

348

8 In a 100-metre race A starts from scratch and B, C, D are allowed starts of 10, 16, 22 metres respectively. How far behind B will C and D be at the finish of a 150-metre race in which A is not taking part?

9 In an 800-metre race A can give B 50 m start, and C can give B 125 m start. By how many metres will C beat A in running 800 metres?

10 In a certain game of skill A can give B 5 points in 20, B can give C 4 points, and C can give D 10 points. How many points can A give D?

11 In a table-tennis tournament (21 points) A gives B 6 points, and C gives B 3 points. How should A and C be handicapped?

12 In a 10-km motor race A passed the post 100 m ahead of B, and B passed the post 400 m ahead of C. If all three cars maintained a steady average speed, by how many metres did A beat C?

13 At billiards A can give B 4 points in 100, B can give C 5 points, and C can give D 10 points. How many should A give D in 100?

14 In a 1 500-metre race A beats B by 100 m and C by 170 m, and B beats D by 151 m. Who wins in a 1 500-metre race between C and D, and by how many metres?

15 A can give B 5 m in 100, and covers the distance in 11·4 s. C can run 100 m in 12·5 s. If B and C race over 100 metres, who wins and by what distance?

Chapter 28

Matrices (2). Mapping

In Book 2, Chapter 9, it was seen that a displacement or **translation** could be performed by adding a vector to each vector representing the points to be translated. A mapping is an example of an operation which can be expressed in terms of an **operator.** The symbol T is frequently used to represent the operator in translation.

If T represents the operation of translating through (4,2) and **a** is (1,2) and **b** is (5,4),

$$T(\mathbf{a}) = \mathbf{b}$$

Similarly $\qquad T(\mathbf{b}) = \mathbf{c}$ where **c** is (9,6)

so that $\qquad T(T(\mathbf{a})) = \mathbf{c}$

which is normally written $T^2(\mathbf{a}) = \mathbf{c}$.

Rotation

Other mappings can be written in a similar way; thus if R represents a rotation through one right angle anticlockwise about the origin and **a** is $\begin{pmatrix} 1 \\ 0 \end{pmatrix}$ and **b** is $\begin{pmatrix} 0 \\ 1 \end{pmatrix}$,

$$R(\mathbf{a}) = \mathbf{b}$$

$R^2(\mathbf{a}) = \mathbf{c}$ where **c** is $\begin{pmatrix} -1 \\ 0 \end{pmatrix}$

$R^3(\mathbf{a}) = \mathbf{d}$ where **d** is $\begin{pmatrix} 0 \\ -1 \end{pmatrix}$

and $R^4(\mathbf{a}) = \mathbf{a}$.

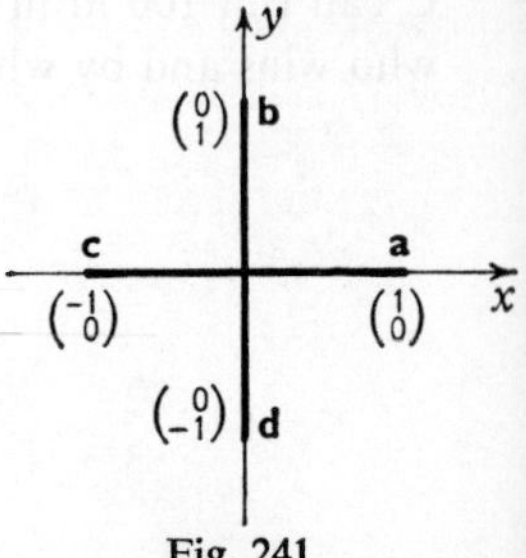

Hence the operator R^4 does not alter the original figure, and so it can be stated that $R^4 = I$ where I is the **identity** operator.

It is possible to represent R by a matrix. Let this matrix be

Fig. 241

called $\begin{pmatrix} p & q \\ r & s \end{pmatrix}$. It is known that R maps $\begin{pmatrix} 1 \\ 0 \end{pmatrix}$ into $\begin{pmatrix} 0 \\ 1 \end{pmatrix}$ and $\begin{pmatrix} 0 \\ 1 \end{pmatrix}$

into $\begin{pmatrix} -1 \\ 0 \end{pmatrix}$.

Hence $\qquad \begin{pmatrix} p & q \\ r & s \end{pmatrix}\begin{pmatrix} 1 \\ 0 \end{pmatrix} = \begin{pmatrix} 0 \\ 1 \end{pmatrix}$

and $\qquad \begin{pmatrix} p & q \\ r & s \end{pmatrix}\begin{pmatrix} 0 \\ 1 \end{pmatrix} = \begin{pmatrix} -1 \\ 0 \end{pmatrix}$

$$\therefore p + 0q = 0$$
$$\therefore p = 0,$$

similarly $\qquad\qquad r = 1,$

$$q = -1,$$

and $\qquad\qquad s = 0.$

$$\therefore R = \begin{pmatrix} 0 & -1 \\ 1 & 0 \end{pmatrix}.$$

The operator R^2 is

$$\begin{pmatrix} 0 & -1 \\ 1 & 0 \end{pmatrix}\begin{pmatrix} 0 & -1 \\ 1 & 0 \end{pmatrix} = \begin{pmatrix} -1 & 0 \\ 0 & -1 \end{pmatrix} = -1\begin{pmatrix} 1 & 0 \\ 0 & 1 \end{pmatrix}$$

which, as expected, changes the sign of each element.

R^4 is $\begin{pmatrix} -1 & 0 \\ 0 & -1 \end{pmatrix}\begin{pmatrix} -1 & 0 \\ 0 & -1 \end{pmatrix} = \begin{pmatrix} 1 & 0 \\ 0 & 1 \end{pmatrix},$

which is the identity matrix I.
Rotations of different angles can be calculated similarly.

Reflection

If M represents a reflection in the y-axis and $\mathbf{a}$ is $\begin{pmatrix} 1 \\ 0 \end{pmatrix}$, $\mathbf{b}$ is $\begin{pmatrix} 0 \\ 1 \end{pmatrix}$

and $\mathbf{c}$ is $\begin{pmatrix} -1 \\ 0 \end{pmatrix}$ as before,

$$M(\mathbf{a}) = \mathbf{c}$$

and $\qquad\qquad M(\mathbf{b}) = \mathbf{b}.$

If M is represented by the matrix $\begin{pmatrix} p & q \\ r & s \end{pmatrix}$, then $\begin{pmatrix} p & q \\ r & s \end{pmatrix}\begin{pmatrix} 1 \\ 0 \end{pmatrix} = \begin{pmatrix} -1 \\ 0 \end{pmatrix}$

and $\begin{pmatrix} p & q \\ r & s \end{pmatrix}\begin{pmatrix} 0 \\ 1 \end{pmatrix} = \begin{pmatrix} 0 \\ 1 \end{pmatrix}$.

$\therefore p = -1, r = 0, q = 0$ and $s = 1$.

$\therefore$ M is $\begin{pmatrix} -1 & 0 \\ 0 & 1 \end{pmatrix}$.

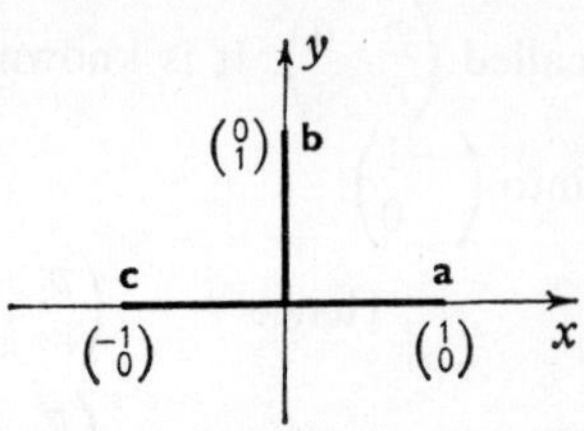

Fig. 242

M^2 is $\begin{pmatrix} -1 & 0 \\ 0 & 1 \end{pmatrix}\begin{pmatrix} -1 & 0 \\ 0 & 1 \end{pmatrix} = \begin{pmatrix} 1 & 0 \\ 0 & 1 \end{pmatrix} = I$, as would be expected.

Example 1 *If the triangle* ABC *where* A *is* $(1,2)$, B *is* $(3,1)$ *and* C *is* $(-2,1)$ *is reflected in the x-axis, what are the co-ordinates of the vertices of the resulting triangle?*

First the operator M for reflection in the x-axis must be found. From the diagram it can be seen that $\begin{pmatrix} 1 \\ 0 \end{pmatrix}$ is mapped into itself and $\begin{pmatrix} 0 \\ 1 \end{pmatrix}$ is mapped into $\begin{pmatrix} 0 \\ -1 \end{pmatrix}$.

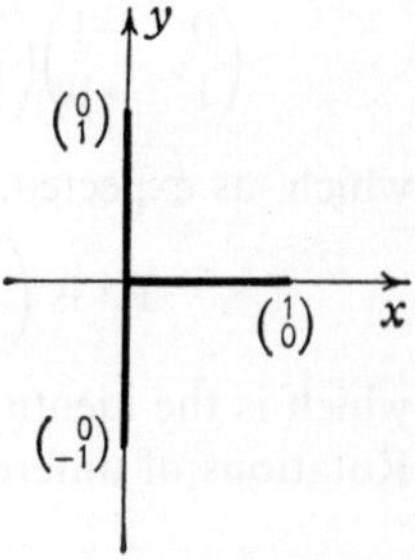

Thus if $M = \begin{pmatrix} p & q \\ r & s \end{pmatrix}$,

then $\begin{pmatrix} p & q \\ r & s \end{pmatrix}\begin{pmatrix} 1 \\ 0 \end{pmatrix} = \begin{pmatrix} 1 \\ 0 \end{pmatrix}$

and $\begin{pmatrix} p & q \\ r & s \end{pmatrix}\begin{pmatrix} 0 \\ 1 \end{pmatrix} = \begin{pmatrix} 0 \\ -1 \end{pmatrix}$.

Fig. 243

$\therefore p = 1, r = 0, q = 0$ and $s = -1$, and hence $M = \begin{pmatrix} 1 & 0 \\ 0 & -1 \end{pmatrix}$.

The co-ordinates of A, B, C are represented by the vectors $\begin{pmatrix} 1 \\ 2 \end{pmatrix}$, $\begin{pmatrix} 3 \\ 1 \end{pmatrix}$ and $\begin{pmatrix} -2 \\ 1 \end{pmatrix}$.

$$\begin{pmatrix} 1 & 0 \\ 0 & -1 \end{pmatrix}\begin{pmatrix} 1 \\ 2 \end{pmatrix} = \begin{pmatrix} 1 \\ -2 \end{pmatrix}, \quad \begin{pmatrix} 1 & 0 \\ 0 & -1 \end{pmatrix}\begin{pmatrix} 3 \\ 1 \end{pmatrix} = \begin{pmatrix} 3 \\ -1 \end{pmatrix}$$

and $\begin{pmatrix} 1 & 0 \\ 0 & -1 \end{pmatrix}\begin{pmatrix} -2 \\ 1 \end{pmatrix} = \begin{pmatrix} -2 \\ -1 \end{pmatrix}$.

Hence the new triangle has vertices at $(1,-2)$, $(3,-1)$ and $(-2,-1)$. Note that the points can equally well be expressed as column or row vectors, and that they must be represented by column vectors during the multiplication process.

Enlargement

If E represents an enlargement of ratio $2:1$ with centre at the origin and **a** is $(1,0)$, **b** is $(0,1)$, **e** is $(2,0)$ and **f** is $(0,2)$,

$$E(\mathbf{a}) = \mathbf{e} \quad \text{and} \quad E(\mathbf{b}) = \mathbf{f}.$$

If E is represented by the matrix
$$\begin{pmatrix} p & q \\ r & s \end{pmatrix},$$

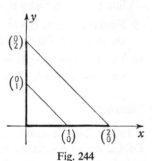

Fig. 244

$$\begin{pmatrix} p & q \\ r & s \end{pmatrix}\begin{pmatrix} 1 \\ 0 \end{pmatrix} = \begin{pmatrix} 2 \\ 0 \end{pmatrix}$$

and
$$\begin{pmatrix} p & q \\ r & s \end{pmatrix}\begin{pmatrix} 0 \\ 1 \end{pmatrix} = \begin{pmatrix} 0 \\ 2 \end{pmatrix}.$$

$\therefore p = 2, r = 0, q = 0$ and $s = 2$.

$$\therefore E \text{ is } \begin{pmatrix} 2 & 0 \\ 0 & 2 \end{pmatrix} = 2\begin{pmatrix} 1 & 0 \\ 0 & 1 \end{pmatrix} = 2I.$$

In general if E is an enlargement in the ratio $r:1$ with centre at the origin,

$$E = rI.$$

Exercise 28a

1 Find a matrix **R** which has the effect of rotation through one right angle clockwise about the origin. Show that $R^4 = I$.

2 Find the co-ordinates of the vertices of the triangle which is the result of mapping the triangle whose vertices are $(1,1)$, $(2,4)$ and $(3,7)$ with the operator **R** of no. 1.

3 Find a matrix **R** which has the effect of rotating through two right angles about the origin. Show that $R^2 = I$.

4 Use the operator **R** of no. 3 to rotate the triangle whose

353

    vertices are (0,0), (1,−1) and (1,1) through two right angles about the origin.

5 Reflect the triangle of no. 4 in the *y*-axis. Compare the answer with that of no. 4.

6 Find the matrix M which has the effect of reflection in the line $y = x$. Show that $M^2 = I$.

7 Use the operator of no. 6 to reflect the rhombus whose vertices are (2,2), (1,−1), (−2,−2) and (−1,1) in the line $y = x$.

8 Find the matrix M which has the effect of reflection in the line $y = -x$. Show that $M^2 = I$.

9 Find the matrix E which has the effect of enlarging with centre the origin in the ratio 3 : 2.

10 Use the operator E of no. 9 to enlarge the rectangle whose vertices are (0,0), (3,0), (0,2) and (3,2) in the ratio 3 : 2.

Shearing

    In Fig. 245 the square OABC is mapped into the parallelogram ODEC by an operation known as **shearing**. Points on the *x*-axis remain where they are while points above it are displaced by an amount proportional to the distance from the *x*-axis. If OABC is the unit square, i.e. $\overline{OC}$ is (1,0) and $\overline{OA}$ is (0,1), and $\overline{OD}$ is $(k,1)$, the matrix S which has this effect can be found in the usual way.

$$\begin{pmatrix} p & q \\ r & s \end{pmatrix}\begin{pmatrix} 1 \\ 0 \end{pmatrix} = \begin{pmatrix} 1 \\ 0 \end{pmatrix}$$

and $$\begin{pmatrix} p & q \\ r & s \end{pmatrix}\begin{pmatrix} 0 \\ 1 \end{pmatrix} = \begin{pmatrix} k \\ 1 \end{pmatrix}.$$

$\therefore p = 1, r = 0, q = k$ and $s = 1$.

$\therefore$ S is $\begin{pmatrix} 1 & k \\ 0 & 1 \end{pmatrix}$.

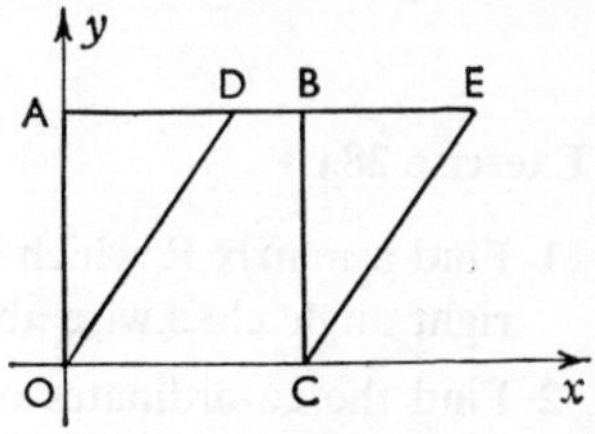

Fig. 245

This can be checked by considering the effect on $\overline{OB}$ (1,1):

$$\begin{pmatrix} 1 & k \\ 0 & 1 \end{pmatrix}\begin{pmatrix} 1 \\ 1 \end{pmatrix} = \begin{pmatrix} 1+k \\ 1 \end{pmatrix} \quad \text{as expected.}$$

Notice that shearing does not affect the area of the figure sheared.

Stretching

Now consider the effect on the unit square of the operator $\begin{pmatrix} 2 & 1 \\ 1 & 2 \end{pmatrix}$.

$$\begin{pmatrix} 2 & 1 \\ 1 & 2 \end{pmatrix}\begin{pmatrix} 1 \\ 0 \end{pmatrix} = \begin{pmatrix} 2 \\ 1 \end{pmatrix},$$

$$\begin{pmatrix} 2 & 1 \\ 1 & 2 \end{pmatrix}\begin{pmatrix} 0 \\ 1 \end{pmatrix} = \begin{pmatrix} 1 \\ 2 \end{pmatrix},$$

$$\begin{pmatrix} 2 & 1 \\ 1 & 2 \end{pmatrix}\begin{pmatrix} 1 \\ 1 \end{pmatrix} = \begin{pmatrix} 3 \\ 3 \end{pmatrix}$$

and $\quad \begin{pmatrix} 2 & 1 \\ 1 & 2 \end{pmatrix}\begin{pmatrix} 0 \\ 0 \end{pmatrix} = \begin{pmatrix} 0 \\ 0 \end{pmatrix}.$

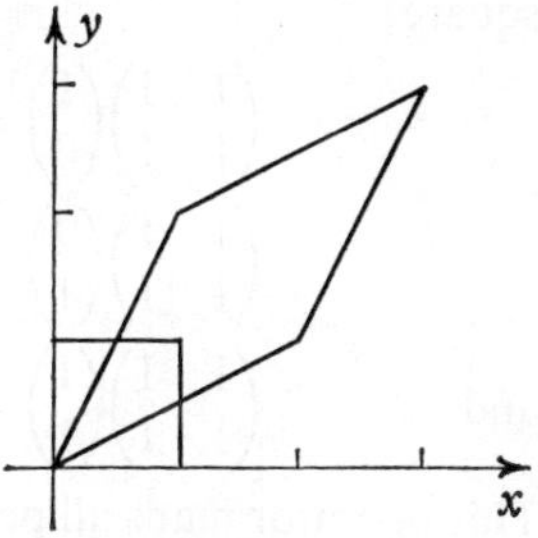

Fig. 246

This process is known as **stretching.**

Note that the origin is always mapped into the origin by an operator which is a multiplying matrix.

Consider now whether it is possible to find a matrix which will map the resulting figure back into the unit square.

Call this $\begin{pmatrix} p & q \\ r & s \end{pmatrix}$.

$$\begin{pmatrix} p & q \\ r & s \end{pmatrix}\begin{pmatrix} 2 \\ 1 \end{pmatrix} = \begin{pmatrix} 1 \\ 0 \end{pmatrix}$$

and $\quad \begin{pmatrix} p & q \\ r & s \end{pmatrix}\begin{pmatrix} 1 \\ 2 \end{pmatrix} = \begin{pmatrix} 0 \\ 1 \end{pmatrix}.$

$$\therefore 2p + q = 1,$$
$$2r + s = 0,$$
$$p + 2q = 0$$
and $\quad r + 2s = 1.$

The solution of these equations gives

$$\begin{pmatrix} p & q \\ r & s \end{pmatrix} = \begin{pmatrix} \frac{2}{3} & -\frac{1}{3} \\ -\frac{1}{3} & \frac{2}{3} \end{pmatrix} = \frac{1}{3}\begin{pmatrix} 2 & -1 \\ -1 & 2 \end{pmatrix}$$

which is the inverse of the original matrix. In general if an object is mapped into an image by a matrix A, then the image can be

355

mapped back into the original object by the inverse A^{-1} because $AA^{-1} = I$ by definition of the inverse matrix.

Consider next the effect of the operator $\begin{pmatrix} 1 & 1 \\ 1 & 1 \end{pmatrix}$ on the unit square;

$$\begin{pmatrix} 1 & 1 \\ 1 & 1 \end{pmatrix}\begin{pmatrix} 1 \\ 0 \end{pmatrix} = \begin{pmatrix} 1 \\ 1 \end{pmatrix},$$

$$\begin{pmatrix} 1 & 1 \\ 1 & 1 \end{pmatrix}\begin{pmatrix} 0 \\ 1 \end{pmatrix} = \begin{pmatrix} 1 \\ 1 \end{pmatrix}$$

and $\quad \begin{pmatrix} 1 & 1 \\ 1 & 1 \end{pmatrix}\begin{pmatrix} 1 \\ 1 \end{pmatrix} = \begin{pmatrix} 2 \\ 2 \end{pmatrix}.$

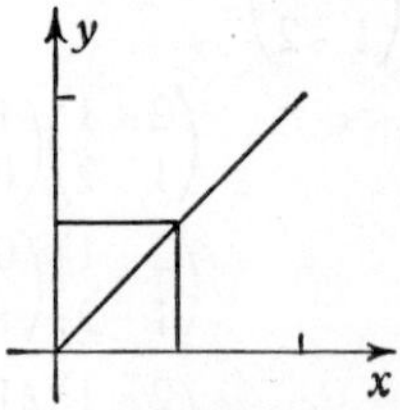

Fig. 247

This operator maps all points onto a straight line from which they cannot be mapped back into the original positions. This occurs because the determinant of the matrix is zero.

Compound mappings

If for example a triangle is to be enlarged in the ratio 2 : 1 with centre the origin, and rotated through one right angle clockwise about the centre, the process is as follows. Let the triangle have vertices at $(0,0)$, $(2,1)$ and $(-1,3)$.

Enlargement in the ratio 2 : 1 with centre the origin is performed by the operator E, $\begin{pmatrix} 2 & 0 \\ 0 & 2 \end{pmatrix}$.

Rotation through one right angle clockwise is performed by the operator R, $\begin{pmatrix} 0 & 1 \\ -1 & 0 \end{pmatrix}$.

Enlarging first,

$$\begin{pmatrix} 2 \\ 1 \end{pmatrix} \text{ is mapped into } \begin{pmatrix} 2 & 0 \\ 0 & 2 \end{pmatrix}\begin{pmatrix} 2 \\ 1 \end{pmatrix} = \begin{pmatrix} 4 \\ 2 \end{pmatrix}$$

and $\quad \begin{pmatrix} -1 \\ 3 \end{pmatrix} \text{ is mapped into } \begin{pmatrix} 2 & 0 \\ 0 & 2 \end{pmatrix}\begin{pmatrix} -1 \\ 3 \end{pmatrix} = \begin{pmatrix} -2 \\ 6 \end{pmatrix},$

then rotating,

$$\begin{pmatrix} 4 \\ 2 \end{pmatrix} \text{ is mapped into } \begin{pmatrix} 0 & 1 \\ -1 & 0 \end{pmatrix}\begin{pmatrix} 4 \\ 2 \end{pmatrix} = \begin{pmatrix} 2 \\ -4 \end{pmatrix}$$

and $\begin{pmatrix} -2 \\ 6 \end{pmatrix}$ is mapped into $\begin{pmatrix} 0 & 1 \\ -1 & 0 \end{pmatrix} \begin{pmatrix} -2 \\ 6 \end{pmatrix} = \begin{pmatrix} 6 \\ 2 \end{pmatrix}$.

This process can be described in general terms as $RE(\mathbf{a}) = \mathbf{b}$.

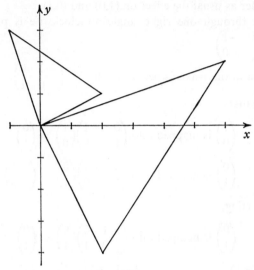

Fig. 248

The product RE is $\begin{pmatrix} 0 & 1 \\ -1 & 0 \end{pmatrix} \begin{pmatrix} 2 & 0 \\ 0 & 2 \end{pmatrix} = \begin{pmatrix} 0 & 2 \\ -2 & 0 \end{pmatrix}$.

Using this operator,

$$\begin{pmatrix} 2 \\ 1 \end{pmatrix} \text{ is mapped into } \begin{pmatrix} 0 & 2 \\ -2 & 0 \end{pmatrix} \begin{pmatrix} 2 \\ 1 \end{pmatrix} = \begin{pmatrix} 2 \\ -4 \end{pmatrix}$$

and $\begin{pmatrix} -1 \\ 3 \end{pmatrix}$ is mapped into $\begin{pmatrix} 0 & 2 \\ -2 & 0 \end{pmatrix} \begin{pmatrix} -1 \\ 3 \end{pmatrix} = \begin{pmatrix} 6 \\ 2 \end{pmatrix}$.

Note that RE means perform E first and then R because

$$RE(\mathbf{a}) = \mathbf{b} \text{ means } R(E(\mathbf{a})) = \mathbf{b}.$$

In this example the order in which the operations are carried out did not matter but in Example 2 it does.

357

New General Mathematics

Example 2 *Show that if a figure is rotated through one right angle anticlockwise and then reflected in the y-axis, the result is different from reflecting first and then rotating.*

Consider as usual the effect on (1,0) and (0,1).

Rotation through one right angle anticlockwise is performed by R, $\begin{pmatrix} 0 & -1 \\ 1 & 0 \end{pmatrix}$.

Reflection in the y-axis is performed by M, $\begin{pmatrix} -1 & 0 \\ 0 & 1 \end{pmatrix}$.

Rotating first,

$$\begin{pmatrix} 1 \\ 0 \end{pmatrix} \text{ is mapped into } \begin{pmatrix} 0 & -1 \\ 1 & 0 \end{pmatrix}\begin{pmatrix} 1 \\ 0 \end{pmatrix} = \begin{pmatrix} 0 \\ 1 \end{pmatrix}$$

and $\quad \begin{pmatrix} 0 \\ 1 \end{pmatrix} \text{ is mapped into } \begin{pmatrix} 0 & -1 \\ 1 & 0 \end{pmatrix}\begin{pmatrix} 0 \\ 1 \end{pmatrix} = \begin{pmatrix} -1 \\ 0 \end{pmatrix},$

then reflecting,

$$\begin{pmatrix} 0 \\ 1 \end{pmatrix} \text{ is mapped into } \begin{pmatrix} -1 & 0 \\ 0 & 1 \end{pmatrix}\begin{pmatrix} 0 \\ 1 \end{pmatrix} = \begin{pmatrix} 0 \\ 1 \end{pmatrix}$$

and $\quad \begin{pmatrix} -1 \\ 0 \end{pmatrix} \text{ is mapped into } \begin{pmatrix} -1 & 0 \\ 0 & 1 \end{pmatrix}\begin{pmatrix} -1 \\ 0 \end{pmatrix} = \begin{pmatrix} 1 \\ 0 \end{pmatrix}.$

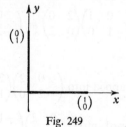

Fig. 249

Reflecting first,

$$\begin{pmatrix} 1 \\ 0 \end{pmatrix} \text{ is mapped into } \begin{pmatrix} -1 & 0 \\ 0 & 1 \end{pmatrix}\begin{pmatrix} 1 \\ 0 \end{pmatrix} = \begin{pmatrix} -1 \\ 0 \end{pmatrix}$$

and $\quad \begin{pmatrix} 0 \\ 1 \end{pmatrix} \text{ is mapped into } \begin{pmatrix} -1 & 0 \\ 0 & 1 \end{pmatrix}\begin{pmatrix} 0 \\ 1 \end{pmatrix} = \begin{pmatrix} 0 \\ 1 \end{pmatrix},$

358

then rotating,

$$\binom{-1}{0} \text{ is mapped into } \begin{pmatrix} 0 & -1 \\ 1 & 0 \end{pmatrix}\binom{-1}{0} = \binom{0}{-1}$$

and $\qquad \binom{0}{1} \text{ is mapped into } \begin{pmatrix} 0 & -1 \\ 1 & 0 \end{pmatrix}\binom{0}{1} = \binom{-1}{0}.$

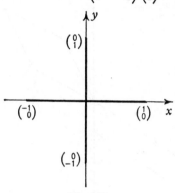

Fig. 250

The difference can be expected from a comparison of RM and MR;

$$RM = \begin{pmatrix} 0 & -1 \\ 1 & 0 \end{pmatrix}\begin{pmatrix} -1 & 0 \\ 0 & 1 \end{pmatrix} = \begin{pmatrix} 0 & -1 \\ -1 & 0 \end{pmatrix}$$

and $\qquad MR = \begin{pmatrix} -1 & 0 \\ 0 & 1 \end{pmatrix}\begin{pmatrix} 0 & -1 \\ 1 & 0 \end{pmatrix} = \begin{pmatrix} 0 & 1 \\ 1 & 0 \end{pmatrix}.$

Example 3 *The rhombus whose vertices are at* (0,0), (1,2), (3,3) *and* (2,1) *is reflected in the x-axis and then sheared by the operator* $\begin{pmatrix} 1 & 2 \\ 0 & 1 \end{pmatrix}$. *Find the vertices of the resulting figure.*

Reflection in the x-axis is performed by $\begin{pmatrix} 1 & 0 \\ 0 & -1 \end{pmatrix}.$

The combined operation is performed by

$$\begin{pmatrix} 1 & 2 \\ 0 & 1 \end{pmatrix}\begin{pmatrix} 1 & 0 \\ 0 & -1 \end{pmatrix} = \begin{pmatrix} 1 & -2 \\ 0 & -1 \end{pmatrix}.$$

$$\binom{1}{2} \text{ is mapped into } \begin{pmatrix} 1 & -2 \\ 0 & -1 \end{pmatrix}\binom{1}{2} = \binom{-3}{-2},$$

$$\binom{3}{3} \text{ is mapped into } \begin{pmatrix} 1 & -2 \\ 0 & -1 \end{pmatrix}\binom{3}{3} = \binom{-3}{-3}$$

and
$$\binom{2}{1} \text{ is mapped into } \begin{pmatrix} 1 & -2 \\ 0 & -1 \end{pmatrix}\binom{2}{1} = \binom{0}{-1}.$$

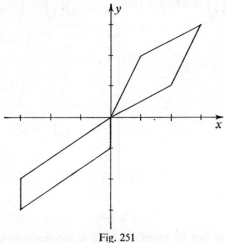

Fig. 251

Example 4 *Find the vertices of the triangle which is the result of translating through* (1,2) *and then enlarging in the ratio* 3 : 1 *with centre the origin the triangle whose vertices are at* (−1,−2), (3,2) *and* (1,1).

Because translation is not performed by a matrix operation this process must be taken in two steps.

Firstly translating,

$$(-1,-2) \text{ is mapped into } (-1,-2) + (1,2) = (0,0),$$
$$(3,2) \text{ is mapped into } (3,2) + (1,2) = (4,4)$$

and $(1,1)$ is mapped into $(1,1) + (1,2) = (2,3)$,

then enlarging using the operator $\begin{pmatrix} 3 & 0 \\ 0 & 3 \end{pmatrix}$,

$$\binom{4}{4} \text{ is mapped into } \begin{pmatrix} 3 & 0 \\ 0 & 3 \end{pmatrix}\binom{4}{4} = \binom{12}{12}$$

and
$$\binom{2}{3} \text{ is mapped into } \begin{pmatrix} 3 & 0 \\ 0 & 3 \end{pmatrix}\binom{2}{3} = \binom{6}{9}.$$

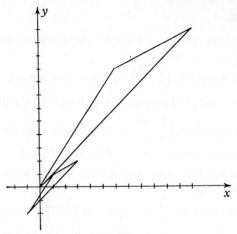

Fig. 252

Note that if the question was to enlarge the triangle in the ratio
3 : 1 with centre $(-1,-2)$ the above process would be performed
and then the triangle mapped back as follows:

$(0,0)$ is mapped into $\quad(0,0) + (-1,-2) = (-1,-2)$,
$(12,12)$ is mapped into $(12,12) + (-1,-2) = (11,10)$
and $\quad(6,9)$ is mapped into $\quad(6,9) + (-1,-2) = (5,7)$.

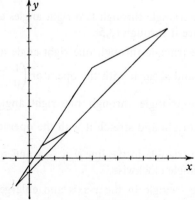

Fig. 253

New General Mathematics

Exercise 28b

The following refer to a triangle whose vertices are at (1,1), (4,2), (2,3):

1 Use the operator $\begin{pmatrix} 1 & 3 \\ 0 & 1 \end{pmatrix}$ to shear the triangle. Find the operator which will map the image back into the object.

2 Use the operator $\begin{pmatrix} 1 & 4 \\ 4 & 1 \end{pmatrix}$ to stretch the triangle. Find the operator which will map the image back into the object.

3 Find the result of first shearing the triangle as in no. 1 and then stretching it as in no. 2.

4 Map the triangle with the operator $\begin{pmatrix} 1 & 2 \\ 2 & 4 \end{pmatrix}$. Is it possible to find an operator which will map the image back into the object?

5 Rotate the triangle clockwise about the origin through one right angle and reflect it in the line $y = x$.

6 Rotate the triangle through two right angles about the origin and reflect it in the x-axis.

7 Rotate the triangle through one right angle anticlockwise about the origin and enlarge it in the ratio 4 : 1 with centre at the origin.

8 Rotate the triangle through two right angles about the origin and displace it through (3,5).

9 Rotate the triangle through one right angle about the origin clockwise and shear it with the operator $\begin{pmatrix} 1 & 2 \\ 0 & 1 \end{pmatrix}$.

10 Rotate the triangle through one right angle anticlockwise about the origin and stretch it with the operator $\begin{pmatrix} 3 & 1 \\ 1 & 3 \end{pmatrix}$.

11 Reflect the triangle in the line $y = -x$ and rotate it through one right angle clockwise.

12 Reflect the triangle in the y-axis and enlarge it in the ratio 3 : 2 with centre the origin.

13 Reflect the triangle in the *x*-axis and shear it with the operator $\begin{pmatrix} 1 & 4 \\ 0 & 1 \end{pmatrix}$.

14 Reflect the triangle in the line $y = x$ and translate it through (2,8).

15 Reflect the triangle in the *y*-axis and stretch it with $\begin{pmatrix} 3 & 1 \\ 1 & 3 \end{pmatrix}$.

16 Shear the triangle with $\begin{pmatrix} 1 & 5 \\ 0 & 1 \end{pmatrix}$ and rotate it through two right angles about the origin.

17 Shear the triangle with $\begin{pmatrix} 1 & 3 \\ 0 & 1 \end{pmatrix}$ and reflect it in the line $y = x$.

18 Shear the triangle with $\begin{pmatrix} 1 & 4 \\ 0 & 1 \end{pmatrix}$ and translate it through $(-1,3)$.

19 Shear the triangle with $\begin{pmatrix} 1 & 2 \\ 0 & 1 \end{pmatrix}$ and stretch it with $\begin{pmatrix} 5 & 1 \\ 1 & 5 \end{pmatrix}$.

20 Stretch the triangle with $\begin{pmatrix} 2 & 1 \\ 1 & 2 \end{pmatrix}$ and rotate it through one right angle clockwise about the origin.

21 Enlarge the triangle in the ratio 3 : 1 with centre the origin and rotate it through two right angles about the origin.

22 Enlarge the triangle in the ratio 4 : 3 with centre the origin and reflect it in the line $y = x$.

23 Enlarge the triangle in the ratio 5 : 3 with centre the origin and translate it through $(4,-5)$.

24 Enlarge the triangle in the ratio 7 : 3 with centre the origin and shear it with the operator $\begin{pmatrix} 1 & 3 \\ 0 & 1 \end{pmatrix}$.

25 Stretch the triangle with $\begin{pmatrix} 3 & 1 \\ 1 & 3 \end{pmatrix}$ and enlarge it in the ratio 3 : 2 with centre the origin.

26 Use the method of Example 4 to enlarge the triangle in the ratio 2 : 1 with centre (1,1).

27 Enlarge the triangle in the ratio 4 : 1 with centre (2,6).

28 Reflect the triangle in the *x*-axis, rotate it through one right angle clockwise about the origin and enlarge it in the ratio 2 : 1 with centre the origin.

29 Rotate the triangle through two right angles about the origin, enlarge it in the ratio 3 : 1 with centre the origin and shear it with the operator $\begin{pmatrix} 1 & 4 \\ 0 & 1 \end{pmatrix}$.

30 Enlarge the triangle in the ratio 4 : 1 with centre (1,1) and stretch it with the operator $\begin{pmatrix} 5 & 1 \\ 1 & 5 \end{pmatrix}$.

Revision examples

XXXI

1 A car travels 3 300 m in 2 min 56 s. What speed is this in km h^{-1}?

2 A thin sheet-metal cone has base diameter 6 cm and slant height 6 cm. What is the angle at the centre of the sector from which the curved surface of the cone is formed, and what is the volume of the cone, to 3 sig. fig.?

3 P and Q are the centres of two circles which touch one another externally, and both circles touch internally a third circle with centre R. If PQ = 14 cm, QR = 10 cm, RP = 8 cm, calculate the radii of the circles.

4 O is the vertex of a symmetrical pyramid on a square base ABCD, the sides of the base being 8 cm long. The edges of the pyramid are all 9 cm long. Calculate (i) the perpendicular height of the pyramid, (ii) the slope of an edge, (iii) the slope of one of the triangular faces.

5 A manufacturer has £3 000 to spend on small machine-tools, but before he buys them the price rises by £5 each, with the result that he is only able to purchase 20 fewer than he had planned. How many had he planned to buy?

6 A wasp is at the bottom of a cylindrical jam jar 8 cm in diameter and 12 cm deep internally, and finds himself unable to fly out or to climb the wall vertically. He therefore goes round the wall in an ascending spiral, and makes three complete circuits of the jar before reaching the rim. At what angle to the horizontal does he rise, and what is the length of his journey? (Take $\pi = 3\cdot142$.)

Fig. 254

7 (i) Simplify $\dfrac{3}{x^2 + 7x + 12} - \dfrac{2}{x^3 + 2x - 8}$.

(ii) Solve the equation $\dfrac{2}{x + 2} = \dfrac{1}{x - 3} - \dfrac{2}{3}$.

365

8 The time of oscillation of a pendulum is given by the formula

$t = 2\pi\sqrt{\dfrac{l}{g}}$, where t seconds is the time, l the length of the

pendulum in cm, and g the gravitational constant.

   (i) Express l as the subject of the formula,

   (ii) Evaluate l when $t = 9.03$, $g = 981$, $\pi = 3.142$.

9 Draw a triangle with sides 8 cm, 7 cm and 5 cm. Construct the incircle of the triangle and measure its radius.

10 The load W and the effort P of a certain machine are connected by the equation $P = aW + b$, where a and b are constants. From the following values of P and W, obtained experimentally, find the most likely values of a and b.

P (kg)	7	8	$9\frac{1}{2}$	$11\frac{1}{2}$	14
W (kg)	322	370	448	545	670

Find also the effort required to raise a load of 600 kg, and the load which can be lifted by an effort of 10 kg.

XXXII

1 In 1952 R. Button (U.S.A.) skated 10 000 metres in 16 min 32 s. Calculate his speed in km h^{-1} to 3 sig. fig.

2 For the rectangular box shown in Fig. 255 find (i) PR, (ii) PC, (iii) the angle between $\overline{PC}$ and the plane PQRS, (iv) the angle between $\overline{PC}$ and the plane DCRS.

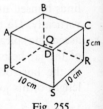

Fig. 255

3 A circle with radius 2 cm touches internally a circle with radius 5 cm. Show how to construct a circle with radius 2·4 cm to touch the smaller of the given circles externally and the greater internally.

4 X is 400 m due north of Y. The bearing of A from X is N 60° E and of B from Y, S 70° E; the distances XA and YB are respectively 200 m and 300 m. By calculating the distance that A is north and east of X, and B south and east of Y, find (i) AB, (ii) the bearing of A from B.

5 Use logarithms to evaluate (i) $\sqrt[4]{0\cdot4} + \sqrt[3]{0\cdot3}$ (ii) $0\cdot762\ 5^{\frac{2}{3}}$.

6 $x = 1 + \dfrac{p}{p-q}$ and $y = 2 - \dfrac{3q}{p+q}$. Find $\dfrac{x}{y}$ and $\dfrac{3}{x} + \dfrac{1}{y}$ in terms of p and q.

7 A conical wine-glass is 6 cm deep and 4 cm in diameter: a wine-bottle is essentially a cylinder 20 cm deep and 8 cm in diameter, all measurements being internal.

How many times can the glass be filled from the bottle?

How many litres does the bottle hold, taking $\pi = 3\cdot142$?

8 A motor-boat goes 10 km against a 4 km h^{-1} current and 10 km back again in 1 h 20 min. How fast can the boat travel in still water?

9 A can just give B 5 m start in a 100-m race, and B can just give C 20 m start. How much start should A give C over the same distance?

10 Draw the graphs of $y = \dfrac{x^2}{4}$ and $y = \dfrac{4}{x+3}$ between $x = -1$ and $x = +4$. Write down the x co-ordinate of the point in which the graphs cut, and show that this number is a solution of the equation $x^3 + 3x^2 = 16$.

XXXIII

1 A point A is 7·2 cm from O, the centre of a circle of radius 5·4 cm, and a tangent from A touches the circle at T. Calculate AT in cm correct to 3 sig. fig., and find also $T\hat{A}O$.

2 A train travelling at 72 km h^{-1} passed a stationary observer in 5 seconds, and went through a station in 15 seconds. How long was the train and how long the station?

3 A sector of a circle of radius 5 cm, the angle at the centre of the sector being 252°, is cut out and formed into a cone by gluing together the two bounding radii of the sector. Find the radius of the base of this cone, and also the vertical angle of the cone.

4 A symmetrical pyramid stands on a base which is a regular hexagon of side 10 m, and all the slant edges of the pyramid are 30 m long. Calculate (i) the inclination to the horizontal of one of the slant faces, (ii) the perpendicular height of the pyramid.

5 Solve the equation $\dfrac{x-1}{x+2} + \dfrac{2x+3}{x-1} = 3$. Check the answer.

6 A housekeeper has £1·20 to spend on jam: she can buy strawberry jam, but if she buys plum, which costs 2p less per pot than strawberry, she will be able to buy one more pot, and will also get 3p change. How much does a pot of strawberry jam cost?

7 The diameter of the top of an ordinary bucket is 30 cm and of the bottom 20 cm, and the bucket holds 25 cm of water when full. What is the capacity of the bucket in litres?

8 Evaluate, using logarithms, (i) $\sqrt[3]{27} + \sqrt[3]{27}$

$$(ii)\ \frac{3·752^2 + 5}{3·752^2 - 5}$$

9 Without using a protractor construct a triangle ABC in which AB = 4 cm, BC = 5 cm and $\hat{B} = 120°$. Measure AC.

Construct also the circumcircle of the triangle and measure its radius.

10 By plotting values of x from 1 to 10 solve the equation $\log x = \dfrac{5}{x}$.

XXXIV

1 Alf could do a certain repair job in 12 days and Bill in 15 days, if each worked alone. They work together on the job for 4 days, and then Alf falls ill. How many more days will it take Bill to finish the job?

2 A door ABCD, hinged in the line $\overline{AD}$, is opened through 60° into the position AXYD (Fig. 256). If the door is 2·1 m high and 1·5 m wide, find (i) the angle that $\overline{CX}$ makes with the floor, (ii) the angle between $\overline{AC}$ and $\overline{AY}$, (iii) the angle that the triangle ACY makes with the floor.

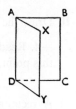

3 O is the centre of a circle, and the tangents at A and B meet at T. Prove that $A\hat{B}T = \frac{1}{2}AOB$.

Fig. 256

4 Solve the equations (i) $2x^2 - 3x - 3 = 0$, to 2 dec. pl.
(ii) $3x - 7y - 8 = 4x - 5y = 7$

5 A hemispherical bowl of internal diameter 12 cm, full of water, is emptied into a cylindrical can 8 cm in diameter. How deep is the water in the can?

6 Draw a trapezium ABCD in which the parallel sides are $\overline{AD}$ and $\overline{BC}$, and AB = 4·2 cm, BC = 6·2 cm, CD = 4·6 cm and DA = 4 cm.

Construct a triangle equal in area to the trapezium and, by constructing an altitude of this triangle and taking appropriate measurements, calculate the area of the trapezium.

7 On a bicycle journey a man went out on by-roads and travelled 15 km altogether. He came back by the main road, which is 2 km longer, but was able to average 2 km h^{-1} faster and save 5 minutes' time on the journey. What were his speeds out and back?

8 Taking log $\pi = 0·497$ 1, find to 3 sig. fig.

(i) the volume of a cone of base-radius 7·9 cm and height 9·6 cm

(ii) the base-radius of a cone of volume 2·74 cm^3 and height 3·07 cm.

9 A square is drawn in a semicircle of diameter 12 cm as shown in Fig. 257, O being the centre of the circle. Calculate (i) the length of the side of the square, (ii) $Y\hat{A}O$, (iii) YA.

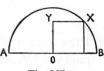

Fig. 257

369

10 Draw the graph of $y = \dfrac{3(x-2)}{x^2+1}$ for values of x from -2 to $+4$. Read off the minimum value of y and the value of x at this point.

XXXV

1 A rectangular box is pushed into the corner of a room as shown in Fig. 258, so that the 50-cm side makes 35° with $\overline{OA}$.

Calculate to the nearest cm the distance of the corner X of the table from (i) $\overline{OB}$, (ii) $\overline{OA}$.

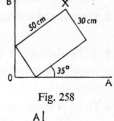

Fig. 258

2 $\overline{OA}$, $\overline{OB}$, $\overline{OC}$ are three mutually perpendicular lines, as shown in Fig. 259. $OA = 24$ cm, $OB = OC = 10$ cm. Calculate (i) AC, (ii) the angle between the planes ABC and OBC.

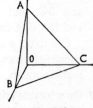

3 Use logarithms to evaluate

(i) $\sqrt[5]{50 + \sqrt[4]{40 + \sqrt[3]{30}}}$

(ii) $\sqrt[3]{0.086\ 7 \times 0.596\ 2^2}$

Fig. 259

4 A lead plummet consists of a hemisphere of diameter 2 cm surmounted by a right circular cone of diameter 2 cm and height 2 cm. Find (i) the volume of the plummet in cm³, (ii) its mass if the density of lead is 11·45 g cm⁻³. (Take $\pi = 3.142$.)

5 Solve the equations (i) $2x + \dfrac{2}{y} = 3$

$$3x + \dfrac{5}{y} = 5$$

(ii) $\dfrac{x}{x-1} - \dfrac{x+2}{x-2} + \dfrac{5}{3} = 0$

6 Draw a sector of a circle of radius 6 cm such that the bounding radii are $\overline{OA}$ and $\overline{OB}$, O being the centre of the circle, and $A\widehat{O}B = 80°$.

Construct a circle to touch $\overline{OA}$, $\overline{OB}$ and the arc AB, and measure its radius.

7 A can trim a length of hedge in 12 days and B in 15: how long will it take them if they work together? If they are joined by C at the beginning, the job takes the three of them 4 days to complete. How long would it take C, working on his own?

8 Two circles touch internally, and a line through their point of contact cuts one circle at A and the other at B. Prove that the radii of the circles to A and B are parallel.

9 ABC is a $\triangle$ in which A is $(-1,-1)$, B is $(2,-1)$ and C is $(1,3)$. The $\triangle$ is reflected in the x-axis and then enlarged in the ratio $3:1$ with centre the origin. What are the new vertices of the $\triangle$?

10 Plot the graph of $y = \dfrac{1-x}{2+x}$ for values of x from -5 to -2.5 and from -1.5 to $+3$. Find from the graph the values of x for which $y = 2x$.

Find also the equation of which these values are roots, and check by solving the equation.

XXXVI

1 (i) Evaluate $\dfrac{1}{\sqrt[3]{0.028\,94}}$.

(ii) The volume of a right circular cone of height 2.97 cm is 29.4 cm³. Find the base-radius of the cone, taking $\log \pi = 0.497\,1$.

2 Construct the incircle of a $\triangle$ with sides 7 cm, 9 cm and 10 cm, and measure its radius.

3 A 'bowl' lampshade (Fig. 260) is suspended from the ceiling by three symmetrically placed chains, each of length 75 cm. The diameter of the bowl is 60 cm.

Find (i) the angle which each chain makes with the vertical, (ii) the angle between two adjacent chains.

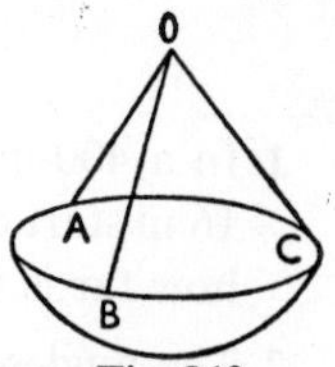

Fig. 260

4 A cylindrical tin 12 cm in diameter and 8 cm deep is filled with 'hundreds and thousands'. These are sold in small conical bags 3 cm in greatest diameter and 6 cm deep. How many bags can be filled from the tin?

5 (i) Simplify $\dfrac{x+3}{x^2-3x+2} + \dfrac{7x+5}{x^2+x-2}$.

(ii) Solve the equation $\dfrac{2x}{x+3} - \dfrac{x-1}{x+1} = \dfrac{1}{2}$. Check both answers.

6 A circle of radius 5 cm is inscribed in an isosceles triangle whose vertical angle is 40°. Calculate the sides of the triangle.

7 Draw a circle 6 cm in diameter with centre O, and mark a point A such that OA = 5 cm. Construct a chord of the circle of length 4 cm which will, when produced, pass through A.
Describe your method briefly.

8 A hollow metal cylinder is 3 cm long, 4 cm in external diameter, and the metal is 5 mm thick. If the density of the metal is 2·8 g cm⁻³, find the mass of the cylinder. (Take $\pi = \frac{22}{7}$.)

9 In Fig. 261 find, using an algebraic method, the ratio of the sides of the large and small squares.

10 Draw the graph of $y = \dfrac{3x^2-8}{3x+8}$ for values of x from -2 to 3. Draw on the same diagram the graph of $y = -\frac{1}{3}x$, and read off the values of x at the intersections.

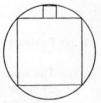

Fig. 261

Of what equation in x are these values the roots?

XXXVII

1 In a 400-m race A can give B 25 m start, and B can give C 16 m start over the same distance. If A, B and C race together, how far is C behind A at the finish if all three start together?

2 The angles of a triangle are 34°, 42°, 104°, and the inscribed circle touches the sides at P, Q and R. Calculate the angles of △PQR.

3 A cylindrical can of internal diameter 8 cm contains 6 cm of water. If 24 000 shot of diameter 2 mm are dropped into the can, how far does the water-level rise?

4 A trapdoor 90 cm by 120 cm, hinged in one of the longer sides, is propped open with sticks $\overline{CX}$ and $\overline{DY}$, each 60 cm long (Fig. 262).

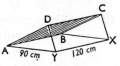

Fig. 262

Find (i) the angle at which the door is propped open, (ii) the angle between the diagonal $\overline{AC}$ and the horizontal plane ABXY.

5 Simplify $\dfrac{4x^2 - 1}{6x^2 - x - 5} \div \left(x + \dfrac{1}{6x + 5}\right)$.

6 Draw a circle of radius 3 cm and a tangent to it.

Construct two circles of radius 2 cm to touch the given circle externally and also to touch the line, all three circles lying on the same side of the line. Measure the distance between the centres of these two circles, and check by calculation.

7 Evaluate by logarithms (i) $\sqrt[3]{0.131\ 4 \times 0.008\ 873}$

(ii) $\dfrac{0.672^3 \times 0.050\ 51}{\sqrt[3]{0.000\ 728}}$

8 A cylindrical tower 7·5 m high is surmounted by a dome 6 m in diameter, on the top of which is a spike (Fig. 263).

A boy whose eye is 1·5 m from the ground can just see the tip of the spike over the curve of the dome when his line of sight is at an elevation of 40°.

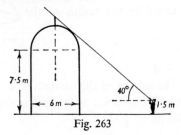

Fig. 263

373

Calculate the length of the spike and the distance the boy is from the nearest point of the tower.

9 ABC is a △ with vertices at (1,2), (2,4) and (3,0) respectively. Reflect the △ in the line $y = x$ and then shear it using the operator $\begin{pmatrix} 1 & 3 \\ 0 & 1 \end{pmatrix}$. What are the new vertices of the △?

10 A trolley is rolling up an incline, and the distance (s metres) that it has travelled beyond a certain point after t seconds is given by the formula $s = 5t - \frac{1}{3}t^2$.

Plot s against t for values of t from 0 to 9, and deduce after what time the trolley first stops.

XXXVIII

1 In three tennis sets A beats B 6–4, 6–1, 6–2; and B beats C 7–5, 1–6, 6–1. How should A and C be handicapped?

2 The base ABC of a tetrahedron ABCD is an isosceles triangle in which AB = AC = 13 cm and BC = AD = 10 cm. The vertex D of the tetrahedron is vertically above the mid-point M of the median $\overline{AX}$ of the triangle ABC. Calculate (i) DM, (ii) the slope of $\overline{DA}$, (iii) the slope of △DBC, (iv) the slope of $\overline{DC}$.

3 Evaluate (i) $2^3 \times 2^{-4}$ (ii) $x^{\frac{2}{3}} \times x^{\frac{4}{3}}$, (iii) $\sqrt[3]{27b^{-6}}$
(iv) $(\frac{9}{4})^{-\frac{3}{2}}$, (v) $2p^{x-1} \times p^{1-x}$

4 ABC is a triangle in which AB = 17 cm, BC = 18 cm, CA = 15 cm, and the inscribed circle of the triangle touches $\overline{BC}$, $\overline{CA}$, $\overline{AB}$ at P, Q, R respectively. Calculate AR, BP, CQ.

5 In Fig. 264 calculate the radius of the sphere.

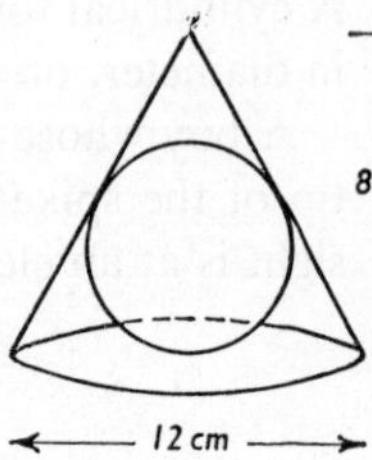

8 cm

12 cm

Fig. 264

6 $e = \sqrt{\dfrac{t - k}{k(1 + kt)}}.$

(i) Change the subject of the formula to t.
(ii) Evaluate t if $k = 0\cdot4$, $e = 0\cdot5$, giving the answer correct to 3 dec. pl.

7 (i) Simplify $\dfrac{4}{3x^2 - 48} - \dfrac{2}{3x^2 - 12x}$.

   (ii) Solve the equation $\dfrac{2}{x + 2} - \dfrac{1}{3} = \dfrac{1}{5x}$.

8 Draw a quadrilateral ABCD in which AB = CD = 5 cm, AD = 6 cm, BC = 4 cm and $A\hat{B}C = 115°$.

   Construct a circle to touch $\overline{AB}$, $\overline{BC}$ and $\overline{CD}$, and measure its radius.

   Does this circle also touch $\overline{AD}$?

9 An aircraft travels from A to B and back again in 144 minutes, while the wind blows steadily from A to B at 50 km h^{-1}. If the distance AB is 350 km, what is the aircraft's air speed?

10 Draw the graph of $y = \dfrac{3x^2 - 2}{x + 10}$ for values of x from -3 to $+4$.

   Use the graph to solve the equation $6x^2 - 3x = 34$, explaining fully how the solutions are obtained.

XXXIX

1 A, B, C are three points on a circle such that AB = AC. Prove that $\overline{AB}$ bisects one of the angles between $\overline{BC}$ and the tangent at B.

2 Fig. 265 shows a writing-slope. Calculate (i) the slope of the plane PADS, (ii) the slope of $\overline{BS}$, (iii) the slope of $\overline{AS}$, (iv) the angle between $\overline{BS}$ and the plane PQRS.

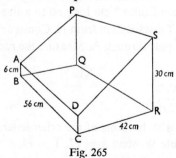

Fig. 265

3 I used to spend £90 a year on coal: when the price rose by £2 per tonne, I found that I saved £10 annually if I used a tonne less than before. How many tonnes did I use annually before the price rose?

4 Blanks for certain steel bolts are of the form shown in Fig. 266. Find the mass of a gross of these blanks if the density of steel is 7·83 g cm^{-3}.
(Take log $\pi = 0.497\ 1$.)

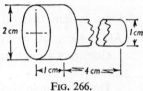

FIG. 266.

5 At billiards A can give B 10 points in 100, and B can give C 10 points in 50. How many can A give C in 100?

6 Two apprentices are told to produce cylinders of a certain material and of given mass. One of them produces a cylinder of diameter 9 cm and 8 cm high, and the other one of diameter 8 cm and height $7\frac{1}{2}$ cm. If the larger cylinder is 20% too heavy, by how much per cent is the smaller one too light?

7 A right circular cylinder of height 4 cm, standing on a circular base, has a total surface area of 165 cm^2. Find the radius of the base, if $\pi = \frac{22}{7}$.

8 $a = 38.4$, $b = 42.7$, $c = 60.1$ and $s = \frac{1}{2}(a + b + c)$.

Evaluate (i) $\sqrt{s(s-a)(s-b)(s-c)}$ (ii) $\sqrt{\dfrac{s(s-b)}{ac}}$

9 $x = \dfrac{2y+3}{3y-2}$. (i) Find y in terms of x.
(ii) Prove that $(3x-2)(3y-2) = 13$.

10 $\overline{AN}$ is a perpendicular 3 cm long on to a straight line $\overline{XY}$. P is a point on $\overline{XY}$ distant 2 cm from N. Construct a circle to touch $\overline{XY}$ at P and pass through A. Measure the radius of this circle.

XL

1 $T - W = \dfrac{Wv^2}{32x}$.

(i) Express W in terms of the other letters.
(ii) Evaluate W when $x = 17$, $T = 74$, $v = 40$.

2 In Fig. 267 $\overline{OB}$ and $\overline{OC}$ represent a pair of shear-legs for raising weights, and $\overline{OA}$ the tie-bar to keep them rigid. In a scale model OA = 37 cm, OB = OC = 17 cm, BC = 16 cm, and the point O is 12 cm above the ground ($\overline{OP}$ is vertical). $\overline{AP}$ and $\overline{BC}$ intersect at M.

Calculate (for the model)
(i) OM and AM,
(ii) the slope of $\triangle OBC$,
(iii) the slope of $\overline{OB}$,
(iv) the slope of $\overline{OA}$.

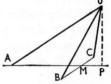

Fig. 267

3 A straight line parallel to the side $\overline{BC}$ of a triangle ABC cuts $\overline{AB}$, $\overline{AC}$ at H, K respectively. Prove that the circle through A, B, C touches the circle through A, H, K.

4 Alf and Bert have to meet at a place 40 km away from their home. Alf has a 'mini-motor' which allows him to average 20 km h^{-1} more than Bert, so he gives Bert 2 hours start and arrives 5 minutes before him. How fast does each go?

5 In a very large industrial concern the number of men earning more than £10 000 a year is shown in the following table:

Salary (before tax)	10 001–12 500	12 501–15 000	15 001–17 500	17 501–20 000	20 001–22 500
Number of employees	70	27	15	6	2

[*N.B.* In this group *no* men earn less than £10 000 p.a.]
Calculate the mean of this distribution.
Draw the cumulative-frequency ogive and explain why it is impossible to estimate from it the median and the inter-quartile range.

6 Simplify (i) $8^{\frac{1}{3}}$ (ii) $2a^2 \times (3a)^3$ (iii) $(2a)^2 \times 3a^{-3}$

(iv) $3^x \times 3^{-x}$ (v) $\dfrac{1}{3^{-2}}$

377

New General Mathematics

7 A small grain-silo consists of a tower 6 m high and 3 m square surmounted by a pyramidal roof 1·8 m high. At one side of the tower and centrally placed is a lean-to building, whose back wall (against the wall of the tower) is 3 m high; front wall 1·8 m high; width 2·4 m; distance between front and back walls 3 m.

Using a scale of 2 cm to 1 m draw the plan of the building, and an elevation on a vertical plane parallel to the plane containing adjacent vertical edges of tower and shed.

8 The number of litres of water that will flow through a pipe in one minute is given by the expression $\sqrt{\dfrac{60\left(\dfrac{d}{8}\right)^5 h}{l}}$, d being the diameter of the pipe in mm, l its length in metres, and h the height in metres of one end of the pipe above the other.

Find in litres per minute, the flow of water through a pipe 88 mm in diameter, one kilometre long, having one end 8 m higher than the other.

9 Fig. 268 shows a semicircle in which are inscribed two equal semicircles and one complete circle. (i) Calculate the radius of the circle. (ii) What fraction of the original semicircle is the shaded area?

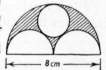

Fig. 268

10 If a cylinder is placed in a hemispherical bowl so that its top edge is level with the top of the bowl, and its lower edge is resting in the bowl (Fig. 269), the volume V of the cylinder and its height h are connected by the formula

$$V = \pi(100 - h^2)h.$$

(i) Prove the truth of this formula.

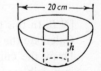

Fig. 269

(ii) By plotting $\dfrac{V}{\pi}$ against h, find the dimensions of the cylinder of maximum volume.

Answers

1 $6a^3$ **2** $18a^3$ **3** $12a^3$ **4** ± 2 **5** 3

6 5 **7** 4 **8** 4 **9** $\frac{1}{4}$ **10** $\frac{1}{27}$

11 ± 3 **12** $\pm\frac{1}{3}$ **13** $\pm 5a$ **14** $\dfrac{2}{a}$ **15** $\dfrac{1}{2a}$

16 ± 8 **17** 2 **18** 16 **19** $\frac{1}{100}$ **20** $\pm 1\frac{1}{4}$

21 $\dfrac{3}{a^2}$ **22** $\dfrac{1}{9a^2}$ **23** ± 9 **24** $\pm\dfrac{1}{a}$ **25** 9

26 ± 2 **27** 9 **28** 9 **29** $\frac{1}{3}$ **30** $\pm 0\cdot 2$

31 $6a$ **32** $\dfrac{3a}{2}$ **33** $18a$ **34** $\pm\frac{1}{64}$ **35** 4

36 $\frac{1}{16}$ **37** $\frac{1}{25}$ **38** 1 **39** $\pm\frac{1}{8}$ **40** $0\cdot 09$

41 $\dfrac{6}{a}$ **42** $\dfrac{2}{9a}$ **43** $\pm\frac{1}{8}$ **44** $2\frac{1}{4}$ **45** 9

46 $\frac{1}{4}$ **47** ± 2 **48** 1 **49** $\pm\frac{1}{32}$ **50** $\dfrac{2}{a^2}$

51 $\dfrac{6}{x^2}$ **52** 2 **53** $\pm\frac{27}{64}$ **54** $\pm\dfrac{2}{a^3}$ **55** $\dfrac{12a^4}{b}$

56 $\dfrac{4a}{9b}$ **57** $\frac{1}{5}$ **58** $\dfrac{15b}{a}$ **59** $4x^5$ **60** $\pm\frac{64}{27}$

61 $\dfrac{1}{a^2}$ **62** $\dfrac{1}{b}$ **63** $\dfrac{1}{c^{\frac{2}{3}}}$ **64** $\dfrac{x}{y}$ **65** $\dfrac{1}{xy}$

66 $\dfrac{b^3}{a^2}$ **67** $\dfrac{a}{b^3}$ **68** $\dfrac{1}{a^3b^3}$ **69** $\dfrac{2}{x^{\frac{1}{2}}}$ **70** $\dfrac{3}{y^{\frac{2}{5}}}$

71 4 **72** 27 **73** $\frac{1}{2}$ **74** $\pm\frac{1}{3}$ **75** 3

76 $\frac{1}{25}$ **77** $\pm\frac{1}{27}$ **78** $-\frac{1}{2}$ **79** 4 **80** 81

1 $10^{0\cdot 423\,2}$, $10^{1\cdot 423\,2}$, $10^{4\cdot 423\,2}$, $10^{2\cdot 423\,2}$

2 $10^{0\cdot 960\,5}$, $10^{3\cdot 960\,5}$, $10^{2\cdot 960\,5}$, $10^{6\cdot 960\,5}$

3 $0\cdot 660\,9$, $2\cdot 660\,9$, $5\cdot 660\,9$, $1\cdot 660\,9$

4 $0\cdot 848\,8$, $7\cdot 848\,8$, $1\cdot 848\,8$, $3\cdot 848\,8$

5 $10^{0\cdot 859\,8}$ **6** $10^{0\cdot 860\,2}$ **7** $10^{0\cdot 860\,1}$ **8** $10^{0\cdot 859\,9}$

9 $0\cdot 710\,6$, $3\cdot 710\,6$, $1\cdot 710\,6$, $5\cdot 710\,6$

10 $0\cdot 924\,5$, $2\cdot 924\,5$, $6\cdot 924\,5$, $4\cdot 924\,5$

New General Mathematics

11 1·875 7   **12** 3·616 7   **13** 2·319 2   **14** 5·468 4
15 7·916 2   **16** 4·814 0   **17** 1·080 9   **18** 2·599 1
19 1·602 3   **20** 2·002 5
21 1·18, 1·67, 1·86, 0·95, 1·96; 3·2, 12·9, 56·2, **21·4, 7·2**

Exercise 1c (p. 6)
 1 4·347, 4 347, 434·7, 434 700
 2 8·948, 894·8, 89 480, 89 480 000
 3 5·178, 51·78, 5 178 000, 5 178
 4 151·8   **5** 16 240   **6** 36·63   **7** 1 987 000
 8 2 808   **9** 120 600   **10** 12·85   **11** 102·1
12 0·699, 0·903, 0·954; 1·41, 2·29, 7·41

Exercise 1d (p. 7)
 1 7·461   **2** 1·545   **3** 7·945   **4** 2·235   **5** 6·921
 6 712·9   **7** 5·298   **8** 735·0   **9** 1·905   **10** 243·5
11 1·872   **12** 17·04   **13** 1 091   **14** 5·589   **15** 385·4
16 4·829   **17** 16·77   **18** 34·30   **19** 60 010   **20** 7·166

Exercise 1e (p. 8)
 1 25·37   **2** 3 724   **3** 25·37   **4** 2 168   **5** 581·5
 6 63 920   **7** 375·3   **8** 105·4   **9** 1 007   **10** 7 053

Exercise 1f (p. 8)
 1 5·120   **2** 2·970   **3** 1·995   **4** 51·20   **5** 1·856
 6 5·010   **7** 2·446   **8** 9·754   **9** 1·112   **10** 1·816

Exercise 1g (p. 10)
 1 149·2   **2** 12 050   **3** 18·86   **4** 14·08   **5** 2 834
 6 7·125   **7** 896·4   **8** 8 523   **9** 383·0   **10** 4·583
11 15·40   **12** 132·9   **13** 70·28   **14** 5·947   **15** 3·024
16 1·995   **17** 74·85   **18** 112·9   **19** 3·979   **20** 138·7
21 26·28   **22** 5·049   **23** 2·164   **24** 2·026   **25** 496·3
26 8·658   **27** 5·866   **28** 3 644   **29** 26·13   **30** 3·169
31 3·025   **32** 2·244   **33** 7·705   **34** 3 852   **35** 3·311
36 71·91   **37** 7·677   **38** 130·6   **39** 4·396   **40** 17·14
41 31·42   **42** 2·248   **43** 92·90   **44** 38·41   **45** 19·59
46 4·998   **47** 9·166   **48** 27·61   **49** 126·8   **50** 7·578
51 2·344   **52** 2·071   **53** 11·27   **54** 1·253   **55** 927·0
56 53·55   **57** 7·716   **58** 1·636   **59** 1·203   **60** 19 050

Exercise 1h (p. 13)
 1 9·12 m²   **2** 8·01 cm²   **3** 559 cm³
 4 27·0 cm²   **5** 7·72 kg   **6** 20·2 cm

7 22·6 cm   **8** 5·06 cm   **9** 276 cm³
10 4·36 m   **11** 31·1 cm   **12** 1·22 ha
13 156 m   **14** 1 852, 61·1 km h⁻¹, 17·3 knots
15 34·8 m²   **16** $8·17, £6·69   **17** 8·40 cm²
18 10·4 cm   **19** 16·5 l   **20** 110 kg
21 21·2 km h⁻¹   **22** 2·23 m

Exercise 2a (p. 19)
  1 35 cm²   **2** 24 cm²   **3** 15 cm²   **4** 63 cm²
  5 14 cm²   **6** 6   **7** 4½   **8** 4
  9 3½   **10** 1⅔   **11** 28·7 cm²   **12** 26·5 cm²
13 15·9 cm²   **14** 31·1 cm²   **15** 25·8 cm²

Exercise 2b (p. 24)
  1 14 cm²   **2** 20 cm²   **3** 31½ cm²   **4** 3·96 cm²
  5 4 cm²   **6** 6   **7** 5   **8** 7
  9 8   **10** 5   **11** 17·6 cm²   **12** 4·23 cm²
13 4·53 cm²   **14** 16·2 cm²   **15** 20·4 cm²

Exercise 2c (p. 26)
  1 15 cm²   **2** 26 cm²   **3** 40 cm²   **4** 37½ cm²
  5 5·31 cm²   **6** 5   **7** 4   **8** 6½
  9 7   **10** 5½   **11** 26·7 cm²   **12** 5·80 cm²
13 17·6 cm²   **14** 38·1 cm²   **15** 31·5 cm²

Exercise 2d (p. 29)
  1 8·94 cm   **2** 4 cm   **5** 15 cm
  7 7·20 cm, 10·14 cm   **8** 28 cm², 5·6 cm   **9** 3·5 cm
14 6·48 cm   **15** 15 cm   **16** 34 500 m²
22 12, 56, 39, 15, 130, 52, 136½, 72½, 107, 72 cm²
24 3·36 cm², 1·92 cm   **25** 26·46 cm², 5·4 cm   **29** 44 cm²
30 12·4 cm   **31** 11·4 cm
34 12·8 cm, 7·5 cm, 96 cm²   **35** 3·53 km²
37 35 cm²   **45** 7·47 cm   **48** 4 cm, 6 cm
51 43° 3′   **54** 3 : 5, 3 : 7, 5 : 7 **55** 4 : 27

Exercise 3a (p. 38)
  1 10 m   **2** 17 cm   **3** 24 m   **4** 7 cm   **5** 40 cm
  6 29 m   **7** 35 m   **8** 11 cm   **9** 53 cm   **10** 33 m
11 13   **12** 15   **13** 17   **14** 61   **15** 16
16 10 m   **17** 61 m   **18** 15 m, 25 m   **19** 9·90 cm
21 5·3 cm   **22** 30 cm   **23** 6·93 cm
24 29 km   **25** 60 m, 65 m, 63 m   **26** 7 cm
27 530 m   **28** 24 cm²   **29** 4·5 cm, 12·6 cm²

New General Mathematics

30 1·45 m   **31** 610 m   **32** 13·9 cm
33 4 cm, 4·8 cm   **34** 17 cm, 14·1 cm   **35** 65 cm², 13·93 cm

Exercise 3b (p. 43)

1 5·434	**2** 1·719	**3** 17·19	**4** 54·34
5 1·976	**6** 0·197 6	**7** 0·624 7	**8** 64·34
9 0·963 5	**10** 6·164	**11** 19·54	**12** 0·029 50
13 11·27	**14** 7·280	**15** 30·51	**16** 10·28
17 8·849	**18** 2·828	**19** 5·385	**20** 21·52
21 8·944	**22** 0·836 7	**23** 7·829	**24** 24·76
25 0·3	**26** 0·948 7	**27** 0·072 11	**28** 20·74
29 50	**30** 15·81	**31** 22·36	**32** 268·9
33 2 437	**34** 0·000 770 7	**35** 0·001 732	**36** 950
37 0·028 46	**38** 0·007 997	**39** 15 490	**40** 61 160

Exercise 3c (p. 44)

1 5·83 cm	**2** 8·06 m	**3** 3·61 cm	**4** 8·32 cm	**5** 8·90 cm
6 18·5 m	**7** 4·24	**8** 3·16	**9** 5·20	**10** 1·73
11 6·93	**12** 9·64	**13** 65·5 m	**14** 2·74 m	**15** 7·83 cm

16 6·71 m, 73° 24′   **17** 11·7 km, N 70° 1′ E
18 12·2 cm   **19** 85·2 m
20 286 km, N 12° 6′ E   **21** 9·80 cm, 8·91 cm
22 4·43 km   **23** 17·5 cm   **24** 4·47 cm
25 436 km, N 54° 15′ E   **26** 5·22 cm
27 5, 5, 5·83, 4·24, 7·21, 7·81, 4·69, 3·61, 6·32, 7 cm
28 5·99 cm   **29** 6·40 cm, 3·75 cm   **30** 66·8 cm

Exercise 3d (p. 49)

6 72 cm²   **7** 16 cm   **11** 1·73, 2·24   **15** $(a^2 + b^2)$ cm

Exercise 4a (p. 52)

1 5, −1	**2** 9, 5	**3** −1, −5
4 3, −7	**5** $1 \pm \sqrt{2}$	**6** $-4 \pm \sqrt{3}$
7 $3 \pm \sqrt{5}$	**8** $-2 \pm \sqrt{2}$	**9** $1\frac{1}{2}, 2\frac{1}{2}$
10 0, 12	**11** $4 \pm \sqrt{10}$	**12** $-4\frac{2}{3}, -5\frac{1}{3}$
13 4, −10	**14** $1 \pm \sqrt{7}$	**15** $8 \pm \sqrt{3}$
16 $\frac{2}{5}, 1\frac{3}{5}$	**17** $\frac{1}{2}, -2\frac{1}{2}$	**18** $-7 \pm \sqrt{6}$
19 $\frac{1}{3}, -1$	**20** $-9 \pm \sqrt{3}$	**21** $6 \pm \sqrt{5}$
22 0, 5	**23** $-10 \pm \sqrt{8}$	**24** $4\frac{1}{3}, 7\frac{2}{3}$
25 $0, -2\frac{1}{2}$		

Exercise 4b (p. 54)

1 $a^2 + 8a + 16 = (a + 4)^2$ **2** $b^2 + 10b + 25 = (b + 5)^2$
3 $c^2 - 4c + 4 = (c - 2)^2$ **4** $d^2 - 6d + 9 = (d - 3)^2$

5 $x^2 + 5x + 6\frac{1}{4} = (x + 2\frac{1}{2})^2$ **6** $y^2 - 3y + 2\frac{1}{4} = (y - 1\frac{1}{2})^2$

7 $z^2 - 7z + 12\frac{1}{4} = (z - 3\frac{1}{2})^2$ **8** $m^2 + 2m + 1 = (m + 1)^2$

9 $n^2 - n + \frac{1}{4} = (n - \frac{1}{2})^2$ **10** $u^2 - \frac{1}{2}u + \frac{1}{16} = (u - \frac{1}{4})^2$

11 $v^2 + \frac{1}{4}v + \frac{1}{64} = (v + \frac{1}{8})^2$ **12** $h^2 + \frac{2}{3}h + \frac{1}{9} = (h + \frac{1}{3})^2$

13 $k^2 - 1\frac{1}{3}k + \frac{4}{9} = (k - \frac{2}{3})^2$ **14** $g^2 - 4\frac{2}{3}g + 5\frac{4}{9} = (g - 2\frac{1}{3})^2$

15 $a^2 + \frac{3}{5}a + \frac{9}{100} = (a + \frac{3}{10})^2$ **16** $b^2 - \frac{4}{5}b + \frac{4}{25} = (b - \frac{2}{5})^2$

17 $c^2 - 1\frac{1}{2}c + \frac{9}{16} = (c - \frac{3}{4})^2$ **18** $m^2 - 8m + 16 = (m - 4)^2$

19 $m^2 - 8mn + 16n^2 = (m - 4n)^2$

20 $a^2 - 6ad + 9d^2 = (a - 3d)^2$

21 $x^2 + 10xy + 25y^2 = (x + 5y)^2$

22 $m^2 + 3mn + 2\frac{1}{4}n^2 = (m + 1\frac{1}{2}n)^2$

23 $u^2 - 1\frac{3}{5}u + \frac{16}{25} = (u - \frac{4}{5})^2$ **24** $v^2 - \frac{3}{4}v + \frac{9}{64} = (v - \frac{3}{8})^2$

Exercise 4c (p. 55)

1 $3, -7$ **2** $-3, 4$ **3** $2 \pm \sqrt{6}$ **4** $-1 \pm \sqrt{3}$

5 -2 twice   **6** $5 \pm \sqrt{10}$ **7** $-5 \pm \sqrt{3}$ **8** 3 twice

9 $-3 \pm \sqrt{2}$ **10** $\dfrac{3 \pm \sqrt{5}}{2}$ **11** $2, 3$ **12** $-1, -4$

13 $\dfrac{5 \pm \sqrt{17}}{2}$ **14** $\dfrac{-5 \pm \sqrt{17}}{2}$ **15** $4 \pm \sqrt{17}$ **16** $\dfrac{1 \pm \sqrt{5}}{2}$

17 $\dfrac{-1 \pm \sqrt{13}}{2}$ **18** $3, -10$ **19** $\dfrac{7 \pm \sqrt{5}}{2}$ **20** $\dfrac{-3 \pm \sqrt{17}}{2}$

21 5 twice   **22** $\dfrac{-9 \pm \sqrt{5}}{2}$ **23** $6 \pm \sqrt{35}$ **24** $7 \pm \sqrt{52}$

25 $-8 \pm \sqrt{5}$ **26** $\dfrac{-7 \pm \sqrt{53}}{2}$ **27** $7, -13$ **28** $-5, 11$

29 $9 \pm \sqrt{17}$ **30** $\dfrac{-13 \pm \sqrt{5}}{2}$

Exercise 4d (p. 56)

1 $9 \cdot 71$ **2** $4 \cdot 85$ **3** $-4 \cdot 85$ **4** $-9 \cdot 71$ **5** $-0 \cdot 55$

6 $-6 \cdot 50$ **7** $1 \cdot 58$ **8** $-3 \cdot 324$ **9** $-4 \cdot 755$ **10** $-0 \cdot 366$

11 $1 \cdot 26$ **12** $-2 \cdot 38$ **13** $-0 \cdot 17$ **14** $-0 \cdot 07$ **15** $3 \cdot 74$

16 $-2 \cdot 73, -9 \cdot 57$ **17** $6 \cdot 89, -3 \cdot 05$

18 $2 \cdot 302, -8 \cdot 548$ **19** $11 \cdot 415, -5 \cdot 583$ **20** $12 \cdot 39, 0 \cdot 47$

Exercise 4e (p. 59)

1 $2 \cdot 73, -0 \cdot 73$ **2** $2 \cdot 41, -0 \cdot 41$ **3** $3 \cdot 24, -1 \cdot 24$

4 $0 \cdot 41, -2 \cdot 41$ **5** $1, -3$ **6** $-1, 5$

New General Mathematics

7 3·73, 0·27	**8** 5·73, 2·27	**9** −1·59, −4·41
10 5·24, 0·76	**11** 1·87, −5·87	**12** −0·59, −3·41
13 1, 2	**14** 5·14, −2·14	**15** 0·19, −5·19
16 2·79, −1·79	**17** 1·71, 0·29	**18** −½, 1
19 2·29, −0·29	**20** 9·47, 0·53	**21** 2·37, −3·37
22 3, −2	**23** 6·46, −0·46	**24** 5·08, −1·08
25 3, −1½	**26** 6·41, 3·59	**27** 8, −5
28 1·87, 0·13	**29** 5, 7	**30** 5·14, −2·14
31 2·11, −7·11	**32** 1, ⅔	**33** 2·32, −0·32
34 2·76, 0·24	**35** 13, −2	**36** 5·10, −1·10
37 −0·07, −2·93	**38** 6·79, 2·21	**39** 4·16, −0·16
40 −0·56, −4·44		

Exercise 4f (p. 62)

1 1, 1⅓	**2** 2, ⅔	**3** imag.	**4** 1, 1⅔
5 2·15, −4·65	**6** 2·19, −0·69		**7** 1·15, −12·15
8 imag.	**9** 2·32, −4·32		**10** 4·73, 1·27
11 3 twice	**12** ⅔, −4		**13** 0·37, −1·37
14 2, −½	**15** imag.		**16** ½, −1½
17 −2 twice	**18** 3·35, −2·69		**19** −3·19, −0·31
20 1·60, −1·10	**21** 2, ½		**22** 7·12, −1·12
23 1¾, −1	**24** ½ twice		**25** 2·84, −1·17
26 −1⅘, 2	**27** imag.		**28** ½, −1½
29 ½, ⅓	**30** −½, 3		**31** 3·65, −1·65
32 −½, 6	**33** 9·29, −1·29		**34** imag.
35 5, −1½	**36** −2·12, −0·28		**37** imag.
38 −2·39, −0·28	**39** imag.		**40** −2, −9
41 2½, 3	**42** 3·63, 0·37		**43** −⅔ twice
44 0·84, −0·59	**45** 3·21, −1·71		**46** 1·46, −4·79
47 −½, 1	**48** 2·18, −3·68		**49** 0·82, −9·82
50 ±1·41			

Exercise 4g (p. 65)

1 2·77, −1·27; 3, −1·50; 0, 1·5; 3·41, −1·91; imag.; 2·35, −0·85
2 4, −1; 2·62, 0·38; imag.; 0, 3; 4·37, −1·37; 3·56, −0·56
3 4·65, −0·65; 5·61, −1·61; 2 twice; imag.; 0, 4; 5·16, −1·16
4 0·56, −3·56; 1·70, −4·70; 1, −4; −1, −2; imag.; imag.
5 0, −5; −7·62, 2·62; imag.; 1·53, −6·53; −1·38, −3·62; 1, −6
6 4, −2; 3·45, −1·45; 1 twice; 0, 2; 5, −3; imag.
7 1·12, −3·12; 2·39, −4·39; −1 twice; 1·55, −3·55; imag.; 0, −2
8 3·23, −0·23; imag.; 1·5 twice; 3·85, −0·85; 2·72, 0·28; 4, −1
9 1·70, −1·37; 1, −0·67; 2·62, −2·29; 3, −2·67; imag.; −2, 2·33
10 1·39, −2·89; 2, −3·5; 0·5, −2; imag.; 2·5, −4; −1, −0·5

Answers

Exercise 4h (p. 68)
1 2	**2** 5 cm	**3** 3
4 0 or 3	**5** 3 m	**6** 44, 11
7 29, 6	**8** 11	**9** 8
10 6·83 cm	**11** 20p	**12** 6 m square
13 2 m	**14** 8, 9 or −9, −8	**15** 10, 12 or −12, −10
16 5 s	**17** 10·8 cm	**18** 8 cm
19 24 cm, 7 cm	**20** 20 cm, 25 cm	**21** 1½ cm
22 3½ cm	**23** 6·62 cm	**24** 2 cm
25 3·82 cm, 1·18 cm	**26** 1 s or 5 s	**27** 2 m
28 7, 9	**29** 4, 6	**30** 16
31 9	**32** 10 cm square	**33** 4 or −9
34 2 or −5	**35** 14 m or 16 m	**36** 8·90 m

Exercise 5a (p. 72)
1 2 : 3	**2** 5 : 3	**3** 2 : 5	**4** 3 : 4	**5** 5 : 3
6 3 : 2	**7** 3 : 7	**8** 5 : 9	**9** 20 : 7	**10** 1 : 6
11 8	**12** 28	**13** 30	**14** 5	**15** 28
16 21	**17** 24	**18** 45	**19** 7	**20** 35
21 28p	**22** 30 m	**23** 1 min 15 s	**24** 75p	**25** 72 km
26 2½ weeks	**27** 1·35 m	**28** £1·17	**29** 49 min	**30** 7 500 cm²

Exercise 5b (p. 73)
1 £2·40 per doz.	**2** £3·15 per week	**3** 66 km h⁻¹
4 26·5 kg m⁻¹	**5** £6·29	**6** £417·25
7 7·2 kg m⁻¹	**8** 11·92	**9** 1·028 g cm⁻³
10 52p per h	**11** £4·30	**12** £76·41
13 £105·78	**14** 51 t m⁻¹	**15** ⅜ kW kg⁻¹
16 37 cars per day	**17** 8p in the £	**18** £6·48
19 24p in the £	**20** £85·50	**21** 10·55 per 1 000
22 11·51 per 1 000	**23** 80·7 kW t⁻¹	**24** 15p in the £
25 36p in the £		

Exercise 5c (p. 76)
1 0·375 : 1	**2** 1·4 : 1	**3** 4·67 : 1	**4** 0·571 : 1
5 7·25 : 1	**6** 0·75 : 1	**7** 1·6 : 1	**8** 2·27 : 1
9 0·4 : 1	**10** 1·7 : 1	**11** 1 : 2·75	**12** 1 : 1·44
13 1 : 0·286	**14** 1 : 0·375	**15** 1 : 1·6	**16** 1 : 32
17 1 : 1 320	**18** 1 : 0·28	**19** 1 : 7 920	**20** 1 : 20 000
21 3·75	**22** 0·625	**23** 13·5	**24** 31
25 2·25	**26** 14·4	**27** 0·333	**28** 7·92 m
29 20 g	**30** 25 cm	**31** Second	**32** Second
33 First	**34** Second	**35** First	**36** Second
37 Second	**38** Second	**39** First	**40** First

41 $\dfrac{1}{1\,000}$ **42** $\dfrac{1}{10\,000}$ **43** $\dfrac{1}{15\,000}$ **44** $\dfrac{1}{30\,000}$

45 $\dfrac{1}{25\,000}$ **46** First **47** Second

48 5 cm to 1 m, 61·5 cm **49** $\dfrac{1}{500\,000}$, 18·8 cm

50 First **51** 2·5 km to 1 cm, $\dfrac{1}{250\,000}$

52 13·59 : 1 **53** C **54** 372 m² **55** Second

Exercise 5d (p. 80)
  1 2·48F, 5·43F; 84p, 61p **4** 0·25, 4 h, 8 km h⁻¹
  5 77p, £2·24, £3·15; 19 litres, 27 litres, 41 litres
  6 4·65 kg, 7·75 kg, 10·85 kg; 5·16 litres, 9·03 litres, 14·19 litres
  7 25, 40p **8** 94 g, 163 g; 39½ cm³, 82 cm³
  9 £80·60, £174·20; 35, 60 **10** 8·32 cm³, 39°C

Exercise 5e (p. 85)
  1 35p, 63p **2** 64p, £1·92, £3·20
  3 24 m, 32 m, 40 m **4** 35 kg, 21 kg
  5 45, 18, 54, 36 **6** £4·22, £10·55, £18·99
  7 6·60 kg, 4·20 kg **8** 6·75 m, 16·20 m
  9 £1·76, 66p, £2·97 **10** 5·2 kg, 6·5 kg, 7·8 kg, 9·1 kg
  11 £13·65, £9·10 **12** £3·50, £2·10
  13 £342·40 **14** £700, £350, £525
  15 155 cm³, 403 cm³, 124 cm³ **16** £7·63
  17 £2·70, £3·78, £1·08 **18** 3·51 kg
  19 6 kg **20** 8p, 12p, 15p
  21 567, 504, 588 **22** £5·70, £2·28, £0·57
  23 After 5 months **24** £1·32, £1·68, £1·80
  25 25·16 kg **26** £285, £190, £380
  27 £7, £1·75, £12·25, £8·75 **28** $\frac{4}{7}$ litre
  29 £604 500, £784 000, £861 500 **30** £459, £621

Exercise 6 (p. 89)
  1 £2 **2** 1¼ kg **3** 6·4 litres **4** 1·08 kg
  5 61p **6** 3·072 litres **7** £1·50 **8** 40½ litres
  9 4 × original surface, ¼ of original thickness
  10 1⅓ cm **11** 90p **12** 2·52 m **13** 2·7 tonnes
  14 4·61 kg **15** 12 500 litres **16** 38·5 m **17** 1 296 m²
  18 32·64 tonnes **19** 675 kg **20** 175 cm²

Exercise 7a (p. 93)

1 $3{\cdot}24 \times 10^1$ **2** $4{\cdot}71 \times 10^{-1}$ **3** $3{\cdot}472 \times 10^6$ **4** $6{\cdot}131 \times 10^{-4}$
5 $4{\cdot}576 \times 10^3$ **6** $5{\cdot}172 \times 10^4$ **7** $4{\cdot}381 \times 10^{-2}$ **8** $2{\cdot}31 \times 10^{-7}$
9 $6{\cdot}23 \times 10^8$ **10** $3{\cdot}471\ 21 \times 10^{-3}$
11 $10^{0{\cdot}400\ 9}$, $10^{\bar{2}{\cdot}400\ 9}$, $10^{\bar{5}{\cdot}400\ 9}$, $10^{\bar{1}{\cdot}400\ 9}$
12 $10^{0{\cdot}863\ 7}$, $10^{\bar{3}{\cdot}863\ 7}$, $10^{\bar{1}{\cdot}863\ 7}$, $10^{\bar{4}{\cdot}863\ 7}$
13 $0{\cdot}715\ 4$, $\bar{2}{\cdot}715\ 4$, $\bar{1}{\cdot}715\ 4$, $\bar{4}{\cdot}715\ 4$ **14** $\bar{2}{\cdot}586\ 8$
15 $\bar{4}{\cdot}294\ 5$ **16** $\bar{1}{\cdot}813\ 2$ **17** $\bar{7}{\cdot}505\ 1$ **18** $\bar{5}{\cdot}400\ 4$
19 $\bar{1}{\cdot}903\ 1$ **20** $\bar{1}{\cdot}903\ 3$
21 $2{\cdot}315$, $0{\cdot}002\ 315$, $0{\cdot}231\ 5$, $0{\cdot}000\ 002\ 315$
22 $0{\cdot}031\ 60$ **23** $0{\cdot}000\ 783\ 2$ **24** $0{\cdot}615\ 5$ **25** $0{\cdot}003\ 749$

Exercise 7b (p. 94)

1 $\bar{5}{\cdot}7 = -4{\cdot}3$ **2** $\bar{2} = -2$ **3** $\bar{2}{\cdot}1 = -1{\cdot}9$
4 $\bar{6}{\cdot}3 = -5{\cdot}7$ **5** $\bar{4}{\cdot}2 = -3{\cdot}8$ **6** $\bar{2}{\cdot}2 = -1{\cdot}8$
7 $\bar{8}{\cdot}6 = -7{\cdot}4$ **8** $1{\cdot}2$ **9** $\bar{3}{\cdot}8 = -2{\cdot}2$
10 $\bar{8}{\cdot}6 = -7{\cdot}4$ **11** $1{\cdot}7$ **12** $\bar{7}{\cdot}4 = -6{\cdot}6$
13 $\bar{1}{\cdot}2 = -0{\cdot}8$ **14** $\bar{1}{\cdot}7 = -0{\cdot}3$ **15** $\bar{4}{\cdot}1 = -3{\cdot}9$
16 $\bar{6}{\cdot}4 = -5{\cdot}6$ **17** $\bar{1}{\cdot}66 = -0{\cdot}34$ **18** $\bar{1}{\cdot}3 = -0{\cdot}7$
19 $\bar{2}{\cdot}8 = -1{\cdot}2$ **20** $\bar{1}{\cdot}4 = -0{\cdot}6$ **21** $\bar{1}{\cdot}45 = -0{\cdot}55$
22 $1{\cdot}8$ **23** $\bar{2}{\cdot}9 = -1{\cdot}1$ **24** $\bar{2}{\cdot}3 = -1{\cdot}7$
25 $\bar{1}{\cdot}4 = -0{\cdot}6$ **26** $\bar{5}{\cdot}2 = -4{\cdot}8$ **27** $\bar{1}{\cdot}425 = -0{\cdot}575$
28 $0{\cdot}9$ **29** $\bar{1}{\cdot}12 = -0{\cdot}88$ **30** $\bar{1}{\cdot}8 = -0{\cdot}2$

Exercise 7c (p. 96)

1 $0{\cdot}124\ 7$ **2** $0{\cdot}268\ 0$ **3** $0{\cdot}624\ 8$ **4** $0{\cdot}810\ 8$ **5** $0{\cdot}066\ 40$
6 $0{\cdot}006\ 621$ **7** $6{\cdot}037$ **8** $0{\cdot}246\ 8$ **9** $0{\cdot}165\ 7$ **10** $0{\cdot}057\ 63$
11 $5{\cdot}631$ **12** $0{\cdot}082\ 17$ **13** $4{\cdot}406$ **14** $0{\cdot}930\ 9$ **15** $123{\cdot}6$
16 $0{\cdot}013\ 2$ **17** $0{\cdot}815\ 3$ **18** $0{\cdot}561\ 0$ **19** $2{\cdot}966$ **20** $0{\cdot}409\ 2$
21 $0{\cdot}424\ 8$ **22** $0{\cdot}022\ 93$ **23** $0{\cdot}121\ 4$ **24** $1{\cdot}344$

Exercise 7d (p. 97)

1 $0{\cdot}479\ 7$ **2** $0{\cdot}120\ 1$ **3** $0{\cdot}294\ 3$ **4** $0{\cdot}002\ 136$
5 $0{\cdot}304\ 2$ **6** $0{\cdot}007\ 516$ **7** $0{\cdot}729\ 8$ **8** $0{\cdot}338\ 8$
9 $0{\cdot}517\ 0$ **10** $0{\cdot}502\ 1$ **11** $0{\cdot}497\ 6$ **12** $0{\cdot}761\ 5$
13 $0{\cdot}795\ 6$ **14** $0{\cdot}405\ 0$ **15** $0{\cdot}483\ 3$ **16** $0{\cdot}716\ 1$
17 $0{\cdot}389\ 0$ **18** $0{\cdot}986\ 3$ **19** $0{\cdot}088\ 47$ **20** $40{\cdot}25$
21 $0{\cdot}062\ 58$ **22** $0{\cdot}511\ 4$ **23** $0{\cdot}123\ 7$ **24** $0{\cdot}344\ 7$
25 $0{\cdot}082\ 17$ **26** $0{\cdot}213\ 5$ **27** $0{\cdot}001\ 035$ **28** $0{\cdot}063\ 56$
29 $0{\cdot}308\ 4$ **30** $0{\cdot}533\ 8$ **31** $3{\cdot}391 \times 10^{22}$
32 $1{\cdot}020 \times 10^{-15}$ **33** $7{\cdot}894 \times 10^{-3}$ **34** $3{\cdot}152 \times 10^{-1}$
35 $2{\cdot}219 \times 10^{-4}$

New General Mathematics

Revision Examples (p. 98)

I

1 (i) $(a - 2)(a + 7)$ (ii) $(x + 5y)(x - 5y)$ (iii) $(a + m)(b - n)$
2 (i) 6·009   (ii) 4·021   3 £99·45$\frac{1}{2}$ 4 5$\frac{5}{8}$ cm
5 5   6 14p   7 (i) 1, 3$\frac{1}{3}$ (ii) 5, $-\frac{2}{3}$
8 6·43 cm, 10·25 cm   10 5

II

1 (i) $(m - 7)(m + 6)$ (ii) $(3a + 4c)(3a - 4c)$ (iii) $(2m - u)(n - 2v)$
2 (i) 34·31   (ii) 124·5   5 $\frac{m - 12}{12}$ 6 £57·73
7 (i) imag.   (ii) 1, 4   8 2$\frac{1}{4}$, 7$\frac{1}{2}$
9 5·6 m, 58° 6′   10 11·7 cm

III

1 (i) $(a - 5b)(a + 3b)$ (ii) $(7x + 10)(7x - 10)$ (iii) $(a - 2b)(c + 3d)$
2 1·875   3 Second   4 5·41 cm   5 $-1, 2$ 6 £1 050
7 (i) 0·63, $-0·80$ (ii) 1·74, $-7·74$ 8 12·43 cm   9 9, 36

IV

1 (i) $(m - 6n)(m + 4n)$ (ii) $(4u + 5v)(4u - 5v)$ (iii) $(2m + u)(3n + v)$
2 75·50   3 275 kg   4 20 cm   5 (i) $3 - 2a$ (ii) $3m + 4n$
6 4%   7 (i) 1, $-\frac{7}{10}$ (ii) $\frac{1}{3}$, 3   8 15, 4   10 2 s and 5 s

V

1 (i) $(x - 5y)(x - 6y)$ (ii) $(a - b)(2c - 3d)$ (iii) $(a + b)(2a - b)$
2 (i) 94·48   (ii) 2·293   3 81p, 45p   5 1$\frac{4}{7}$ 6 2·16 kg
7 (i) 1·79, $-0·08$ (ii) $-2, 7$ 8 3·77 cm   10 8 cm

VI

1 (i) $(2a - 3)(a + 4)$ (ii) $3(m + n)(m - n)$ (iii) $(a + 2m)(2b - n)$
2 (i) 3·043   (ii) 5·109   3 £2·80   4 9·49 cm   5 $\frac{x - 4}{2}$
6 (i) 78 : 1   (ii) 40 : 1   7 (i) 2·24, 0·76   (ii) imag.
8 12·6 cm, 7·2 cm   9 25 cm, 16·8 cm   10 4 or -9

VII

1 (i) $(3u + 5)(u - 1)$ (ii) $3a(a + 2b)$ (iii) $(a + b)(a + b - 3c)$
2 23·42   3 15·1, 14·5   4 1·05 km²   5 3, -2 6 6 yr
7 (i) imag.   (ii) 1$\frac{1}{3}$, $-2\frac{1}{2}$ 8 3·78 m   10 24

VIII

1 (i) $(2a - 9)(a + 6)$ (ii) $(c - 2d)(3c - 4d)$
(iii) $(2a - b + 2c)(b - 2c)$
2 (i) 22·77   (ii) 12·76   **3** About 4 kg
5 (i) $2a + 5b$ (ii) $-x + 15y$ **6** 45%
7 (i) imag. (ii) 0·48, $-10·48$
8 14, 15   **9** 305 km, S 10° 23′ E   **10** 3·5 m

IX

1 (i) $(2m - 3u)(3m - 2u)$ (ii) $4(a + b)(2a - b)$
(iii) $(a - 3b)(2m + n)$
2 (i) 58·68 (ii) 7·936   **3** £432, £216, £384   **4** 2·94 ha
5 1   **6** 77p   **7** (i) 1·26, $-0·16$ (ii) $-1·33, 0·23$
8 5·83 cm   **10** 36 cm, 15 cm

X

1 (i) $(2a - 3b)(4a + 5b)$ (ii) $(m - n)(7m + n)$
(iii) $(2a + b)(m - 2n)$

2 5·474   **3** £1·30, £3·90, £5·85   **5** $\dfrac{15a - 35}{12}$

6 £24·10, £23·20   **7** (i) 1·90, $-2·10$ (ii) 4·48, $-2·23$
8 $2\frac{1}{2}$, 4   **10** 1·5 m

Exercise 9a (p. 119)
1 4·25   **2** 6·26   **3** 8·54   **4** 8·06
5 7·86   **6** 11·04   **7** 12·58   **8** 25·9
9 10·79   **10** 18·63   **11** 328   **12** 1 410
13 167 000 **14** 8·07   **15** 0·078 5 **16** 0·004 08
17 612   **18** 81·0   **19** 5·59   **20** 0·004 54
21 3 580 000 **22** 28 400 000 **23** 75 200 **24** 283 000 000
25 37 000   **26** 0·000 444 **27** 4 510   **28** 8·54
29 4·47   **30** 2 330 000

Exercise 9b (p. 122)
1 1·4   **2** 0·714   **3** 2·86   **4** 0·561
5 1·232   **6** 1·002   **7** 1·155   **8** 0·955
9 0·620   **10** 1·28   **11** 1·060   **12** 1·87
13 0·889   **14** 2·80   **15** 11·96   **16** 12·44
17 0·482   **18** 0·157 5 **19** 0·000 099 2 **20** 23 000
21 146   **22** 0·138   **23** 1·935   **24** 0·000 232
25 0·001 47 **26** 134·6   **27** 0·998   **28** 111 800
29 0·019 7 **30** 922 000

New General Mathematics

Exercise 9c (p. 124)

1 9·33	**2** 18·9	**3** 8·79	**4** 5·90
5 8·96	**6** 4·43	**7** 7·69	**8** 6·62
9 1·99	**10** 1·90	**12** 36	**13** 42·9
14 520	**15** 1·012	**16** 14·9	**17** 245
18 0·291	**19** 0·004 06	**20** 7 250	**22** 21·6
23 56·0	**24** 105·3	**25** 0·968	**26** 288
27 105·4	**28** £670	**29** £325	**30** No

Exercise 9d (p. 128)

1 6·10	**2** 61·0	**3** 458	**4** 1 030
5 0·523	**6** 0·168	**7** 0·001 043	**8** 54 800
9 1 790	**10** 0·000 000 116 3		**11** 2·83
12 8·94	**13** 2·88	**14** 9·02	**15** 15·2
16 30·2	**17** 269	**18** 78·25	**19** 0·458
20 0·179	**21** 3·46	**22** 0·775	**23** 150·8
24 69·1	**25** 1·155	**26** 0·602	**27** 3·71
28 2·70	**29** 1·898	**30** 0·005 33	

Exercise 10a (p. 130)

1 1·376 3, 1·455 4	**2** 1·377 1, 1·454 5	**3** 1·375 5, 1·456 3
4 1·670 1, 1·248 6	**5** 1·672 6, 1·247 5	**6** 1·124 0, 2·190 1
7 1·018 1, 5·319 5	**8** 2·096 8, 1·137 7	**9** 1·344 2, 1·496 4
10 1·032 3, 4·025 6	**11** 1·202 7, 1·799 9	**12** 1·149 4, 2·028 7
13 3·654 1, 1·039 7	**14** 1·807 8, 1·200 4	**15** 2·045 5, 1·146 3
16 3·436 4, 1·045 2	**17** 1·617 7, 1·272 2	**18** 1·255 7, 1·653 4
19 2·616 8, 1·082 1	**20** 1·100 1, 2·399 1	

21 25° 30′	**22** 25° 35′	**23** 71° 25′	**24** 39° 2′
25 46° 46′	**26** 75° 50′	**27** 8° 32′	**28** 32° 41′
29 68° 16′	**30** 27° 8′	**31** 39° 32′	**32** 45° 37′
33 28° 45′	**34** 18° 1′	**35** 77° 23′	**36** 29° 55′
37 61° 14′	**38** 68° 26′	**39** 25° 22′	**40** 11° 43′

Exercise 10b (p. 130)

1 $\dfrac{BC}{AB}$, $\dfrac{PQ}{QR}$, $\dfrac{XY}{YZ}$, $\dfrac{YZ}{XZ}$, $\dfrac{QR}{PR}$, $\dfrac{AC}{BC}$

2 sin R, cos P; sec Y, cosec X; cot B, tan C; tan X, cot Y; cosec B, sec C; tan P, cot R

3 6·62, 4·35 cm; 4·53, 2·13 cm; 22° 37′; 72° 54′

4 50° 17′; 56° 11′; 100° 34′

5 4·35, 1·72 cm; 3·63, 8·79 cm; 4·08, 2·77 cm

6 13·3 cm; 23·9 cm; 19·1 cm; 9·03 cm

Exercise 10c (p. 135)

1 0·407	**2** 0·533	**3** 0·692	**4** 0·091
5 0·044 7	**6** 0·568	**7** 0·923	**8** 0·990
9 0·071 5	**10** 0·055 6	**11** 0·625	**12** 2·45
13 0·936	**14** 3·25	**15** 1·409	**16** 0·087
17 0·075	**18** 0·069	**19** 0·048 6	**20** 0·033 0
21 0·012 2	**22** 31·8	**23** 0·185	**24** 1·356
25 3·094	**26** 0·036 4	**27** 22·2	**28** 15·0
29 0·735	**30** 0·048 1		

Exercise 10d (p. 137)

1 46° 24′	**2** 183 m, 204 m	**3** 7·78 cm	**4** 27° 32′
5 93·2 m	**6** 14·6 m	**7** 5·32 cm	**8** 40° 32′
9 3·61 km, 53° 42′		**10** 15 m	**11** 41°
12 8·50 cm, 12·1 cm, 14·8 cm		**13** 25° 46′	**14** 2·93 m
15 4·69 m, 100° 24′		**16** 33° 28′, 87° 4′, 59° 28′	
17 1 080 m	**18** 16° 6′	**19** 14·2 m, 22°	**20** 13° 12′
21 39° 43′, 1·25 m		**22** 3·45 cm	**23** 7·79 km
24 6·67 km	**25** 14° 2′	**26** 213 m	**27** 5·76 cm
28 697 m	**29** 20° 44′	**30** 2 370 m	

Exercise 11a (p. 144)

1 £16·20, £41·40	**2** £1·53, £19·71, £3·78, £2·43	**3** £3 625·16
4 34·2% (approx.)	**5** £162	**6** 1p
7 £6 525	**8** 73p	**9** £35·32	**10** £18 less

Exercise 11b (p. 146)

1 £3·80, £2·69	**2** £8·58	**3** £15·18	**4** £24·38
5 £16·80	**6** 0·625p	**7** £6·99	**8** £8·86
9 £45·39	**10** £14·52		

Exercise 11c (p. 149)

1 £13·25	**2** £22·25	**3** £84·80	**4** £12·33
5 £26·25	**6** £22·56		
7 £20·30, £22·60, £25·55, £29·20, £32·60			**8** £14·22
9 £54·08	**10** £777·60	**11** £1 640	**12** £2 094, £3 500

Exercise 11d (p. 153)

1 £273·20	**2** £546·20	**3** £217·34	**4** £27·50
5 £59	**6** £128·30	**7** £1 178·30	**8** £208·94
9 £168·62	**10** £345·23	**11** £1 566·80	**12** £2 522·30

Exercise 12a (p. 156)

1 $2x^3 - 3x^2 - 7x + 3$ **2** $6y^3 - 5y^2 - 13y + 12$

3 $9z^3 - 31z - 10$ **4** $2a^3 + 8a^2 - 18$

New General Mathematics

5 $6b^3 - 13b^2 + 3b + 2$

6 $3m^3 - m^2n + mn^2 + 2n^3$

7 $6a^3 - 8a^2b + 2b^3$

8 $2x^3 - 5x^2y + 8xy^2 - 3y^3$

9 $2c^3 + 7c^2d + cd^2 - d^3$

10 $6h^3 - 27hk^2 + 6k^3$

11 $m^2 - n^2 - 2n - 1$

12 $u^2 + 2uv + v^2 - 1$

13 $4a^2 - b^2 + 6b - 9$

14 $6 + 15m - 2n + 9m^2 - 4n^2$

15 $3m^4 - 8m^3 + 7m + 2$

16 $2n^4 + n^3 - 11n + 3$

17 $a^5 - 3a^4 + 2a^3 + 3a^2 - 9a + 10$

18 $2b^5 + 5b^4 - 7b^3 - 8b^2 + 8$

19 $4c^5 - 29c^3 - 18c^2 - 27$

20 $3d^5 + 10d^4 + 5d^3 - 2d - 4$

21 $6x^5 + 15x^2 - 6x + 15$

22 $2a^4 + 3a^3m + a^2m^2 - 4am^3 - 2m^4$

23 $m^4 - 2m^3u - 2m^2u^2 + 8u^4$

24 $2x^4 - 9x^3y + 9x^2y^2 - xy^3 + 3y^4$

25 $2m^4 - 3m^3n - 6m^2n^2 + 13mn^3 - 6n^4$

26 $2x^5 - 3x^4y - 6x^3y^2 + 9x^2y^3 + 2xy^4 - 3y^5$

27 $2u^2 - 2v^2 + 9w^2 - 3uv - 9uw + 3vw$

28 $c^2 - 4d^2 + 25e^2 - 10ce$

29 $a^5 + ad^4 - d^5$

30 $p^3 + q^3 + r^3 - 3pqr$

31 $m^2 + 1$

32 $2x^2 + 2y^2 + 2z^2 - 4yz$

33 $3a^2 - 3b^2 + 6a - 6b$

34 $13 - 3a^2$

35 $2u^3 + 6uv^2$

Exercise 12b (p. 159)

1 $a^2 + a - 1$

2 $m^2 - m + 2$

3 $x^2 + 2x - 4$, rem. 2

4 $u^2 - 2u + 3$, rem. -4

5 $m^2 - 3mn - 2n^2$

6 $x^2 + 2xy - y^2$

7 $b^2 + 2bc - 3c^2$, rem. $3c^3$

8 $a^2 - 3ad + 2d^2$

9 $3x^2 - 2x - 4$, rem. -2

10 $3y^2 - 4y + 6$, rem. -3

11 $a - 2b$

12 $2m - u$

13 $3h^2 + 4hk - 2k^2$

14 $2m^2 + 5mn - 3n^2$

15 $3b - 2$, rem. -1

16 $3a - 1$, rem. 4

17 $m^2 + mn + n^2$

18 $m + n$

19 $3u - 4v$

20 $4m - 5n$

21 $4a^3 - 6a^2 - a + 1$, rem. 5

22 $2x^3 + x^2 + 3x - 1$

23 $m^3 + m^2 + m + 1$

24 $y^3 - y^2 + y - 1$

25 $a + b$

26 $m - n$

27 $3x^2 - 2x + 2$, rem. -3

28 $b^2 - b + 1$

29 $4u^2 + 3uv - v^2$

30 $2y^2 - 2yz - 3z^2$

31 $a^2 - 2a - 8$

32 $2x^2 + 7x + 3$

33 $3m^2 - 10m - 8$

34 $12e^2 + 7ef - 12f^2$

35 $6u^2 + 5uv - 6v^2$

Exercise 12c (p. 162)

1 $(x + 1)(x^2 - x + 1)$

2 $(1 - y)(1 + y + y^2)$

3 $(a - 2)(a^2 + 2a + 4)$

4 $(3 + b)(9 - 3b + b^2)$

5 $(c - 5)(c^2 + 5c + 25)$ **6** $(d + 4)(d^2 - 4d + 16)$
7 $(u + 3v)(u^2 - 3uv + 9v^2)$ **8** $(2m - n)(4m^2 + 2mn + n^2)$
9 $(4a + d)(16a^2 - 4ad + d^2)$ **10** $(2c + 3d)(4c^2 - 6cd + 9d^2)$
11 $(3e - 4f)(9e^2 + 12ef + 16f^2)$ **12** $(5x - 2y)(25x^2 + 10xy + 4y^2)$
13 $(am + n)(a^2m^2 - amn + n^2)$ **14** $(x - yz)(x^2 + xyz + y^2z^2)$
15 $(a - 2de)(a^2 + 2ade + 4d^2e^2)$
16 $(3mn + u)(9m^2n^2 - 3mnu + u^2)$
17 $(a - 3bc)(a^2 + 3abc + 9b^2c^2)$
18 $(4mn - 3uv)(16m^2n^2 + 12mnuv + 9u^2v^2)$
19 $(x + \frac{1}{4})(x^2 - \frac{1}{4}x + \frac{1}{16})$ **20** $(1 + a^2)(1 - a^2 + a^4)$
21 $(b + 1)(b - 1)(b^2 - b + 1)(b^2 + b + 1)$

22 $\left(\dfrac{m}{n^2} - 1\right)\left(\dfrac{m^2}{n^4} + \dfrac{m}{n^2} + 1\right)$ **23** $\left(\dfrac{u}{2} + \dfrac{v}{3}\right)\left(\dfrac{u^2}{4} - \dfrac{uv}{6} + \dfrac{v^2}{9}\right)$

24 $3(x - 2y)(x^2 + 2xy + 4y^2)$
25 $2(3m - n)(9m^2 + 3mn + n^2)$ **26** $(a + b^2)(a^2 - ab^2 + b^4)$
27 $(3x - y^2)(9x^2 + 3xy^2 + y^4)$ **28** $(m^2 + u^2)(m^4 - m^2u^2 + u^4)$
29 $(2h + k)(2h - k)(4h^2 + 2hk + k^2)(4h^2 - 2hk + k^2)$
30 $(3x^3 - 2y^3)(9x^6 + 6x^3y^3 + 4y^6)$
31 $m(m^2 + 6mn + 12n^2)$ **32** $(a + 4b)(a^2 - ab + 7b^2)$
33 $(4u - v)(4u^2 - 2uv + v^2)$ **34** $y(27x^2 - 9xy + y^2)$
35 $2d(3c^2 + d^2)$ **36** $2a(a^2 + 3b^2)$
37 $9x(x^2 - x + 1)$
38 $(2m - 3n)(13m^2 + 3mn + 3n^2)$
39 $(5a - 3b)(7a^2 - 12ab + 9b^2)$ **40** $(a + 2b)(19a^2 - 14ab + 4b^2)$

Exercise 12d (p. 163)
1 $(h + u - v)(h - u + v)$ **2** $(a - 2b)(5a - 2b)$
3 $(d + 1 + e)(d + 1 - e)$ **4** $(h + 3 - a)(h + 3 + a)$
5 $3a(a + 2)$ **6** $(x + 4)(x - 4)$
7 $(a + 2b - x)(a + 2b + x)$ **8** $(x + y)(x - y - z)$
9 $(x - 3y + a)(x - 3y - a)$ **10** $(a + x + 1)(a - x - 1)$
11 $(b - y + 3)(b + y - 3)$ **12** $-8y(3x + 2y)$
13 $16a(a + 2d)$ **14** $(m + n)(m - n + p)$
15 $(m - n - 2p)(m - n + 2p)$ **16** $(a + 4b + 3m)(a + 4b - 3m)$
17 $(u - v)(u + v - 2m)$ **18** $(h + x - y)(h - x + y)$
19 $(k + a + 3b)(k - a - 3b)$ **20** $(4 + a - b)(4 + a + b)$
21 $(3a - 5b)(m + 2n)$ **22** $4c(4c - 3d)$
23 $(5 - b + c)(5 - b - c)$ **24** $(3x + a - 2)(3x - a + 2)$
25 $(l - n)(l + m + n)$ **26** $(3x - 2y)(3x + 2y + 2)$
27 $(a - 3)(a - 7)$ **28** $(3m - 4)(2m - 7)$
29 $(2a - m + 2n)(2a + m - 2n)$ **30** $(3m - n + h)(3m - n - h)$
31 $(2a + 3m + 2k)(2a + 3m - 2k)$
32 $(m + 2)(m - 2)(m^2 + 3)$

33 $(x + 3y)(x - 3y)(2x + y)(2x - y)$
34 $(3b + u + 5v)(3b - u - 5v)$
35 $(5x + 2y + 3m)(5x + 2y - 3m)$
36 $(5d - 3m + 2n)(5d + 3m - 2n)$
37 $(4a + 3b)(4a - 3b + c)$ 38 $(9m + n)(3m - 5n)$
39 $(m + 2n + u + 2v)(m + 2n - u - 2v)$
40 $(a + m - b + 3n)(a + m + b - 3n)$
41 $(a - b + 4)(a + b - 2)$ 42 $(4n - 1)(5n - 3)$
43 $3(4a + 5)$
44 $(4u + 5v - 2m + 3n)(4u + 5v + 2m - 3n)$
45 $(2m + 5n + 2a + 5b)(2m + 5n - 2a - 5b)$

Exercise 13a (p. 166)
 1 $a + 3, 6(a + 3)$ 2 $b - 1, 12(b - 1)$
 3 $2(c - 2d), 12(c - 2d)$ 4 $3(3e + 2f), 6(3e + 2f)$
 5 $m + n, mn(m + n)$ 6 $u - v, uv(u - v)$
 7 $c - e, c(c + e)(c - e)$ 8 $x - 2y, 6xy(x - 2y)$
 9 $h + k, 3h(h + k)(h - k)$
10 $2(m + 2n), 4m(m + 2n)(m - 2n)$
11 $a - 3b, 2(a + 3b)(a - 3b)$
12 $2ab(2a - 3b), 12a^2b^2(2a - 3b)$
13 $u - v, (u + v)(u - v)(u - 2v)$
14 $x - 3, (x - 2)(x + 2)(x - 3)$
15 $a - 5, (a - 1)(a + 2)(a - 5)$
16 $2(m + 2n), 12(m - 2n)(m + 2n)(m - 3n)$
17 $c + d, 6(c - d)(c - 2d)(c + d)^2$
18 $a - 2d, 4a^2(a - 2d)(a + 3d)(a + d)$
19 $(a - b)(a - 2b), (a - b)(a - 2b)(2a - b)(2a + b)$
20 $m(m - n)(m + n), mn(m - n)^2(m + n)$

Exercise 13b (p. 168)

 1 $\dfrac{m}{v}$ 2 $\dfrac{4x}{5y}$ 3 No simpler form

 4 $\dfrac{b + c}{d + e}$ 5 $\dfrac{a + b}{a + c}$ 6 No simpler form

 7 $\dfrac{u}{v}$ 8 $\dfrac{h - k}{k}$ 9 $\dfrac{1}{3dnv}$

10 $-\dfrac{c}{d}$ 11 $-\dfrac{a + b}{b}$ 12 $\dfrac{x}{x - y}$

13 $\dfrac{4cd^2}{5e^2}$ 14 No simpler form 15 $\dfrac{c - d}{c}$

16 $\dfrac{m+n}{m-n}$ **17** $\dfrac{c+3}{c+2}$ **18** $\dfrac{d+3}{d-4}$

19 $-\dfrac{m}{n}$ **20** $\dfrac{y}{x-y}$ **21** No simpler form

22 No simpler form   **23** $\dfrac{h+k}{h-k}$ **24** $\dfrac{u-2v}{u+4v}$

25 $\dfrac{x+3y}{x-y}$ **26** $\dfrac{a^2-ab+b^2}{a+c}$ **27** $\dfrac{a^2+ab+b^2}{a+b}$

28 $-\dfrac{x+3}{x+5}$ **29** $-\dfrac{3a+m}{a+m}$ **30** $-\dfrac{a+4}{2a+1}$

31 $\dfrac{a-n}{a+n}$ **32** $\dfrac{a-n}{a+n}$ **33** $\dfrac{w+u-v}{w-u+v}$

34 $\dfrac{a+b+c}{b-a-c}$ **35** $\dfrac{1}{m+2n}$ **36** $\dfrac{m(m-a)}{a(m+a)}$

37 $\frac{3}{5}$ **38** $\dfrac{b+c}{b-c}$ **39** $\dfrac{x+y-a}{a-x}$

40 $\dfrac{a-b}{c-a}$

Exercise 13c (p. 170)

1 $\dfrac{a}{e}$ **2** $\dfrac{8n^2}{9c^2}$ **3** $\dfrac{n}{3}$ **4** $\dfrac{4}{3u}$

5 $\dfrac{b}{2}$ **6** $\dfrac{a+2}{a}$ **7** $\dfrac{m+3}{m}$ **8** $\dfrac{3u^3v}{16m^2}$

9 $-2a$ **10** $\dfrac{a}{2}$ **11** $\dfrac{n-3}{n}$ **12** $-\dfrac{n}{m}$

13 $\dfrac{a+2b}{a+3b}$ **14** $\dfrac{d(d-2)}{2}$ **15** $2c$ **16** $-\dfrac{c^2}{d^2}$

17 1 **18** $\dfrac{2e(e-2)}{3(e-1)}$ **19** $\dfrac{u-2}{3u}$

20 $\dfrac{(x+1)(x+2)}{x(x-2)}$ **21** $\dfrac{a(a-b)}{b(a+b)}$ **22** $m+4$

23 $\dfrac{a}{b}$ **24** $\dfrac{m-3n}{m+n}$ **25** $\dfrac{(m-3n)(m+n)}{(m-2n)^2}$

Exercise 13d (p. 174)

1 $\dfrac{8a + 9c}{6abc}$ **2** $\dfrac{5c - a + b}{c}$ **3** $\dfrac{3c - 14b}{30bc}$ **4** $\dfrac{7}{6(x + y)}$

5 $\dfrac{2}{a - 2b}$ **6** $\dfrac{3a - b}{a - b}$ **7** $\dfrac{x + 4y}{x + 2y}$ **8** $\dfrac{9}{20(u - v)}$

9 $\dfrac{u - 9v}{2u + 3v}$ **10** $\dfrac{6a - b}{2(2a + b)}$ **11** $\dfrac{19mn}{6(m^2 + n^2)}$ **12** $\dfrac{3}{2(2x - y)}$

13 $\dfrac{c - a}{ac}$ **14** $\dfrac{u(u - 2v)}{v^2}$ **15** $\dfrac{5d + 7}{6(d - 4)}$

16 $\dfrac{5a + 7}{(a + 1)(a + 2)}$ **17** $\dfrac{3x^2 + 2x + 4}{(x - 1)(x + 2)}$ **18** $-\dfrac{4}{(e + 2)(e + 3)}$

19 $\dfrac{4m}{(m - n)^2}$ **20** $\dfrac{c - d}{(2c + d)^2}$ **21** $\dfrac{2a - b}{(a - 2b)^2}$ **22** $\dfrac{3}{c - d}$

23 $\dfrac{2}{4m + 3n}$ **24** $-\dfrac{m + n}{n}$ **25** 1

26 $\dfrac{2}{(c + 5)(c - 2)}$ **27** $\dfrac{7d - 6}{(d + 2)(d - 2)(d - 4)}$

28 $-\dfrac{a + 11b}{6(a + b)(a - b)}$ **29** $\dfrac{7d + 12}{(d - 4)(d + 4)^2}$ **30** $\dfrac{2}{x - 3}$

31 $\dfrac{u - 2v}{u^2 - uv + v^2}$ **32** $\dfrac{4(a - m)}{a^2 + am + m^2}$

33 $\dfrac{a^2 + 7a + 5}{(a - 2)(a - 3)(a + 4)}$ **34** $\dfrac{x - 1}{x^2 - x + 1}$

35 $\dfrac{1}{(a - c)(b - c)}$ **36** 0   **37** d

38 $\dfrac{4a + 5}{5a + 8}$ **39** $-\dfrac{5}{3m}$ **40** $\dfrac{3w - 8}{8w - 5}$

Exercise 13e (p. 178)

1 $3, -1$ **2** $\frac{1}{2}, 2$ **3** $3, -\frac{2}{3}$ **4** $1, -3$ **5** $-2, 1\frac{1}{3}$
6 $-1, -6$ **7** $-\frac{1}{3}, 2$ **8** $5, 1$ **9** $-1, -2$ **10** $0, 2$
11 $5, -\frac{2}{3}$ **12** 1   **13** $2\frac{1}{5}$ **14** $1, 3$ **15** $6, -1\frac{1}{3}$
16 1   **17** $-\frac{1}{4}$ **18** $5, 8\frac{1}{2}$ **19** $3, 1\frac{3}{4}$ **20** $-2, 1\frac{3}{7}$
21 $3, -7\frac{3}{8}$ **22** $3, 1\frac{1}{19}$ **23** $2\frac{1}{2}$ **24** $2, -3$ **25** $-\frac{3}{4}$
26 $-1\frac{1}{6}$ **27** 0   **28** -9 **29** $-\frac{1}{3}$ **30** -2

Exercise 13f (p. 180)

1 6 **2** $\dfrac{3(a-6)}{(a+4)(a-2)}$ **3** $\dfrac{3}{b+3}$ **4** $1\frac{2}{3}$

5 $\dfrac{3c-5}{(c+1)(c-1)}$ **6** $1\frac{1}{3}$ **7** $\dfrac{4-3a}{(a+2)(a-3)}$

8 $\dfrac{2}{(n-4)(n-5)(n-6)}$ **9** $2, -\frac{2}{3}$

10 $\dfrac{2x}{(3+x)^2}$ **11** 0 **12** $-1\frac{1}{2}$

13 $\dfrac{2(2m+3)}{(m+1)(m+2)(m+3)}$ **14** $\dfrac{2}{2m+3}$

15 $2, -7\frac{1}{2}$ **16** $9\frac{1}{2}$ **17** $\dfrac{19-2a}{(a-2)(a+3)(a-5)}$

18 -12 **19** $\dfrac{2n-15}{(2n-5)^2(2n+5)}$ **20** $-\frac{2}{3}$

21 $\dfrac{3(3b+2)}{(b+3)^2(b-4)}$ **22** -3 **23** $-\dfrac{3(t+3)}{(t+2)(2t-1)}$

24 $\dfrac{3}{3d-1}$ **25** $\dfrac{3(b-5)}{2(b+1)(b-3)}$ **26** 5

27 $-\dfrac{3}{2h+3}$ **28** 4

29 $\dfrac{m-4}{(m-1)(m-2)(m-3)}$ **30** -3

31 $\dfrac{5(x+3)}{(x+1)(x+2)(x-2)}$ **32** 3 **33** 3

34 $\dfrac{2(m-3)}{(2m-3)(3m+2)}$ **35** $-\dfrac{4d}{(d+1)(2d-1)(3d+1)}$

36 0 **37** $-\frac{1}{3}$ **38** $\dfrac{3a+1}{(a-1)(a-2)(a+3)}$

39 $\dfrac{3}{2m+7}$ **40** $-\dfrac{a+8}{(a+2)(a-2)(a+3)(a-3)}$

Exercise 13g (p. 186)
1 £4 **2** 11 **3** 10 **4** 36 km h⁻¹
5 15 km h⁻¹ **6** 10 km h⁻¹ **7** 24 **8** 16
9 15p **10** 28 **11** £5 **12** 19
13 $2\frac{1}{2}$ h **14** 11 km h⁻¹ **15** £11 **16** 9 km h⁻¹

17 22	**18** 10.48	**19** 10 km h^{-1}	**20** 18
21 20	**22** 12 km h^{-1}	**23** 8 cm	**24** 15p
25 21	**26** 15	**27** 120	**28** 16
29 25	**30** 45p		

Exercise 14a (p. 192)
 9 42 m   **23** 88 cm

Exercise 14b (p. 200)
 1 Two; 6·72 cm   **2** Four   **4** 2·66 cm, 8·66 cm
 5 1·76 cm, 6·24 cm   **6** 23°, 56½°   **7** 5·74 cm
 8 6 cm   **9** 4·04 cm   **10** 7·42 cm
 12 42 m   **17** 8 cm   **18** 7·20 cm

Revision Examples (p. 204)

XI

1 (i) $3n^3 - 14n^2 - 14n - 3$ (ii) $m^2 - 3m - 2$
2 (i) 0·054 20   (ii) 0·402 1   **3** £145·64

4 (i) $-\dfrac{a + 2b}{b(a + b)}$ (ii) $\dfrac{1}{a + b}$ **5** 9 cm   **6** 3·51

7 $30\frac{2}{3}\%$ **9** 47° 10′; 55 cm   **10** $2\frac{1}{2}$p

XII

1 (i) $6(2a - 5)(2a + 5)$ (ii) $(2m - 3n)(3x + 4y)$
 (iii) $(a + b + c)(a + b - c)$

2 (i) 0·247 4   (ii) 0·928 3   **3** $10\frac{1}{2}$ cm   **4** $\dfrac{5}{6(x - 2)}$ **6** -3

7 £1 200   **8** (i) $1\frac{1}{2}$, $-1\frac{2}{3}$ (ii) 2·36, $-0·11$
9 3·05 cm, 2·58 cm

XIII

1 (i) $4b^3 + 4b^2 - 41b + 15$ (ii) $a^2 - 2a + 3$ **2** 2·27 cm^2

3 8 m   **4** $\dfrac{a^2 + 4a + 6}{(a + 1)^3}$ **5** 48 cm   **6** -4

9 4·96 m   **10** 69

XIV

1 (i) $(a - 2b)(c + 4a)$ (ii) $(3x - 2y)(4x + 5y)$
 (iii) $(x + a + 2m)(x - a - 2m)$

2 (i) 0·227 1   (ii) 0·605 7   **3** 29 m   **4** $\dfrac{a + b}{b}$ **6** 1

7 $2x = 3y$; 32, 64   **8** (i) 0·14, −1·44   (ii) −2, −3, −9
9 8·52 cm   **10** 19

XV

1 (i) $3c^3 - c^2d + cd^2 + 5d^3$ (ii) $x^2 + 5x - 2$, rem. −4

2 (i) 0·116 3   (ii) 6·558   **3** 39 m; £107·25   **4** $\dfrac{1}{m - 2n}$

5 2·60 cm   **6** 4, $4\frac{1}{2}$ **7** $\frac{2}{7}$ **9** 1·86 m   **10** 15

XVI

1 (i) $3(x + 3y^2)(x - 3y^2)$ (ii) $(x - 5y)(9x + 4y)$
(iii) $(u + 2v + 4)(u + 2v - 2)$

2 (i) 0·355 0   (ii) 0·705 7   **3** 5 m   **4** $\dfrac{1}{a + 2}$ **6** −1, 3

7 $\frac{2}{3}$ **8** (i) −1·54, −0·26   (ii) 3, $-\frac{1}{2}$, −2   **9** 5·10 cm
10 28

XVII

1 (i) $4h^3 - h^2k - hk^2 - 2k^3$ (ii) $2u^2 - 5u - 3$, rem. 5

2 (i) 0·062 27   (ii) 0·806 0   **3** 183 cm³   **4** $\dfrac{2d - 1}{d + 1}$ **5** 2·5 cm

6 $-\frac{1}{2}$, 1   **7** 54·27   **9** 6·22 cm   **10** 1 h 12 min

XVIII

1 (i) $(x + 3y - 3)(x + 3y + 1)$ (ii) $(x + 2)(x - 2)(x^2 + 4)$
(iii) $(4 + c - 3d)(4 - c + 3d)$

2 (i) 0·519 0   (ii) 0·396 5   **3** $2\frac{1}{2}$%   **4** $\dfrac{7c + 12}{(c - 4)(c + 4)^2}$

6 $-1\frac{1}{2}$, −5   **7** $2\frac{5}{6}$ **8** $\dfrac{m + 3}{3m + 1}$ **9** 122 cm   **10** 15

XIX

1 (i) $9u^2 - v^2 + 4v - 4$ (ii) $3a^2 - 5ab + 2b^2$

2 (i) 0·506 9   (ii) 4·646   **3** £119·25   **4** $-\dfrac{3}{d + 2n}$

5 7 cm   **6** 3, −2   **7** 26·90
9 11·6 cm by 5·8 cm by 6 cm   **10** 9 or $9\frac{1}{3}$

XX

1 (i) $\pi(R + 2r)(R - 2r)$ (ii) $(3a - 4b)(5a + 6b)$ (iii) $3a(5d - 2a)$
2 3·907   **3** 8 years 3 months

4 $\dfrac{2a - 5b}{(a - 2b)(2a - b)(2a + b)}$ **6** $3\frac{1}{2}, -5$ **7** $7\frac{1}{2}$

8 $\dfrac{6m + 1}{2m + 3}$ **9** (i) 16·49 m (ii) 5·07 m   **10** 16 km h⁻¹

Exercise 15 (p. 215)

1 3·5 cm	**2** 1·2 cm	**3** 7·2 cm	**6** 5·66 cm
7 420 cm²	**12** 10·4 cm		**13** 14 cm
14 4·4 cm, 0·4 cm	**17** 5·3 cm		**20** 7·04 cm
21 8·66 cm	**22** 8·54 cm		**27** 8·1 cm, 2·5 cm
28 $\sqrt{r^2 - \frac{1}{4}c^2}$ cm	**32** 30 cm		**35** 25 cm
36 10·6 cm	**40** 18 cm		**42** 2·92 cm, 1·75 cm

Exercise 16a (p. 221)

1 $b - a$ **2** $a - b$ **3** $\dfrac{b}{a}$ **4** $\dfrac{c}{a + b}$ **5** $\dfrac{b}{1 - a}$

6 $\dfrac{a}{b}$ **7** $\dfrac{a}{c - b}$ **8** $a(c - b)$ **9** $\dfrac{ab}{a + b}$

10 $a + b$ **11** $\dfrac{c}{a} - b$ **12** $\dfrac{bc}{a - b}$ **13** $\dfrac{ab}{a + c}$ **14** $\dfrac{6ab}{5}$

15 $\dfrac{bc}{a}$ **16** $b - \dfrac{a}{c}$ **17** $\dfrac{b(3a - 2)}{2a + 3}$ **18** a^2

19 $\dfrac{a^2}{2}$ **20** $\dfrac{a^2}{4}$ **21** $2a^2$ **22** $4a^2$ **23** $\dfrac{b^2}{a^2}$

24 $\dfrac{b^2}{a}$ **25** ab^3 **26** $\pm a^2$ **27** $\pm\sqrt{a}$ **28** $b^2 - a$

29 $(b - a)^2$ **30** $\pm\sqrt{b^2 - a^2}$ **31** $\pm 2a\sqrt{2}$ **32** $a - \dfrac{b}{2}$

33 $1 + \dfrac{b^2}{a^2}$ **34** $\left(\dfrac{1 + b}{a}\right)^2$ **35** $\dfrac{a}{a - b}$ **36** 0

37 $b - a$ **38** $a^2 + ab + b^2$ **39** $-\dfrac{a + b}{2}$

40 $\pm\dfrac{a}{b}\sqrt{b^2 - y^2}$ **41** $2a + b$ **42** $\pm\sqrt{b^2 - a^2}$

43 $\dfrac{3b}{4}$ **44** a **45** $-a$ **46** $\dfrac{2ab}{2a - b}$ **47** $\dfrac{b}{2}$

48 $-\dfrac{a^2}{b}$ **49** $2a$ **50** a or $a + b$

Exercise 16b (p. 223)

1 $N = PD - 2$ **2** $b = \dfrac{kv}{k + rt}$ **3** $r = \dfrac{c}{2\pi}$

4 $W = \dfrac{P - b}{a}$ **5** $n = \dfrac{2S}{a + l}$; $l = \dfrac{2S}{n} - a$

6 $P = \dfrac{100A}{100 + RT}$; $T = \dfrac{100(A - P)}{PR}$ **7** $h = \dfrac{S}{2\pi r} - r$

8 $s = \dfrac{v^2 - u^2}{2a}$; $u = \pm \sqrt{v^2 - 2as}$ **9** $W = \dfrac{LaP}{h - La}$

10 $R = \dfrac{2aE}{L} + r$ **11** $x = \dfrac{P + R^2Q}{a - R^2b}$ **12** $h = \dfrac{2D^2}{3}$

13 $r = \pm\dfrac{1}{2}\sqrt{\dfrac{S}{\pi}}$ **14** $M = \dfrac{4\pi^2 I}{HT^2}$

15 $u = \pm\sqrt{v^2 - \dfrac{2A}{m}}$ **16** $H = \dfrac{Nd^3}{a^3}$

17 $l = \dfrac{d}{2} + \dfrac{4M}{wd}$ **18** $l = \dfrac{wd^2}{2(wd - S)}$

19 $t = T - \dfrac{275H}{\pi Rn}$ **20** $r = \pm\sqrt{R^2 - \dfrac{2gH}{w^2}}$

21 $b = \dfrac{T^2(a^2 + 4)}{Ph}$; $a = \pm\sqrt{\dfrac{Pbh}{T^2} - 4}$

22 $a = \dfrac{b(3x - 2h)}{h - 3x}$ **23** $x = \pm\sqrt{a^2 - \dfrac{v^2}{w^2}}$

24 $h = \pm\sqrt{\dfrac{A^2}{\pi^2 r^2} - r^2}$

25 $H = T^2 - \dfrac{w^2 l^2}{4}$; $l = \pm\dfrac{2}{w}\sqrt{T^2 - H}$ **26** $u = \dfrac{vf}{2v - f}$

27 $S = 2\sqrt[3]{9\pi V^2}$ **28** $P = \pm Q\sqrt{\dfrac{2 + A^2}{1 - 2A^2}}$

29 $h = \pm\dfrac{\sqrt{A^2 - 2A\pi r^2}}{\pi r}$ **30** $q = \pm\sqrt{r^2 - rf}$

31 $T = \dfrac{100I}{PR}$; 6 **32** $y = \dfrac{xR}{x - R}$; 14·4

33 $r = \sqrt{\dfrac{A}{\pi}}$; $3\frac{1}{2}$ cm **34** $h = \dfrac{3V}{\pi r^2} - 2r$; 3·4 cm

New General Mathematics

35 $L = \dfrac{8S^2}{3l} + l$; 16·06 m   **36** $l = \dfrac{21T}{4B^2} + \dfrac{3}{5}B$; 71·1 m

37 $v = \pm\sqrt{\dfrac{2E}{m} - 2hg}$; 14 m s⁻¹   **38** $d = \dfrac{2(S - an)}{n(n - 1)}$; $-1\frac{1}{2}$

39 $r = \sqrt{\dfrac{3V}{\pi h}}$; $2\frac{1}{2}$ cm   **40** $h = \pm\sqrt{\left(\dfrac{A}{\pi r}\right)^2 - r^2}$; 24 cm

Exercise 16c (p. 227)

1 $-2, -3$	**2** $1, 4$	**3** $5, -1$	**4** $-1, -1\frac{1}{2}$
5 $1, \frac{1}{3}$	**6** $2, -\frac{1}{3}$	**7** $1, -\frac{2}{5}$	**8** $-2, \frac{1}{4}$
9 $-\frac{2}{3}, -1\frac{1}{2}$		**10** $5, -\frac{2}{3}$	
11 $-2·62, -0·38$	**12** $3·24, -1·24$	**13** $0·39, -3·89$	
14 $2·14, -0·47$	**15** $1·58, -0·38$	**16** $0·22, -1·82$	
17 $-1·77, -0·57$	**18** $2·82, 1·18$	**19** $2·39, 0·28$	
20 $-1·13, 0·53$	**21** $3·80, 0·20$	**22** $3·89, -0·39$	
23 $1·54, -0·87$	**24** $-1·84, -0·41$	**25** $-2·29, 0·29$	
26 $0·55, -1·22$	**27** $2·30, -1·30$	**28** $0·89, -0·56$	
29 $4·30, 0·70$	**30** $0·68, -0·58$		

Exercise 17a (p. 232)

4 $50°$	**5** $32°$	**6** $23°$	**7** $33°$	**8** $79°$
9 $117°$	**10** $60°$	**11** $22°$	**12** $124°$	

Exercise 17d (p. 241)

1 (i) $1 : 2 : 3$ (ii) $4 : 1$ (iii) $5 : 15 : 16$

2 (i) $2\pi, 4\pi, 6\pi$ cm;   (ii) $\dfrac{48}{5}\pi, \dfrac{12}{5}\pi$ cm;   (iii) $\dfrac{5}{3}\pi, 5\pi, \dfrac{16}{3}\pi$ cm

3 (i) $36°, 72°, 72°$;   (ii) $18°, 72°, 90°$;   (iii) $40°, 60°, 80°$

4 (i) $18°$,   (ii) $72°$,   (iii) $90°$,   (iv) $72°$

5 (i) $60°$,   (ii) $45°$,   (iii) $132°$,   (iv) $105°$,   (v) $37\frac{1}{2}°$

6 $72°, 36°, 72°, 108°, 36°$

Exercise 18b (p. 247)

1 $\sqrt{12}$	**2** $\sqrt{18}$	**3** $\sqrt{8}$	**4** $\sqrt{27}$	**5** $\sqrt{50}$
6 $\sqrt{45}$	**7** $\sqrt{28}$	**8** $\sqrt{96}$	**9** $\sqrt{108}$	**10** $\sqrt{125}$
11 $\sqrt{300}$	**12** $\sqrt{90}$	**13** $\sqrt{44}$	**14** $\sqrt{72}$	**15** $\sqrt{175}$
16 $2\sqrt{5}$	**17** $4\sqrt{2}$	**18** $4\sqrt{3}$	**19** $5\sqrt{3}$	**20** $6\sqrt{2}$
21 $2\sqrt{6}$	**22** $3\sqrt{7}$	**23** $3\sqrt{6}$	**24** $10\sqrt{2}$	**25** $2\sqrt{21}$
26 $3\sqrt{11}$	**27** $5\sqrt{6}$	**28** $7\sqrt{2}$	**29** $12\sqrt{2}$	**30** $7\sqrt{3}$

31 $5\sqrt{2}$ **32** 4   **33** 6   **34** $5\sqrt{6}$ **35** 6

36 48   **37** $2\sqrt{2}$ **38** $6\sqrt{5}$ **39** $8\sqrt{6}$ **40** $9\sqrt{3}$

41 28   **42** 60   **43** 60   **44** $24\sqrt{3}$ **45** $24\sqrt{10}$

46 $\sqrt{2}$ **47** $3\sqrt{2}$ **48** $2\sqrt{5}$ **49** $\sqrt{2}$ **50** $\dfrac{7\sqrt{6}}{2}$

51 $5\sqrt{3}$ **52** $\dfrac{2\sqrt{5}}{5}$ **53** $\dfrac{3\sqrt{7}}{7}$ **54** $3\sqrt{7}$ **55** $\sqrt{2}$

56 $\dfrac{4\sqrt{2}}{3}$ **57** $\dfrac{\sqrt{6}}{5}$ **58** $\dfrac{3\sqrt{5}}{5}$ **59** $2\sqrt{3}$ **60** $\dfrac{5\sqrt{2}}{2}$

61 $3\sqrt{3}$ **62** 0   **63** $\sqrt{7}$ **64** $\sqrt{5}$ **65** 0

66 $12\sqrt{2}$ **67** $2\sqrt{6}$ **68** $2\sqrt{6}$ **69** $7\sqrt{7}$ **70** 6

71 $\dfrac{\sqrt{6}}{2}$ **72** $\dfrac{11\sqrt{3}}{9}$ **73** $\dfrac{3\sqrt{2}}{2}$ **74** $2\sqrt{6}$ **75** $\dfrac{\sqrt{2}}{2}$

Exercise 19 (p. 253)

1 3 cm, $3\sqrt{2}$ cm   **2** $\dfrac{5\sqrt{2}}{2}$ cm, $\dfrac{5\sqrt{2}}{2}$ cm   **3** $2\sqrt{3}$ cm, 4 cm

4 5 cm, $5\sqrt{3}$ cm   **5** $\dfrac{7\sqrt{3}}{3}$ cm, $\dfrac{14\sqrt{3}}{3}$ cm   **6** $2\frac{1}{2}$ cm, $\dfrac{5\sqrt{3}}{2}$ cm

7 $\dfrac{2\sqrt{3}}{3}$ cm, $\dfrac{4\sqrt{3}}{3}$ cm   **8** 14 cm, $7\sqrt{3}$ cm   **9** 2 cm, $2\sqrt{2}$ cm

10 12 cm, $6\sqrt{3}$ cm   **11** $\sqrt{2}$ cm, 2 cm   **12** $\dfrac{\sqrt{3}}{2}$ cm, $1\frac{1}{2}$ cm

13 $\dfrac{\sqrt{3}}{3}$ cm, $\dfrac{2\sqrt{3}}{3}$ cm   **14** $\dfrac{3\sqrt{2}}{2}$ cm, $\dfrac{3\sqrt{2}}{2}$ cm   **15** $\sqrt{3}$ cm, $2\sqrt{3}$ cm

16 $\dfrac{5\sqrt{3}}{3}$ cm   **17** $4\sqrt{3}$ cm   **18** $5\sqrt{2}$ cm   **19** 6 cm

20 $3\sqrt{2}$ cm   **21** $2\sqrt{2}$ cm   **22** $\sqrt{2}$ cm   **23** 6 cm

24 $2\sqrt{3}$ cm   **25** $2\sqrt{6}$ cm   **26** $\dfrac{\sqrt{6}}{2}$ cm   **27** $4\frac{1}{2}$ cm

28 $6\sqrt{2}$ cm   **29** $(3 - \sqrt{3})$ cm   **30** 2 cm   **31** $13\sqrt{3}$ m

32 $8\sqrt{3}$ cm   **33** $110\sqrt{2}$ m, 2·42 ha   **34** $14\sqrt{3}$ cm, 462 cm²

35 $2(2 - \sqrt{3})$ cm   **36** $9(2 - \sqrt{3})$ cm   **37** $3\sqrt{3}$ m

38 $80(\sqrt{3} - 1)$ m, 160 m   **39** 32 m   **40** $8(3 - \sqrt{3})$ m

New General Mathematics

Exercise 20a (p. 257)

1 2	**2** 3	**3** 2	**4** 4	**5** 2
6 3	**7** −1	**8** 3	**9** $1\frac{1}{2}$	**10** $\frac{2}{3}$
11 $-\frac{1}{2}$	**12** $\frac{1}{2}$	**13** $\frac{1}{3}$	**14** $-1\frac{1}{2}$	**15** $-\frac{1}{2}$
16 $-1\frac{1}{2}$	**17** $-1\frac{1}{2}$	**18** $-1\frac{1}{3}$	**19** 3	**20** −2

Exercise 20b (p. 258)

2 (i) 0·699 0, (ii) 0·903 0, (iii) 1·690 2, (iv) 1·146 1, (v) 1·544 1,
(vi) 1·623 2, (vii) 0·574 1

3 (i) 2·58, (ii) 0·92, (iii) 1·58, (iv) −0·06

4 (i) log 12, (ii) log $\frac{4}{3}$, (iii) log 125, (iv) log 5, (v) log $\frac{1}{3}$, (vi) log 30,
(vii) log 2, (viii) log 18, (ix) log 25, (x) log 8

5 (i) 1 000, (ii) 0·01, (iii) 3, (iv) $1\frac{1}{2}$

6 (i) 2, (ii) $1\frac{1}{3}$, (iii) $\frac{1}{4}$, (iv) $-\frac{1}{2}$

7 (i) $x = a^b$, (ii) $xy = a$, (iii) $ax = 1$, (iv) $xy^2 = a^3$, (v) $x = yz$

8 (i) log 2, (ii) $1\frac{1}{2}$, (iii) 5 log 2, (iv) 1

9 (i) 0, 1; (ii) 1, 3; (iii) ±1

10 $x = 2, \frac{1}{2}; y = \pm 0·69$

Exercise 20c (p. 259)

1 126·8	**2** 2·989	**3** 10·32	**4** 0·384 3	**5** 5·443
6 0·145 3	**7** 0·887 6	**8** 7·691	**9** 0·095 66	**10** 0·015 5
11 0·014 52	**12** 0·631 0	**13** 0·587 8	**14** 0·336 2	**15** 15·74
16 0·035 71	**17** 8·324	**18** 2·419	**19** 0·135 1	**20** 6·190
21 3·496	**22** 0·141 6	**23** 652·1	**24** 2·527	**25** 2·054
26 0·413 2	**27** 31·04	**28** 0·964 5	**29** 0·599 2	**30** 0·682 8
31 0·398 1	**32** 0·468 4	**33** 0·464 1	**34** 1·585	**35** 1·218
36 1·540	**37** 0·559 5	**38** 0·659 8	**39** 0·001 245	**40** 1·058
41 0·477 1	**42** 2·096	**43** 2·861	**44** 2·672	**45** −0·092 17
46 0·138 7	**47** −2·322	**48** 0·162 4	**49** 12·34	**50** 65·03

Exercise 20d (p. 261)

1 3·326	**2** 0·148 0	**3** 2·372	**4** 0·718 cm
5 0·327 1	**6** 0·798 cm		

7 (i) 373·2, (ii) 14·1, (iii) 0·980 9, (iv) 2·282   **8** 0·518

9 (i) 96·94 cm³, (ii) 1 406 cm³, (iii) 3·731 m³

10 15 280   **11** 1·794 s   **12** 249 mm   **13** 0·984 6 cm

14 12·77 kg   **15** 42·78 cm³

Exercise 21a (p. 264)

1 <5	**2** >3	**3** >2	**4** <6	**5** <3	**6** >3
7 < −1	**8** <2	**9** >3	**10** >0	**11** > −9	**12** > −12

404

Exercise 21b (p. 264)

1 $\leqslant 8$ **2** $\geqslant 2$ **3** $\geqslant -1$ **4** $\geqslant 3$ **5** $\leqslant 1$ **6** $\leqslant -1$

7 $\geqslant -1$ **8** $\geqslant 1\frac{1}{2}$ **9** $\geqslant 5\frac{1}{2}$ **10** $\leqslant -2$ **11** $\leqslant 2$ **12** $\leqslant -5\frac{5}{8}$

Exercise 21d (p. 269)

2 (3,5) or (4,3). The second; 1p   **3** 93; (72,21) or (73,20). (60,30)

4 (96,34). (140,20); £13   **5** 10; 4A and 6B. 4A and 6B

6 (i) (4,12)   (ii) (2,11) or (4,2) weekly.   12 ways

Revision Examples (p. 271)

XXI

1 (i) $6a$ (ii) $\frac{2}{5}a$ (iii) $\dfrac{a^4}{4}$ (iv) 25   (v) 2^{3x} (vi) 1

2 $2\sqrt{6}$ cm, 6 cm   **3** 87°   **4** 4

5 (i) $1\cdot33 \times 10^7$ (ii) $1\cdot47 \times 10^{-10}$ (iii) $6\cdot91 \times 10^6$ **6** 15° 43′

7 $l = \dfrac{ea}{k - e}$ **8** 3·73, 0·27   **9** (i) 6, 45, 0   (ii) $\sqrt{5}, \dfrac{\sqrt{2}}{5}$

10 $1\frac{1}{3}, 1\frac{1}{2}, -2$

XXII

1 $r = \dfrac{V}{\pi h^2} + \dfrac{h}{3}$; 3·9 cm   **2** 8 cm

3 (i) $3(p + 5q)(p - 5q)$ (ii) $(4x - y)(4y - x)$ (iii) $(a + c)(a - 2b)$

4 $20(\sqrt{3} - 1)$ m   **5** 23

6 (i) $81\sqrt{3}, 8\sqrt{3}, \sqrt{11}$ (ii) $\dfrac{5\sqrt{2}}{3}, \dfrac{\sqrt{2}}{2}$ **7** $-2\cdot64, 1\cdot14$

8 65°   **10** -5; 2·58, $-0\cdot58$

XXIII

1 (i) $(2x - 1)(x - 2)$ (ii) $a(3a + 1)(3a - 1)$ (iii) $(3a + 2)(2x - 3y)$

    (iv) $(5 + 4r)(2 - 3r)$

2 (i) 5·944   (ii) 0·497 1   (iii) 0·481 2   **3** 3 cm, $\sqrt{6}$ cm

4 $\frac{3}{5}$ **5** 6·32 cm   **6** $L = \dfrac{l(1 - et)}{1 - eT}$

7 7·32 cm, 11·04 cm   **8** (i) $\dfrac{\sqrt{3}}{2}, 8, 5\sqrt{2}$ (ii) $\sqrt{5}, \dfrac{\sqrt{21}}{5}$

9 31·7 m   **10** 1·585

New General Mathematics

XXIV

1 12 m, 20 m

2 $H = \dfrac{V^2}{2g(1 - E)}$

3 (i) $14\sqrt{6}, 250\sqrt{2}, 30\sqrt{2}$ (ii) $\dfrac{2\sqrt{3}}{5}, 8\sqrt{2}$

5 $-2\cdot58, -1\cdot42$ **6** 17%   **7** $7, -8$ **8** $\sqrt{3}$ cm

9 6 m by 15 m *or* 7·5 m by 12 m   **10** $(4,1\frac{1}{2}), (4\frac{1}{2},1); 5\frac{1}{2}$

XXV

1 $d = \dfrac{v^2 - 3hg}{g}$

2 (i) 2   (ii) 17, 10

3 (i) $18, 3\sqrt{7}, 11\sqrt{2}$ (ii) $2\sqrt{2}, 6\sqrt{3}$

4 $104° 2'; 1\cdot46$ cm   **5** 40 km h^{-1}, 48 km h^{-1}

7 (i) $0\cdot196\ 1$ (ii) $0\cdot646\ 8$ **8** $5\sqrt{3}$ cm, $10\sqrt{2}$ cm

9 $2\cdot28, 0\cdot22$ **10** $1\cdot29$

XXVI

1 (i) 1 twice (ii) 0, 2 (iii) $\frac{1}{2}$ (iv) 1, 2   **2** (i) 13·6 cm (ii) 22 cm

3 $1\cdot43, 0\cdot23$ **4** $74\frac{1}{2}; 70; 64\frac{1}{2}–81\frac{1}{2}$

5 $k = \pm\sqrt{\dfrac{hg\text{T}^2}{2\pi^2} - h^2}$ **6** $2:3$

7 (i) $15\sqrt{3}, 42, \sqrt{6}$ (ii) $3\sqrt{5}, \dfrac{\sqrt{6}}{2}$

9 $1\cdot336$ **10** 45, 10

XXVII

1 (i) $24\sqrt{5}, 75, 2\sqrt{3}$ (ii) $\sqrt{3}, 2\sqrt{6}$

2 $a = \pm\dfrac{bc}{\sqrt{c^2 + 2gb^2}}$ **3** $\dfrac{5}{(x - 3y)(x + 2y)}$

4 $28° 30'$ **5** $10\sqrt{3}$ m   **6** (i) $6\cdot808$ (ii) $0\cdot724\ 3$

7 $2\cdot59, -0\cdot26$ **8** 35p   **10** $-0\cdot239\ 6$

XXVIII

1 (i) $3, -2$ (ii) 1, 4   (iii) -10 (iv) $2\frac{1}{2}, \frac{2}{5}$

2 $u = \pm\sqrt{v^2 - \dfrac{2g\text{E}}{m}}$ **3** (i) $\frac{2}{3}\sqrt{6}, 28, \sqrt{7}$ (ii) $5\sqrt{7}, \frac{3}{5}\sqrt{5}$

4 $11\cdot2$ cm, $4\cdot28$ cm   **5** (i) $\dfrac{1 + x^2}{x - 3}$ (ii) $\dfrac{1 + y^2}{y - 3}$

6 $50(3 + \sqrt{3})$ m   **7** $2 \cdot 58$, $-0 \cdot 58$

8 (i) £31·86   (ii) 15 000 litres   (iii) 40 cm

9 (i) 18° 26′   (ii) 5·51 cm   **10** 0, 1

XXIX

1 (i) $10\sqrt{6}$, 147, $\frac{1}{2}\sqrt{2}$ (ii) $3\sqrt{2}$, $4\sqrt{2}$

2 $m = \dfrac{2(c + 3k)}{3k - 2c}$ **3** (i) 67·8   (ii) 0·782

4 $2\frac{3}{4}$ **5** 5·54 cm, 5·79 cm

6 (i) 14.36   (ii) 8 km h^{-1} (iii) 11.54, 14.26   **8** 2·718

9 66·3 cm   **10** 2·59, $-0 \cdot 26$; $-6\frac{1}{12}$

XXX

1 (i) $\frac{1}{3}\sqrt{6}$, $\frac{4}{5}\sqrt{5}$, $3\sqrt{6}$ (ii) $2\sqrt{5}$, $\sqrt{5}$ **2** 75 km h^{-1}, 90 km h^{-1}

3 25 cm by 18 cm   **4** 4·94 cm

5 110 min, 12 people   **7** $d = \dfrac{g\mathrm{D}^2}{2v^2 - g\mathrm{D}}$

8 69 s   **9** ± 1

10 (i) V $= x^2 - 3x$ (ii) 9 cm by 12 cm   (iii) 8·73

Exercise 22a (p. 286)

1 (i) 6 cm, 60°   (ii) 4 cm, 47° 10′   (iii) 5 cm, 112° 53′

   (iv) 2 cm, 28° 58′

2 (i) 72π cm²   (ii) 40π cm²   (iii) 30π cm²   (iv) 16π cm²

3 288°   **4** 16π cm³; 20π cm²   **5** 38° 56′

6 48 cm³; 7 cm   **7** 195π cm²; 700π cm²   **8** 218π cm³

9 500 m³, 468 m³   **10** 1 552 cm³; 143 cm²

Exercise 22b (p. 289)

1 (i) 120 cm³   (ii) 100π cm³   (iii) 480 cm³   (iv) 48 cm³   (v) 120 cm³

   (vi) 18π cm³   (vii) 8π cm³   (viii) 420 cm³   (ix) 20 cm³

2 (i) 158 cm²   (ii) 90π cm²   (iii) 528 cm²   (iv) 96 cm²   (vi) 27π cm²

3 $\dfrac{129\pi}{4}$ m³   **4** $\dfrac{64\pi}{3}$ m³   **5** $\dfrac{61\pi}{2}$ cm³   **6** 1 500

7 5   **8** 1 728   **9** 1·4 cm   **10** 5·12 cm

11 9 cm   **12** $31\frac{1}{4}$ cm   **13** $2\frac{1}{4}$ cm   **14** $5\frac{1}{3}$ cm

15 12·7 cm   **16** 1 cm   **17** 2 cm

18 1 232 cm³; 550 cm²   **19** 100·8°   **20** 1 040 litres

21 275 kg   **22** 650 kg   **23** 9 612 cm³   **24** 181 000 l h^{-1}

25 11·4 cm approx.   **26** 225 m³   **27** 5·55 km

28 0·006 3 cm   **29** 16·54 kg   **30** 121 mm   **31** 0·343 kg

32 20·9 kg

New General Mathematics

Exercise 24 (p. 307)
 1 130 cm; 67° 23′ **2** 44·7 cm; 63° 26′
 3 (i) 7 cm; (ii) 51° 4′; (iii) 60° 15′
 4 (i) 14 cm; (ii) 63° 26′, 71° 34′
 5 (i) 5 cm; (ii) 53° 8′; (iii) 57°
 6 (i) 15 cm; (ii) 17 cm; (iii) 28° 4½′; (iv) 44° 54′;
    (v) 31° 58′; (vi) 41° 38′; (vii) 56° 19′
 7 (i) 31° 36½′; (ii) 51° 49½′; (iii) 22° 37′; (iv) 41° 3′
 8 22° 41′   **9** 16° 16′, 11° 12′
10 (i) 2·54 m; (ii) 29° 22′; (iii) 57° 38′; (iv) 55° 48′
11 (i) 60° 15′; (ii) 63° 40′ **12** 20° 42½′; 1 in 2·8
13 (i) 38° 56′; (ii) 22° 9′ **14** (i) 36° 52′; (ii) 21° 6′
15 (i) 26° 45′; (ii) 21° 6′ **16** (i) 0°; (ii) 16° 40′; (iii) 29° 47′
17 (i) 8·24 cm; (ii) 62° 46′ **18** 30° 41′
19 55° 28′   **20** (i) 71° 12′; (ii) 67° 41′
21 62° 2′   **22** 63° 17′ **23** (i) 30 m; (ii) 11° 51′
24 (i) 19° 36′; (ii) 65° 53′ **25** 10·88 cm; 32° 56½′

Exercise 25 (p. 315)
 1 2·12; $x^3 - x^2 = 5$ **2** −2, −0·41, 2·41
 3 1·41   **4** −2·49, 0·66, 1·83
 5 −3·05, 1·36, 1·69 **6** 1·78
 7 −2·57, −0·14, 2·71 **8** 2·26
 9 −1·45, 3·45   **10** −2·85, 0·35; $2x^2 + 5x - 2 = 0$
11 0·23, 4·27   **12** $y = 3·17$; $x = 4·47$
13 21·5 km h⁻¹, £692 **14** −1·79, 1·12; $3x^2 + 2x - 6 = 0$
15 2·59 **16** 3·92 **17** 32 cm, 6·93 s
18 31·25 m, 22·36 m **19** 14·2 cm³, 2⅔ cm × 2⅔ cm × 2 cm
20 2 m

Exercise 26a (p. 323)
 1 63°   **2** 57°   **3** 96° **4** 32° **5** 23°
 6 4·5 cm   **7** 3·3 cm **8** 141° **9** 5 cm, 4 cm, 2 cm
10 5 cm, 6 cm, 14 cm **11** 16 cm **12** 5·8 cm
13 14 cm, 4 cm   **14** 43° **15** 3·25 cm
16 35°; 35° or 145° **17** 106° **18** 59° or 121°
19 8 cm   **20** 9·6 cm

Exercise 26c (p. 328)
 1 56°   **2** 52°   **3** 43° **4** 102°
 5 78°   **6** 82°, 49°, 49° **7** 72° **8** 40°
 9 101°, 74° **10** 34°, 77°, 69° **11** 50°, 60°, 70° **12** 44°, 108°

Answers

Exercise 26e (p. 335)
1 8·78 cm   **2** 4·12 cm   **3** 4·58 cm   **4** 6·24(5) cm
5 1·91 cm   **6** 2·22 cm   **7** 1·36 cm   **8** 2·03 cm
9 2·83 cm   **10** 1·16 cm   **11** 1·33 cm, 2·40 cm, 4·00 cm
12 3·5 cm, 2·5 cm, 4·5 cm   **13** 3 cm, 4 cm
14 60°, 50°, 70°; 60°, 65°, 55°   **15** 120°, 20°, 40°
19 2·48 cm   **21** 2·07 cm   **22** 6·33 cm   **24** 8·99 cm, $73\frac{3}{4}$°
25 9·22 cm or 3·19 cm   **26** 4·12 cm, 6·42 cm
27 4·06 cm, 6·23 cm   **29** 2·66 cm   **32** 7·52 cm

Exercise 27a (p. 341)
1 (i) 90 km h⁻¹ (ii) 0·036 km h⁻¹ (iii) 96 km h⁻¹ (iv) 83 km h⁻¹
   (v) 108 km h⁻¹
2 (i) 25 m s⁻¹ (ii) 40 m s⁻¹ (iii) $26\frac{2}{3}$ m s⁻¹ (iv) $2\frac{1}{2}$ m s⁻¹
   (v) $6\frac{1}{4}$ m s⁻¹
3 3 min 18 s   **4** 54 km h⁻¹   **5** $12\frac{1}{2}$ s   **6** 19·8 s
7 13.09   **8** 10.42; 10·2 km from start   **9** $7\frac{1}{2}$ s
10 240 m   **11** 54 km h⁻¹   **12** $11\frac{1}{4}$ s   **13** 63 km h⁻¹
14 41 km h⁻¹   **15** 12 min   **16** (i) 96 min (ii) 36 min
17 $2\frac{1}{2}$ h   **18** $8\frac{1}{2}$ km h⁻¹   **19** 2 km h⁻¹   **20** 1 min

Exercise 27b (p. 343)
1 1 : 2   **2** 11 : 1   **3** 2 : 3   **4** 6 : 1
5 3 a penny   **6** £1·95   **7** 50%   **8** 1 : 4 : 4
9 72p   **10** £1·40 per litre   **11** 25%   **12** $11\frac{1}{2}$p

Exercise 27c (p. 345)
1 4 min   **2** 4 min   **3** 3 days   **4** 3 min   **5** 40 min
6 36 h   **7** 1 min   **8** $1\frac{4}{5}$ days   **9** $1\frac{1}{2}$ days
10 A 6, B 12, C 4 days   **11** 3 days   **12** $2\frac{1}{2}$ min   **13** $2\frac{1}{2}$ days
14 Sid, in just under 14 h   **15** 32 men

Exercise 27d (p. 348)
1 10 m   **2** 20 m   **3** 11 m approx. ($11\frac{1}{3}$)   **4** 28
5 28 m   **6** 1   **7** 3   **8** 10 m, 20 m
9 80 m   **10** 14   **11** A gives C 3 points ($3\frac{1}{2}$) and wins
12 496 m   **13** 17   **14** C, by 80 m   **15** B, by 4 m

Exercise 28a (p. 353)
1 $\begin{pmatrix} 0 & 1 \\ -1 & 0 \end{pmatrix}$ **2** (1,−1), (4,−2), (7,−3)

3 $\begin{pmatrix} -1 & 0 \\ 0 & -1 \end{pmatrix}$ **4** (0,0), (−1,1), (−1,−1)

409

New General Mathematics

5 (0,0), (−1,−1), (−1,1)

6 $\begin{pmatrix} 0 & 1 \\ 1 & 0 \end{pmatrix}$

7 (2,2), (−1,1), (−2,−2), (1,−1)

8 $\begin{pmatrix} 0 & -1 \\ -1 & 0 \end{pmatrix}$

9 $\begin{pmatrix} 1\frac{1}{2} & 0 \\ 0 & 1\frac{1}{2} \end{pmatrix}$

10 (0,0), (4$\frac{1}{2}$,0), (0,3), (4$\frac{1}{2}$,3)

Exercise 28b (p. 362)

1 (4,1), (10,2), (11,3). $\begin{pmatrix} 1 & -3 \\ 0 & 1 \end{pmatrix}$

2 (5,5), (12,18), (14,11). $-\dfrac{1}{15}\begin{pmatrix} 1 & -4 \\ -4 & 1 \end{pmatrix}$

3 (8,17), (18,42), (23,47)   **4** (3,6), (8,16), (8,16). No
5 (−1,1), (−4,2), (−2,3)   **6** (−1,1), (−4,2), (−2,3)
7 (−4,4), (−8,16), (−12,8)   **8** (2,4), (−1,3), (1,2)
9 (−1,−1), (−6,−4), (−1,−2)   **10** (−2,2), (−2,10), (−7,3)
11 (−1,1), (−4,2), (−2,3)   **12** (−1$\frac{1}{2}$,1$\frac{1}{2}$), (−6,3), (−3,4$\frac{1}{2}$)
13 (−3,−1), (−4,−2), (−10,−3) **14** (3,9), (4,12), (5,10)
15 (−2,2), (−10,2), (−3,7)
16 (−6,−1), (−14,−2), (−17,−3)
17 (1,4), (2,10), (3,11)   **18** (4,4), (11,5), (13,6)
19 (16,8), (42,18), (43,23)   **20** (3,−3), (8,−10), (8,−7)
21 (−3,−3), (−12,−6), (−6,−9) **22** (1,1), (2,5), (4,2)
23 (5$\frac{2}{3}$,−3$\frac{1}{3}$), (10$\frac{2}{3}$,−1$\frac{2}{3}$), (7$\frac{1}{3}$,0) **24** (9$\frac{1}{3}$,2$\frac{1}{3}$), (23$\frac{1}{3}$,4$\frac{2}{3}$), (25$\frac{2}{3}$,7)
25 (6,6), (21,15), (13$\frac{1}{2}$,16$\frac{1}{2}$) **26** (1,1), (7,3), (3,5)
27 (−2,−14), (10,−10), (2,−6) **28** (−2,−2), (−4,−8), (−6,−4)
29 (−15,−3), (−36,−6), (−42,−9)
30 (6,6), (70,38), (34,50)

Revision Examples (p. 365)

XXXI

1 67$\frac{1}{2}$ km h^{-1} **2** 180°; 49·0 cm^3 **3** 8 cm, 6 cm, 16 cm
4 (i) 7 cm (ii) 51° 4′ (iii) 60° 15′   **5** 120

6 9° 3′; 76·4 cm   **7** (i) $\dfrac{x-12}{(x-2)(x+3)(x+4)}$ (ii) 4, −4$\frac{1}{2}$

8 (i) $l = \dfrac{gt^2}{4\pi^2}$ (ii) 2 030 cm (2 026)   **9** 1·73 cm

10 $a = 0·02$, $b = 0·6$; 12·6 kg; 470 kg

XXXII

1 36·3 km h⁻¹ (36·29)

2 (i) 14·1 cm (ii) 15 cm (iii) 19° 28′ (iv) 41° 49′

4 (i) 612 m (ii) N 10° 14′ W   **5** (i) 1·017 (ii) 0·897 3

6 $\dfrac{p+q}{p-q}$; 2   **7** 40 times, 1·01 litres (1·006)

8 16 km h⁻¹   **9** 24 m   **10** 1·8

XXXIII

1 4·76 cm; 48° 36′   **2** 100 m; 200 m   **3** 3·5 cm; 88° 51′

4 (i) 72° 58′ (ii) 28·3 m (20√2)   **5** −6½

6 15p   **7** 12·4 litres   **8** (i) 3·108 (ii) 2·101

9 7·81 cm; 4·51 cm   **10** 6·27

XXXIV

1 6 days   **2** (i) 54° 28′ (ii) 33° 48′ (iii) 58° 15′

4 (i) 2·19, −0·69 (ii) (−2,−3)   **5** 9 cm

6 21·36 cm²   **7** 10 km h⁻¹, 12 km h⁻¹

8 (i) 627 cm³ (ii) 0·92 cm

9 (i) 4·24 cm (ii) 35° 16′ (iii) 7·35 cm   **10** −6·35; −0·24

XXXV

1 (i) 41 cm (ii) 52 cm   **2** (i) 26 cm (ii) 73° 35′

3 (i) 2·209 (ii) 0·313 4   **4** (i) 4·19 cm³ (ii) 48·0 g

5 (i) (1¼,4) (ii) 4, $\frac{4}{5}$ **6** 2·35 cm

7 6⅔ days; 10 days   **9** (−3,3), (6,3), (3,−9)

10 −2·69, 0·19; $2x^2 + 5x - 1 = 0$

XXXVI

1 (i) 3·257 (ii) 3·08 cm (3·075)   **2** 2·35 cm

3 (i) 23° 35′ (ii) 40° 32′   **4** 64

5 (i) $\dfrac{4(2x+1)}{x^2-4}$ (ii) 1, 3   **6** 14·3 cm, 20·9 cm, 20·9 cm

8 46·2 g   **9** 5 : 1   **10** 1·12, −1·79; $3x^2 + 2x - 6 = 0$

XXXVII

1 40 m   **2** 38°, 69°, 73°

3 2 cm   **4** (i) 38° 56′ (ii) 22° 9′

5 $\dfrac{2x-1}{(x-1)(3x+1)}$ **6** 9·80 cm

7 (i) 0·105 2 (ii) 0·170 4   **8** 91·6 cm; 8·82 m

9 (5,1), (10,2), (9,3)   **10** 7½ s

New General Mathematics

XXXVIII

1 A gives C 4 games per set
2 (i) 8 cm (ii) 53° 8′ (iii) 53° 8′ (iv) 45° 41′

3 (i) $\frac{1}{2}$ (ii) x^2 (iii) $\frac{3}{b^2}$ (iv) $\frac{8}{27}$ (v) 2

4 7 cm, 10 cm, 8 cm   **5** 3 cm

6 (i) $t = \dfrac{k(1 + e^2)}{1 - e^2k^2}$ (ii) 0·521   **7** (i) $\dfrac{2}{3x(x + 4)}$ (ii) 3, $\frac{2}{5}$

8 2·40 cm; yes   **9** 300 km h⁻¹   **10** 2·65, −2·15

XXXIX

2 (i) 29° 45′ (ii) 23° 12′ (iii) 18° 55½′ (iv) 33° 28′   **3** 5 tonnes
4 7·09 kg (7·086)   **5** 28   **6** 11⅓%   **7** 3·5 cm

8 (i) 816·2 (ii) 0·923 9   **9** (i) $y = \dfrac{2x + 3}{3x - 2}$

10 2·17 cm

XL

1 (i) W = $\dfrac{32xT}{v^2 + 32x}$ (ii) 18·78

2 (i) 15 cm, 26 cm (ii) 53° 8′ (iii) 44° 54′ (iv) 18° 56′
4 32 km h⁻¹, 12 km h⁻¹   **5** £12 980

6 (i) 2 (ii) 54a^5 (iii) $\dfrac{12}{a}$ (iv) 1 (v) 9

8 278 litres per min   **9** (i) 1⅓ cm (ii) $\frac{5}{18}$
10 (ii) Radius 8·16 cm; height 5·77 cm